The New York Times

ROAD TRIP CROSSWORDS

The New York Times

ROAD TRIP CROSSWORDS
150 EASY TO HARD PUZZLES

Edited by Will Shortz

ST. MARTIN'S GRIFFIN · NEW YORK

For information, address St. Martin's Press,
175 Fifth Avenue, New York, NY 10010.

www.stmartins.com

ISBN 978-1-250-11898-1

Our books may be purchased in bulk for promotional, educational, or business use.
Please contact your local bookseller or the Macmillan Corporate and
Premium Sales Department at 1-800-221-7945, extension 5442,
or by e-mail at MacmillanSpecialMarkets@macmillan.com.

First Edition: March 2017

10 9 8 7 6 5 4 3 2 1

The New York Times

ROAD TRIP CROSSWORDS

EASY 1

ACROSS

1 Makes eyes at
6 Start of four TV drama titles of the 2000s
9 Twisted, as a wet towel
14 Entry in the Rose Parade
15 "Winnie-the-Pooh" baby
16 Course you hardly have to study for
17 Brand of orange or grape soda
18 Misbehaving
20 Unit of work in physics
21 N.F.L. team that plays in Jersey, strangely enough
23 Marquis ___ (French writer)
25 Regarding
26 ___ News (Roger Ailes's former channel)
29 Tool for laying cement
31 Locale for mobile campers
33 ___ jacket (denim top)
34 Pie ___ mode
36 "Miss" of TV's "Dallas"
37 Jazz group
38 "Yo"
39 Caramel-filled candies
40 Server overseer, informally
41 Conan O'Brien's network
42 Romulus or Remus
43 Put (together), as a jigsaw puzzle
45 "Little" folk tale character with lazy friends
47 One of the Kennedys
48 "Stumblin' In" singer Quatro
50 Didn't give a definitive answer
53 Something bid on on "The Price Is Right"
55 Drunk motorist's infraction, for short
56 California's says "Eureka"
59 Sag
61 Speakers' platforms
62 ___ and outs
63 Stares (at)
64 Emmy or Espy
65 Sporty Pontiac
66 Minuscule, informally

DOWN

1 Took care of, mob-style
2 What a sun visor reduces
3 Like some wineglasses and roses
4 Dine
5 Perform an inverted feat
6 Rocky outcropping
7 Alcohol, per its effect at a party
8 Smidgens
9 Lost one's sanity
10 From ___ to riches
11 Military entertainment grp.
12 Sch. on Manhattan's Washington Square Park
13 Gun, in old mob slang
19 Like some verbs: Abbr.
22 Tree whose name sounds like a letter of the alphabet
24 Language of Yemen and Oman
26 Like the contents of this puzzle's circled squares, in a nursery rhyme
27 Hunter of myth
28 Sporty Jaguars
30 "It is the ___, and Juliet is the sun": Romeo
32 Prepared for planting, as a field
33 Actress Foster
35 Cathedral recess
37 Lt.'s superior
44 Twosomes
46 Some A.L. sluggers
49 Stefan ___, influential Austrian writer of the 1920s–'30s
51 Furry "Star Wars" creatures
52 ___ Doodles (snack brand)
53 Kerfuffle
54 In addition
56 Health resort
57 Pull to a pound
58 Nabokov novel
60 Singer Carly ___ Jepsen

by Jacob Stulberg

2 EASY

ACROSS

1 President who ended "don't ask, don't tell"
6 Women's suffrage leader Carrie Chapman ___
10 Swanky
14 Fortuneteller's deck
15 "Famous" snack maker
16 Teeny
17 Overboard, to a sailor
19 Maryland athlete, for short
20 Talk back to
21 Actress Skye of "Say Anything . . ."
22 Jazz vocalist Carmen ___
23 Data storage devices
25 "Let me take care of that"
29 Function
30 Kathmandu's land
31 Chicken of the Sea product
34 ___ team (police unit)
38 Punch in the mouth, slangily
41 Neither good nor bad
42 To whom God said "For dust you are and to dust you will return"
43 Nintendo character who hatches from an egg
44 Prefix with athlete
46 Website that investigates urban legends
47 Bright sort
53 International court site, with "The"
54 Jagged cliff
55 ___ fide
59 With 2-Down, star of 2003's "Hulk"
60 Backpack containers where you can find the ends of 17-, 23-, 38- and 47-Across
62 No-longer-fashionable fur
63 Common ingredient in lotions
64 Dance move added to the O.E.D. in 2015
65 Things to hang coats on
66 "What a ___!" ("Too bad!")
67 Meanders

DOWN

1 Soul singer Redding
2 See 59-Across
3 The "A" of B.A.
4 ___ scale (measure of hardness)
5 Had dinner
6 Rebound on a pool table
7 ___ acid (protein builder)
8 Photocopier powder
9 "Naughty!"
10 Is a romancer, old-style
11 Former "S.N.L." comic Cheri, whose last name rhymes with her first
12 Bridle rein, e.g.
13 Promotes, with "up"
18 Weight-loss program
22 Show hosts, in brief
23 Skim or 2%
24 Chinese money
25 Signs, as a contract
26 Jets quarterback Smith
27 Grand work
28 Street vendors selling Mexican food
31 Senator Cruz
32 Made in ___
33 Place of service for John McCain, briefly
35 Bit of smoke
36 Aftereffect from working out
37 "___ ends here!" (fighting words)
39 Of the flock
40 Unit of force
45 GPS calculation: Abbr.
46 [Ah, me]
47 Oldest of the Three Stooges
48 ___ Antoinette
49 Getting into a gray area?
50 Eyes: Lat.
51 Words after "like it" and "ready"
52 Singer Musgraves who won a 2013 Grammy for Best Country Album
55 Heavyweight champ Riddick
56 Headstrong animals
57 Do 10 crosswords in a row, say, with "out"
58 Questions
60 Once around the track
61 "Oh, before I forget . . . ," in a text

by Sam Buchbinder

Easy 3

ACROSS

1 Numbered things in a hotel hallway
6 Not fully closed, as 1-Across
10 Sicilian volcano
14 Cry to a battlefield medic
15 Pasta sauce "trusted since 1937"
16 "Um, pardon me"
17 Airborne animal with a monstrous name
19 Not medium or well done
20 "Who knows the answer?"
21 Mare's mate
23 Pod fillers
25 Site with the option "Shop by category"
26 Top choice, informally
29 Anonymous John
31 Exclamation when raising one's champagne glass
35 University of Maine town
37 Airborne animal with a monstrous name
39 Zilch
40 12:00
42 Spot for a cat
43 Undersea animal with a monstrous name
45 Lessen
47 Much
48 Remove from a no-parking zone, say
50 High/low cards
51 ___-serif font
53 Singer who starred in "Moonstruck"
55 Beret-wearing individualists of the 1950s–'60s
59 U.S. moon-landing program
63 Play's start
64 Undersea animal with a monstrous name
66 "For ___ the Bell Tolls"
67 Half: Prefix
68 No longer in the closet, and not by choice
69 Brain or ear part
70 Fearsome dino
71 Must-haves

DOWN

1 Performer inclined to throw tantrums
2 Muscat is its capital
3 "Goodness gracious!"
4 Tear the wrapping off
5 Children's writer R.L. ___
6 "___ you kidding me?!"
7 Quick punches
8 Banded rock
9 Relative of a turnip
10 In the beginning stages
11 Bangkok resident
12 Emperor accused of starting the Great Fire of Rome
13 "I'll second that, brother!"
18 Enjoy a book
22 One of the Jacksons
24 "Ditto"
26 Hollywood's Henry or Jane
27 "The Little Mermaid" mermaid
28 Swedish car whose name is Latin for "I roll"
30 German artist Max
32 Insurer with a duck in its commercials
33 Something to write on with chalk
34 Uses a computer keyboard
36 Borrowed, as artwork between museums
38 For one particular purpose, as a committee
41 Subpar performance for a team or musician, say
44 "We've waited long enough"
46 Ornate architectural style
49 "___ the heck"
52 One going down a slippery slope
54 Printer brand
55 Cry like a baby
56 Canyon rebound
57 Very limited range
58 "Ditto"
60 Troubadour's stringed instrument
61 Told untruths
62 10:1 at a racetrack, e.g.
65 Veto

by Patrick Merrell

4 EASY

ACROSS

1 Hawaiian greeting
6 Growth on the forest floor
10 Seller of the Söderhamn sofa
14 Like three NASA rovers
15 "This is disastrous!"
16 Lima's home
17 PowerPoint slide with fake data?
20 Hershey bar with toffee
21 Go to the mall
22 "Duty, ___, Country" (West Point motto)
23 Fancy affair
25 Pressing business?
26 Sliced serving with ritzy crackers?
31 Restaurant basketful
32 Stir-fry vessel
33 Octagonal sign
37 Everybody
38 Rag covered in dirt?
42 Pal of Piglet and Pooh
43 "Holy moly!"
45 Bill ___, the Science Guy
46 Japanese auto import
48 Pep squad member's lament?
52 Cotton fabric
55 Flying circus performer?
56 ___ Sam
57 Eatery with sidewalk tables, often
59 Breckinridge of fiction
63 Briefs from Walmart or Target?
66 Biggest city on the Big Island
67 Length x width, for a rectangle
68 Innocent's reply to "Who did this?"
69 Store sign
70 Like morning grass
71 From Zurich, e.g.

DOWN

1 "Woe is me"
2 Stand in the shadows
3 Not fooled by
4 What may keep a Mohawk in place
5 Dog's yap
6 Latte alternatives
7 Lima's home
8 "Oh, ___!" ("Good one, girlfriend!")
9 Fa follower
10 Products featuring Siri
11 "The Family Circus" creator Bil
12 Goof
13 Cowboy singer Gene
18 Capri or Man
19 Something a thoughtful person strokes
24 Lead-in for prof. or V.P.
25 Reference page edited by a group
26 Steep rock face
27 Golfer's target
28 Glamour rival
29 It gives a little hoot
30 Rock's ___ Fighters
34 "You make a good point"
35 Primordial muck
36 Rain really hard
39 Unknown source, informally
40 School about 40 miles from S.L.C.
41 "God does not play ___ with the world": Einstein
44 Ginormous number
47 Cloth made famous by infomercials
49 Appearance
50 When nothing seems to go right
51 Escape (from)
52 A ton, in Tijuana
53 Square
54 Item on many a bathroom floor
57 Successfully treat
58 From square one
60 Supposed sighting in Tibet
61 Aries animals
62 God who sounds like he was mentioned in the preceding clue
64 ___ sack
65 E.R. staffers

by Samuel A. Donaldson and Doug Peterson

EASY 5

ACROSS

1 Ten to one, for one
6 "I Am ___" (Jenner's reality show on E!)
10 "Madam, I'm ___" (palindromic introduction to Eve)
14 Something "walked" on a pirate ship
15 Merry-go-round or roller coaster
16 Nevada's so-called "Biggest Little City in the World"
17 *Serving between appetizer and dessert
19 Puts out, in baseball
20 Dedicated poems
21 Confuse
22 Politically left-leaning
26 Hairstyle with straight-cut bangs
28 Mrs. whose cow supposedly began the Great Chicago Fire
29 Philosopher who tutored Nero
30 ___ Claus
31 James of "The Godfather"
32 Germany's von Bismarck
35 Abbr. at the bottom of a letter
36 *It's signaled by a white flag on the racetrack
39 Austin's home: Abbr.
40 Witty Mort
42 Hearts of PCs, for short
43 "Me, Myself & ___" (Jim Carrey film)
45 Punch hard
47 Offset, as costs
48 Exchange, as an old piece of equipment for a new one
50 "Aren't I the fortunate one!"
51 Fruit-filled pastries
52 Window frame
53 Prefix with sphere
54 Plan that has no chance of working . . . or the answer to each starred clue?
60 Stay fresh
61 Winter ailments
62 Wet, weatherwise
63 Does wrong
64 Toy block brand
65 "___ Boots Are Made for Walkin'" (1966 Nancy Sinatra hit)

DOWN

1 33⅓, for an LP
2 In the manner of
3 ___ chi (martial art)
4 Bed-and-breakfast
5 Shootout site involving the Earp brothers
6 Mean, mean, mean
7 Is broadcast
8 Check-cashing requirements, for short
9 Golf peg
10 Design style of the 1920s and '30s
11 *Reason for jumper cables
12 ___-Saxon
13 Putter (along)
18 Anita of jazz
21 Get on in years
22 Finishes with fewer votes
23 Glazer of "Broad City"
24 *Athlete who "rides the pine"
25 Chow down
26 Rings, as church bells
27 Kournikova of tennis
29 Stopped lying?
31 Bill also called a benjamin
33 Brunch time, say
34 Common daisy
37 Free speech advocacy grp.
38 Infographic with wedges
41 Go-with-you-anywhere computers
44 D.C. stadium initials
46 The "L" of L.A.
47 Attic accumulation
48 Vampire hunter's weapon
49 H_2O
50 Rodeo rope
52 Close-fitting
54 Lombardi Trophy org.
55 Stadium cheer
56 Stadium cheer
57 Suit accessory
58 U.S.N. officer: Abbr.
59 Whiskey type

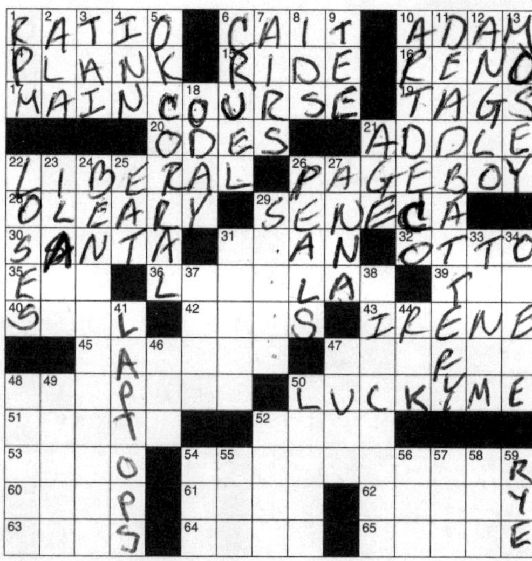

by Damon Gulczynski

EASY

ACROSS

1 Plumbing problem
5 Gulf of ___ (arm of the Red Sea)
10 Progeny: Abbr.
14 Flying start?
15 Stock of words, informally
16 Country's McEntire
17 1961–75
19 Asia's disappearing ___ Sea
20 ___ Master's Voice
21 Reprimand to a dog, maybe
23 Prank
26 Cigarette stat
28 Manipulators
29 Public transportation system in the capital of Catalonia
32 Carnival city, casually
33 Time of one's life?
34 I-85 and I-77 to get from Atlanta to Cleveland, e.g.: Abbr.
35 National Historic Landmark in Pearl Harbor
42 Tattoo parlor supply
43 Egg: Prefix
44 Rap's Dr. ___
45 Marvel Comics superhero wielding a nearly indestructible shield
50 Ralph ___ Emerson
51 Wine: Prefix
52 What birds of prey do
53 Clarinet need
55 "___ Little Teapot"
56 Roasted: Fr.
57 What 50-Across is . . . or a clue to 17-, 29-, 35- and 45-Across
63 Belarussian, e.g.
64 Change from "I do" to "I don't"?
65 Illusionist Henning
66 3M product
67 Guess things
68 Additionally

DOWN

1 Cleveland player, for short
2 Hawaiian shirt go-with
3 Bank deposit?
4 "Wuthering Heights" genre
5 Actress Gardner and others
6 Iranian holy city
7 Top fighter pilot
8 Singer Streisand
9 Rhyme scheme in the last verse of a villanelle
10 "The Fast and the Furious" racer
11 More spooky
12 Italian restaurant chain
13 "Safe!" and "You're out!"
18 French city named after the Greek goddess of victory
22 As a result of
23 Start of a magician's cry
24 Commercial alternative to waxing
25 Enterprise counselor
26 Attire for Atticus
27 Tentacled marine creature
30 Sri ___
31 1983 Michael Keaton comedy
36 Obsolescent data storage device
37 En pointe, in ballet
38 ___ Spiegel, co-founder of Snapchat
39 Prefix with -syncratic
40 Gas brand rendered in all capital letters
41 ___ of faith
45 Olive oil alternative
46 Pub fixture
47 What I may stand for?
48 Salinger title girl
49 Neighbor of Tanzania
50 Razzie Award word
54 Key with four sharps: Abbr.
55 Woes
58 Subject for Watson and Crick
59 Grayish-brown
60 The "A" of AIM
61 Followers of lambdas
62 Id's counterpart

by Mary Lou Guizzo

EASY

ACROSS

1 Small jump
4 Burrito alternative
10 Lion's sound
14 April is the only month that has one
15 Backbone-related
16 Border
17 Attila or one of his followers
18 Gifts for guests
20 Seeks answers
22 Caddie's bagful
23 Cap for a Special Forces member
24 Alternative to Spot or Rover
26 "$&#@" and "%*&!"
27 Friendly scuffles at sleepovers
32 Hoity-toity sort
33 Jimi Hendrix hairdo
34 Poems featuring 39-Across
38 Dangerous, as winter sidewalks
39 Acts of bravery
42 Mare : horse :: ___ : sheep
43 Actress Thompson of TV's "Family"
45 Double agent
46 Group of eight
48 Not good with large sums of money, in a saying
51 Furnishes with new weapons
54 Foot or yard
55 Fire-setter's crime
56 ___ Jemima
59 Scoffer's sound
62 Real name of the Pillsbury Doughboy
65 Rowboat propeller
66 Thought: Prefix
67 Harass, as a witness in court
68 Gun in an action film
69 TV rooms
70 Outer parts of pizzas
71 Agent, for short

DOWN

1 Response to a joke
2 "This one's ___" ("Our treat")
3 "The Wall" rock band
4 Amount of cough syrup: Abbr.
5 Judd who wrote and directed "Knocked Up"
6 Muck
7 One or two poker chips, maybe
8 Brand of chips
9 Sprite
10 What the numbers 9, 8, 7, 6, 5, 4, 3, 2 and 1 are in
11 Scents
12 Be of the same mind
13 Observes the Sabbath
19 Share a border
21 Farm storage building
25 Performs, to Shakespeare
26 One of the three flavors of Neapolitan ice cream, for short
27 Letters between chis and omegas
28 Ancient alpaca herder
29 ___ Young, singer with the #1 country hit "Live Fast, Love Hard, Die Young"
30 "Uncle," in poker
31 Mourning
35 Small frosted cake
36 Is indebted to
37 MacFarlane of "Family Guy"
40 Cousins of ostriches
41 Any second now
44 Fittingly
47 Trim, as a hedge
49 Prefix with potent
50 Beginning
51 Swift
52 Wear away, as soil
53 Colorado ski town
56 At a distance
57 Official language of Pakistan
58 Darkroom masters, for short
60 Discombobulate
61 Voyage
63 Airer of the Olympics since 1988
64 9 a.m. and 12 p.m.: Abbr.

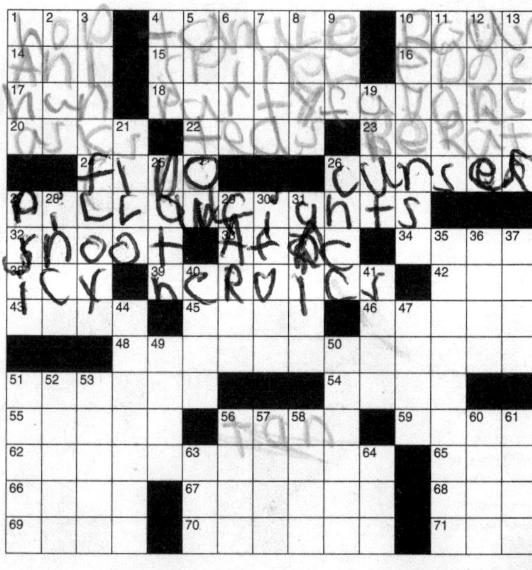

by Herre Schouwerwou

8 EASY

ACROSS

1 Marital ___
6 Food thickener
10 Mineral spring
13 ___ Burr, major role in "Hamilton"
14 Something to be settled
15 ___ Aviv
16 Major telecom's corporate headquarters?
18 1950s presidential nickname
19 "Little red" animal in a children's tale
20 Intensely longed (for)
21 One listed in a fundraising report
23 Grazing grounds
24 Dense grove
26 Early history of a drafting tool?
30 Force out of bed
31 They're big among the stars
32 Ending with web or spy
35 Skip over
36 Dutch shoe
38 Musical finale
39 Still
40 Where baby Moses was found
41 Focused beam
42 Demeanor during a kid's outdoor game?
45 Identify incorrectly
48 Part of a spider's description, in a children's song
49 Gives off
50 Entire range
52 Many a pre-med's major
55 Response to an Internet meme, maybe
56 Sending of invoices for removable car roofs?
59 Ancient dynastic ruler, briefly
60 ___-surface missile
61 Treacherous peak in the Alps
62 Filthy place
63 Tampa Bay ballplayers
64 Final ceramic layer

DOWN

1 Room often next to a bedroom
2 Not cool, informally
3 Spinach is rich in it
4 [Boo-hoo!]
5 Hit with zingers
6 Ice pack target
7 All set
8 Extension
9 Goes over again, as copy
10 Perform abysmally
11 Orange ___ (tea type)
12 It can be red or amber
14 Have a feeling for
17 Type who might say "The dog ate my homework"
22 Where future mil. leaders are trained
23 One of the seven deadly sins
25 Highly amusing experience
26 Movie in which Brad Pitt plays Achilles
27 Not all
28 Ctrl+Q function
29 Refuse to conform
32 "___ Fan Tutte"
33 Yemen seaport
34 Actress Helgenberger of "CSI"
36 Where Anna met the king
37 "Animal Farm," for one
38 Grant for moviemaking?
40 Kobe Bryant, e.g.
41 Final phase of a trip
42 Explosive initials
43 Reductive film trope for a blonde
44 Sewing accessory
45 Gets all gooey
46 Poker declaration
47 Like river deltas
51 Bldg. units
52 Nickname for New York's Aqueduct Racetrack
53 Don Juan's mother
54 Folklore villain
57 Aunt, in Andalusia
58 Rapper ___ Wayne

by Jim Holland

ACROSS

1 Online pics that often move
5 Flowed back, as the tide
10 European automaker
14 Black-and-white cookie
15 Place to be in the hot seat?
16 See 38-Across
17 Colorado River landmark dedicated by F.D.R.
19 Elects (to)
20 Sundance Film Festival entry
21 Bucks
23 Honorees on the third Sunday in June
26 Amtrak guess, for short
27 ___ Speedwagon
28 Inquire
31 Novelty B-52's song with the lyric "Watch out for that piranha"
34 Measurement for a bird
36 Title for Paul McCartney or Mick Jagger
37 Environmental sci.
38 With 16-Across, Susan Lucci's "All My Children" role
41 Carnival
44 John who directed "Mission: Impossible II"
46 Temporarily
48 California locale of several golf U.S. Opens
52 Bagel and ___
53 Ron who played Tarzan
54 Prior to, poetically
55 Hammer-wielding deity
57 Friendless
60 Lift
64 October birthstone
65 One covering a big story?
68 Big rig
69 Compound found in wine and olive oil
70 Clark ___ (Superman's alter ego)
71 ___ of March
72 Heads of classes?
73 "The Sweetest Taboo" singer

DOWN

1 Mongolian desert
2 Fe, to chemists
3 Ongoing dispute
4 Cube or sphere
5 Suffix with Brooklyn or Japan
6 Tavern
7 BFFs
8 Tooth cover
9 Former New York senator Alfonse
10 "All right already, I get it!"
11 Series of leads for a white-collar crime investigator
12 Main course
13 Landlord
18 Loved ones
22 Uber competitors
24 Ignoramus
25 Reminder of surgery
28 Wonderment
29 [not my mistake]
30 Be familiar with without having met
32 Switchblade, e.g.
33 Search (through), as evidence
35 Liquidy lump
39 Layer of paint
40 St. Louis ___ (landmark)
42 "As I see it," in textspeak
43 "Oedipus ___"
45 Some World Cup cheers
47 Now, en español
48 Former House speaker Nancy
49 Said "I do" without the to-do
50 Eaten away, like the first words of 17-, 31-, 48- and 65-Across in order?
51 Flummox
56 Oven shelves
58 Whitney and Manning
59 It is, en español
61 Furniture store that also sells Swedish meatballs
62 What to click after finishing an email
63 Suffix with cigar
66 Number starting many a countdown
67 11th graders: Abbr.

by Howard Barkin

10 EASY

ACROSS

1 Like "War and Peace," famously
5 Exposed
10 StubHub's parent
14 Instrument that begins an orchestra's tune-up
15 Gushes onstage, say
17 Tip of Italy, once?
18 Most of the leading characters in "Babe"
20 To-do
21 Recipe no.
22 Queen of Sparta
23 Downed, as a meal
25 Tiny bit
26 Fitness program popularized in the 1990s
28 Things kids make in the winter
31 Skip over
33 Sitting room
34 Where Oman Air is headquartered
37 Apiece
38 Refs. that may occupy whole shelves
41 Elle Decor reader . . . or any of the names hidden in 18-, 28-, 52- and 66-Across?
45 Casting need
46 His, to Hilaire
47 "See?!"
48 ___-Lorraine
51 Hard-to-read character
52 Aerial navigation beacon
55 "In my view . . ."
59 Poehler of "Sisters"
60 Birthplace of the Baath Party: Abbr.
61 Any of las Filipinas
63 Towing org.
64 Karate studio
66 Serious setback for a kicker
69 Youngest player ever to hit 500 home runs, familiarly
70 Think creatively
71 Tiny matter
72 Lee side, informally
73 Dashboard array
74 Trait origin

DOWN

1 Lite, on labels
2 Michelle in the White House
3 El ___ (the United States, to Central Americans)
4 Masterpiece
5 Nota ___
6 In the thick of
7 Like the numerals V and I
8 Gate info
9 The Blue Hen State
10 1994 P.G.A. Tour Rookie of the Year
11 Conclusion of an arduous process
12 Plain font
13 Things gained and lost in football
16 Cool red giant
19 Roberto in Cooperstown
24 Blowup: Abbr.
27 "Time to Say Goodbye" tenor Andrea
29 Many David Brooks pieces
30 Looked up, in a way
32 "Lord, is ___?"
34 Old Russian space station
35 Jean-Luc Godard's "___ Femme Coquette"
36 Reliable source of money
37 Hog the mirror, maybe
39 Susan of "L.A. Law"
40 Madeira Mrs.
42 Recognition from the Academy
43 Poker great Ungar
44 ___ Sea (Italy/Greece separator)
49 Message that might be laid out in coconuts on a beach
50 Early Indo-European
51 Scalp
52 Missile tracker
53 Love, to Casanova
54 Radner of comedy
56 Brown a bit
57 Sorkin who created HBO's "The Newsroom"
58 "I rock!"
62 Tells a tale
65 Has too much, in brief
67 ___ pond (ornamental pool)
68 Spree

by Zhouqin Burnikel

EASY **11**

ACROSS

1 Bread with a pocket
5 Ivan the Terrible, for one
9 Positive, as an attitude
14 Tiny building block
15 Down-on-his-luck wanderer
16 Farewell that's "bid"
17 Rebels
19 Copenhageners, e.g.
20 2002 Tom Cruise sci-fi film
22 ___ Khan
23 "___-Man," 2015 superhero movie
24 Related to fireworks
30 Alias
33 All of them lead to Rome, in a saying
34 Right of way, at law
36 Greek liqueur
37 Square, triangle or circle
39 On the Pacific, say
40 Boss
42 Small hill
43 Put money into, as a meter
44 They know how to have a good time
47 Smith who sang the theme for "Spectre"
48 Ages and ages
49 Sublime physical performance . . . or a hint to this puzzle's circled letters
57 Relish
58 Violent vortex
60 Note taker
61 Forest scent
62 Surrender
63 Lost on purpose
64 Lost traction
65 Rio de Janeiro, for the 2016 Olympics

DOWN

1 It's not easy to shoot
2 Agenda listing
3 Tennille of pop music's Captain & Tennille
4 "So be it!"
5 Cry to the cavalry
6 It starts with Aries
7 Assist with a heist, say
8 Like Santa's cheeks
9 Rhythm
10 Change with the times
11 El ___ (weather phenomenon)
12 Bambi, for one
13 Boot from power
18 Nannies and billies
21 Employee's reward
24 Prosecutor's burden
25 "___ got mail"
26 Torn down
27 Aroma
28 Valentine symbol
29 Snooze
30 Creator of "The Tortoise and the Hare"
31 Mournful ring
32 Dickens's "___ of Two Cities"
35 Hand, to José
37 Sordid
38 Counterpart of his
41 Fictional pirate who shares his name with a bird
42 Smallville family
45 Saudi neighbor
46 Put together, as funds
47 Slingshot missile
49 "Hey, you!"
50 Vow
51 Second-to-last word in a fairy tale
52 Little rascals
53 Something chewed by a nervous person
54 Yen
55 Brand touted as "Milk's favorite cookie"
56 Go-aheads
59 New York baseballer

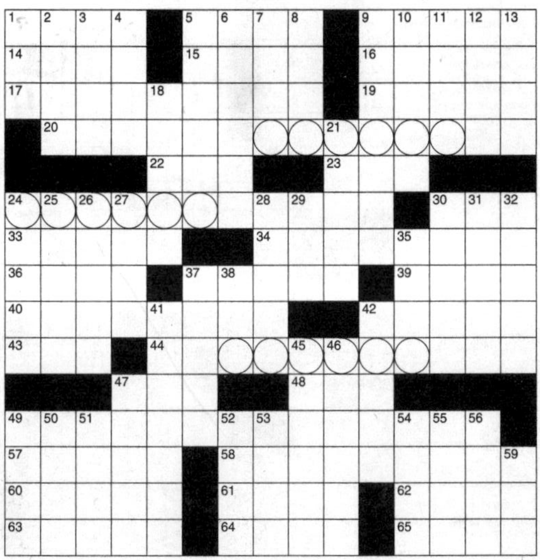

by Kathy Wienberg

EASY

ACROSS

1 Boots, backpack, tent, etc.
5 Triangle on a pool table
9 "You ___" ("Sure thing")
15 ___ Reader (alternative digest)
16 Maker of Arctic Blast and Java Freeze beverages
17 Arthurian island
18 Some PC screens
19 Criticized nigglingly
21 Roosted on
23 Mentalist Geller
24 Ticks off
25 Tattered
28 Travelers with paddles
31 Gun, slangily
34 Mideast ruler
35 Landlord's counterpart
36 Struggled to make progress
42 Digs deeply (into)
43 Beano competitor
44 Bull session?
45 Halite formations that might be oil reservoirs
50 How-to book
52 Address of Juliet's balcony?
54 Umberto ___, author of "The Name of the Rose"
56 Proceeded without trying very hard
59 Classic out-of-office sign . . . or what this puzzle's author has done?
62 "C'mon, be ___"
63 Nearest target for a bowler
64 Fashion designer Klein
65 Repetitive means of learning
66 Hitting high in the air
67 Colors, as Easter eggs
68 Did 80 on the highway, say

DOWN

1 Swallows deeply
2 ". . . and on and on and on"
3 Newswoman Mitchell
4 Make another image of
5 They get the paddy started
6 Part of U.S.C.G.A.: Abbr.
7 "Juno" actor Michael
8 Avoided phoniness
9 Celeb's arrest report, to the celeb, say
10 Actress Mendes of "2 Fast 2 Furious"
11 Neighbor of Caps Lock
12 Bumbling detective of film
13 "Spring forward, fall back" unit
14 One in opposition
20 Time immemorial
22 Aetna offering, briefly
26 Mimic
27 ___ Torretta, 1992 Heisman Trophy winner
29 "___ Mine" (George Harrison autobiography)
30 Noble knight who found the Holy Grail
32 Wolf Blitzer's employer
33 You may be asked to arrive 90 mins. prior to this
35 Sneaky shelters
36 Pres. who recuperated at Warm Springs, Ga.
37 Sign before Virgo
38 Aristocratic ancestry
39 Eye layer whose name derives from the Latin for "grape"
40 Gas in signs
41 "Spring forward, fall back" inits.
45 Fifth Avenue retailer
46 13-Down, in Italian
47 Grinding teeth
48 Fall Out Boy genre
49 Where John Kerry and Bob Kerrey served
51 On drugs
53 Eyed caddishly
54 They benefit from boosters
55 Crash, with "out"
57 Minuscule
58 Feminine suffix
60 Prefix with center
61 1950s car feature

by Byron Walden

EASY 13

ACROSS

1 Liberals, with "the"
5 Too
9 Basics of education
13 A pupil is in the middle of it
14 Finnish-based telecom
16 Screwdriver or hammer
17 *Party with disguises
19 Build one's muscles, with "up"
20 Something an e-cig lacks
21 ". . . and yet, here we ___"
22 Like the glass in some church windows
24 Emphasis
27 Bowling lanes
28 Endings of chess games
30 Cosmic destiny
32 Like devoted fans
33 What Grizzlies and Timberwolves play in
35 Enemy
38 Plug-in in an amp
39 Puppy amuser . . . or the end of the answer to each starred clue
40 Sch. founded by Thomas Jefferson
41 Act as a quizmaster
42 Crime that Joan of Arc was charged with
43 Change for a five
44 Casual eatery
45 Job for Mrs. Doubtfire or Mary Poppins
46 Pilgrimage site
49 It's worth two points in football
52 Conductor Bernstein
54 Hot off the presses
55 Move like a buoy
58 Icicle site
59 *Barrier outside a popular nightclub
62 "For the first time ___ . . ."
63 AOL service
64 Burden
65 Money in Mexico
66 Birds whose heads can move 270°
67 Toward sunset

DOWN

1 World capital whose name is a kind of bean
2 Noteworthy periods
3 *Food item often dipped in ketchup or tartar sauce
4 " 'Tis a pity"
5 Actor Braugher of "Brooklyn Nine-Nine"
6 Lower parts of 18-Down
7 Jamaican music genre
8 Lubricates
9 Notable Hun
10 Frontiersman Daniel
11 New York's ___ Island
12 Winter coasters
15 Mass assistant
18 Headphones cover them
23 Cosmetics brand owned by Revlon
25 Kennedy who said "Frankly, I don't mind not being president"
26 Shish kebab holders
28 Call from a crib
29 Hertz rival
31 Insects in colonies
33 "Where does that guy get off?!"
34 "___ comes trouble!"
35 *Inaptly named part of the elbow
36 Where a cake is baked
37 "Piece of cake"
39 Shanghai's land
43 Cereal grain
44 Money, in Mexico
45 Politico Gingrich
46 Snooze
47 Throw, as an anchor
48 Wanders around
50 Blacksmith's block
51 Senses
53 Floor model
56 ___ Dei (Catholic group)
57 A+++
60 Bill, after being signed by the president
61 Column's counterpart

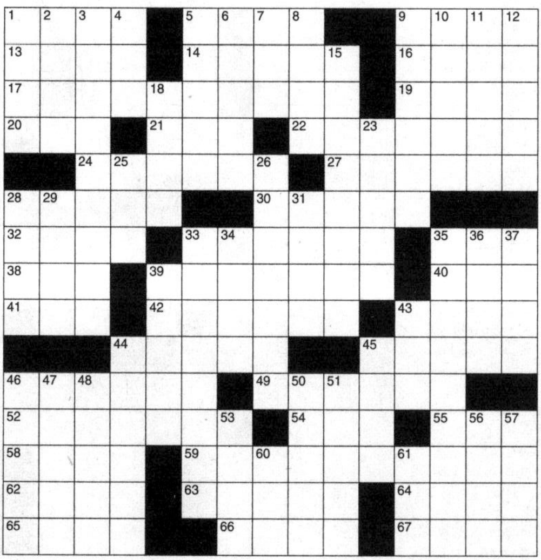

by Ian Livengood

14 EASY

ACROSS

1 Hearty har-hars
5 "Keep ___ the D.L." ("Don't tell anyone")
9 Jockey's attire
14 Slightly
15 Marathon runner's stat
16 Burger King or Costco
17 "Little" Dickens girl
18 Subject of the 2013 documentary "Blackfish"
19 Temporary skin decorator
20 Results of some unexciting at-bats
23 Rock band that gets fans charged up?
24 Micromanager, say
26 "Well, aren't you something!"
29 Celebratory cry
30 Natural radiation?
31 Pond dweller that can regenerate its eyes
35 With 43-Across, singer of the lyric formed by the first parts of 20-, 24-, 40-, 51- and 58-Across
39 N.Y.C. subway overseer
40 As you like it, in a recipe
42 Forest animal
43 See 35-Across
45 Paul who sang "Eso Beso"
46 German refusal
47 Leader who said "Once all struggle is grasped, miracles are possible"
49 DVD alternative
51 Snafu
57 No longer anonymous, in brief
58 High jinks
62 "Dead serious!"
64 Compton's state, to hip-hoppers
65 The duck in "Peter and the Wolf"
66 It's just below C level
67 Country between Sudan and Niger
68 ___ pants (earth-toned apparel)
69 Really put one's foot down
70 ___ 'n Honey (granola bar option)
71 Didn't just guess

DOWN

1 Positive Chinese principle
2 Competitor of Lyft
3 Drug bust quantity, casually
4 Caribbean island whose capital is Castries
5 Product that once bore a click wheel
6 Holder of The Hermit, The Devil and The Magician
7 Befall
8 Quaint cousin of "Suh-weet!"
9 Colgate, but not Crest: Abbr.
10 "Yep, that's clear"
11 Weapon held on horseback
12 "Yes 'n no"
13 Twinkies or Pringles
21 Silent assent
22 Like some winks
25 Lose vividness
26 Meat often served with mint jelly
27 Prefix with complete
28 Action in go fish
32 Sched. figure
33 Sickly-looking
34 "That's bad!"
36 Zig or zag
37 Heroine princess of Mozart's "Idomeneo"
38 Big Apple fashion inits.
40 Rip
41 Papers covered with dirt?
44 Antidiarrheal brand
46 Key near the upper-right corner of a PC keyboard
48 Go (for)
50 Shortest zodiac sign, lexically
51 They may be blown by a magician
52 Ratify
53 Easy-to-digest dessert
54 Son of Madonna and Guy Ritchie
55 City NE of Lincoln
56 Starting key of 35-/43-Across's "Starman"
59 Abba of Israel
60 "When in ___ . . ."
61 "That HURT!"
63 Mind reader's skill, for short

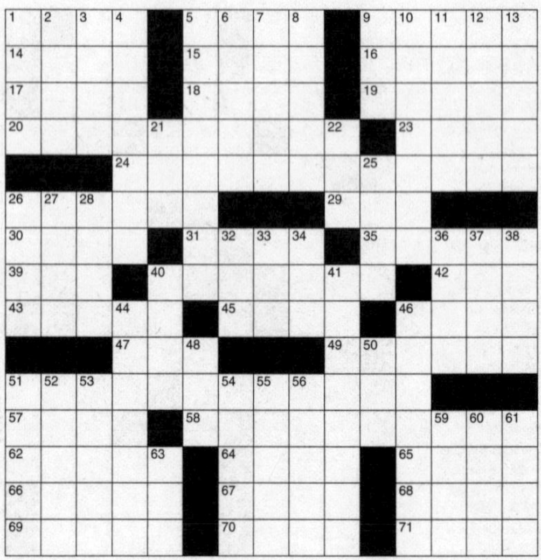

by Sam Ezersky

EASY 15

ACROSS

1 Switch that changes bands on the radio
5 Memo
9 Frequently
14 ___ Crawley, countess on "Downton Abbey"
15 One of the Great Lakes
16 Cut, as a pumpkin
17 Like most college dorms nowadays
18 Title locale in a 1987 Oliver Stone drama
20 U-turn from WNW
21 Animal hide
22 Four-baggers
23 Sandbars
25 Any old Joe
26 Title locale in a 1950 Billy Wilder film noir
33 Youth org. since 1910
34 Make a selection
35 Longtime N.B.A. coach Pat
36 Hawaiian shindig
38 "$500 on the roan nag," e.g.
39 "You and who ___?" (fighting words)
40 "Love Story" author Segal
42 "Hey ___, what's up?"
43 A, in Berlin
44 Title locale in a 2001 David Lynch thriller
49 Doctor's charge
50 "Time is money" and "Knowledge is power"
51 Floating aimlessly
55 "Well, what do we have here!"
57 F.D.R.'s successor
58 "Bonnie and Clyde" and "Thelma & Louise" . . . or a hint to 18-, 26- and 44-Across
60 Lead-in to boy or girl
61 Sleep disorder
62 Dot on an ocean map
63 Trounce
64 Started
65 Topic of a pre-election news story
66 Detective fiction writer ___ Stanley Gardner

DOWN

1 Means of entry
2 Kind of pork at a Chinese restaurant
3 Conditionally released from custody
4 Seeing red
5 Most modern
6 Spoken, not written
7 ___ at windmills
8 Sushi selection
9 Month with Columbus Day
10 Old MacDonald's place
11 Arborist's focus
12 "Have I ___ told you . . . ?"
13 Brooklyn hoopsters
19 Jewish house of worship
21 Earnest request
24 In that capacity
25 Campaign giveaway
27 Move up and down, as a doll's head
28 "Carmen" or "Rigoletto"
29 Meredith of daytime TV
30 Crammer's last chance
31 Hi-___ image
32 Easter egg coating
36 Moon landing craft, for short
37 Neighbor of Arg. and Braz.
41 Dustin who won an Oscar for "Rain Man"
43 Mini-whirlpool
45 Actor Jared of "Dallas Buyers Club"
46 Distressed maiden, in fairy tales
47 ___ virgin
48 Home for a Rockefeller or a Vanderbilt
51 Mideast native
52 Narcotize
53 Tolled, as a bell
54 Notion
55 Japanese soup
56 Scream
59 Big cheese
60 Face on a fiver

by Gary Cee

16 EASY

ACROSS
1 Something seen in the 6-Across
6 Blue expanse
9 Melee
14 Chick of jazz
15 Whom Uncle Sam wants, on an old poster
16 "___ en Rose" (song classic)
17 Genius's head?
18 Yule quaff
19 Gems with kaleidoscopic colors
20 Group found above the 37-Across
23 Field worker, e.g.
26 Old atlas inits.
27 Things spotted in a casino
28 Paul ___, 1993 World Series M.V.P.
30 Prop for the Tin Man
32 ___ Mix
33 Dealer buster
36 Politburo refusals
37 Line dividing 6- and 70-Across
39 Thermonuclear experiment of the '50s
43 Dutch cheese
44 "Didn't you get the ___?"
48 Poker declaration
50 Muslim holy month
52 Go separate ways
53 Mani-pedi spot
56 "Hey, wait your turn in line!"
57 Group found below the 37-Across
60 Express appreciation for
61 Zilch
62 Request forgiveness for
66 Strangely coincidental, say
67 Hip-hop's Dr. ___
68 "If ___ a Carpenter"
69 Dog-eared
70 Blue expanse
71 Something seen in the 70-Across

DOWN
1 Windows runners
2 Bathroom, in Bath
3 Bark
4 Big name in on-demand media
5 Bald baby?
6 Coordinate
7 Nutcases
8 Cheap 1980s car imports
9 Lump
10 At a clip
11 One of the seven deadly sins
12 University of Kentucky athlete
13 Alleviates
21 Maine university town
22 1960s Angela Davis do, informally
23 Channel for cinephiles
24 "How delightful!"
25 ___ de France
29 Like a 1913 Liberty Head nickel
31 Quaint lodging
34 Expunge
35 Peter or Ivan
37 Brooklyn ___, N.Y.: Abbr.
38 Saudi neighbor
39 Trendy urbanite
40 Windpipe
41 Aviation's Amelia
42 "Oh, shut up!"
44 Supersonic speed
45 Follower of indiana., ohio. or colorado.
46 Wrestling need
47 Clip-___ (some sunglasses)
49 Immigrant's course, for short
51 Subway artwork, maybe
54 Skin cream brand
55 Blazing
58 "___-doke!"
59 Bother for Bowser
63 Anthem contraction
64 2nd Amendment advocate
65 Slippery swimmer

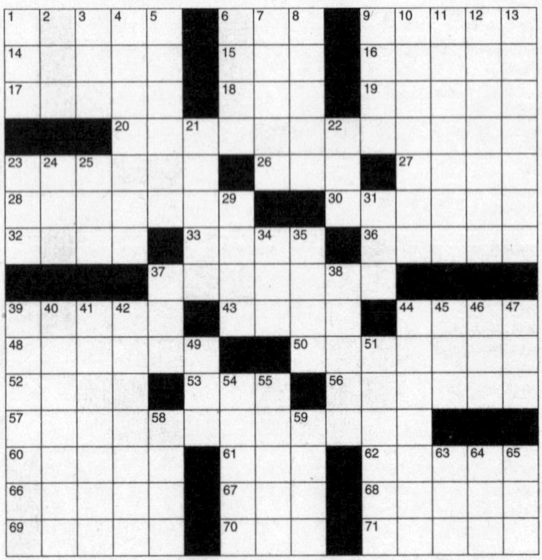

by Peter A. Collins

ACROSS

1 Gift tag word
5 Golden calf, e.g.
9 Comes to earth
14 Use the oven
15 Goya's "The Naked ___"
16 Mythical hunter
17 *Like a nursery rhyme spider
19 Paris transport system
20 Queen in "Frozen"
21 Setting for much of "Breaking Bad"
23 Boxing decision, for short
24 Typists' timesavers
27 What sets things in motion
29 Palindromic girl's name
30 Host Banks of TV's "America's Next Top Model"
32 Fussy sort
33 Daddy-o
35 Galley propellers
37 Laura of "The Fault in Our Stars"
39 *Big seller for Sports Illustrated
43 Sci-fi phaser setting
44 1962 007 villain
45 Palindromic boy's name
46 Diva's delivery
48 Brainstorm
50 "No one wants to hear about that!"
51 Gesture of sarcastic support
54 Buffy, to vampires
56 Duke's athletic grp.
57 "Keeping Up With the Kardashians" sister
58 Psych 101 subjects
59 Fixture at a subway entrance
61 Tabloid twosomes . . . or a hint to the answers to the starred clues
66 Name repeated before "pumpkin eater"
67 Manhattan neighborhood next to TriBeCa
68 Boater's haven
69 Eye sores
70 Part of the Grim Reaper's getup
71 "I'd like 'The New York Times Crossword' for $200, ___"

DOWN

1 Org. with a Most Wanted list
2 Pied Piper's follower
3 Gives the go-ahead
4 "Twilight" author Stephenie
5 Long-distance lover's lament
6 Figures to be processed
7 Breakfast drinks, briefly
8 1972 hit for Eric Clapton
9 Coach who said "The dictionary is the only place that success comes before work"
10 "Gone ___ the days . . ."
11 *Basics, informally
12 Dweebs
13 Stuck-up sort
18 Rorschach test element
22 Org. for Nadal and Federer
24 Atlas contents
25 Boldly states
26 *Place often marked with a star on 24-Down
27 Something to pack up the trunk for
28 Intentionally mislead
31 "Kills bugs dead!" brand
34 Blue creature of old Saturday morning TV
36 Transmit
38 "You're looking at the wrong guy"
40 3 Musketeers alternative
41 Volunteers, gives to charity, etc.
42 Dark film genre
47 Boxer Muhammad
49 Baseball's Moises or Jesus
51 "Oh no you didn't!" sounds
52 Singing eightsome
53 Barn-raising group
55 Pet-protecting org.
58 Talk back?
60 Gen. Robert E. ___
62 When repeated, pretentious
63 [That is so funny]
64 New Year's ___
65 Possible reason for an R rating

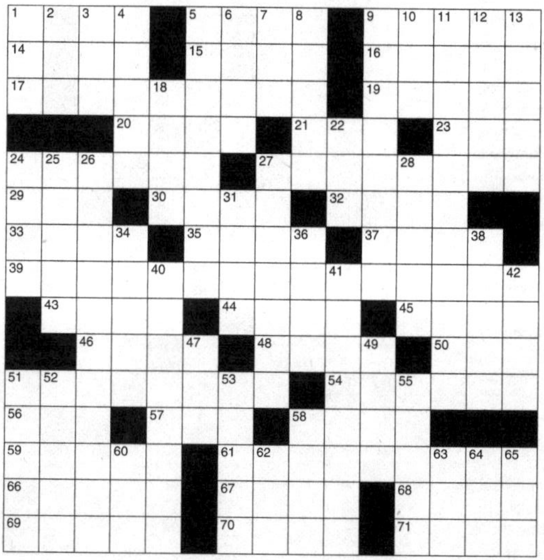

by Paolo Pasco

18 EASY

ACROSS

1 Soapy powder mineral
5 Vague
9 Ohno on skates
14 Valhalla's ruling god
15 Malarial fever
16 Gore who wrote "Lincoln"
17 Detonates a weapon in the underworld?
19 Came about
20 Construct
21 Raises the price of some pastries?
23 "By all means!"
24 Pep rally shout
27 Candidate's quest
28 Adjust, as a watch
30 Junkyard jalopies
34 Clocks trainees for a fabled race rematch?
38 Branch of Islam
39 They all lead to Rome, it's said
40 With 43-Down, Apple C.E.O. beginning in 2011
41 Where some athletes need guards
42 Something calamine lotion alleviates
43 Cuts up little bloodsuckers?
45 Get along
47 Camera attachment, often
48 Landing spot for Santa
50 Over there, quaintly
51 Poke
54 Puts up with one's family?
58 Vulgar
60 Parts of hearts
61 Scrutinizes the underworld?
64 Cops' crook-catching hoax
65 Beringer Vineyards' county
66 Saved for later
67 Equivocate
68 W.W. II turning point
69 Vittles

DOWN

1 Maguire of "The Great Gatsby"
2 Be nuts about
3 Citrus supply at a bar
4 Network for market monitors
5 "I told ya!"
6 Wine or cheese concern
7 Bantu speaker of southern Africa
8 Sounds from pounds
9 James Cameron megahit of 2009
10 Transport for William Kidd or Jack Sparrow
11 Skunk's defense
12 Hold out
13 Exuberant flamenco cries
18 Emphasize
22 Takes part in a bee
25 Mount Etna emission
26 Moor
28 Purposeful misdirection
29 Musketeers and blind mice
31 Stylish
32 Glitch
33 Bratty retort
34 Clip or snip
35 Teeny bit
36 Big name in trucks
37 Unoccupied
41 Stop the flow of
43 See 40-Across
44 Unwelcome sign for latecomers
46 Proper medicine amount
49 Diabolical sort
51 Southern region of ancient Palestine
52 Skilled
53 One-ups
54 Shindig
55 Diminutive suffix
56 Unlikely to get rain
57 Long-distance swimmer Diana
59 Tool with teeth
62 U.S. asbestos regulator
63 "You don't ___!"

by Lynn Lempel

EASY 19

ACROSS

1 President after Tyler
5 Quantities: Abbr.
9 Contradicted
15 Microwave, e.g.
16 Excess spending by Congress
17 Change over time
18 "Othello" villain
19 Opposite of work
20 Doesn't just throw away
21 Cut with a knife
22 Enter gradually
24 New York's Washington Square ___
25 Canon camera brand
26 ___ horse (surprise candidate)
27 Job for a sleuth
29 Swings wildly
31 Blowgun ammunition
32 Letters between O and S
35 Young deer
36 "Peter Pan" girl
37 Yes, to Yves
38 President-elect, e.g.
39 Touched in the head
40 Like sneakers and corsets
42 Earth-friendly prefix
43 Stealing
45 Nominates
46 Gen ___ (boomer's child)
47 President after Roosevelt
48 Blow a ___ (lose one's temper)
49 Prefix with dynamic
50 Mini-pie
51 "___ well" (George Washington's last words)
53 Legal wrong
56 Tell
58 Swear to
59 Chorus after "Who wants ice cream?"
61 Black, to a bard
62 Former late-night host Jay
63 Used a rotary phone
64 Baltimore's ___ McHenry
65 Roman road
66 Gossipy types
67 Chuck
68 President after Nixon

DOWN

1 Composure
2 President's workplace
3 Senator or representative
4 End of one's rope?
5 Takes to a higher court
6 Grinding teeth
7 Cal ___, Dean's "East of Eden" role
8 Terrier type
9 St. ___ (dog)
10 Adam's madam
11 Jeweler's magnifying glass
12 "Casablanca" woman
13 For all time
14 2-Down fixture
23 Quitter's words
26 Breakfast alcove
28 Coif creator
30 Shoemaker's tool
31 Like a magician's hands
32 President's option for an unwanted bill
33 Participant at a presidential press conference, say
34 Clear (of)
36 Float, as an aroma
38 Home for G. W. Bush
39 Daniel who wrote "Robinson Crusoe"
41 Comic strip cry of dismay
44 Famous London department store
45 Mom and dad
48 Swamp critters
49 Slanted
50 Off-limits
52 Zorro's weapon
53 Neat
54 "Garfield" dog
55 Horse color
57 Liberals, with "the"
58 A, in Arabic
60 Anti-trafficking org.

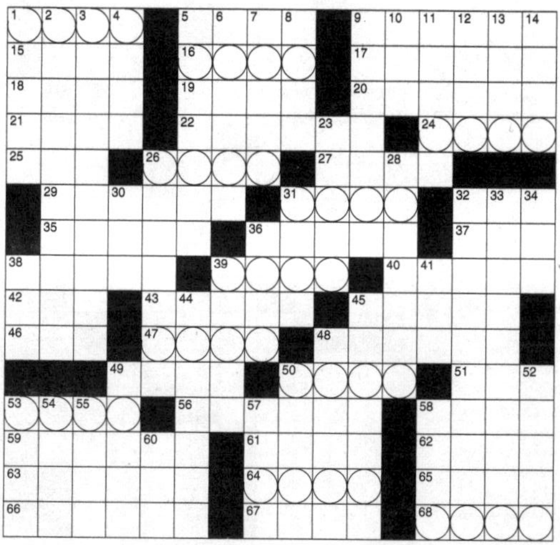

by David J. Kahn

20 EASY

ACROSS

1 Record label for Bing Crosby's "White Christmas"
6 Greek R's
10 Mets' home before Citi Field
14 "Too rich for my blood"
15 Ice dam site
16 Brick carriers
17 Banned wrestling hold
19 Dr. ___, Austin Powers's foe
20 Andrea ___, ship that sank in 1956
21 Big concert venue
22 Together, musically
25 Aid in accomplishing a goal
28 The Sunflower State
30 Actress Thompson of "Family"
31 Guest you might not want to stay for too long
32 Pop singer from 27-Down
34 Inits. on an airport uniform
37 "Don't give up the fight!"
40 Workplace often surrounded by trailers
41 Seize (from)
42 Gives stars to, say
43 ___ to middling
44 Actress Anderson of "Baywatch"
45 Risk everything
50 Slippery
51 Gold star or silver medal
52 Realty listing data
54 The "B" in Roy G. Biv
55 Carved decoration on a ship's prow . . . or a hint to the first word of 17-, 25-, 37- and 45-Across
60 Something you can see through
61 "Dark Sky Island" singer, 2015
62 "May the ___ be with you"
63 Coup d' ___
64 Indian royal
65 Many a middle-schooler

DOWN

1 "What's the ___?"
2 Bird that can run up to 30 m.p.h.
3 One of 15 in a typical weekday crossword: Abbr.
4 Dead-end street
5 1 for hydrogen or 2 for helium: Abbr.
6 Linotype machine, nowadays
7 Starts, as a big job
8 Egg: Prefix
9 Rand Paul or Marco Rubio: Abbr.
10 Everest guide
11 Homely home
12 Minneapolis suburb
13 Symbol of Jesus Christ in the "Narnia" series
18 Historical periods
21 Only country in which Catalan is the official language
22 Half of S.W.A.K.
23 Who wrote "Let us not speak of them, but look, and pass on"
24 Dark
26 "All ___ lost"
27 Honolulu's island
29 All thumbs
32 Red Sox Hall-of-Famer Bobby
33 Yiddish cries
34 Private pupil
35 Part of a fishing line to which a hook is attached
36 Analyze, as ore
38 Oakland paper, for short
39 Where you might hear "Ding ding ding!"
43 Setting for "Little Red Riding Hood"
44 Czech form of the French "Pierre"
45 One of seven in a Hawthorne title
46 Small hooter
47 Animals, collectively
48 Delivery person?
49 Island neighbor of 27-Down
53 Test by lifting
55 "Oh, ___ cryin' out loud!"
56 "___ perfect world . . ."
57 Before, poetically
58 Star pitcher
59 Cub Scout group

by Ron and Nancy Byron

EASY 21

ACROSS

1 Indian in many an old western
7 Prix ___ (restaurant offering)
11 "Who cares"
14 More ritzy
15 The Almighty
16 "___ Baba and the 40 Thieves"
17 Teasing
19 Decide not to join, with "out"
20 Put-ons
21 The first "R" of R&R
22 1/8 fluid ounce
23 Things "counted" when taking attendance
25 Fictional Plaza Hotel girl
27 The "R" of I.R.S.
30 Former "Family Feud" host Richard
31 Like a game that's played on the road
32 155, in ancient Rome
34 When Presidents' Day is always celebrated: Abbr.
35 747s, e.g.
36 Japan's so-called "City of Ten Thousand Shrines"
38 Immediately, on an order
42 Like Willie Winkie
44 Las Vegas's home: Abbr.
45 "Uh-uh"
46 Come into view
49 State of thinking
51 Fabricated
52 Miles per hour, e.g.
53 Fall over one's feet
54 Russia's ___ Mountains
56 Bone below the knee
60 "Cool, man!"
61 Coalition with no infighting
63 Interject
64 Start of a play
65 Power failure
66 C minor, for Beethoven's Fifth
67 Word following "If not now"
68 Presidential palace in Paris

DOWN

1 iTunes Store purchases
2 Winnie-the-___
3 "___ silly question . . ."
4 *One "as lucky as lucky can be," in "Mary Poppins"
5 Kermit creator Jim
6 Unit of work
7 Fireplace smoke escapes through them
8 + and – particles
9 *Showing at an adult film theater
10 Summer hours in N.Y.C.
11 Native New Zealanders
12 Texas city on the Mexican border
13 Ones used by the Mafia
18 Without restraint
22 Done in a quick but effective manner . . . or like the answers to the three starred clues?
24 *Sudden, unprovoked slug
26 Mekong native
27 Period of British rule in India
28 Mother sheep
29 Winery container
33 ___ Trapp family ("The Sound of Music" group)
37 The Parthenon, for one
39 Emergency transmission
40 Gorilla
41 Animal with a collar
43 Water: Fr.
46 Northeast Corridor service
47 Veterans Day event
48 Onetime stage name for Sean Combs
50 Shrimper's catch
52 Smooth sheet material
55 Bar mitzvah or communion
57 Constrictors
58 Playwright William
59 Suit to ___
61 Detroit labor org.
62 Buck's mate

by Ed Sessa

22 EASY

ACROSS

1 It's often said with a smile
7 Madrid-to-Lisbon dir.
10 Black & Decker competitor
14 Medium for Michelangelo
15 Characters on a wanted poster
16 Bone parallel to the radius
17 Remove from practice
18 Loved, as archaeological work?
19 Forbid
20 "Gentlemen Prefer Blondes" blonde
23 Word with cream or cutie
24 Volley
28 Inquires about
30 Come out on top
32 Call on a dairy farm
33 Non-pro?
34 Tiniest leftover
38 Ones watching their plates?
41 2012 election name
42 One of two in a Big Mac
43 ___ land
44 Bombard
45 Makeshift ghost costume
46 One for Caesar?
47 Countless centuries
49 Bowling
51 Pink shade
56 One terminus of a Japanese bullet train
57 Former ember
58 Aids for some urban commuters
60 Evil "Get Smart" group
62 Office PC setup
63 Epoch when modern mammals arose
68 It's a small whirl after all
69 Sundial three
70 Stick : punishment :: ___ : reward
71 Simon ___
72 BlackBerry, e.g., briefly
73 Freeloader

DOWN

1 Military authority: Abbr.
2 Beijing's river basin
3 Nurse settings, briefly
4 Flow back
5 Skiing event with gates
6 Dulles airport designer Saarinen
7 Goes in up to one's knees, say
8 Hide in the shadows
9 Fights, as war
10 Direction opposite nord
11 Problem with lifting?
12 Belly button type
13 With 51-Down, description of the circled answers?
21 Enthusiastic
22 Sam-___ (Seuss character)
24 Passport certification
25 Golfer Palmer, informally
26 Another nickname for the Ocean State
27 Big name in luxury bags
29 Bunglings
31 H.M.O. doctor designations
35 Southwest Indian
36 Virgil described its eruption in the "Aeneid"
37 Tiny storage unit
39 Drop heavily
40 "The Metamorphosis" protagonist
48 Slap handcuffs on
50 "Can't do it"
51 See 13-Down
52 Carne ___ (Mexican restaurant order)
53 Black flower in a Dumas title
54 "Let me repeat . . ."
55 In ___ paratus (ready for anything)
59 Muscles above the abs
61 Part of DOS: Abbr.
64 ___-Magnon man
65 Suffix with north
66 Nutmeg-topped drink
67 Summer on the Seine

by Elizabeth C. Gorski

ACROSS

1 Exterior
6 Acronym on an online help page
9 Treat cruelly
14 Toy company that gave us Frisbee and Slip 'N Slide
15 Sch. in Tempe
16 Type of composition that Bach is noted for
17 They're taken in punishment, so to speak
18 *Hairstyle popularized by Jennifer Aniston's character on "Friends"
20 Omar who portrayed Dr. Zhivago
22 Happy as a ___
23 In a cheerful and pleasant manner
26 Write permanently
30 Mysterious sightings that hover
32 Compete (for)
33 The ___ Kid (Willie Mays)
35 Tennis match units
36 A low one is good in baseball, in brief
37 Words written by a teacher on a failed test, perhaps
38 Nelson Mandela's org.
39 What the answers to the four starred clues are
42 Fellows
43 So not cool
45 Tell a whopper
46 Mom's mom
47 Tremors
49 Female sheep
50 Does stage work
51 "Oh, one more thing . . ."
52 Set of info about sets of info
55 Opposite of quiet
57 Little blue cartoon characters whose adversary is named Gargamel
60 *Boots brand big in grunge fashion
65 Shatter
66 Sharper than 90°
67 Trivial gripe
68 Jouster's weapon
69 "War and Peace" famously has more than 1,200
70 Crafty
71 Thrill

DOWN

1 Avian hooters
2 "Forget it!"
3 *Hand-held "pets" with digital faces
4 Catherine the Great, for one
5 Bagful on a pitcher's mound
6 Obese
7 Baseball bat wood
8 Stop, as an uprising
9 Many miles off
10 Ohio State student
11 "Blech!"
12 "A Boy Named ___" (1969 song)
13 Fish that is long and thin
19 Fish that are flat and wide
21 TV's "Hawaii ___"
24 Puts on TV
25 Printed handout
27 *Dance associated with a #1 Los del Rio hit
28 Sidewalk material
29 "Laughing" animals
30 Patriotic Olympics chant
31 Herb sometimes called "sweet anise"
34 Donkey
39 2100, in civilian time
40 Onetime big name in Japanese electronics
41 Monopoly cards
44 Quarantine
46 Word before gas or disaster
48 Obscene material
53 Perfect places
54 Mosey along
56 Metals from lodes
58 Fiction's opposite
59 ___-Ball (arcade game)
60 Fist bump
61 ___ Victor
62 Make a face for the camera
63 Zero, in a soccer score
64 Very messy room

by Damon Gulczynski

24 EASY

ACROSS

1 Unable to escape
8 Double helix parts
15 Cuckoo, from the Yiddish
16 Hard work
17 Something to check if the lights go out
18 Tree whose berries flavor gin
19 Memorable hurricane of 2011
20 Disneyland locale, briefly
21 Rebellious Turner
22 Lay out plates, silverware, napkins, etc.
28 Princess in "Frozen"
30 ___ shark
31 Cabbage for miso soup?
32 Where Samsung is headquartered
34 Cut out (for)
37 "Anatomy of a Murder" director
40 The Taj Mahal, for one
41 Mrs. Eisenhower
42 One of the five W's
43 Poetic measure
44 Step on a ladder
48 Quick-cooking cut of meat
53 An eagle beats it
54 Fracking material
55 Major artery
57 Placate
60 Wrap "worn" by 17-, 22-, 37- and 48-Across?
62 Cafeteria worker's wear
63 Opening on the side of a vest
64 Toads and kangaroos
65 Sci-fi weapon

DOWN

1 "Nothing's broken!"
2 ___ network (term in anatomy and artificial intelligence)
3 Building, inventory, cash on hand, etc.
4 Now's partner
5 Unsophisticated sorts
6 Previously
7 ___ Romana
8 Virgin Island that's 60% national park
9 Armistice
10 Stampeded toward
11 Walled Spanish city
12 40 winks
13 Game cube
14 Camera inits.
20 No-win chess outcome
23 Marry a cutie on the q.t., maybe
24 Get the show on the road
25 Tiny memory unit
26 Wolfish look
27 Crusty bread slice
29 Sparkling wine region
33 Word found in "time on end," appropriately
34 "The Lion King" lion
35 Prefix with brow
36 Disney bigwig Bob
37 "Fancy seeing you here!"
38 Video game film
39 Broadway auntie
40 Certain bachelor, in personal ads
43 Archipelago parts
45 Pull from the ground
46 Christmas, in Italy
47 Gadget for Parmesan
49 Seize unlawfully
50 ___ of Fife (Macduff's title)
51 Like a beaver
52 Destiny
56 Adolph in New York Times history
57 "That feels amazing!"
58 ___ Tomé and Príncipe
59 Drink hot chocolate, maybe
60 Like the Beatles, in 1960s lingo
61 Bookmarked thing

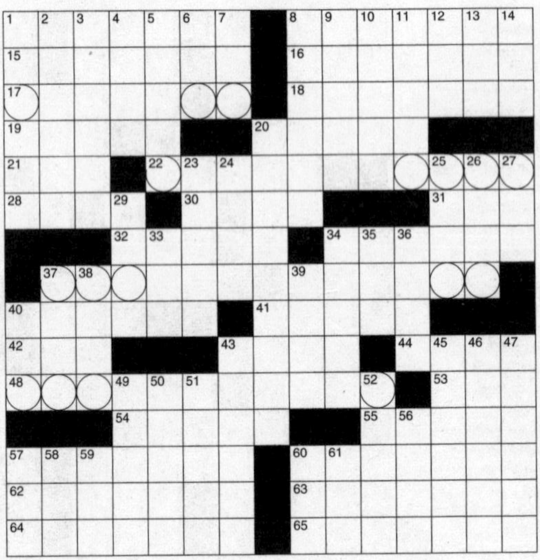

by David Steinberg

EASY 25

ACROSS

1 "Away with you!"
5 Snide
10 Skier's lift
14 "Nah!"
15 Hawaiian hi
16 Southwest tribe
17 Cheese in spinach pies
18 "Wilbur, get in the game!"
20 "Elijah, press your clothes!"
22 Woman who lent her name to a business-locating "list"
23 Philosopher Immanuel
24 2005–08 position held by Barack Obama: Abbr.
26 Employees at the Times or Post, for short
27 Wuss
30 Fought head to head, like bighorns
32 End of a univ. email address
33 "Eric, give some to us!"
38 McEntire at the Grand Ole Opry
40 Manage to avoid
41 Glutton's desire
42 "Sally, keep up the fight!"
45 Become the champ
46 Introduction
47 Possessed
49 Ginger ___
51 Reverse of NNW
52 Clown's name
54 Potato treat for Hanukkah
56 "Larry, shoot!"
60 "Emma, do that sexy dance!"
63 The "B" of Roy G. Biv
64 Chevy that's now called the Sonic
65 Slow, in music
66 Arm or leg
67 A.L. division for the Yankees
68 "Omigosh!"
69 Talks one's head off

DOWN

1 One practicing a mystical form of Islam
2 Sonny's old singing partner
3 Chevy, e.g.
4 "That was so nice of you!"
5 Rooster destined for dinner
6 Apportion
7 Amphibian that doesn't really cause warts
8 "Frailty, ___ name is woman!": Hamlet
9 Deviate erratically from a course
10 Slender
11 Mired
12 Crop-destroying insect
13 Bat mitzvahs and baptisms
19 Totaled, as a bill
21 House Committee on ___ and Means
24 Velvety leather
25 Merman in old musicals
27 Novak Djokovic, for one
28 Notion
29 Easy-to-overlook details
30 Boston pro on ice
31 Victim of a bark beetle barrage
34 Considers carefully, as advice
35 Title role for Michael Caine or Jude Law
36 Lake on Ohio's northern border
37 Tear apart
39 Chowed down
43 Cut with an intense light
44 Nod off
48 Unsteady
49 Organisms that cause red tide
50 Tadpole or caterpillar
52 Spree
53 Things to "Twist, Lick, Dunk" in a game app
55 Tie that's hard to untie
56 Decision point in a road
57 Largest pelvic bones
58 Posterior
59 Socialites having a ball
61 Furtive
62 Mai ___ (bar order)

by Lynn Lempel

26 EASY

ACROSS

1 Tori who sang "Cornflake Girl"
5 Inspiring part of the body?
9 Shot the bull
14 Handed-down tales
15 Bibliographic abbr.
16 As a friend, in France
17 Nut from Hawaii
19 Certain nonviolent protest
20 Elements' various forms
22 Wanna-___ (copycats)
23 Have on
24 Ottoman bigwig
28 Tapioca or taro root
31 "Eternally nameless" Chinese concept
34 Places where knots are tied
36 ___ chi
37 "The Magic Mountain" novelist Thomas
38 Places to do figure eights
41 One preparing for a coming flood
42 Sports org. with a five-ring logo
43 Rudely interrupt, as a comedian
44 "Cheers" bartender
45 Like mud, in an idiom
47 Under siege
48 Lacking adornment
50 Mil. mail center
52 Three main 20-Across . . . with examples included in 38-Across and 11- and 26-Down
59 Parts of combination locks
60 Bursting with joy
61 Leading the pack
62 Middle's middle?
63 Sell
64 Like much chili
65 Greased auto part
66 Just manages, with "out"

DOWN

1 Help for the poor
2 Ring around a castle
3 Toothed whale
4 Ticket specification
5 Alternative to buy
6 Nth degree
7 Babe in the woods
8 Early rock genre for David Bowie
9 Court entertainer
10 ___ Bath (prank call name)
11 Large containers often found atop buildings
12 Abu Dhabi dignitary
13 Loud noise
18 Go down the gangplank
21 Just free of the sea bottom
24 Annoying sorts
25 Giant in lightweight metals
26 Some Mississippi River traffic
27 This-and-that dish
29 City on the Erie Canal
30 The U.N.'s ___ Ki-moon
32 Site for a parolee tracking device
33 Get-go
35 Went by sloop, say
37 Computer alternatives to touchpads
39 "Piggy"
40 Bring to 212° again
45 Fried chicken option
46 Welch of "Myra Breckinridge"
49 Divvy up
51 A vital sign
52 It's 1 for 90°
53 Mother of Helen of Troy
54 Alpine goat
55 Run-down tavern
56 Show one's nerdy side, with "out"
57 Youngest Brontë
58 Yardsticks: Abbr.
59 Qty. at a bakery

by Gordon Johnson

EASY 27

ACROSS

1 Psychedelic drug
4 Davenport
8 Messy
14 Not their
15 Billiards game
16 Knuckle rub
17 #1 success
19 Two of them don't make a right
20 Author Zola
21 Jean ___, old-time French pirate with a base in New Orleans
23 Lady of Lima
25 Likeliest time for a traffic jam
28 Fury
29 Santa's little helper
31 Hi-___ graphics
32 G.I. entertainers
33 Banks of "America's Next Top Model"
35 Baseball hit that doesn't go far
37 English class assignment
39 Rubbish pile
42 "Goodbye, mon ami!"
45 Luge, e.g.
46 "Be on the lookout" messages, for short
50 Score in baseball
51 Baking meas.
53 No longer in the game: Abbr.
55 Deserter of a sinking ship
56 It's at the end of the line
59 Dawning period
61 Beer can opener
63 "That's enough out of you!"
64 Criticized angrily, with "out"
66 Top-secret . . . or a hint to 17-, 25-, 39-and 56-Across (AND 66-Across!)
68 Not filled, as a part
69 Not fat
70 Grp. that meets after school
71 Nevertheless
72 Not fooled by
73 Oscar- and Grammy-winning singer Smith

DOWN

1 Goes bonkers
2 Suitable for warm weather
3 Sink-side rack
4 Ball, geometrically
5 "That's amazing!"
6 Wrap for leftover food
7 Place for a bride and groom
8 Foolhardy
9 Body of water between Denmark and Scotland
10 A candy lover has a sweet one
11 Like granite and basalt
12 Like, in slang
13 "I agree"
18 ___-mo
22 Advance, as a cause
24 Jessica of "Sin City"
26 ___ Today
27 Cowboy Rogers
30 Hard-to-please sort
34 Consumed
36 Org. in which Ducks play with pucks
38 Relaxing getaway
40 Cold-blooded
41 Garden with forbidden fruit
42 Relative of "Bowwow!"
43 Busted boozer's offense, for short
44 Where "no one can hear you scream," per "Alien"
47 Union agreements, informally?
48 Coffee shop employee
49 Action star Jason
52 Did some business with
54 Electronic music genre
57 What "to err is"
58 Artist Frida
60 "Do ___ Diddy Diddy" (1964 #1 hit)
62 Good, in Guatemala
64 Regret
65 Part of S.A.S.E.: Abbr.
67 Used a davenport

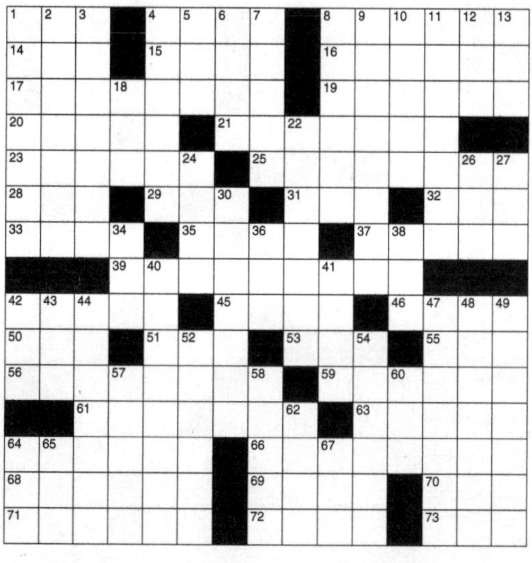

by Michael Hawkins

28 EASY

ACROSS

1 Fail big-time
5 To any degree
10 Cash caches, briefly
14 "Garfield" drooler
15 Artoo-___
16 Pan handler
17 ___ Raton, Fla.
18 Clear, in a way
19 Once-popular roadside chain, familiarly
20 Losing some love handles, say
22 "Yes sir" overseas
24 Manhattan neighborhood next to SoHo
26 ___ bear
30 Maxim magazine's intended audience
31 Arouse, as curiosity
36 French female friend
37 The "common" sort is said to be not so common
39 Yawn-provoking
40 Walmart competitor
42 Fiji competitor
44 Where scrubs are worn, for short
45 "Mazel ___!"
47 Floor coat
48 Bosox great Carl, familiarly
49 They're never away
52 Pet lovers' org.
55 Precollege exams
56 Car radio button
60 Tiniest bit
62 Commercial ending with Water
63 Botanist's specialty
64 One way of ordering things, like all the consonants in rows three, six and nine
67 Unexpected hit
68 Just as good
69 Sister fast-food chain of Carl's Jr.
70 Browning's "How Do I Love Thee?" and others

DOWN

1 Common clown name
2 Consume too much of, in brief
3 Sheet rock?
4 Rosary part
5 Puff ___
6 Golf reservation
7 Org. shifted to the Dept. of Justice in 2003
8 Eases
9 Sudoku solver's need
10 Arthritis symptom
11 SpongeBob or Scooby-Doo
12 Self-confidence, slangily
13 Hershey toffee bar
21 "Give ___ rest!"
23 Easy mark
25 Title rat of a 1972 film
26 Bruce Lee's role in TV's "The Green Hornet"
27 Longtime Sudanese president ___ al-Bashir
28 Puts on TV
29 One of six for an insect
32 Fingers, as a perp
33 Where ships get loaded
34 Bone below the elbow
35 Part of QE2: Abbr.
37 Defeat soundly
38 Red-coated cheeses
41 D.D.E.'s charge in W.W. II
43 Timber feller
46 Sunset prayer service
47 New York's ___ Glen State Park
49 Discussed, with "out"
50 Trot or canter
51 California's ___ Sea
52 Cut drastically, as prices
53 Big name in windows
54 Lark
57 Wavy-patterned fabric
58 Concern for a fall gardener
59 Thick locks
61 3M product
63 Be a toady
65 Stinger
66 Workplace for some veterinarians

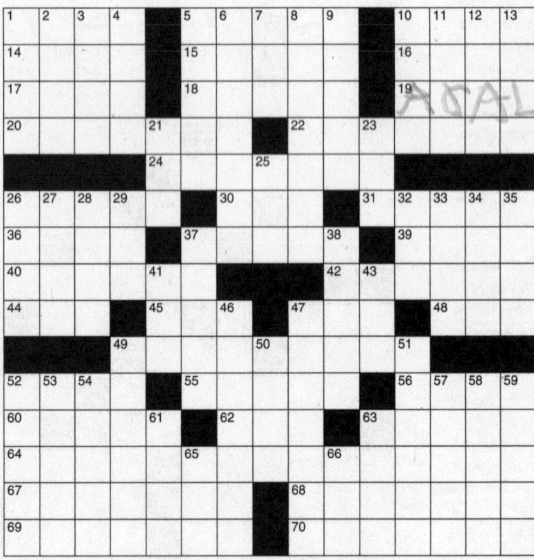

by Don Gagliardo and Zhouqin Burnikel

ACROSS

1 Bills and coins
5 Light punishment on wrists
10 Sumptuously furnished
14 Pear-shaped stringed instrument
15 Hebrew school reading
16 Throw a chip in the pot
17 Bump on the neck
19 Letter-shaped girder
20 Like monkeys and 59-Downs
21 Key with no sharps or flats
23 What angry bees do
24 Issue that's too dangerous to touch
27 Charged particle
28 Quickly
30 Connected to the Internet
31 Constant complainer
33 State-of-the-___
34 Tennis champ Agassi
35 Winsome . . . or like the ends of 17-, 24-, 51- and 58-Across, to a punster?
39 Steeple
42 Sloe ___ fizz
43 Completely gratify
47 Having a gun
48 Like the numerals I, V, X and L
50 Highest setting, informally
51 Grand pooh-bah
53 100-meter dash or shot put
55 Itzhak Perlman's instrument
56 Come out
57 Huckleberry ___
58 Hand-blown wine bottle that's also the title of a 1968 Beatles song
61 Favorable margin
62 Increase the energy of
63 Scored 100 on
64 Sleep indicators in the comics
65 Many a middle schooler
66 Young fellows

DOWN

1 Like rock music from the 1950s–'70s, now
2 Tax fraud investigator
3 Something a long-distance runner needs
4 Encircle
5 ___ Lee of Marvel Comics
6 Cut (off)
7 Painter/poet Jean ___
8 Gourmet's heightened sense
9 Curly's replacement in the Three Stooges
10 "Sunflowers" and "Water Lilies"
11 In a plane or train
12 Opposite of a bench player
13 His counterpart
18 Multigenerational tale
22 Early caucusgoer
24 Aesop character who lost a race
25 Shape of a stop sign
26 Appreciative poem
29 Easy-to-chew food
32 Nitty-gritty
36 One of two on a bike
37 Capital of Peru
38 Any port ___ storm
39 Used a bench
40 Bring home the bacon, so to speak
41 Encroach (on)
44 "Sweet land of liberty," in song
45 Did a stylized ballroom dance
46 Widens
48 Was almost out of supplies
49 "Finding ___" (2003 Pixar film)
52 When one sees stars
54 Open to bribery
56 Channel that describes itself as "The worldwide leader in sports"
57 Hat with a tassel
59 Jungle swinger
60 Begin litigation

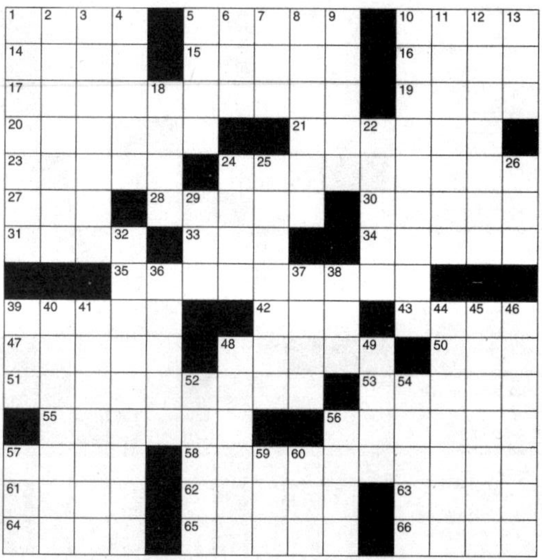

by Gary Cee

30 EASY

ACROSS

1 Volleyball actions between bumps and spikes
5 Name on an orange-and-white truck
10 "Hey, buddy!"
14 "What ___" (1996 Sublime hit)
15 Some chip dip
16 Ceremony
17 What red markers may indicate on 59-Acrosses
19 Altar exchange
20 Even (with)
21 Cat in a record store
23 To date
24 Musician Reed or Rawls
26 Tripoli's land
27 Musical name after Tori or before Lee
29 Ancestor of the harmonica
31 Supporter
32 Top-shelf
33 1960s Egyptian president
37 "___ My Children"
38 Some links holes . . . with a hint to the circled letters
40 ___-Magnon
41 Capital of Saudi Arabia
43 Capital of Norway
44 Big export of Saudi Arabia and Norway
45 Lithe
47 When summer officially starts
48 Like a disciplinarian's talk
51 Luau instrument, informally
52 Symbol of power, with "the"
53 Like some lights
55 Scored, as on a 59-Across
58 "Out of Africa" author Dinesen
59 18 holes, often
62 Suffix with disk
63 Indian ___
64 Pipeline problem
65 Animal that's sometimes frozen in the headlights
66 Like a chimney sweep
67 Nobel winner Wiesel

DOWN

1 Missile ___
2 Op-ed columnist Timothy
3 "Act quickly! This offer will end very soon!"
4 Supporting stalks
5 Country in a classic Beatles title
6 Overhead expense?
7 Pub order
8 Exhausts
9 Z's position
10 Outhouses
11 Obsolescent designation in the music business
12 Expressionless
13 Girl's name that's a benefit in reverse?
18 Sup
22 Texas home of the Sun Bowl
24 Early filmmaker Fritz
25 It just took this before "I fell so hard in love with you," in a 1960s hit
27 Way off
28 Burkina Faso neighbor
29 Some stuffed bears
30 Hearth
32 Doing sums
34 Rascal
35 "___ go bragh!"
36 Something cast
39 Salinger title girl
42 Morning TV weatherman
46 Gas brand with an arrow in its logo
47 "Always on Time" rapper
48 Recoiled (from)
49 Flavor
50 Thrill
52 World leader with a distinctive jacket
54 Divas have big ones
55 Sch. overlooking Harlem
56 Morales of "La Bamba"
57 Hockey feint
60 Many an August birth
61 What beef marbling is

by Peter A. Collins

EASY 31

ACROSS

1 Republican grp.
4 Owns up to
10 That guy
13 "Cat ___ Hot Tin Roof"
14 Billionaire Aristotle
15 Point of no return?
16 Lunar New Year in Vietnam
17 Actor who portrayed Newman on "Seinfeld"
19 Be behind
21 "Honest!"
22 Obvious indication
26 Fascinated by
27 Explore, as the Internet
28 Mortarboard attachment
31 Glock, e.g.
34 It may keep cafeteria food warm
38 In time past
39 Red or yellow card issuer
41 Channel for Anderson Cooper
42 Neither's partner
43 Billiards variant
46 Prefix with intestinal
48 "Come on, no cheating"
50 Went in haste
51 Commotion
54 Ushers' offerings
57 Native of Akron or Cleveland
60 Dante's "La Vita ___" ("The New Life")
61 Rural area . . . or what can be found in each set of circled letters?
64 Spoiled
67 "Able was I ___ I saw Elba"
68 Notable products of Persia
69 Poem "to" somebody or something
70 Thumbs-up response
71 Helping after seconds
72 Heed the coxswain

DOWN

1 Understood
2 Result of dividing any nonzero number by itself
3 James whose novels have sold more than 300 million copies
4 Diarist Nin
5 Naturally illuminated
6 Yahoo alternative
7 Suffix with expert
8 Kind of torch on "Survivor"
9 ID thieves' targets
10 Actress Uta
11 Apple messaging software
12 The first "M" in MGM
14 Man ___
18 Volunteer's response
20 Flat floater
22 Channel with hearings
23 Mario's video game brother
24 Exasperated cry
25 Tiny div. of a minute
29 Serenaded
30 One of three active volcanoes in Italy
32 "Kill ___ killed"
33 Thumb (through)
35 Like 1947's Taft-Hartley Act
36 Edible mushroom
37 Herders' sticks
40 Commotion
44 Kindle download
45 Rap's ___ Kim
47 Prison weapon
49 ___ and raved
51 Maguire of Hollywood
52 Midway alternative
53 Does some kitchen prep work
55 Mongolian tents
56 All students at Eton
58 A debit card is linked to one: Abbr.
59 "The Daily Show" host Trevor
62 Mentalist Geller
63 "Wait Wait . . . Don't Tell Me!" airer
65 Commotion
66 It might get your feet wet

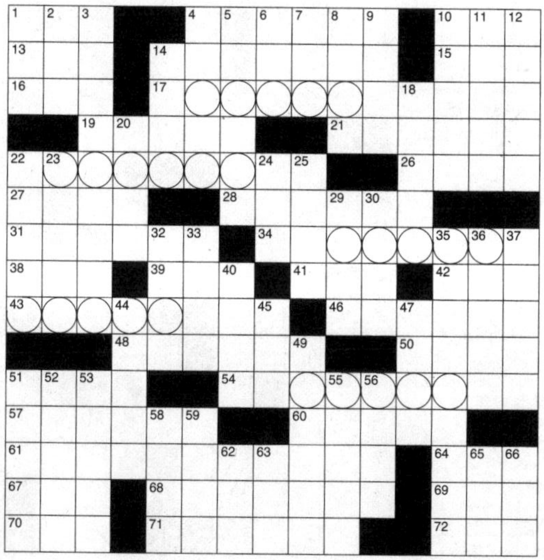

by David Kwong

32 EASY

ACROSS

1 Like the best kind of vacation
5 Look over
8 Olympian's achievement
13 First James Bond film
14 Crew chief
15 "You think I won't try that?!"
16 Pagoda placement consideration, often
18 Reddish-brown
19 Climate features of equatorial countries
21 What a mute button affects
24 Radon regulators, in brief
25 ___ Tin Tin
26 Savior, in popular parlance
30 Release
32 Fluffy trio?
33 Big name in bandages and hardware
34 Baked or stoned
35 Prognostication tool
40 First female Nobelist, 1903
42 LinkedIn profile, e.g.
43 Band-___
46 Onetime center of Los Angeles
47 Clumps of sugar on a stick
50 Kind of school
51 Anaheim nine, on scoreboards
53 Loosen, as a knot
54 Cards #53 and #54 in a deck . . . or a hint to the answers to 19-, 26-, 35- and 47-Across
59 Home of the National Gallery of Canada
60 Partied like it was 1999
64 Pete who co-wrote "If I Had a Hammer"
65 Home of the Burning Man festival: Abbr.
66 Rim
67 Broke off
68 James Bond, e.g.
69 Speckled steed

DOWN

1 JPEG alternative
2 "___ we done here?"
3 It might have a bed icon on a highway sign
4 Doesn't give one's full effort
5 Reverberate
6 B.Y.O.B. part
7 Freeway sign
8 It last erupted in 1984
9 Once, once
10 Cactus, for one
11 Explorer Vespucci
12 Turndown to the suggestion "We should . . ."
15 Sound that can prevent sleeping at night
17 Loafer, e.g.
20 Itsy-bitsy
21 Knock the socks off
22 TV band above channel 13, in brief
23 Damaged the reputation of
27 Dines on
28 Mo. when the Supreme Court reconvenes
29 Two-time Grammy winner Bryson
31 Photo blowup: Abbr.
36 Inlet
37 Like old newspaper clippings
38 D.M.V. issuance: Abbr.
39 ___ choy
40 Write music
41 Like leftovers
44 Dictator Amin
45 Bottleful at a salon
47 Rule Gandhi opposed
48 Terse
49 R.S.V.P.
52 Many miles away
55 Road hazard?
56 Dominates, informally
57 Stay good
58 Go green?
61 Engagement-ending words
62 Airport alternative to JFK
63 ___ of iniquity

by Dan Schoenholz

EASY 33

ACROSS

1 *With 9-Across, loose-fitting bottoms
6 Mini-albums, briefly
9 *See 1-Across
14 Hate
15 Prefix with liberal or conservative
16 Legend automaker
17 Incline
18 Grade of wine
19 Who thought of "The Thinker"
20 ___ Sabe (the Lone Ranger, to Tonto)
21 Tedious task
23 Ready for picking
24 *Where you can hear a pin drop
27 Kind of tip, in baseball
28 Emulates Jay Z
29 Small recipe amt.
32 Unfiltered and unpasteurized brew
34 Grp. holding after-school events
37 Island ring
39 Guacamole or salsa
40 Soft-serve ice cream shape
42 Sounded like a cow
43 Corroded
44 Up to the point that
45 Versailles and others
47 Vacationers to Vail may carry them
49 Wed. follower
50 Run up ___ (owe)
51 Maidenform product
53 Keeps for oneself . . . or features of the answers to all the starred clues
57 Snitch (on)
60 Features of biology classes
62 "Kiss me, I'm ___" (T-shirt slogan)
63 Jay who preceded Jimmy Fallon
64 Hideous
65 "Won't you let me?"
66 The "O's" of Cheerios
67 Deeply regretted
68 "Oh, shucks!"
69 Poetic paeans

DOWN

1 Poe's "The ___ of Amontillado"
2 Having what it takes
3 Diamond shape
4 Magically vanish
5 It might be found in a deposit
6 Stuffed tortillas
7 Evita of "Evita"
8 Reaction from a sore loser
9 4, maybe, on a golf hole
10 Nuts from oaks
11 Skin flick
12 Stumble
13 Rational
21 One of 77 in this puzzle
22 Carrier to the Holy Land
25 Quadrennial soccer event
26 Hairy Halloween rentals
29 Drive (down)
30 Athenian colonnade
31 *Where you might be behind the eight ball
33 Illuminated
34 *Falafel holder
35 Pre-calc course
36 "___ fair in love and war"
38 Wife of Jacob
41 Lady hoopsters' org.
46 Beethoven's Symphony No. 3
48 ___ Lee Gifford (morning TV host)
51 Image of a speeding car, maybe
52 Prego competitor
54 Stick in one's ___
55 Double-decker checker
56 Villa d'___
58 Get into a poker game, say
59 Something to do to a salad or coin
61 Hip-hop's ___ tha Kyd
63 Place to go in Britain?

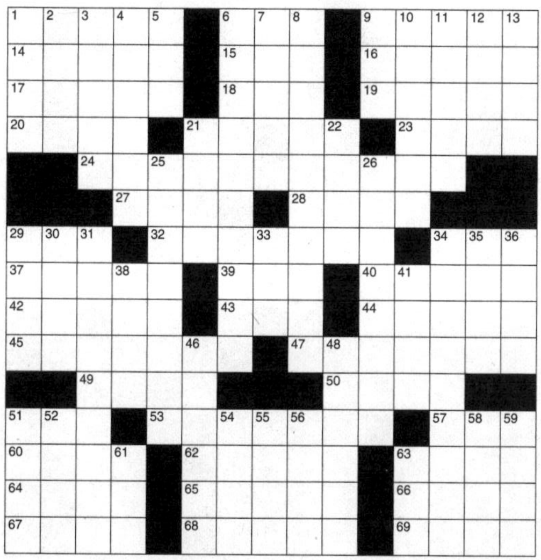

by Ron Toth and Zhouqin Burnikel

34 EASY

ACROSS

1 Playwright Fugard
6 Airline to Stockholm
9 Narnia nabob
14 SeaWorld attraction
15 Legendary boy king
16 Belt holder
17 Fast-food kitchen fixture
18 A retirement party might toast the end of one
19 Jon of "Two and a Half Men"
20 Anthem preposition
21 Heartthrob Zac
23 Kind of admiral
24 Dancer and Prancer
26 Drill attachment with teeth
28 Like a fully initiated Mafia member
29 Like good soil
31 Place for a chaise longue
32 Culinarian who cries "Bam!"
34 Bunker fill
36 Eastern path
37 Tip, as a hat
39 Brief admission of responsibility
41 "The Racer's Edge"
44 Sandwich with toothpicks
46 Look for truffles as a pig might
50 Faux
52 National alternative
54 Relative of "Smash!"
55 Most twisted, as humor
57 Common deli order . . . or a literal occurrence five times in this puzzle
59 "Shoot!"
60 53-Down product
61 Always, poetically
62 Say something bleep-worthy
63 Bran source
64 ___ of Strength (Festivus rite)
66 Firearm, slangily
67 Actress Long
68 "Is there no ___ this?"
69 Longest continental range in the world
70 Director Lee
71 Either of the twin child stars of "Full House"

DOWN

1 "In my opinion . . ."
2 Time to which you "spring forward" in daylight saving
3 Tractor-drawn fall activity
4 Kipling's "Follow Me ___"
5 Brought in
6 Non-mono, say
7 Night lights
8 "South Park" boy
9 Capital of Ghana
10 Sharp
11 Wager
12 Another name for "My Country, 'Tis of Thee"
13 "All Things Considered" network
22 Didn't land, as a joke
25 Dorkmeister
26 Pattern of symptoms
27 Fight-ending letters
30 ___ tai
33 Quadrennial games org.
35 One worshiped in Rome
38 Suffix with pocket
40 In the dumps
41 Opposite NNE
42 Add haphazardly
43 Give careful attention
45 Kingdom on the Persian Gulf
47 Clothes, slangily
48 Complete outfit for a newborn
49 Poet/essayist who wrote "To be great is to be misunderstood"
51 Threaten
53 Kenmore alternative
56 Tender spots
58 "___ ed Euridice" (Gluck opera)
60 Spanish lady
62 Where one might hear oohs and aahs
65 Blowup: Abbr.

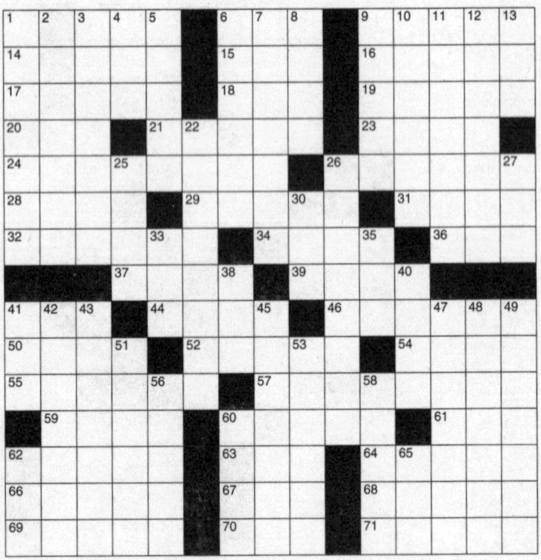

by Alan Derkazarian

ACROSS

1 Smooth-talking
5 "___ and Punishment"
10 Number in a quartet
14 Capital of Italia
15 Fable writer
16 "___ Karenina"
17 Send ___ errand
18 *1938 Horse of the Year
20 Relax
22 Artificial jewelry
23 Unsophisticated sort
24 See 45-Across
26 Actress/singer Pia
29 Mensch
32 Praise highly
33 Scarlett O'Hara, for one
34 "___ the land of the free . . ."
36 Window base
37 Moolah . . . or the makeup of the ends of the answers to the starred clues
38 Lion's locks
39 Bathwater tester
40 "The Lorax" author
41 About 39 inches, in England
42 Onetime rival of Facebook
44 Untrustworthy sort
45 With 24-Across, body of water that's in four African countries
46 Condé ___ (magazine company)
47 Watering spot in the desert
50 KEY USED FOR THIS CLUE
54 *Hunk
57 Like most businesses between 9 to 5
58 There's no place like it
59 Orchard
60 Prefix with dynamic
61 Roman god of love
62 Idiot, in Canadian lingo
63 Source of linseed oil

DOWN

1 Grasp, in slang
2 Actress Anderson who was once married to 21-Down
3 Popular desktop computer
4 *Provide funds for
5 Yellow-skinned melon
6 Athlete/model Gabrielle
7 Dinesen who wrote "Out of Africa"
8 Flash ___ (faddish assembly)
9 Prefix with -dermis
10 Building front
11 Burden
12 Corporate division
13 Put on a scale from 1 to 10, say
19 Garden shovel
21 Actor Reynolds who was once married to 2-Down
24 Pepsi and RC
25 "Please ___" (operator's request)
26 Verve
27 Universal truth
28 Longtime name in Chicago politics
29 V fliers
30 Farm animals that butt
31 Romance or science fiction
33 Actor Willis
35 Fishing line holder
37 A toucan has a colorful one
38 *"Bat Out of Hell" singer
40 Jerk
41 Pigsty
43 Mini-burger
44 Original judge on "The People's Court"
46 Trustingly innocent
47 Employee protection org.
48 Part of a molecule
49 Heavyweight wrestling
50 Corp. money managers
51 German auto make
52 Michael of "Arrested Development"
53 Kentucky's Fort ___
55 "Yuck!"
56 To's partner

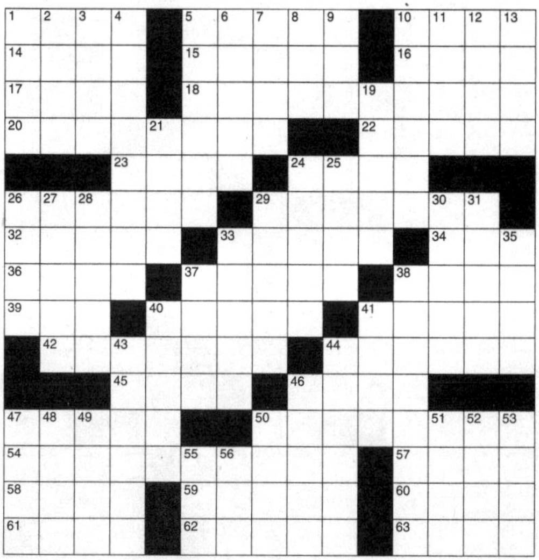

by Janice Luttrell

36 EASY

ACROSS

1 Practice boxing
5 Dr. who's done 19-Down for Dr Pepper
8 Tree houses?
13 Auricle's site
15 Produced, as coins
16 Breadwinner
17 Kitchen covers
18 Former House leader Nancy
19 "The Fox and the Crow" storyteller
20 Cheerleader's cheer
21 2011 World Series champs, informally
24 Office V.I.P.
27 Pageant winners' wear
29 Alternative to Enterprise
30 Call letters?
33 Tizzy
34 Navy student, informally
35 Be rough with, in a way
36 Warning appropriate for this puzzle?
38 90° turn
39 Moon of Mars
41 Tombstone lawman
42 Father's study: Abbr.
43 Go ___ for (defend)
44 Agreed
46 Circus performer with a ball
47 Veil material
48 Jodie Foster and Meryl Streep, collegiately
52 Reason to use a visor
54 Opera's Tebaldi
56 Name repeatedly sung in Rossini's "Largo al factotum"
58 One of the "E's" in E.E.C.
60 Stranded due to frigid weather
61 Shoal
62 Anatomical pouch
63 Christmas ___
64 Some savings, for short

DOWN

1 Too sentimental
2 Food processor setting
3 Bikini, for one
4 Not take it anymore
5 Names in someone's honor
6 Girl's name that's a homophone for a boy's name
7 Make a goof
8 Barely beats
9 Attired, as a judge
10 "Buy" or "sell" directive at a specified price
11 Start of a countdown
12 1960s protest grp.
14 Sue Grafton's "___ for Ricochet"
15 Fannie ___ (securities)
19 Commercials
22 Locality
23 Unfair treatment
25 Arena entrance feature
26 George ___, longtime maestro of the Cleveland Orchestra
28 "___ the Sheriff" (1974 #1 hit)
29 Land animal whose closest living relatives include whales
30 Data in a daily planner: Abbr.
31 North America's largest alpine lake
32 Double, in baseball lingo
34 Certain homicide, in police lingo
37 Something that may be trimmed or rigged
40 "Oh! Susanna" and others
44 Take to court
45 Obi-Wan ___
47 High-tech 1982 Disney movie
49 Tennessee senator ___ Alexander
50 Turner autobiography
51 Fires
53 Rossini's "Largo al factotum," e.g.
55 Not continue
56 Lie a little
57 Hosp. locale
58 Suffix with Japan
59 Cleveland cager, for short

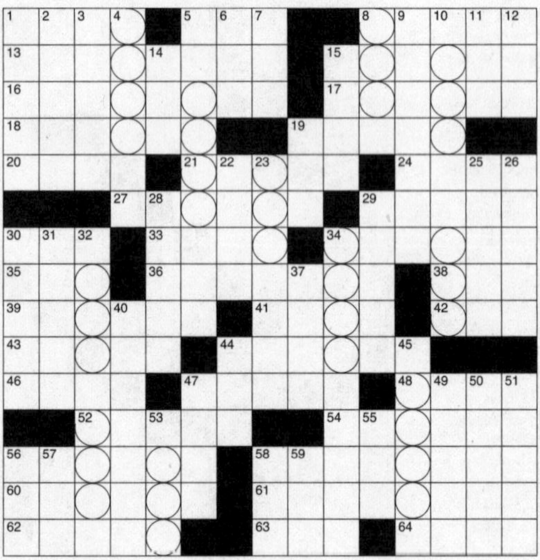

by David J. Kahn

ACROSS

1 Go out with ___
6 Toy with a tail
10 "Get ___ writing"
14 "Vive ___!" (old French cry)
15 Score after deuce
16 U2 lead singer
17 Walter who created Woody Woodpecker
18 64-, 65- and 66-Across, in this puzzle
20 Heavy vehicle that smooths a road surface
22 Time in history
23 Ernie of the P.G.A.
24 Antipoverty agcy.
25 Goof up
26 Samurai sash
27 ___ Trueheart, Dick Tracy's love
29 The year 2051
31 Rotisserie rod
32 TV series with "NY," "Miami" and "Cyber" spinoffs
34 Thoroughfare in the name of Springsteen's band
37 "Don't mess with" him, per an old song lyric . . . or a hint to 18-, 20-, 55- and 58-Across
39 College or company starter
40 Big name in ice cream
41 Putter or 9-iron
42 Promotional hoopla
44 Court legend Arthur
48 Thornton Wilder's "___ Town"
49 "I love," to a Latin lover
51 Sixteenths of lbs.
53 Dress (up)
54 K-O connector
55 Means of fortunetelling
58 Audio feature that comes standard on cars
60 Provoked
61 Gloomy
62 Card with the headings "Appetizers," "Entrees" and "Desserts"
63 Overly anxious
64 Rotating car part
65 Mumbai titles
66 Proverbial waste maker

DOWN

1 Completely ready
2 John, Paul, George or Ringo
3 James of "Gunsmoke"
4 The "N" of N.B.
5 Thingamabob
6 Explosion sound
7 TV's discontinued "American ___"
8 Big name in golf balls
9 Exit's opposite
10 "Let's Build a Smarter Planet" co.
11 Ripped the wrapping off
12 Circling the earth, say
13 "Oh, hang on a minute!"
19 Former Bruin Bobby
21 Jog the memory of
28 Use elbow grease
30 Apprehensive
31 "Ciao!"
33 One of the seven "deadly" things
35 Pluck, as an eyebrow
36 Crimson, e.g.
37 Heavy-hearted
38 Witness
39 Discombobulate
41 Piña ___ (fruity drink)
43 Permeable
45 Beach building supports
46 "I kid you not!"
47 Easter dip
49 Mo. before May
50 Sirs' partners
52 Politico Palin
56 5×5 crossword, e.g.
57 Actress Merrill
59 Field fare for a G.I.

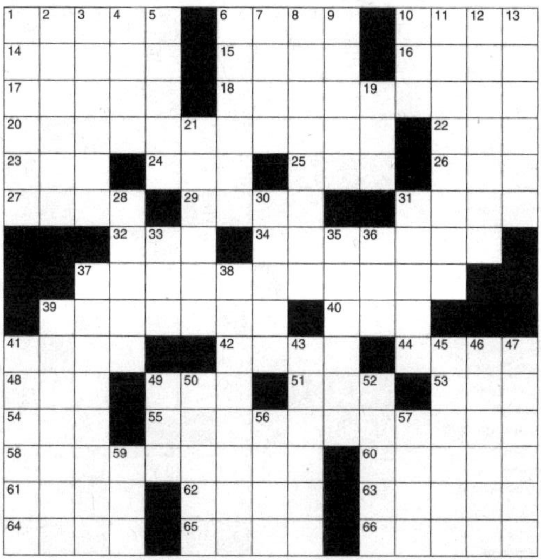

by Betty Keller

38 EASY

ACROSS

1 Medieval drudges
6 Word before shot or season
9 Imbecile
13 Gives a heads-up
15 Protection provided by military planes
17 Watch in astonishment
18 Scandal surrounding copy editors' proofreading marks?
19 Scandal involving Tesla C.E.O. Musk?
21 Completely fine
22 Some hosp. tests
23 Facilitate
25 Storyteller Wilhelm or Jakob
28 Scandal affecting iPhone owners?
33 ___ Canyon Park (running spot in the Hollywood Hills)
35 Restaurant dip for bread
36 Do the breaststroke, say
37 N.Y.C. subway inits.
38 "Hamilton," e.g.
41 Sleeve filler
42 Title on "Downton Abbey"
44 TV-watching room
45 Rink game
47 Scandal in the aftermath of a tsunami?
50 Removes, as a layer
51 Small, brown songbird
52 "Toodles!"
54 Words of sympathy
57 Scandal that implicates a detective?
61 Scandal depicted in "Avatar"?
64 "Amen to that!"
65 Popular strength-training program
66 Be a pilot
67 Warmonger
68 Shirt for a workout
69 Come after

DOWN

1 Wise one
2 Its inaugural flight was in 1948
3 Pickup that gets picked up, perhaps
4 Ally who's not completely an ally
5 Aggressive manager for a child star
6 Lose vibrancy
7 Bit of fiction
8 Address you can't enter into a GPS
9 Angled golf holes
10 Shape of the president's office
11 Jared of "Dallas Buyers Club"
12 Long hike
14 Doe's mate
16 Desist
20 Decidedly not-lax grp. at LAX
23 Filmdom's "The Bible," e.g.
24 Deity to 1.5+ billion
25 "Good ___!"
26 Nonurban
27 Course that might be labeled "101"
29 North, south, east or west
30 Up from bed
31 Ready for bed
32 TV's "Oscars"
34 Wink accompanier
39 Actor Bean, whose first name looks like it rhymes with his last, but doesn't
40 Frequent theme for Adele
43 Not having much chance of failure
46 "Much to my ___ . . ."
48 Bottom-of-the-barrel stuff
49 Hellenic "H"
53 Former Sanyo competitor
54 Ruler division
55 ___ mia (Italian term of endearment)
56 Declare assuredly
57 Head of the French department?
58 Ones helping a public prosecutor, for short
59 Ballerina's wear
60 Olympics sword
62 Back on board
63 Suit accessory

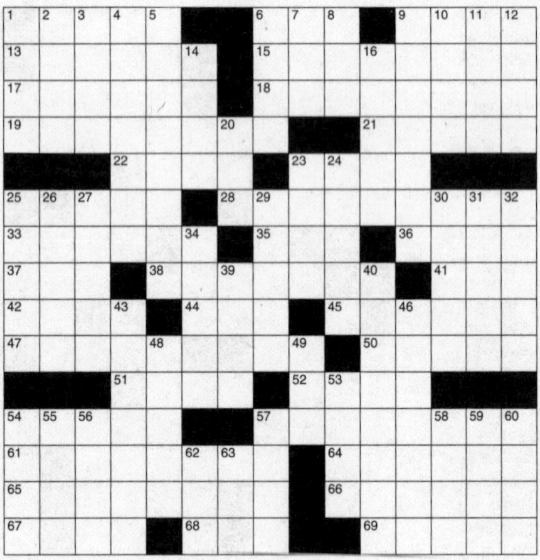

by Finn Vigeland

ACROSS

1 Coke rival
6 Popular hairstyle in the 1960s
10 "No ifs, ___ . . ."
14 Birdlike
15 Next year's jr.
16 Wife of Jacob
17 Electric car maker
18 8:00–11:00 p.m., TV-wise
20 Anticipate
22 Actress Strahovski of "Dexter" and "Chuck"
23 ABAB in a poem, e.g.
27 Tax form ID
28 Superiors of sarges
29 Wildcat with tufted ears
31 "So gross!"
32 D-E-A-D dead
35 Harmonizes, informally
39 Large or extra-large
41 Copycat's comment . . . or, phonetically, a hint to this puzzle's theme
43 Émile of the Dreyfus Affair
44 Mattress brand
46 "Thanks," in Deutschland
48 Letter between sigma and upsilon
49 Roman marketplaces
51 Breaks off a romantic relationship
53 Lawyers' org.
56 Greeting to a returning soldier, maybe
59 V.I.P.
61 Coffee shop lure
62 What a finger-pointer "plays"
64 Robbery at a police station, e.g.
68 Abbr. in a footnote
69 Prefix with -logical
70 Roast host
71 Many millennia
72 Those, in Mexico
73 One side of a Faustian bargain

DOWN

1 Butter serving
2 Night before a holiday
3 Detectives, for short
4 Deli meat
5 Seven days from now
6 Savory jelly
7 ". . . and so on and so ___"
8 Sch. in Troy, N.Y.
9 "Good heavens!"
10 Choir voice
11 Dresden denials
12 Curses
13 Luster
19 Odds' opposite
21 Indian state known for its tea and silk
23 Like non-oyster months
24 Comic Mandel
25 "Holy moly!"
26 John who sang "Philadelphia Freedom"
30 End run of the alphabet
33 Power a bike
34 Tony winner Hagen
36 "On the contrary!"
37 Demand by right
38 Pan-frying instruction
40 Santa's little helper
42 Vermont skiing destination
45 "Ouch, that hurts!"
47 All the people attacking you
50 Jackson who was on five World Series-winning teams in the 1970s
52 Cosmic order, in Buddhism
53 Hoffman of 1960s radicalism
54 "The Hobbit" hero Baggins
55 Once more
57 One of many Hitchcock appearances in his own films
58 Sandwich cookies now sold by Mondelez
60 Iraq war concerns, for short
63 Commercials
65 Halloween mo.
66 Teachers' org.
67 Tokyo currency

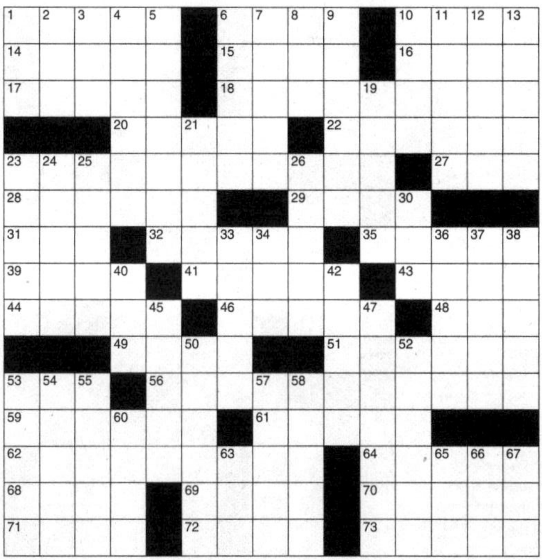

by Paula Gamache

40 EASY

ACROSS
1 Laid up
5 Toward a boat's wake
10 Kindergarten lesson
14 Big name in denim
15 Equestrian, e.g.
16 Lummox
17 Wax makers
18 Dough
19 Political columnist Klein
20 How the Great Emancipator got around?
23 Controversially patented thing
24 Source of a common allergy
25 How the star of the Indiana Jones films got around?
31 Leveled
32 See 41-Across
33 "Leave!"
35 Give proper attribution
36 Embroidery loop
38 "Hey, ___" (casual greeting)
39 Gobbled up
40 Mother of Helen
41 With 32-Across, place to snorkel
42 How a Seattle Mariner great got around?
46 "Sure"
47 ___ empty stomach
48 How Queen's former frontman got around?
56 Word before window or end
57 Its capital is Oranjestad
58 List-ending abbr.
59 ___ buco
60 City near Avignon
61 All the ___
62 Underworld river
63 Something a composer composes
64 Bogus

DOWN
1 Actress Jessica
2 Channel that airs "Sherlock," with "the"
3 ___ since
4 Clash (with)
5 Giorgio of fashion
6 Wetlands and tundra, e.g.
7 Kerfuffles
8 Cut down
9 Something to keep track of?
10 One of the Furies
11 Buffoon
12 Permanent thing?
13 "South Park" boy
21 What's rounded up in a roundup
22 "___ said!"
25 Where Toussaint L'Ouverture led a revolt
26 Coyolxauhqui worshiper
27 Penguin predators
28 Prefix with realism
29 Howard ___, "The Fountainhead" protagonist
30 Home of the world's tallest building, completed in 2009
31 Panasonic competitor
34 ___ Avivian
36 Xerxes' people
37 Swear words?
38 They might bar bargoers
40 Emulated Pinocchio
41 Peter the Great, for one
43 Longtime Oreo competitor
44 Like the mood in a losing locker room
45 Agita
48 Big dos
49 Staff break?
50 Like one-star puzzles
51 "South Park" boy
52 ___ wrestler
53 Salt flats location
54 Music of Mumbai
55 Proto-matter of the universe

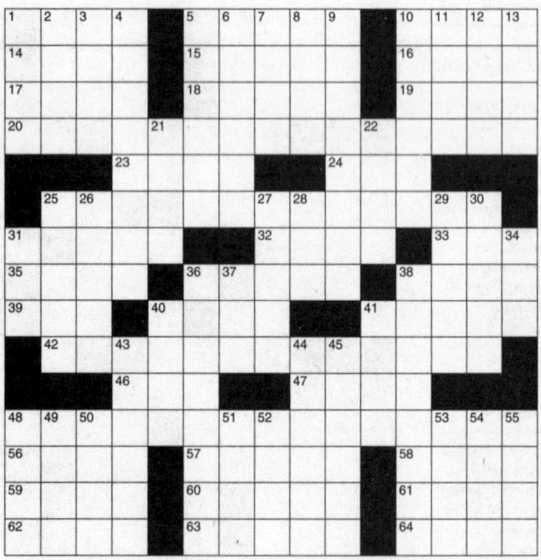

by John Westwig

ACROSS

1 Protein-rich bean
5 Prices
10 Nursery school, informally
14 "Wait ___!" ("Hold on!")
15 "Tiny Bubbles" singer
16 "Arsenic and Old ___"
17 Article of tropical apparel . . . whose start is a state nickname for the state indicated by the circled squares
19 Arthur who was king of the court?
20 Julie ___, portrayer of Claire on "Modern Family"
21 Go from one social gathering to another
23 Facebook ___ (collection of posts)
26 Sought legal redress
27 Catchphrase shouted in "Jerry Maguire" . . . whose start is a state nickname for the state indicated by the circled squares
33 1/24 of a day
34 Designer's degree, for short
35 Samsung Galaxy, e.g.
36 Naval leader: Abbr.
37 Secretariat's mother, for one . . . whose start is a state nickname for the state indicated by the circled squares
40 Boise's state: Abbr.
41 Officer below a captain, slangily
43 Punk rock subgenre
44 A-1 tennis server
45 Emergency worker . . . whose start is a state nickname for the state indicated by the circled squares
49 ___ Lee, creator of Spider-Man
50 Secretariat's father, for one
51 Succession
55 Dressed to the ___
59 Detective's lead
60 Biblical idol . . . whose start is a state nickname for the state indicated by the circled squares
63 Landed
64 Peeved
65 Excursion
66 Seized vehicle, informally
67 Superbright colors
68 Whole lot

DOWN

1 Discontinued Swedish car
2 Norwegian capital
3 "Ouch!"
4 Want badly
5 Conservative investments, briefly
6 La-la lead-in
7 Little scissor cut
8 Beat handily
9 "You can say that again!"
10 Moldable kids' stuff
11 Impulsive
12 Returned call?
13 Not go bad
18 All over again
22 Arizona home of the nation's largest public university
24 Madame Bovary
25 Stand up to
27 "Me, too!"
28 Funny business
29 Domesticates
30 Feature of a neat drink
31 What can follow week or rear
32 2016, e.g.
33 50%
37 Davis of "What Ever Happened to Baby Jane?"
38 Volume enhancers
39 Cheer (for)
42 Give, as a passport or parking ticket
44 Druggies, e.g.
46 Welcomed, as the new 32-Down
47 "We want more!," at a concert
48 Sam for whom Georgia Tech's School of International Affairs is named
51 Surgery memento
52 Palindromic fashion magazine
53 Witticism
54 Nevada city
56 Pusher buster
57 Kazan who directed "On the Waterfront"
58 Law force in 1960–'70s TV's "Ironside"
61 Lair
62 Paper cutters, briefly?

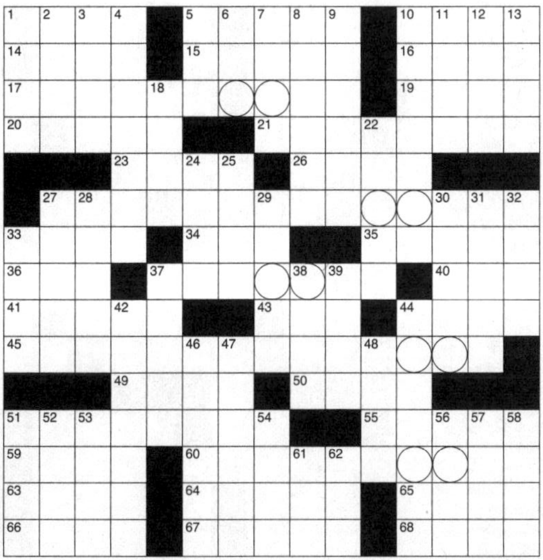

by Dan Schoenholz

42 EASY

ACROSS

1 Some rote learning
5 Cutup
10 Not ___ many words
14 "You make me laugh"
15 Sponsorship
16 Oracle
17 Bosnian, e.g.
18 Longtime Orioles manager in the Baseball Hall of Fame
20 El-overseeing org.
21 TV Guide chart, for short
22 "Buenos ___!"
23 Co-author of the Federalist Papers
25 Fathers, to tots
27 More foolish
28 Big name in skateboarding
31 "Dude!"
32 9-3 automaker
33 Covert org.
34 "The Broken Tower" poet
38 "Annie" characters
41 Alsace assents
42 Havens
46 Boy genius of old teen fiction
49 Team esteem
50 Relative of a blintz
51 Best Picture of 2014 . . . or what 18-, 23-, 28-, 34-, 46- and 56-Across each is?
52 Parts of small intestines
53 Famed synthesizer
55 Genre first included in the Rock and Roll Hall of Fame in 2007
56 "Network" Oscar winner
58 ___ Minor
60 Like fine wines and cheeses
61 Put into office
62 Appearance
63 Mouthfuls of chewing gum
64 Poking around in other people's business
65 Lead-in to masochism

DOWN

1 Sounds of comprehension
2 One set in a "Romeo and Juliet" production
3 Georgia county of which 4-Down is the seat
4 Oldest city in Georgia
5 "Veni, vidi, vici" speaker
6 Like a faulty pipe
7 Shrek, e.g.
8 Word repeated before "West" in a film and 1960s TV series
9 Its capital is Sydney: Abbr.
10 Book after Song of Solomon
11 Many a resident on Lake Tahoe
12 Vacillates
13 Boston Bruin great
19 Turning point?
23 Brown or Rice
24 Actress Malone of "The Hunger Games"
26 Cousin of reggae
28 Implied but not stated
29 Sculls
30 Magic and Wizards org.
32 Double ___ Oreos
35 Reine's husband
36 Former queen of Jordan
37 Catchers of some waves
38 And everything else, for short
39 Former dictator of Panama
40 Refined
43 Biblical city of Palestine
44 Passed, as time
45 Jack Reed or Harry Reid: Abbr.
47 Barrels along
48 Have on
49 Powerful
51 Lawn game
53 Minderbinder of "Catch-22"
54 Cash register compartment
56 Manhandle
57 Swamp
59 Enero begins it

by David Kwong

EASY 43

ACROSS

1 Picking out of a lineup, informally
6 Magazine with a "Person of the Year"
10 Former "Meet the Press" host Marvin
14 Craze
15 Freshly
16 French lady friend
17 Reason for a cast
19 Spanish newborn
20 Period after dark, in poetry
21 Fifth-century pope known as "the Great"
22 Impressionist Claude
23 Ugandan tyrant Idi ___
25 Piece of sports equipment that's spiked
28 Grand ___ National Park
30 Pie ___ mode
31 Insect with a stinger
32 Cozies keep them hot
36 Cutlass or 88, informally
37 Family gathering place
39 Leopard's marking
41 Starts liking
42 Skillet, e.g.
43 It's thinner as you go up
44 City-related
48 Device with a snooze button
53 Idiot
54 "I agree"
55 Emmy winner Perlman
57 Call of Duty: Black ___ (video game)
58 Hermes' mother
59 "Ready to go!" . . . or a description of 17-, 25-, 37- and 48-Across?
62 Tesla co-founder Musk
63 Opera part
64 Tin or titanium
65 Scouting groups
66 Something rising in a gentrifying neighborhood
67 Choice plane seating

DOWN

1 "Man, what a day!"
2 Comment after "You think I'm chicken?"
3 Part of a prank, say
4 Suffix with peace or neat
5 Certain Scotsman
6 Off-limits
7 How foods are often fried
8 All Supreme Court justices until 1981
9 Ram's mate
10 Meat on a skewer
11 Willing to go along
12 Defamed in print
13 Small VWs
18 Home to Vegas: Abbr.
22 R&B singer with the hit "It's All About Me"
24 Cry in a game of tag
26 Foamy coffee order
27 "___ Dream" (63-Across from "Lohengrin")
29 Former All-Star closer Robb
33 Shenanigan
34 Gem whose authenticity can be checked by rubbing it against the teeth
35 Mork's birthplace, on TV
36 Prayer starter
37 Gift to a nonprofit
38 A/C measure, for short
39 Sent millions of emails, say
40 Brew with a rhyming name
43 ___, amas, amat
45 Raises
46 Take to a higher court
47 Snuggle
49 Speckled horses
50 Utah's Sen. Hatch
51 Have an affair
52 Mauna ___ (Hawaiian peak)
56 ___ mater
59 Card game that can go on and on
60 Before, to a bard
61 Gift given while saying "Aloha!"

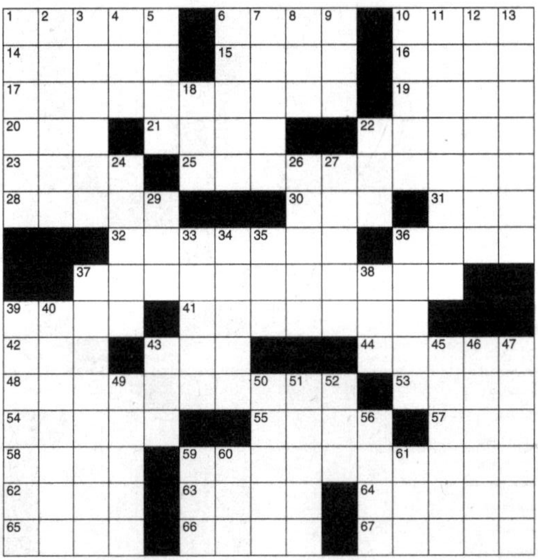

by Sam Buchbinder

44 EASY

ACROSS

1 Thing on a string
5 Listening device?
9 ___ bag
14 One of several on a big rig
15 Poet Teasdale
16 Brother of Prometheus
17 *Especially memorable, as a day
19 Burner holder
20 Garbage transporters
21 *Campground amenity
23 Beings, in Bretagne
25 A dress line
26 Pictionary company
29 It's carbonated
33 *Feature of a carpenter's level
36 Valley with many cabs?
37 Last: Abbr.
38 Naval base builders
41 [Damn, this is annoying!]
42 Gamboling spots
44 *Beef alternative in many countries
46 Gamblers use them
49 Low-end
50 Obsolescent mobile device, briefly
51 186,000 miles/second, for light
53 *Basic china color
57 Courage
61 Hit musical set in Buenos Aires
62 "Don't wait for me to proceed" . . . or what either part of the answer to each starred clue can do?
64 Arrest
65 Writer Sarah ___ Jewett
66 Eugene O'Neill's "___ Christie"
67 Dummy Mortimer
68 Breather
69 Quaint affirmative

DOWN

1 Criminals may be behind them
2 Corner office type
3 Designer Gucci
4 Big name in retirement community development
5 Suffix with human
6 Company that invented newsreels
7 They can be crushed for a pie crust
8 It may be thrown at a corkboard
9 Ruined, as dreams
10 ___ Empire (land of Suleiman the Magnificent)
11 What fireflies do
12 Handed over
13 River to the North Sea
18 Stage when an animal is in heat
22 HBO rival
24 Spa amenity
26 Fisherman's takes
27 Alvin of American dance
28 Mex. misses
29 Oracle
30 Website parts
31 O of the magazine world
32 Part of G.O.P.
34 Dismissive cries
35 Wall St. debt deal
39 Villa d'___
40 A Williams sister
43 Heavenly gatekeeper
45 Seized the opportunity
47 One of eight English kings
48 ___-jongg
51 Mall tenant
52 Drudges
53 Hospital capacity
54 Kiln
55 Dark time, in ads
56 Prince of opera
58 Actor Auberjonois
59 Some shuttles
60 Dutch export
63 Part of a soccer goal

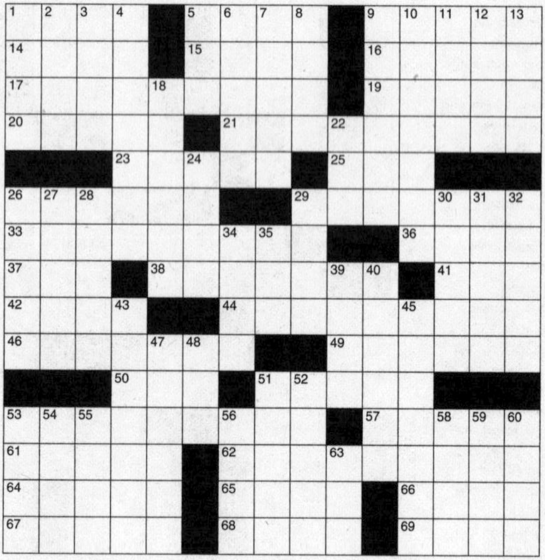

by Paula Gamache

ACROSS

1 ___ browns (breakfast order)
5 Golf target
9 Where "they tried to make me go," in an Amy Winehouse hit
14 Red Muppet on "Sesame Street"
15 Last word of grace
16 Wear away, as soil
17 Defeat decisively
18 ___ Payne, One Direction heartthrob
19 Turn on one foot, in basketball
20 One being laughed at
23 "A Nightmare on ___ Street"
24 "Help!," at sea
25 Cheese-loving pest
28 Where Mom or Dad sits at dinner
33 "___ sells" (advertising maxim)
34 Take to the skies
35 Not walk completely upright
36 Mama's mate
38 Org. co-founded by W. E. B. Du Bois
41 When doubled, a Hawaiian fish
42 Each and ___
44 Place after win and place
46 Totally cool
47 Locale
51 Building blaster, for short
52 R&B's ___ Hill
53 Cub Scout unit
54 Where it's calmest in a hurricane
61 Part of a bicycle or loom
63 An hour before office closing time, maybe
64 Cookie in cookies-and-cream ice cream
65 Actress Berry
66 Brink
67 Space race competitor, for short
68 Clothesline alternative
69 Word that follows steel, open or pigeon
70 Boring way to learn

DOWN

1 Oregano, for one
2 Baseball's Felipe
3 Filth
4 Good drink for a sore throat
5 First or last quarter in the lunar cycle
6 Exclude
7 Jacob's wife
8 Catch in a net
9 Shares on Facebook, maybe
10 "The Phantom of the Opera" lead role
11 Futuristic mode of transportation in the "Back to the Future" films
12 Big fuss
13 Wager
21 Early automaker Ransom E. ___
22 "Average" guy
26 Greetings in Honolulu
27 Lukewarm
28 What's beyond the Pearly Gates
29 As predicted
30 Flight watchdog org.
31 Get rid of
32 Cash dispenser, briefly
33 Exhausted
37 Animal house?
39 Guerrilla Guevara
40 Like some doughnuts and wigs
43 One calling from a Swiss mountaintop
45 Troubles
48 Questlove's hairdo, for short
49 Nursery rhyme seat
50 Doing concerts here and there
55 Connecticut Ivy
56 Kind of list
57 Ginormous
58 Approximately
59 Slumber
60 "Encore!"
61 Prof's degree
62 Corn unit

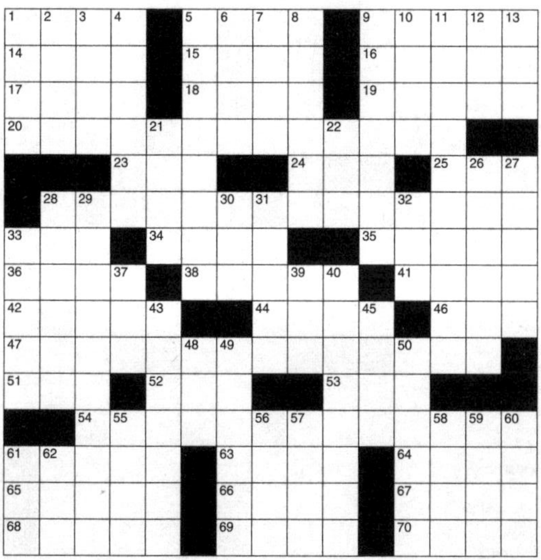

by Ori Brian

46 EASY

ACROSS

1 Frat party staples
5 Wrote a four-star review
10 Open a smidge
14 TV's "___ Betty"
15 Singer Turner's memoir
16 Doughnut feature
17 It can be left 10-Across
18 "Open" things for a call-in show
20 Not recommended
22 Resort near Venice
23 Get rid of
24 "___ bet?"
26 "Huh?"
28 Scare word
30 ___ buco (veal dish)
32 China's Chou En-___
33 End in ___ (not be resolved)
35 Places for shawls
40 Canyon vantage points
41 Phony
42 O.T. book before Daniel
43 Coal and natural gas
45 Like bratty comments
46 Reverse of SSW
47 Rebuke to a traitor
49 Unusual
50 Petite dress specification
54 Absorb, as gravy
56 "Il était ___ fois" ("Once upon a time": Fr.)
57 Kids' guessing game
59 Some vintage photos
62 Syrup comes from them
65 Suddenly lose patience
66 Competitor of Pedigree
67 Totally wipe out
68 Poet Pound
69 Blood worry
70 Safari sighting, for short
71 Bugle tune . . . or what one does to 1-, 18-, 35-, 43- and 62-Across

DOWN

1 African antelope with curvy horns
2 Dr. ___ Spengler, "Ghostbusters" role
3 Luminescent larvae
4 Origin of much 2015–16 emigration
5 Gets redder, say
6 N.C.A.A. part: Abbr.
7 Baroque stringed instrument
8 ___ Del Mar, "Brokeback Mountain" role
9 Icarus' father, in myth
10 Hawaiian yellowfin tuna
11 Biblical prophet who had a whale of a time?
12 Vega of "Spy Kids"
13 Put back to 0, say
19 True-blue
21 Forecast eagerly awaited by schoolkids
25 N.C.A.A. part: Abbr.
27 Make broader
28 Roseanne of "Roseanne"
29 Slobbering cartoon character
31 "Well, I'll be!"
34 In unison
36 Ejects from office
37 "South Pacific" co-star
38 Comic Foxx
39 Timetable, informally
41 William ___, Pilgrim Father
44 Loosen, as neckwear
45 Apartment building V.I.P., for short
48 Throw at
50 Poison oak cousin
51 Entirely
52 One of Groucho's brothers
53 Show on which Dr. Phil became famous, familiarly
55 Surprise win
58 Himalayan mystery
60 ___ The Magazine (bimonthly with 35+ million readers)
61 Massage spots
63 Parking area
64 German article

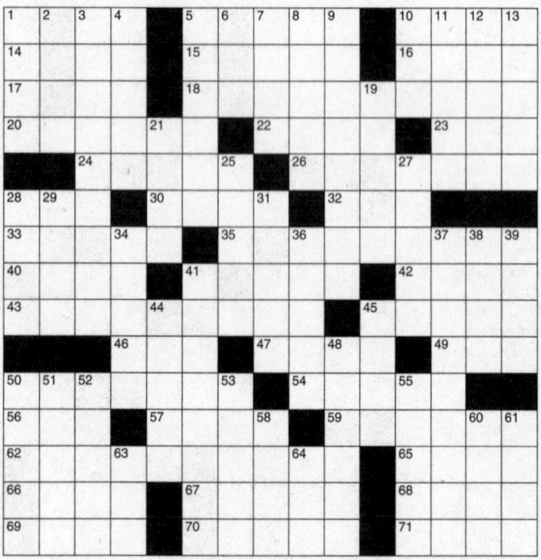

by Jonathan Gersch

ACROSS

1 Funny Groucho or Harpo
5 Lover of Tristan, in legend
11 Place with R.V. hookups
14 Swear
15 GoDaddy purchase
16 90° bend
17 Tropical drinks often served with umbrellas
19 ___ Period (time in Japanese history)
20 Lustful deity of myth
21 Rooster's mate
22 Store sign during business hours
23 Spicy ballroom activity?
27 Communication for the deaf, in brief
30 Try to win, as a lover
31 Baseball Hall-of-Famer Mel
32 Finishing eighth out of eight, say
35 Strain the body too much
38 Stupefy
39 Baby horses
41 Nipple
42 Rococo and Postmodernism
44 Application to highways before a winter storm
46 Take to court
47 Actress Thurman
48 Zodiac lion
49 "The Hitchhiker's Guide to the Galaxy" author
55 Boleyn, Brontë or Bancroft
56 Prof helpers
57 Earl or baron
61 2012 #1 album for Taylor Swift
62 Common first course . . . or what's literally contained in 17-, 23-, 32-, 44- and 49-Across?
65 Maker of the Optima and Sorento
66 "Hey!," from someone who's hiding
67 Wander
68 Foxy
69 Butcher's implement
70 The Ugly Duckling, actually

DOWN

1 Rand McNally items
2 Big name in running shoes
3 $2,000 for Boardwalk, with a hotel
4 Penetrating looks?
5 Declaration made with a raised right hand
6 Note between fa and la
7 Warren Buffet, the Oracle of ___
8 Stowed on board
9 Singer Ross with the Supremes
10 Coast Guard rank: Abbr.
11 Stay authentic, colloquially
12 Of yore
13 See 18-Down
18 With 13-Down, move at a snail's place
22 Groups of eight
24 Hangs around and does nothing
25 Just all right
26 Thanksgiving's mo.
27 Does sums
28 Bench or chair
29 Relaxing time after church, say
33 Downpour
34 Paver's supply
35 Target of a decade-long manhunt, informally
36 Over hill and ___
37 Germany's ___ von Bismarck
40 Eardrum-busting
43 Squirmy fish
45 Curses
49 Opposite of whites, laundrywise
50 Longtime NBC newsman Roger
51 Do penance (for)
52 An Obama girl
53 Thing in the plus column
54 Goes way, way up
58 Erupt
59 What a volcano erupts
60 Biblical garden
62 Dickens's Tiny ___
63 Long, long time
64 Showtime's serial killer protagonist, familiarly

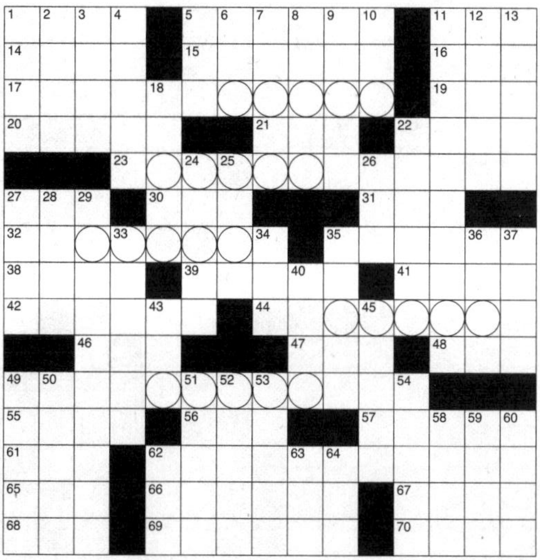

by David Woolf

EASY

ACROSS

1 "Gotta run!"
6 Cretan peak: Abbr.
11 Home of George W. Bush's library, for short
14 Potty-mouthed
15 Rowed
16 ___ and feather
17 Bruce Springsteen's group
19 Sheepskin boot name
20 Jazz combo, often
21 Advantage
22 Vodka brand
26 Offensive football lineup
30 Makes happy
32 Longtime New York Times film critic
33 Adele song with the lyric "I must have called a thousand times"
34 Letters associated with a rainbow flag
35 Phrase on the back of a buck
41 Move, in real-estate lingo
42 Subject of discussion
44 Gourd-shaped rattles
48 Respectful term for a conductor
50 Cole Porter classic from "Can-Can"
52 Earring shape
53 "___ here!"
54 Folkie Phil
56 Top-left button on most keyboards
57 Surprise ending, as in "The Gift of the Magi"
64 11-Down that made "King Kong"
65 Picture book character lost in a crowd
66 "Oh no!"
67 Frodo's best friend
68 Fishline material
69 Children's song refrain found at the starts of 17-, 26-, 35-, 50- and 57-Across

DOWN

1 ___ Palace (Elsa's hide-out in "Frozen")
2 "___ Doubtfire"
3 Publicly 34-Across
4 New Deal prez
5 Pedicure targets
6 Recurring musical ideas
7 No-no
8 Glass of "This American Life"
9 Lion's hide-out
10 Stir in
11 Where to find a soundstage
12 Housefly larva
13 Subject heading for an important email
18 Buffalo's county
21 "Yadda, yadda, yadda"
22 Globe shape: Abbr.
23 "Red Balloon" painter Paul
24 App with restaurant reviews
25 Informal pronoun
27 Prego alternative
28 Unruly crowds
29 Quick on the uptake
31 Reporter's contact
34 Corp. takeover
36 Gather what's been sown
37 Ingrid Bergman's "Casablanca" role
38 Snack
39 "What've you been ___?"
40 Joan of art
43 Bobby : U.K. :: ___ : U.S.
44 Scrooge types
45 U.S. state closest to the International Date Line
46 "My Big Fat Greek Wedding" or "When Harry Met Sally . . ."
47 "___ Maria"
48 One-millionth of a meter
49 Like a barbecue pit
51 Last movement of a sonata
55 Eye irritation
57 Part of B.Y.O.B.
58 Cushion material for some horse-drawn rides
59 Building wing
60 Rival of Xbox
61 "I Like ___" (old campaign slogan)
62 Due × tre
63 Chinese menu general

by Sarah Keller

ACROSS

1 Common lunchbox sandwich, for short
4 Florida home to Busch Gardens
9 Equally distant
14 Prevaricate
15 Wears, as clothing
16 Serviceable
17 Outcome
19 Ankle bones
20 From east of the Urals
21 Indication that someone's home at night, say
23 Chicago exchange, briefly
26 Found's opposite
27 The first "A" in N.C.A.A.: Abbr.
30 Bird on a weather vane
33 "Wanna ___?"
36 Midday
38 Six-time N.B.A. champion Steve
39 How kids are grouped in school
40 Damage
41 Texas A&M student
42 Alan who played Hawkeye
43 Return to a former state
45 "Go team!"
46 Roman goddess of wisdom
47 "N.Y. State of Mind" rapper
48 John Kasich's state
50 Capital of Norway
52 Stair rail
56 Voices above tenors
60 Money sometimes said to be "filthy"
61 Like 17-, 36- and 43-Across as well as 11- and 29-Down
64 Not this or that
65 Not reacting
66 Room that needs a serious cleanup
67 Merchandise
68 Australian "bear"
69 Chi-town team

DOWN

1 ___ bargain
2 Trash receptacles
3 User of the Force
4 "What gall!"
5 Batteries in TV remotes
6 The Spartans of the N.C.A.A.
7 Voting place
8 ___-aging cream
9 Stephen King or Ellery Queen
10 Rebounds and field goal average
11 Started
12 Too
13 Free ___ (total control)
18 Symbol of Aries
22 Secluded valley
24 ___ v. Wade
25 Scam artists
27 Being litigated
28 Choreographer Tharp
29 Top dog
31 Dry, white Italian wine
32 Matador
34 Writer Jong
35 Odysseys
37 N.Y.C. airport code
38 C.I.A. : U.S. :: ___ : Soviet Union
41 Maiden who raced Hippomenes, in myth
43 Uproar
44 Mobile accommodations, for short
46 Scrooges
49 Put on the payroll
51 Long in the tooth
52 Modern journal
53 Volvo or Volt
54 ___ the Red
55 City at the foot of the Sierra Nevada
57 Itar-___ news agency
58 "I'm ___ you!"
59 River to Hades
62 Traffic-stopping org.
63 It might be bookmarked

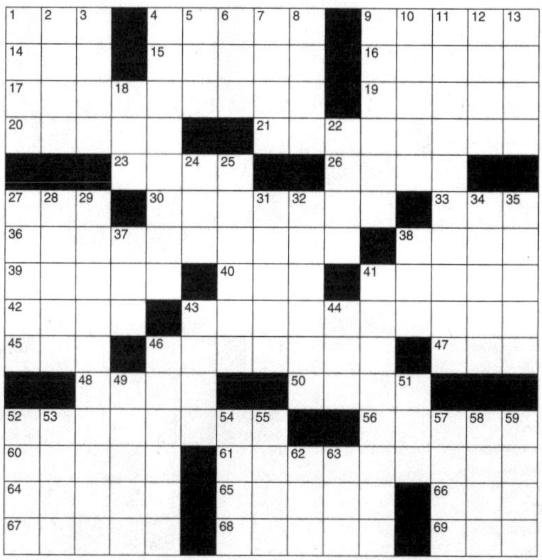

by Mary Lou Guizzo

50 EASY

ACROSS

1 Shapes of bacilli bacteria
5 Snug
10 North-of-the-border station
14 State that voted Republican by the highest percentage (73%) in the 2012 presidential election
15 River to the Rhône
16 Sporty car feature
17 With 18- and 19-Across, classic song that starts "'Mid pleasures and palaces though we may roam"
18 See 17-Across
19 See 17-Across
20 Company shake-up, for short
22 Hero war pilot
23 Suit coat feature
24 Popular setting for 17-/18-/19-Across
27 Hagen of stage and screen
29 Fanatic
30 GPS suggestion: Abbr.
31 Was down with
34 Swinger's target at a party
36 Yale, affectionately
38 Façade feature
40 Small flycatchers
41 Korean performer with a monster 2012 international hit
42 Jeanne d'Arc, e.g.: Abbr.
44 1974–75 pigskin org.
45 Pastoral poem
47 With 53- and 56-Across, certain abode
49 Certain military hazards, for short
52 Evening, in ads
53 See 47-Across
54 Q*___ (1980s arcade game)
55 Homer Simpson cry
56 See 47-Across
57 "___ Rosenkavalier"
58 Bygone Ugandan despot
61 Oxide in rubies and sapphires
64 Harvesting machines
65 Possession of property
66 What initials on something may signify
67 Where femurs are located

DOWN

1 Germany's ___ Valley
2 Indian tribe that lent its name to a county in Nebraska
3 Classical exemplars of steadfast friendship
4 Hite of "The Hite Report"
5 Modern prefix with gender
6 Comedian Patton ___
7 Little rodents, jocularly
8 Having one's business mentioned in a news article, e.g.
9 Up to now
10 Patriot Allen
11 Avert more serious losses
12 Four or five, say
13 German-based G.M. subsidiary
21 How George Harrison's guitar "weeps"
23 Hide out
25 Like many exhausts
26 "Looking at it a different way," in texts
27 Something a scanner scans, in brief
28 20-20, e.g.
32 Stein filler
33 Insult, informally
35 Dairy ___
37 "Clear!" procedure, for short
39 Actor Kutcher and others
40 Watches intently
43 Pants, in slang
45 Former Indian P.M. Gandhi
46 Semiconductor devices
47 Improper attire at a fancy restaurant
48 Hole in one's shoe
50 Make sopping wet
51 Humane Society pickups
59 Hairy primate
60 Not-so-hairy primates
62 Durham sch.
63 ___ tai (drink)

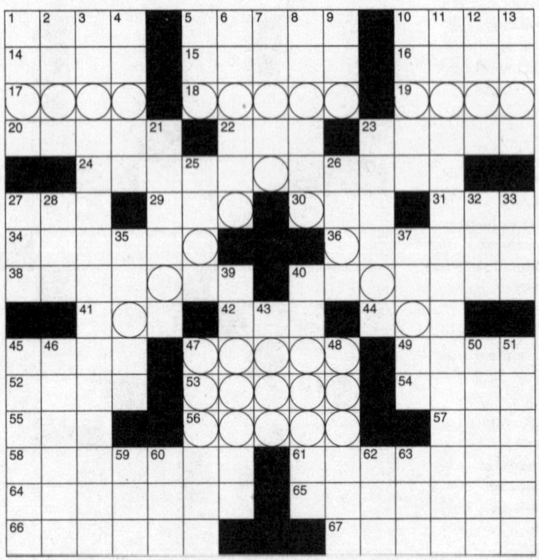

by Peter A. Collins

MEDIUM 51

ACROSS

1 *Mac-vs.-PC during the early 2000s, e.g.
6 *Give a worn appearance to, as jeans
14 Not neutral
16 Securer of locks
17 Verdi work that was the first opera to be recorded in its entirety
18 Going nowhere
19 New York rail and bus inits.
20 Austrian city where Kepler taught
21 Distance ÷ time: Abbr.
22 *Road to ancient Rome
26 Villainous "Get Smart" group
27 26-Across, to Maxwell Smart
28 Sushi bar tuna
29 Islam's largest branch
31 Brouhahas
34 Pacific Ocean phenomenon
36 *Tucson collegians
41 How police may investigate
42 "Alrighty then . . ."
43 Dirty-looking
45 A GPS coordinate: Abbr.
47 Turf ___ (football ailment)
48 "Me too"
49 *Holy Communion drink
52 Cool ___ cucumber
53 Former U.N. secretary general ___ Annan
55 "Bali ___"
56 Mississippi's state tree
58 Oldest entertainment awards ceremony
62 Like barely spicy chili
63 Makes a lasting impression?
64 *Radio medium
65 Classic root beer brand . . . or a hint to the answers to this puzzle's starred clues

DOWN

1 Broadway's Burrows
2 Co. board member
3 Sickly-looking
4 "Me too"
5 Lead-in to cop or car
6 *Salem witch trials accuser
7 Altima or Accord alternative
8 Rombauer of cookery
9 Health adviser on talk TV
10 Where to use a browser
11 Anxiety-treating medication
12 Canonized fifth-century pope
13 Formal footwear
15 Roman goddess of the hunt
22 Mennen product
23 D-worthy
24 Lead-in to cab
25 Bread choice
26 Sound eliciting a "Who's there?"
29 R.S.V.P. part
30 Word processing command
32 A greenhouse gas
33 Spotify selection
35 Bite playfully
37 Roll-call call
38 37-Down caller
39 Animator's creation
40 ___'Pea
43 Aquafina competitor
44 Graphics-capturing device
46 Chevy model
48 Pago Pago's locale
49 Flambé, say
50 Dreads sporter
51 Religion with pentagrams
53 Caffeine-laden nut
54 Norway's patron saint
57 Rustic denial
59 "Kung Fu" actor Philip
60 Visibly abashed
61 202.5°

by Michael Dewey

52 MEDIUM

ACROSS

1 Bedridden
7 Enclosed, old-style
11 "___ on Melancholy"
14 Not so current
15 Clue
16 Children's author Asquith
17 Give an "Odyssey" character a trim?
19 Some media coverage
20 Old Testament book that asks "Does a lion roar in the thicket when it has no prey?"
21 Take it easy
22 Japanese writing system
24 Back muscle, informally
25 Ecosystem components
27 Threaten
28 Cover story
30 Favorite whack job?
32 Windshield decorations
34 Act of sedition
35 Be a crowd
37 Hurrahs
38 Slummy building
41 Rhythmic Cuban dance: Var.
45 Invoice a whole Mideast peninsula?
47 OPEC dignitaries
48 Annual New York honor
49 Letter sign-off
51 Talk smack about
52 Shadow
54 Barrio greeting
55 Cruising along
56 PBS backer
57 Motto of a huge "Star Wars" and "Star Trek" fan?
60 One hailed by city dwellers
61 Meticulous to a fault
62 Washington in "Philadelphia"
63 Ticket info
64 Carnival ride provider
65 Silver and others

DOWN

1 Small business purchase, perhaps
2 Like Wabash College
3 Not worth considering
4 Ballroom maneuvers
5 The Gamecocks of the N.C.A.A.
6 They're found within kingdoms
7 Controversial fish catcher
8 Blind love
9 Sales ___
10 Charge
11 River that's home to the black spot piranha
12 "Much Ado About Nothing" villain
13 White house occupant?
18 Masterstroke
23 "Sweet" plant of the mustard family
25 Sole orders
26 ___ gun
29 Conflicted sort?
31 Willie Mays descriptor
33 Letter embellishment
36 "Holy cow!"
38 Barbecuer's supply
39 Hero of a tale told by Scheherazade
40 Impressive collection
42 Neither large nor small . . . or a phonetic hint to 17-, 30-, 45- and 57-Across
43 Brought up to speed
44 Tears into
45 Pep in one's step
46 Take it easy
50 Enriches, in a way
53 "This can't wait!"
55 Bumps on the head?
58 Collaborator on several David Bowie albums
59 Fixed

by Timothy Polin

Medium

ACROSS

1 Ladies' night attendee
7 "It's all good"
13 Light-colored brew
14 Condo building employees
16 Canada's first province alphabetically
17 Prepare, as a musical score
18 Lack of supply
19 Join
20 Possible response to "Can you pick up the kids from school?"
24 Like Beethoven's Symphony No. 6
27 What an Ironman has to battle
28 Place
31 Mazda roadster
33 "___ out walkin' after midnight" (Patsy Cline lyric)
34 Boxer Ali
36 Model in 10 straight Sports Illustrated swimsuit editions, familiarly
37 Summer setting in Seattle: Abbr.
38 Get tats
39 Big name in precision cutting
40 ___ capita
41 Asparagus spears, e.g.
42 "___ durn tootin'!"
43 Luau souvenir
44 Bottom of bell bottoms
45 Like a zoot-suiter
47 A Marx brother
49 Possessive often containing a mistaken apostrophe
52 Color of the Dodge Charger on "The Dukes of Hazzard"
55 Land created by C. S. Lewis
58 Surgical asst.
60 Insects on a 17-year cycle
61 Exciting romantic prospect
62 Ones defrauding museums
63 Weaponry storehouse
64 Vitamin brand with an instructive name

DOWN

1 High wind
2 Actress Jessica
3 Satyr's stare
4 Item in a swag bag
5 Gibson who was the first person of color to win a tennis Grand Slam event
6 Bucolic locale
7 Journalist Wells
8 Title "Dr." in an H. G. Wells story
9 Southern side dish made with kernels off the cob
10 Spoken test
11 Marriott competitor
12 Last parts drawn in hangman
13 Crib
15 Something cut down during March Madness
21 Go completely dotty?
22 Push oneself to the max
23 Bout of swellheadedness
24 Where to see pictures on the big screen?
25 Ship of 1492
26 Pretentiously high-class
28 Thinking similarly
29 Many a college applicant's interviewer, for short
30 Flaps one's gums
32 Spot for un chapeau
35 Pay to play
45 Hullabaloo
46 Wild throw, e.g.
47 Keebler saltine brand
48 Sometimes-caramelized food
50 Part of Wonder Woman's outfit
51 Impertinent
53 Like Venus in "The Birth of Venus"
54 Nickname for Mom's mom
56 A lot of land, maybe
57 Bit of Bollywood music
59 Jellied delicacy
60 Exec. money manager

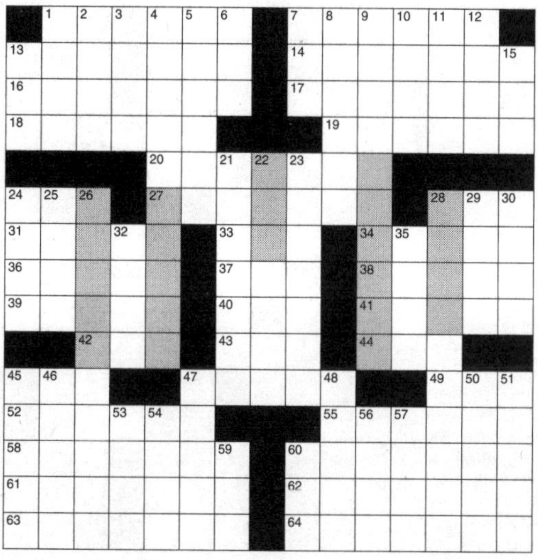

by Jeff Chen

54 MEDIUM

ACROSS

1 Much police paperwork
8 From Kigali, e.g.
15 Intrinsically
16 French locale of fierce W.W. I fighting
17 Baked chocolaty treat
18 Hefty item
19 Arabic name part
20 Nos. at the beach
22 Blew one's horn
23 Crushed, as a test
25 Creative works utilizing the landscape
27 Supermarket section
28 "Caddyshack" director
30 D.C. pro
31 Cleaner brand
32 Ready to retire
34 Part of N.Y.C. once derisively called Hell's Hundred Acres
36 Yank
37 Angered
39 Draft choice
41 Ft. Benning training facility
44 Early 20th-century abdicator
46 Magical creatures in Jewish folklore
50 Tracks
52 One who keeps the beat?
54 Lay out differently, in a way
55 "___ la Douce" (1963 film)
56 Public recognition
58 Apportion
59 Roll the dice, so to speak
61 Not in use
63 Ocasek of the Cars
64 About 25 years, for N.F.L. players
66 What a spray may provide
68 Ones shaking to the music?
69 Comic legend
70 Chic
71 N.B.A. team since 2008

DOWN

1 Places for oysters and clams
2 On the up and up
3 Basic linguistic unit
4 Antipoverty agcy. created under L.B.J.
5 Some performances at the Apollo
6 Baloney
7 Two-time Wimbledon winner Edberg
8 Lively piano tune
9 One of the seven deadly sins
10 Prefix with business
11 Emily Dickinson, self-descriptively
12 Aid in genealogy
13 Poet who wrote "You may shoot me with your words, / You may cut me with your eyes"
14 Bereft of
21 Sp. ladies
24 Per ___
26 Corvette feature
29 Old-fashioned fashion accessories
31 Sorrowful state
33 Abbr. by a golf tee
35 Halloween costume
38 Per
40 ___ sch.
41 Crane construction?
42 Vacation vehicle
43 Keeps on low, say
45 It may be slated
47 ___ City (memorable film destination)
48 Something never seen at night
49 Spirit
51 Small test subject
53 Stickler
56 "Love Story" novelist
57 First extra inning
60 Like some tablecloths
62 He married two Hittites to the chagrin of his parents, in Genesis
65 Suffix with legal
67 Channel that became Heartland in 2013

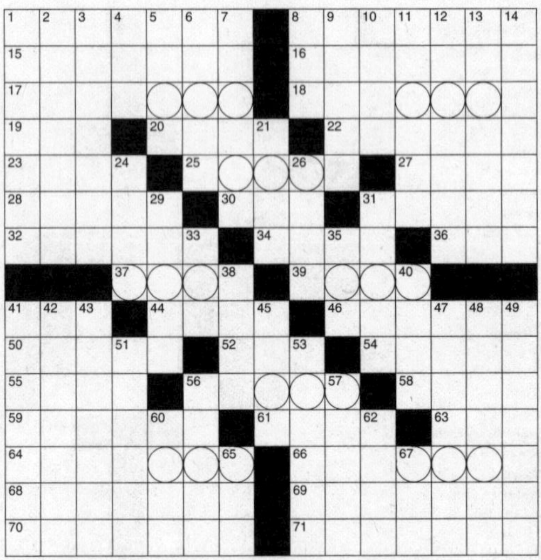

by Don Gagliardo and Zhouqin Burnikel

ACROSS

1 Twosome on TMZ, e.g.
5 Level
9 Put down for the count
13 Touch emotionally
14 Bakery employee
15 Mazatlán mister
16 SAT administrator, by trade?
18 City where Galileo taught
19 Cremains holder
20 "I did it!"
21 Game one
23 Fiddle (with)
25 Doctor, by trade?
27 Biblical garden
28 Word before bump or pump
29 Great Lakes canal name
30 Dizzying designs
33 Marzipan component
36 Apt title for this puzzle
38 Sweetie pie
40 Politico Perot
41 With 10-Down, lead vocalist and flutist for rock's Jethro Tull
42 Perlman of "Cheers"
44 Beige-ish
48 Model, by trade?
51 Boozehounds
53 Claptrap
54 Candy in a dispenser
55 Farm mama
56 Last word of "The Star-Spangled Banner"
57 Manicurists and tax preparers, by trade?
60 Bit of gossip
61 Green shade
62 Jacob's womb-mate
63 One of a Latin trio
64 Risqué, maybe
65 Captain Sparrow portrayer

DOWN

1 Attribute (to)
2 Hot and then some
3 Goolagong who won seven Grand Slam singles event titles
4 Ran into
5 Choir's support
6 Doesn't just talk
7 Waltz ending?
8 Using "effect" for "affect" and vice versa
9 "The Matrix" star Reeves
10 See 41-Across
11 "I'll take that bet!"
12 ". . . man ___ mouse?"
15 Something a journalist may work on
17 Feature of a 22-Down
22 Something to make a hash of?
24 Bouillon brand name
25 Pub purchase for the table
26 Implement for an angler
28 To's opposite
31 Dish baked in an imu
32 Disinclined (to)
34 Fleur-de-___
35 Person who had a major part in the Bible?
36 View through a wide-angle lens
37 Coach Parseghian
38 Bad news in the polls
39 Part of the body studied by otolaryngologists
43 "S O S"
45 Word that brings a smile
46 Fix, as a bandage
47 Consumes
49 Cagey debater's tactic
50 "Your turn to talk," on radio
51 Liberal, disparagingly
52 Israeli gun
54 Beer ___
56 Commercial ending with Wonder
58 Dispose (of)
59 Was like Fred Astaire to Ginger Rogers

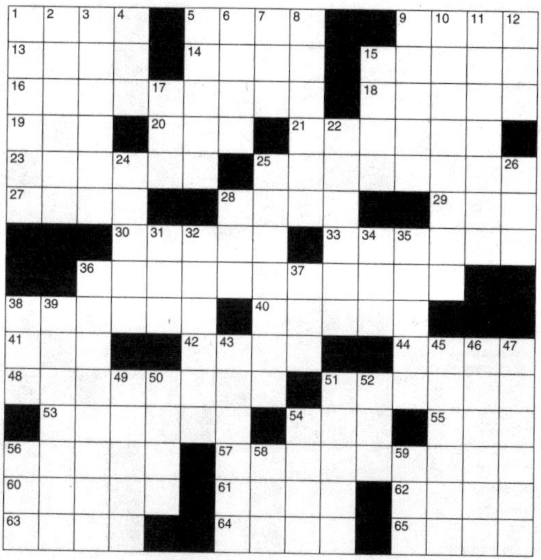

by Tom Pepper

56 MEDIUM

ACROSS

1 "Yep, you're right."
8 Set opening?
11 Boxer, e.g., for short
14 Appealing in appearance
15 Poetic preposition
16 Stage legend Hagen
17 "It's my understanding that . . ."
18 Worker who may skim off the top?
20 Passing remark?
21 Zulu, e.g.
23 Dense
24 Interoffice email abbr.
26 Decide (to)
28 Colorado tributary
29 Large numbers
31 Sum for keeping mum
33 Lassoed
34 With 36- and 40-Across, organization whose name hints at some missing letters in this puzzle
35 Site for a famed garden
36 See 34-Across
37 Think (over)
40 See 34-Across
41 Diner option
42 Literature Nobelist between Hermann Hesse and T. S. Eliot
45 1950s sex symbol
46 Actress Singer
47 I
48 Banana ___
49 Political commentator Molly
51 Eats (at)
53 Boxer's achievement, for short
56 India's national anthem was originally written in it
58 Walgreens competitor
60 Variety
61 See the humor in
62 Totally far-fetched
63 Draft letters
64 Unspecified amount
65 Mom and dad, slangily

DOWN

1 King's little cousin
2 Pirate-fighting org.
3 Bearded
4 Non-P.C. add-on?
5 Questions
6 Abdullah I made it a capital city
7 ___ idol
8 Short-term retail location, nowadays
9 Chocolaty goodie
10 Round numbers?
11 "Juno and the Paycock" setting
12 French star
13 Cry for help, or a time for celebration
19 Apple's apple and others
22 Mentioned
25 Former Alaska politico Stevens
27 Cleveland's bills, for short
29 Staff
30 Expose, in verse
31 "Hallelujah!"
32 Star of the short-lived reality show "I Pity the Fool"
34 Strains with sadness
36 Blue state?
37 Jacket flap
38 Sweets alternative
39 Terminal listing, in brief
40 Come with
41 Cupped apparel
42 Stand outs?
43 Much of a literature class's studies
44 What you might meet someone for
45 Closest friend, informally
48 Result of a perfect shot
50 TV host who inspired Neil deGrasse Tyson
52 "How now!" follower in "Hamlet"
54 Variety
55 Wordsmiths' paeans
57 Longtime leader in late-night
59 Musician Brian

by Andrew J. Ries

Medium 57

ACROSS

1 Wraps around the subcontinent
6 The Rocksteady 7 genre
9 Hermès rival
14 Market not to be bullish in?
16 Courtier who invites Hamlet to a duel
17 Frost mixed with pebbles?
18 Ebb away
19 Bud in Burgundy
20 Dated
21 Scatter
23 Bad spot for taking prom pictures
24 Authors of fiction?
27 Having a propensity to dig
29 Priest getting what's coming to him?
33 Don't do it
36 High on hwys.
37 Title Mr. of literature
38 Post-operation site, for short
39 Elementary education . . . or feature of the last words punned upon in 17-, 29-, 49- and 66-Across
43 "Y" wearer
44 Poet Lazarus
46 Equine nibble
47 City by the Wasatch Mountains
49 Pond admired from the back porch?
53 Pair for some Winter Olympians
54 Eclipse
58 Juice drink brand
60 Expected hr. at the airport
62 That ship
63 The Horned Frogs of the N.C.A.A.
64 First name in infamy
66 Chiffon mishap?
69 Home of the Imperial Palace
70 Volunteer's affirmation
71 Villain's look
72 Currency unit, briefly
73 Feeling sexually aroused

DOWN

1 Jettison
2 "Oh, give me ___ . . ."
3 Poison used on TV's "Breaking Bad"
4 Tats
5 Speaks volumes
6 April weather event
7 Org. for R.V. lovers
8 Lenders' figs.
9 Vanish, in a way
10 Type of laptop-to-printer connection
11 Loony-looking
12 New York's ___ Field
13 "Home Invasion" rapper
15 "For ___!"
22 Studio alert
25 PX patron
26 "Hello Goodbye" to "All You Need Is Love" on the Beatles' "Magical Mystery Tour" album
28 "Put a cork in it!"
30 Maestro's signal
31 Do nothing
32 Jockey strap
33 Grand ___ (opera house section)
34 Tiptop
35 Pick from another's pack
40 Give a lift
41 Funny Charlotte
42 Enchanting sort
45 Couples' getaway?
48 Come together
50 Try to win
51 Oil spot?
52 Old anesthetic
55 Dined at home
56 Burn, as milk
57 Irritably sullen
58 New England football team, informally
59 Use in great excess
61 It's west of the Pacific
65 Corrosive stuff
67 D.D.E.'s predecessor
68 Old "You're going to like us" sloganeer

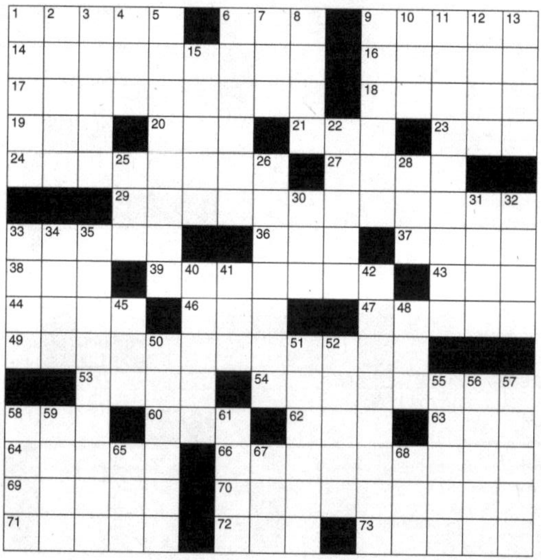

by Jeremy Newton

58 MEDIUM

ACROSS

1 Arctic resident
5 Who sings "Climb Ev'ry Mountain" in "The Sound of Music"
11 Co. bought by G.E. in 1986
14 NASA's ___ Research Center
15 Give, as instructions
16 Sushi fish
17 Like limes
18 One who might cause a spill at a cafeteria?
20 Some TV drama locales, for short
21 Yellow-card, e.g.
22 Patches, in a way
23 Dog attacking a newsstand?
27 Jungian concept
28 See 26-Down
29 Show of pride
30 Stadium vendor's offering
32 Answer to "What's her job in the garden supply store?"?
39 Oodles and oodles
40 "___ a stinker?" (Bugs Bunny catchphrase)
41 Longtime "Law & Order" actor
45 Goes soft
46 What happens after getting in Vivien's way on a movie set?
50 Viperidae family member
51 State
52 Some choice words
53 Group whose songs get spoonerized in 18-, 23-, 32- and 46-Across
56 With 25-Down, women's fashion designer
57 Might
58 Part of a presidential motorcade
59 Certain bakery worker
60 Paris's ___-Chapelle
61 Puts aside
62 Bygone Ottoman rulers

DOWN

1 School allowance?
2 "Immortal" flower in "Paradise Lost"
3 Make beads, say
4 It's observed in L.A.
5 Natural perfume
6 The catcher in the wry?
7 Like most lait et riz
8 English cathedral city
9 Criterion: Abbr.
10 "Indeed, yes"
11 Drake, e.g.
12 "Down the hatch!"
13 Highfalutin attitude
19 Crostini topping
21 ___ of God
24 Big birds
25 See 56-Across
26 With 28-Across, schlemiels
30 Features of urban ancient Rome
31 President Morales of Bolivia
33 Pricing word
34 One frequenting arcades
35 "That's utter slander!"
36 How we experience our first kiss
37 Mason, notably
38 Language manglers, e.g.
41 Stale
42 Unwanted photo effect
43 "Boyfriend" singer, to fans, with "the"
44 Matches
47 Fire-suppressing compound
48 Unhidden
49 Police protection
50 You might be recorded using them
54 Blaze evidence
55 Fort Worth campus, for short
56 Succor

by Jeffrey Wechsler

ACROSS

1 Soaks so as to extract flavor
7 Late-night host before Carson
11 Fare for the toothless
14 "Clearly Different" eye care chain
15 Aunt of Prince William
16 Sénat accord
17 Like some top-quality kitchen oil
19 Org. originally known as the National Congress of Mothers
20 Sci-fi visitors
21 Cross-dressing Streisand character
22 Arsenal stock
24 Refusing to listen
26 Delta locale
29 "Loot" playwright Joe
31 Word abbreviated on fight cards
32 Branch out
37 Slangy rebuttal to 65-Across
38 Exchange program for preschoolers?
41 Help for the puzzled
42 Adopts, as a stray
43 Treat, as table salt
45 Schnapps flavoring
49 Cocktail made by combining the ends of 17-, 26- and 38-Across
54 Battle of Normandy town
55 Passed with ease
56 Charles who wrote "Peg Woffington"
58 Unedited, as footage
59 Online Q&A session
60 Dickens classic . . . and, phonetically, two garnishes for a 49-Across?
63 Place for pickles
64 Fall clearance item?
65 "Quite correct"
66 Nativity scene beast
67 Declare
68 Some decaf orders

DOWN

1 Brand of skimpy swimwear
2 One who might type "OMG" or "CYA"
3 Bothers no end
4 Veer off course
5 Ump's call after "Time!"
6 Break off completely
7 Fifth installment of a miniseries
8 Con man's scheme
9 DiFranco who created Righteous Babe Records
10 Label again, as a file
11 Top 40 fare
12 Pitch-correcting audio processor
13 With 44-Down, "Butterfly" Golden Globe winner
18 Common pasta suffix
23 Deposits of glacial debris
25 Temporarily
27 Many KOA patrons
28 "The buck stops here" prez
30 Tennis ball fuzz
33 Stave off
34 Tax planner's recommendation, for short
35 The first "A" of 59-Across
36 Plumbing joint
38 Scenes in shoeboxes, say
39 Vehicles for the Unsers
40 Big wheel
41 Went underground
44 See 13-Down
46 Under threat
47 Top-shelf
48 Guides for D.I.Y.'ers
50 Toddler's wheels
51 "When will ___ learn?"
52 Lassie's turndown
53 "The Wire" actor ___ Elba
57 James who sang "At Last"
59 Steely Dan album of 1977
61 Where many people solve crosswords, for short
62 Successfully woo

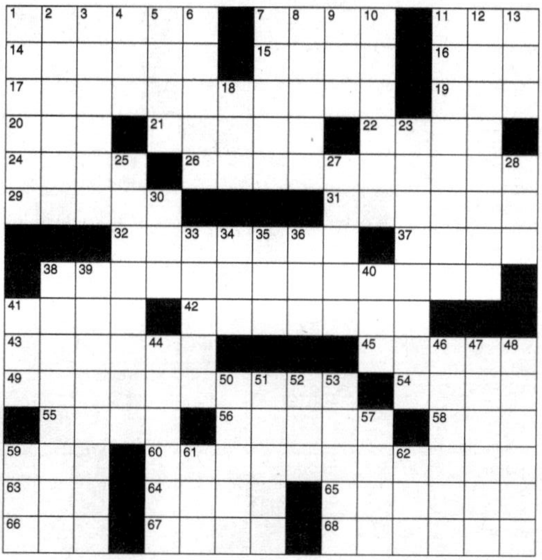

by Herre Schouwerwou

60 MEDIUM

ACROSS

1 Edit, as tape
7 Pro-___
10 Bill issuer, for short
13 3 Musketeers filling
14 Some trophies
16 Mauna ___
17 "Gosh darn it!"
18 Ford aircraft of the 1920s–'30s
20 Hand over
21 Flame-colored gemstones
22 Hindu god pictured playing a flute
25 It might save your skin
26 Like Liederkranz cheese
28 Parcel of land
32 Outburst accompanying a facepalm
35 With 44-Across, off-the-record discussions . . . or 12 answers in this puzzle?
36 "Want me to?"
37 ___ Air
39 Alternative to Mega Millions
41 Spa session
42 Minor, as a sin
44 See 35-Across
46 "Didn't need to know that"
47 Georgia of "The Mary Tyler Moore Show"
48 Sink to the bottom
50 Onetime Mustang option
52 Like elephant seals
56 Hospital conveyance
60 Auto parts giant
61 Superior, as investments go
62 Brutish sort
64 Big mfr. of 10-Acrosses
65 North Atlantic hazard
66 Six Nations tribe
67 Jane in court cases
68 Kickoff aid
69 "He hath ___ the fateful lightning . . ." ("The Battle Hymn of the Republic" lyric)

DOWN

1 Concession stand
2 High-carb bite
3 Day before mardi
4 "Well . . . probably"
5 One notably entertained by a laser pointer
6 French connections
7 Play starter
8 Andy who won Olympic gold in tennis in 2012
9 Pitcher's delivery
10 Province bordering Sask.
11 It might include "copy" and "paste"
12 Chocolate treat since 1932
15 Hairless
19 Works with librettos
21 Golf Channel analyst Nick
23 Royal Navy letters
24 Sam of "Jurassic Park"
27 Not disturb
29 Jillions
30 Place for steamers
31 Place to order a mai tai, maybe
32 Low-class watering hole
33 Feature of many a wedding reception
34 Loiter, with "out"
36 In a way, informally
38 Certain New Year's resolution follower
40 ___ Tots
43 PC task-switching shortcut
45 Camera with a mirror-and-prism system, for short
48 Round figure
49 Weather phenomenon named for baby Jesus
51 Eightsome
53 Furniture designer Charles
54 It's below "C V B N M"
55 Sneeze guard locale
56 Beach formation
57 Buffet with shells
58 Steak request
59 Barely beat
62 Hand communication, for short
63 Prefix with cortex

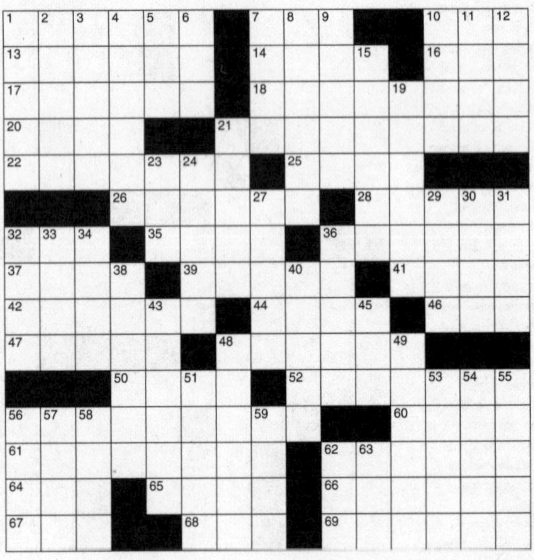

by David Phillips

ACROSS

1 *Do in, old-style
6 Org. for Janet Yellen, with "the"
9 *Grocery line count
14 Suffix with Obama, once
15 One more than due
16 Judge's determination
17 SeaWorld frolicker
18 Club selection factor
19 *Tiny biters
20 Phil who sang "Draft Dodger Rag"
21 Overlook, as a fault
23 With 38- and 52-Across, 1964 Bob Dylan song . . . or a hint to the answers to this puzzle's starred clues
25 Sine, for example
28 Midtown Manhattan cultural attraction, for short
29 Bigger than big
31 G.I. address
33 Symbol of penance
36 Nutritional figs.
37 Make a run for it
38 See 23-Across
41 "Need ___ on?"
42 When Brutus struck
44 Make even slicker
45 Some refrigerators
46 Foot-long sandwich option
49 "See ya!"
51 5 for B and 6 for C
52 See 23-Across
56 Affair that led to Scooter Libby's 2007 conviction, informally
58 Steering wheel option
59 *Gives off
62 You, impersonally
63 Number of strikes in a turkey
64 Lash of old westerns
65 Nabokov heroine
66 Canasta plays
67 *Answer to "Who's there?"
68 Pro ___ (for now)
69 *"No more, thanks"

DOWN

1 ___-Hawley Tariff Act of 1930
2 One of 20 in a book
3 How Buddhists strive to live
4 Connects with
5 Musical gift
6 N.J. town next to Palisades Park
7 Great Lakes tribesmen
8 How a daring quarterback may throw
9 2001 Sean Penn movie
10 Service with a bird logo
11 The "E" of 12-Down
12 Army fare, for short
13 1960s antiwar org.
21 Flop's opposite
22 Place for a shot
24 "___ my wit's end!"
26 "Colorful" folk duo
27 River to the Missouri
29 Golf's Aoki
30 Those, in Taxco
31 Touched down
32 "The Taming of the Shrew" setting
34 Rosemary, for one
35 Part of a Masonic symbol
39 Nouveau ___
40 Director Kazan
43 Place of privacy
47 "Obviously"
48 2015 FIFA Women's World Cup champs
50 Reason to take off one's hat
52 "Hoarders" airer
53 Third-stringers
54 ___-France (region including Paris)
55 Bikini blast, briefly
57 Target of blame
59 "Y"-sporting collegian
60 Antislip protection
61 Recipient of much Apr. mail
63 Texter's "Didn't need to know that"

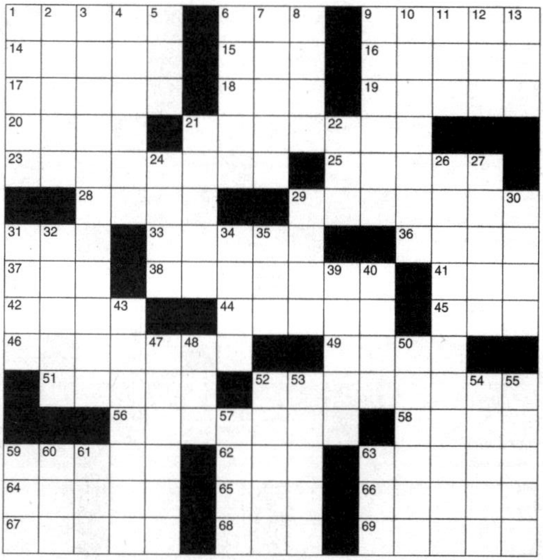

by Adam G. Perl

62 MEDIUM

ACROSS

1 Stop daydreaming
7 Fowl territory?
11 Speaker's position?
14 Betray, in a way
15 Starting now
16 Bagel shop order
17 Lumberjack contests
18 Takes back
20 Response to "How'd you get the answer so fast?"
22 Boil
23 Dessert wine
24 Hirsuteness, for one
26 Both, for openers
29 Emulate Snidely Whiplash
31 Mineral suffix
32 Kind of separation
33 Twofold
35 Raises
36 Ostrichlike bird
39 Party staple suggested by connecting this puzzle's special squares
41 Mother of Eos and Selene
42 Available, as for work
44 Actress Laura of "ER"
46 "What ___ surprise!"
47 Good name, informally
48 Pillowcases
52 High-end Swiss watch
53 Candidate of 1992 and 1996
55 Toolbar image
56 39-Across filler
58 Fishy deli order
60 Where service is lacking
63 Within walking distance, say
64 Approved
65 Church offering
66 It's found under an arch
67 Wide receiver Welker
68 Yellow stick
69 Became bitter

DOWN

1 Prepares to streak
2 Former liberal, informally
3 Present, groupwise
4 Like some skirts and lampshades
5 Tugboat's greeting
6 Word go
7 "Burlesque" co-star, 2010
8 Toddler's wear
9 This puzzle's special squares, e.g.
10 Van Gogh's "Portrait of ___ Tanguy"
11 Seeker of the elixir of life
12 Monsieur Marceau spoke the only one in all of Mel Brooks's "Silent Movie"
13 G.I. suppliers
19 Big name in games
21 Fire safety measure
25 Drawing room?
27 Take a dip
28 Ingrid's "Casablanca" role
30 Souvenir of a Russian trip
32 Mutes, with "down"
34 Homeboy
35 Babe
36 Simba's warning
37 Dyeing wish?
38 Frequent trip takers
40 Cannabis-using
43 "Feed ___, starve . . ."
45 Spa offering
47 Out-of-studio broadcast
49 Want in the worst way
50 Team leader's concern
51 Was obviously asleep
53 Homework assignee
54 Home of Carthage Palace
57 Words in an analogy
59 "Tsk, tsk" elicitor
60 Financial average
61 Just get (by)
62 One of TV's Huxtables

by Elizabeth C. Gorski

MEDIUM 63

ACROSS

1 Infomercial presentation, e.g.
6 Many fourth-down plays
11 Take to the hills?
14 Scaly wall-scaler
15 HI hi
16 QB Brady
17 Seize the reins
19 Bauxite or galena
20 Fall guy?
21 What pi may be used to find
22 Female lead in "Gattaca" and "Kill Bill"
26 Drive away
30 Tirade
31 Bourgeoisie . . . or a description of each group of circled letters?
34 Sound from a terrier
37 Genre of Isaac Asimov's "Foundation"
38 Avail
39 Concur
41 Adjust, as a watch
42 Baseball position . . . or a description of each group of circled letters?
45 Barn neighbor
46 Itty-bitty
47 In eager anticipation
52 F.B.I. action
53 Superstate in "1984"
59 Avail oneself of
60 Followers of Lord Voldemort
63 Beseech
64 Go around in circles
65 What might get an A1 application?
66 "What ___ the odds?!"
67 Some Arizona flora
68 Grosses

DOWN

1 Pepper and others: Abbr.
2 Maximum
3 Gross
4 Barely obtained, with "out"
5 Focal points
6 "The Hunger Games" nation
7 Very, very
8 "Neither snow ___ rain . . ."
9 However, in brief
10 "My Gal ___" (song classic)
11 Hurricane, e.g.
12 Land partitioned in 1945
13 "That is to say . . ."
18 Future seed
21 "___ washes away from the soul the dust of everyday life": Picasso
23 Commerce
24 Owns
25 Hazardous
26 Source of about 20% of the calories consumed by humanity
27 Work with 31-Down
28 File name ending in Adobe Acrobat
29 Draw out
31 Some submissions: Abbr.
32 Group of established works
33 Put a match to
34 God whose name is a homophone of a zodiac sign
35 Count (on)
36 Made dinner for
40 Cotton ___
43 ___ Whitney
44 Witherspoon of "Legally Blonde"
45 Down
47 Dutch Caribbean island
48 Surgical beam
49 Feudal lord
50 Question sometimes accompanied by an elbow jab
51 Christine of "Chicago Hope"
54 Shock, in a way
55 The U.N.'s Kofi ___ Annan
56 Forward-looking person?
57 Persia, nowadays
58 Requests, with "for"
60 File name ending in Word
61 Long time
62 Epitome of simplicity

by Tom McCoy

64 MEDIUM

Note: The four long Across answers are affected by a literal interpretation of the circled boxes.

ACROSS

1 Loads
6 What a pitcher is full of?
9 Atlas's disciples
14 Yale after whom Yale was named
15 "___ Kingdom Come" (2005 Coldplay song)
16 Patient of a 10-Down
17 Ace
19 Battlefield yell
20 Cousin of "um"
21 Like some barrels used for aging whiskey
23 KO
24 B.A. of the 39-Across
26 River mentioned in Yosemite Sam's self-introduction
28 Marvel Comics group
32 Circuits
35 Essence
36 Peat source
37 Leaves for dinner?
38 Cubs' home
39 Special Forces unit court-martialed for a crime they didn't commit
41 Padre's hermana
42 Scottish seaport known for its single-malt Scotch
44 Accrete
45 Elated
48 Principle of cosmic balance
49 The notorious Deepwater Horizon and others
53 What a mule may carry
55 Unstable subatomic particles
57 Lhasa ___
58 "West Side Story" woman
60 Milestone birthday
62 Martini's partner
63 What precedes the season?
64 Nostalgia evoker
65 Lead-in to hound, in the canine world
66 Wanting for nothing
67 Imperatives

DOWN

1 It's a sobering process
2 "Hi, Ho!"
3 Secretarial sort
4 Powerful offers?
5 Fashion designer Anna
6 Best man's opening
7 Surprise volleyball shot
8 Lies and lies some more?
9 "That's odd . . ."
10 Provider of contacts, informally
11 Reasonable charge
12 Having immense implications
13 Make out
18 Words ending in "o" in Esperanto
22 Snags
25 Small flap, maybe
27 Bulwark
29 Chemical ___
30 Sport
31 "I'm buying!"
32 Regarding
33 Ocean
34 Bar in Hollywood
38 Cabaret Voltaire iconoclasts
40 Cold war weapon?
43 Baby ___
44 Pop up
46 Father of Taoism
47 Level
50 Touch things?
51 "The Martian" garb
52 Results of chafing
53 Big name in corn syrup
54 Playing extra minutes, for short
56 Boo-boo
59 Word before China or India
61 Ford of fashion

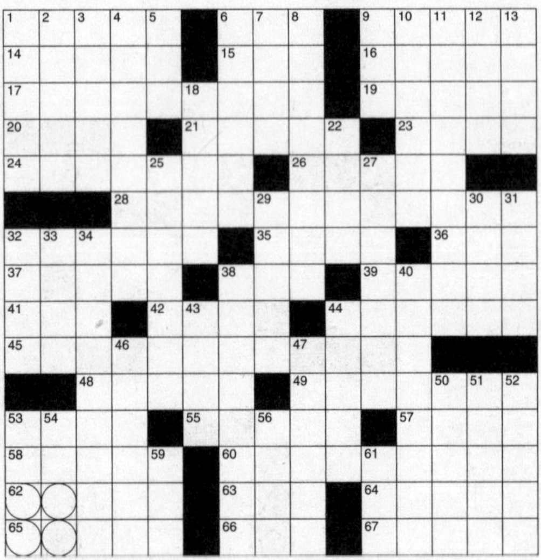

by Jeff Chen

MEDIUM 65

ACROSS

1 Many Latin ones end in -are
6 Some jazz sessions
10 Doorstep item
13 Right-leaning
15 The munchies, e.g.
16 Homage in verse
17 Tsunami, for one
20 Bone-chilling
21 Hobos' conveyances
22 Grinder input
27 Caucus locale
28 Mansard overhang
29 Regatta teams
31 Attack from a blind, say
33 Airer of Super Bowl 50
36 "This is ___" (TV slogan)
37 The first parts of 17- and 22-Across are always this, the first part of 46-Across is sometimes this, and the first part of 55-Across is never this
39 Back talk
40 ___-backwards
41 Doggy
42 Problem for a comb
44 Pronoun in letter greetings
45 Relative of contra-
46 Sound judgment
53 Hatch of Utah
54 Blow one's top
55 Hobbes, in "Calvin and Hobbes"
61 ___ Pérignon
62 Scrubbed, as a mission
63 Leno's late-night successor
64 '16 people in '16, e.g.
65 ___ Goose vodka
66 Broom-___ of the comics

DOWN

1 Car registration fig.
2 H, on a fraternity house
3 Mob hit victim, sometimes
4 Sunday shopping ban
5 "No ___, Bob!"
6 Herod's realm
7 "Exodus" hero ___ Ben Canaan
8 Classic British sports cars
9 Pirates, or their ships
10 Dominant theme
11 Singer with the 2015 album "25"
12 Hardly long-winded
14 Potato or pasta, informally
18 It's not true
19 Something behind a painting, maybe
22 Pagan belief
23 Most big band instruments
24 Jesse of the 1936 Olympics
25 Sound from a stable
26 Superhero accessory
30 Stealing, as gasoline
31 Leaf pore
32 Japanese PC maker
33 Trolley sound
34 Blessed event
35 The 7–10 is a nasty one
38 It comes before one
43 Spiral-shelled mollusks
44 Kristen of "Bridesmaids"
46 Bodybuilder's dirty secret, informally
47 Hard wear?
48 J.F.K.'s AirTrain and others
49 "Bad, bad" Brown of song
50 Have a go at
51 Fit of pique
52 Celeb parodied by Maya Rudolph on "S.N.L."
56 ___'easter
57 Dating site datum
58 90° bend
59 Oscar nomination, informally
60 "CSI" evidence

by John Guzzetta

66 Medium

ACROSS

1 Undergoes recession
5 Dining tip?
10 Works at the Guggenheim
14 Cut crops
15 Hooch
16 Have the answers
17 Malady?
20 1968 Heineken acquisition
21 Prairie predator
22 Tamale?
26 ___ II (Gillette razor)
28 Con opener?
29 Popular fragrance that's a girl's name
32 One way to run
33 Let in
35 Pain in the neck
37 Outfit for newborns
39 Adventure's end?
41 Brian who scored "The Lovely Bones"
42 Reddit Q&A session, briefly
43 Jimmy Eat World genre
44 Dragon's locale
45 Secret identity of Dick Grayson
47 Perfect Elements maker
49 James who can jam
51 Sports Illustrated's 2015 Sportsperson of the Year, to fans
54 "Wow!!"
56 Odyssey, e.g.
57 ___ Nostra
58 Dweller on the upper Mississippi
60 Hunger indicator
61 Oodles
62 Took a shot, say
63 Big pizza chain, informally
64 Part of the eye
65 Dulls, as pain
66 [You over there!]

DOWN

1 First name in home humor
2 Put on a happy face
3 Monkey ___
4 "You did WHAT?" reaction
5 Number of churchgoers?
6 Appeared (in)
7 Caught off base
8 Sgt., for example
9 Progressive competitor
10 "Alrighty then"
11 Keen on
12 Former senator Trent
13 ___'Pea
18 Fair-hiring watchdog, for short
19 Chuck who won four Super Bowl rings
23 Like quinoa growers
24 Sleep stage
25 Bangs and clangs
26 Fake bill tracer
27 Roman?
30 Legal?
31 Something to give a kitty?
32 Belgian red, e.g.
33 Sign on a convenience store window
34 Mindless but addictive app games, e.g.
36 Knowledge range
38 Gifting someone with a clock in China, e.g.
40 "Marriage Italian-Style" actress
46 They may have many stops
48 Cause to blunder
49 Like some subway stops
50 Really act out?
52 Thin iPods
53 Teen sensation?
55 Romanian wedding dance
56 Equestrian's handhold
59 Never-___ (unsuccessful sort)

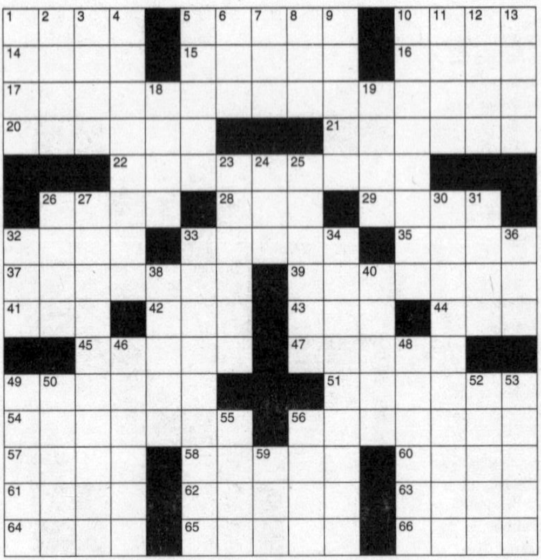

by Zhouqin Burnikel

ACROSS

1 Derby sound
6 Evidence of injury
10 Some football linemen
14 Golfer Palmer, to fans
15 ___ Romeo
16 HBO hit starring Julia Louis-Dreyfus
17 Cuddly-looking "bear"
18 One of 100 on a football field
19 Not home
20 Informant trapped after an icy storm?
23 Twisted Sister frontman Snider
24 "Who doesn't know that?!"
25 Ones with a lot of pull in the agricultural world?
26 Actress with an icy stare?
31 Repeated musical themes
34 Mary Lincoln's maiden name
35 Treasure on the Spanish Main
36 Chicago mayor Emanuel
37 "Weekend Update" co-anchor Michael
38 "Two for me. None for you" candy bar
39 Pronoun in several Beatles titles
40 Basilica part
42 Like a trampoline
44 Pitcher of ice?
47 "Would I ___!"
48 A, in Spanish
49 Grp. concerned with global warming
52 Next Republican nominee after Dwight D. Ice in Shower left office?
56 Garment usually with two buttons
57 Chutzpah
58 Part of a drum kit
59 Ticklish "Sesame Street" character
60 Sunny honeymoon site, maybe
61 Venerated ones
62 Offering in The New Yorker
63 Somewhat
64 Not neat

DOWN

1 Obvious, as ambition
2 Crumble over time
3 Dumbstruck
4 ___ monster
5 Generally known
6 Waves, say
7 Whole extended family
8 Old hairdo for Diana Ross
9 Something bleeped
10 Doesn't answer directly
11 Like a recent transplant
12 School overseer
13 Secret admirer?
21 Toggery
22 Gen. follower
26 "Huckleberry Finn" character
27 Neighbor of Lucy on "I Love Lucy"
28 One alternative of a sentry's challenge
29 ___ the Red
30 Common theater name
31 Richie's mom, to Fonzie
32 Locale of Kaneohe Bay
33 Who I am inside
37 Long-running CBS drama
38 Pull
40 One scoring on a serve
41 Realm of King Midas
42 Tie up
43 Just because
45 Where a Nintendo might be hooked up
46 Soothed
49 Group values
50 Sounds from a bell tower
51 Affected
52 Skinny tie
53 Museum dinosaur skeleton, say
54 Jar for stews
55 White House worker
56 Get-up-and-go

by Kyle Mahowald

68 MEDIUM

ACROSS

1 Long Island university
7 Agenda starter
13 Well-read folks
15 Cube source
16 "Me too"
17 Like some radiation
18 Rihanna's first #1 single
19 Windsurfing mecca
20 Suffix with class
21 Fair-hiring inits.
22 Carlo in the film business
23 Land of ancient Ephesus
25 England's last Catholic king
28 Sign of stress
32 Quarreling
33 Vague reason for a social turndown
37 Verb-to-noun suffix
38 Martial arts rank
39 "So THAT'S the trick here!"
40 Popular
41 At one time, once
43 Jack
45 It may start with "Starters"
46 Composer Rimsky-Korsakov
48 One might get you in
50 Don-turned-con
52 Storyteller's admission
53 Johns
56 "Star Trek: T.N.G." role
57 Whit
58 Charge
61 Food item that may be eaten on a dare
63 Per se
65 Modus ___
66 "Forget they said that"
67 Follower of the Bushido code
68 Lights

DOWN

1 "I wish it weren't so"
2 Rat Pack nickname
3 Airport data, for short
4 French article
5 Trailers, e.g.
6 Sampled the sauce
7 Flat population?
8 Iago's wife
9 ___ Kanata, "Star Wars: The Force Awakens" character
10 "The Grapes of Wrath" migrant
11 Rarest of the 50 state birds
12 So
14 Ballyhoo
15 First name in fashion
22 Stroke
24 Bitter ___
25 Will Smith's actor son
26 Space Invaders maker
27 Eastern European capital
29 Laid up, say
30 Sharing mail with, in a way
31 Transition
34 First name in horror
35 "Now I see!"
36 Halloween follower: Abbr.
42 Deck (out)
43 Devastating name in 2005 news
44 There are two Oscars for it
45 "___ Men"
47 Mandrake the Magician's sidekick
49 Pummel
51 Squealed
52 Past the baseline, in tennis
53 ". . . but ___ counting?"
54 Lola's club, in brief
55 Hold back
58 Stocking stuffers
59 "Night" memoirist Wiesel
60 New newts
62 Grand ___ (wine phrase)
64 Title of respect that's an anagram of another title of respect

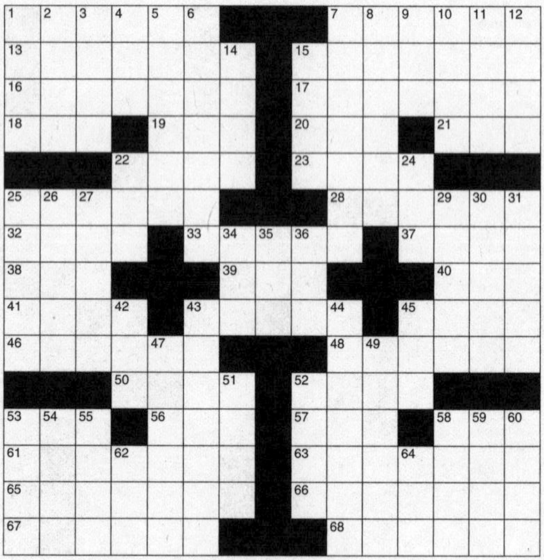

by Bruce Haight

MEDIUM 69

ACROSS

1 Lofty in thought or manner
5 Like the area between city and farm
10 Puts down by force
14 Apple originally marketed to schools
15 Blackmore's Doone
16 M.I.T. part: Abbr.
17 M.I.T. part: Abbr.
18 Make impure
19 City on the Arno
20 S.U.V. named for a lake
22 Football legend Amos Alonzo ___
24 Number of states that border the Mississippi
25 Composer of music "as ignorable as it is interesting"
26 D-Day vessels, for short
28 With all judges present
30 Greet, as the new year
32 Popular Bach piece for the lute
33 Twinings in London is one
36 Super Bowl highlights, to many
37 Goes underwater . . . or a hint to the answers on the perimeter of this puzzle
40 "Six-pack" muscles
42 Talent show judge, often
45 LP protectors
48 Bow respectfully
50 Fruitcake fruit
51 Eartha who sang "C'est Si Bon"
53 Mani-pedi spot
54 Mens ___ (criminal intent)
55 "Star Wars" droid, informally
57 Upper reaches of space
59 "You've Got a Friend ___"
61 Yoga posture
63 Diva ___ Te Kanawa
64 Wasabi ___ (bar snack)
65 Politico lampooned by Fey
66 Sign to heed
67 Underlying theme
68 Take away
69 Become less intense

DOWN

1 Renter from a renter
2 "This is no joke!"
3 Speed of sound
4 Guitar amp effect
5 Extreme: Abbr.
6 Comedians' shindig
7 Yanks' allies in W.W. I and II
8 Visitor to Siam, on stage and film
9 "Explorer" channel
10 Stock market fluctuation
11 Acrobat's wear
12 Dead Sea Scrolls sect
13 Meat of the matter
21 College benefactor Yale
23 Serengeti antelope
27 Hoity-toity sort
29 Rio's land, to natives
31 Thigh-slapper
32 Capital on the Aare
34 World Series game sextet
35 Triton's domain
38 Tale of adventure
39 Send over the moon
40 Property recipient, in law
41 Loser to VHS
43 Sushi bar option
44 Like the pointed end of a pencil
45 The "2" in the formula for water, e.g.
46 U.S. broadcaster overseas
47 Totally absorbed
49 U.S.S. Nautilus, for one
51 Eucalyptus-munching animal
52 Column style
56 Central figure in a Mussorgsky opera
58 Ring stoppages, for short
60 Guinness suffix
62 Formicide's target

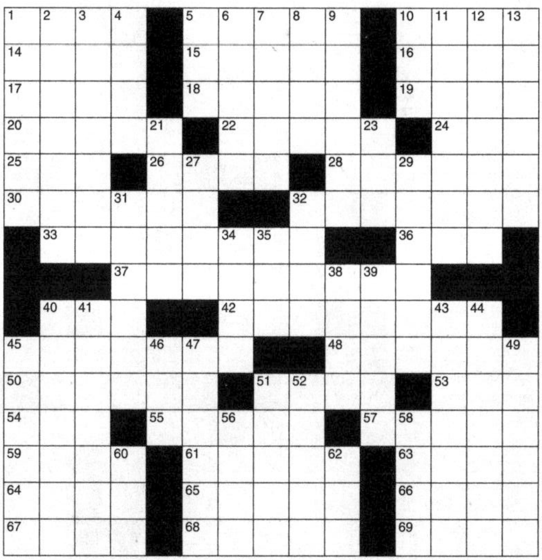

by Ruth Bloomfield Margolin

70 Medium

ACROSS

1 Squelch
7 Landlord on "Three's Company"
14 Jumped up and down, perhaps
15 Towering over
16 One of the rooms in Clue
17 Neighbor of Miss Gulch
18 South American monkey's handhold?
20 Mount that's a poker term when read backward
21 Urge
22 Give ___ whirl
23 Verizon FiOS, e.g., for short
24 [Insert your least favorite congressman here]?
31 Second-class person, informally?
32 "Quit your excuses"
33 "___ con Dios" (Spanish farewell)
35 Affectation
36 "Junk"
38 Veterinarian's branch of sci.
40 Bird watcher upon spotting the rare California condor?
43 Bobs and buns
44 ___ Fridays
45 Friend of Fidel
47 Types
49 Focal points of many F.A.A. investigations . . . or a description of 18-, 24- and 40-Across?
53 Figure in Matisse's "Le Bateau"
55 Soften
56 Boston specialty
57 Out of service?
58 Landlocked European
59 "America's diner is always open" sloganeer

DOWN

1 Spread out
2 Pennsylvania senator Pat
3 Cactus flower eaters
4 Epitome of cool, with "the"
5 Small construction company
6 ___ Prairie, Minn.
7 View from Hilo
8 Baseball Hall-of-Famer Sandberg
9 Word that can precede or follow pack
10 2015 award for "Hamilton"
11 Aristotle work that began literary theory
12 "Yeah, but still . . ."
13 Update, cartographer-style
15 Serve
19 A-lister
25 Shack
26 Style with illusory motion
27 "Silly goose!"
28 One of the Balearic Islands
29 Best-selling author of legal thrillers
30 "No worries"
34 J.F.K. conveyance
36 More burly
37 Render invalid
39 Stand taken by one making a speech
40 1958 hit with the lyric "Your love has given me wings"
41 Grunts
42 Watery, as eyes
43 Checkers, e.g.
46 They're given for Best Upset and Best Play
48 Sidewalk section, e.g.
49 Setting of a top 10 Barry Manilow hit
50 Be mindful of
51 ___-Altenburg (old German duchy)
52 "This ___ outrage!"
54 Ratio involving height and weight, for short

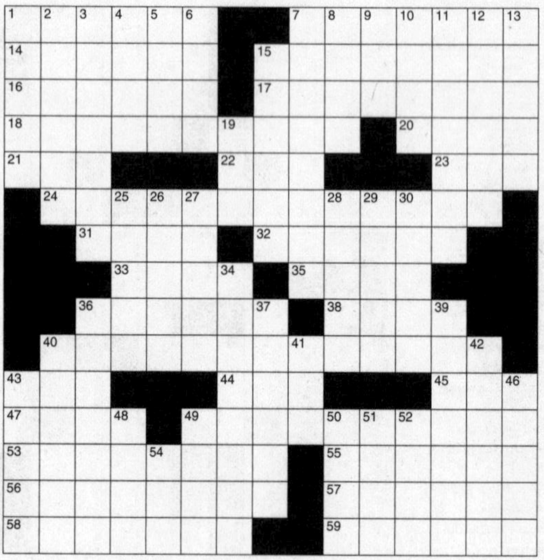

by Joel Fagliano

MEDIUM 71

ACROSS

1 "Beg pardon . . ."
5 Help in a heist
9 Looked slack-jawed
14 Like a neat bed
15 King noted for saying "How sharper than a serpent's tooth it is / To have a thankless child!"
16 Still in the running
17 "This won't hurt ___!"
18 Setting for the highest-grossing movie of 1939
19 George whose name is a lead-in to "film"
20 Politician in charge of pasta?
23 Early anesthetic
24 ___-Drive, popular light-powered watch
25 Dice tosses
29 Hang in there
34 Comfy shoe
37 Means of transportation in "Cinderella"
39 "Am I my brother's keeper?" brother
40 Pasta, apparently?
44 Circus horn honker
45 Cotton candy, mostly
46 Original "King Kong" studio
47 Corrida combatant
50 Some used cars, informally
52 Hole maker
54 Orchard Field, today
58 Card game with pasta for stakes?
64 Philip Morris brand
65 Word said with a handshake
66 Latvia's capital
67 In the same way
68 1996 Gwyneth Paltrow title role
69 H H H
70 Knight's mount
71 "Angels We Have Heard on High," e.g.
72 Mentally together

DOWN

1 Wow
2 Something to kick or break
3 British poet/critic Sitwell
4 Job at which one excels
5 Certain sax
6 Lover boy
7 Yield, as interest
8 Tiny amount
9 Tank unit
10 Reunion attendee, briefly
11 12-point type
12 Hunter who wrote "The Blackboard Jungle"
13 ___ Moines
21 Spring blooms
22 Cap material?
26 Sotheby's collection
27 There are three for motion
28 Search all over
30 Court figures, briefly
31 Foe of the taxi industry
32 Stink to high heaven
33 Muppet who speaks in a falsetto
34 Ending with second or upper
35 Dessert item that was clued as "Mountain: Comb. form" in old crosswords
36 White House policy chief
38 Donald Trump catchword
41 Bullring cheer
42 Cat's seat, maybe
43 Show exhaustion
48 Went on a tirade
49 Be in hock
51 Beach resort locales
53 Filled with cargo
55 Muscular Japanese dog
56 Daughter of 15-Across
57 Expunge
58 Clobber with snowballs, say
59 The Gem City, so-called because of its sparkling lake
60 Greek figure on many a trophy
61 Jules Verne captain
62 Broken, as a bronco
63 President Chaim Weizmann was on its first flight
64 Some postgrad degrees

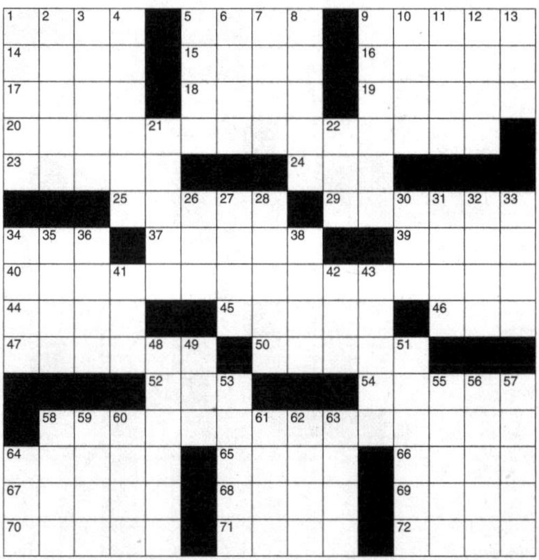

by Fred Piscop

72 MEDIUM

ACROSS

1 Police rounds
5 Anne, par exemple: Abbr.
8 Transfix
12 Hail
13 ___ jazz (fusion genre)
15 America's Cup, for one
16 Home to many stuffed animals
19 Son-in-law of Muhammad
20 Tar water, as seen in medieval medicine
21 Cargo unit
22 What the second letter of 17-Down stands for: Abbr.
24 Bark up the wrong tree
25 In times of yore
27 Port city on the Red Sea
29 Virtual city dweller
30 Porto-Novo is its capital
33 Having no legal force
34 They may be stretches
36 Ruler preceding the Year of the Four Emperors
37 Trunk attachment?
38 First first family of Alaska
39 Field of competition, for short?
40 Early Japanese P.M. Hirobumi ___
41 Certain geek
43 Japanese P.M. Shinzo ___
44 Petro-Canada unit
46 Mo
47 Pointer
49 Shade of blue
50 Challenges
51 Mill runoff
54 Got nothing back from?
56 Salade ___
59 Floating
63 "Seriously"
64 Nook, e.g.
65 Dressed neatly and fashionably
66 Gridiron scandal of 2015, informally

DOWN

1 ___ mater
2 Savage
3 One added to the staff?
4 Thomas Gray's "The Bard," e.g.
5 "50% off" and "Sorry, we're closed"
6 High-tech home gadget company
7 Having the same pitch but written differently, in a score
8 Fixed
9 Dichromatic fad of the 1950s
10 Aviation-related prefix
11 ___ Mawr
13 Ypsilanti sch. whose initials name a bird
14 Big U.S. import
17 Five-time Rose Bowl winner, for short
18 Hunk
23 Skillful
26 Kind of pool
27 Blacksmiths' needs
28 "Stop that!"
31 Sci-fi classic featuring Dr. Susan Calvin
32 "Haven't heard a thing"
34 Pastoral setting
35 Map abbr. before 1991
41 Film director from whose work the word "paparazzi" is derived
42 Library penalty
45 Let stand in water again
48 Sale item indicator
52 Explanatory words
53 Suffer some tire damage
54 Wonderstruck
55 One adept with a deck
56 Zero
57 Personally speaking, in a text
58 Top of an outfit?
60 Neighbor of Mont.
61 Bring in
62 M.A. hopeful's hurdle

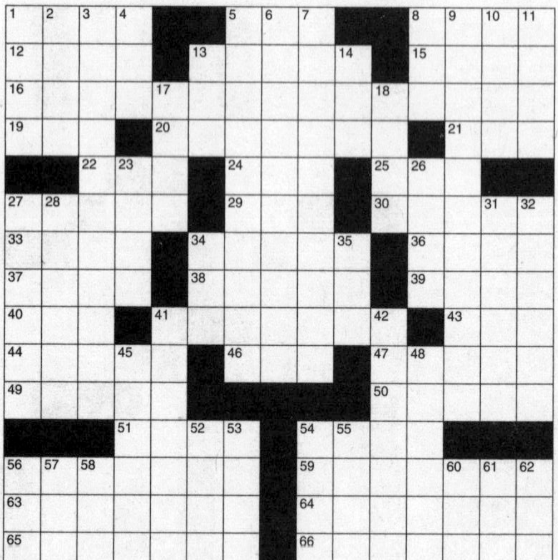

by Andrew Zhou

MEDIUM 73

ACROSS

1 Gift from 1-Down
5 See red?
8 Took a turn on "Wheel of Fortune"
12 "The Hares and the Frogs" writer
14 Death ___
15 Place where you need an ID to get mail?
16 Wildlife refuges
19 Robin Hood's target
20 Fatigue
21 Word that becomes its own synonym when its first letter is moved to the end
22 Curvaceous
24 Pulls a certain prank on, informally
25 Translucent sea creature that drifts with the current
27 Partner of Simon and Theodore, in cartoons
30 "Dulce et Decorum ___" (Wilfred Owen poem)
31 Jeweler's tool
35 Go on either side of
37 Kind of turn
39 Latin dance in 3/4 time
40 Colorado county or its seat
41 Capable, jocularly
42 R&B/soul ballad
46 No-goodnik
47 Author Silverstein
49 Crashed ignominiously
50 Beer purchase
51 "Thinking is the hardest work there is, which is probably the reason why ___ engage in it": Henry Ford
53 Miller who directed "Deadpool"
54 Readers of the Daily Mirror or the Sun, mainly
55 #1 hit of 1975 and 2001
58 Prohibition of strip mining, e.g.
59 More angry
60 Roman who originated the phrase "What fools these mortals be"
61 Firmly plants

DOWN

1 Noted gift giver
2 Longtime Vermont senator
3 Woman's name that sounds like two French letters
4 Gloomy
5 Like Jane Eyre or Harry Potter
6 What polemology is the study of
7 Some canines
8 Put out
9 Abrupt realignment of policy priorities
10 Deplete
11 Egg containers
13 Cons
15 Fourth element on the periodic table
17 Not an original thought
18 Place to set a candle, maybe
23 Something to go out in?
25 Karaoke need
26 Days long past
27 Mother figure
28 Legislative oversights
29 Complete reversal
32 Took to task
33 Ornamental columns
34 Online provider of study guides
36 The Big Easy
38 Give ___ on the back
43 Ontario/Quebec border river
44 Small dam
45 Six-time Nascar champion Johnson
48 Gave the wrong idea, say
50 Shipping unit
52 Noah of "Falling Skies"
54 Talk, talk, talk
56 Bub
57 Auxiliary group

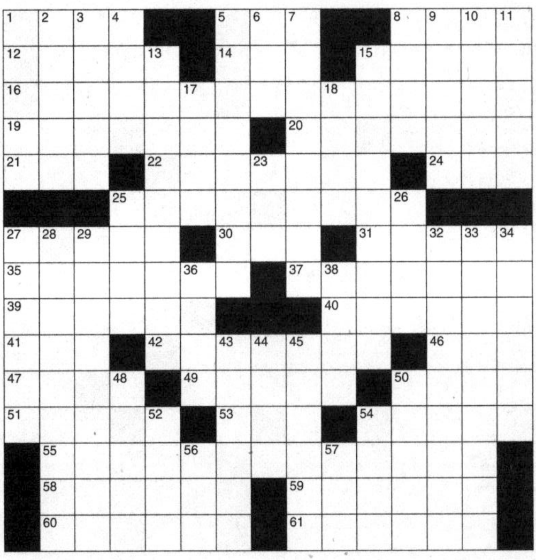

by John Guzzetta

74 MEDIUM

ACROSS

1 Not much
5 French writer who co-founded the newspaper Combat
10 Adriatic port
14 Pronoun in "America the Beautiful"
15 It covers the globe
16 Had too much ecstasy, for short?
17 Former C.I.A. director Panetta
18 Donizetti's lady of Lammermoor
19 Rolls for dogs
20 Old jalopy
22 Spanish uncle
24 Pasture
25 Mounts
26 Proficient, computerwise
28 Pro vote
29 Jai ___
31 Overplays one's role
32 In: Fr.
34 Former British P.M. Douglas-Home
36 Old Olds
37 Subject of medical research since the 1980s
40 Big cat in Narnia
43 It's inclined to provide entertainment for kids
44 It holds 5,148 potential flushes
48 "Will it play in ___?"
50 Exchange at the altar
52 Hawaiian bowlful
53 Gunning
55 Attack
57 Former communications corp.
58 Where Dodge City is: Abbr.
59 Mufti
60 Answer to the old riddle "What's round on the ends and high in the middle?"
62 "Taking you places" network
64 1999 Ron Howard satire
66 Foxx of "Sanford and Son"
67 Emphatic follower of yes or no
68 Evolved
69 ___ fixe
70 "O.K., you caught me"
71 "Antenna"

DOWN

1 N.B.A. div.
2 John Donne poem with a line starting "It suck'd me first . . ."
3 Wind-blown
4 Blue material
5 One side of a diner?
6 Shade of bleu
7 Soft shoe, for short
8 Marxist exhortation to "workers of the world"
9 Polar bear habitat
10 Head motion
11 Put on a pedestal
12 Longtime subscriber, maybe
13 "Sounds right"
21 Ring master's org.
23 "Jeez!"
25 Dancer Charisse
26 Item often kept with cuff links
27 Did a cobbler's job on
30 "Ah, well"
33 Lewis who voiced Lamb Chop
35 Sent a dupe email to
38 How contracts are signed
39 Put on a pedestal
40 Based on deduction rather than experience
41 Smoldered with rage
42 When a sandbar may appear above the waterline
45 F.D.A.-banned weight-loss supplement
46 The drink's on me
47 Young fox
49 Andre who wrote "Open: An Autobiography"
51 Perform some millwork
54 Up to
56 Wait-'em-out strategy
59 Saskatchewan native
61 Shelley's "To a Skylark," for one
63 Jackie O's man
65 Bugs, e.g. . . . or a hint to this puzzle's theme

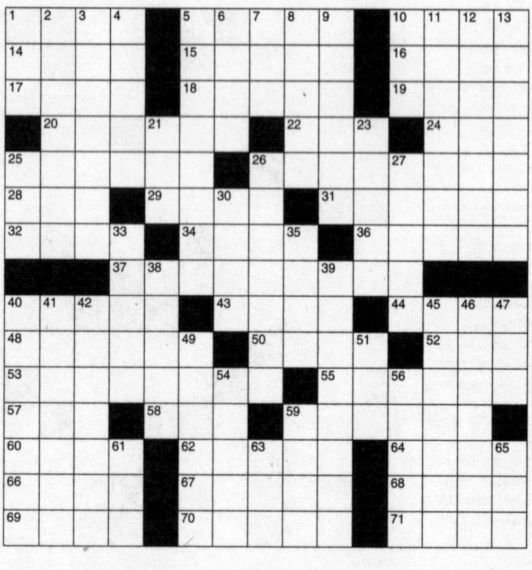

by Ed Sessa

ACROSS
1 Upstate New York city where Mark Twain was buried
7 Laughing matter
11 Fraternity letter
14 Tap
15 Skating feat
16 Chicago's ___ Center
17 Serving with liver
19 One-third of tres
20 Fish said to be named for a Mediterranean island
21 Pan coating
23 Kind of blockade
26 Hockey speedster Bobby
27 Food in a tongue-twister
33 Buds
34 Martini's partner in winemaking
35 Tennessee athlete, informally
36 More hideous
39 Actress Bassett of "Olympus Has Fallen"
41 Bird's beak
42 Cancels
46 Paris's ___ Airport
47 Chili ingredient
51 The Jazz, on scoreboards
52 SeaWorld whale
53 Wild side of a split personality
56 Be made up (of)
61 With 48-Down, kind of street
62 Preparer of 17-, 27- and 47-Across?
65 For each
66 Gillette brand
67 "Get outta here!"
68 Before, old-style
69 Online site for business reviews
70 Where sacrifices may be made

DOWN
1 Bad grades
2 ___ Croft, "Tomb Raider" role
3 News anchor David
4 Bumped off
5 Business losses, informally
6 Hard-to-hum, in a way
7 ___ alai
8 Brand of kitchenware
9 ___ State
10 "Who ___?"
11 Title hero of a Longfellow poem
12 Dean's lists, e.g.
13 Close ___ (approach)
18 "Not in a million years!"
22 Sharp dresser
24 Ruckus
25 Hi-fi supply
27 Book you can't put down
28 1970 #1 Jackson 5 song
29 TV's "___: Cyber"
30 That, in Spanish
31 Bowler's target
32 Leave in stitches
33 Some crossword clues
37 Thanksgiving ___
38 Reel holder
40 Icky stuff
43 Word often wrongly apostrophized
44 Cry made with a head slap
45 Big kiss
48 See 61-Across
49 Certain protozoan
50 Subway, basically
53 Sulk
54 Critical time
55 Art Deco illustrator
57 "Get outta here!"
58 Tiny bit
59 "Bon" time in France
60 Speeders' comeuppances: Abbr.
63 Dot-com's address
64 Take a time out?

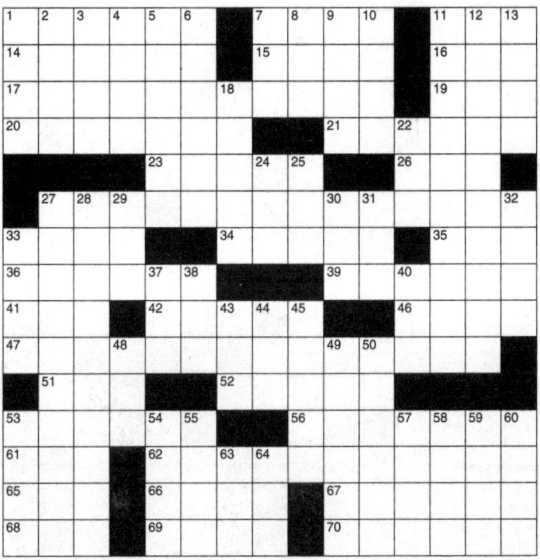

by David J. Kahn

76 MEDIUM

ACROSS

1 Sauce for linguine
6 Performances that may evoke bravas
11 Drift off
14 Better
15 Home invasion, in police shorthand
16 Ending for all Facebook logins until late '05
17 Like many disasters, in hindsight
18 Without consideration
20 Devilish sorts?
22 Winter hrs. in Winter Park
23 "How awful!"
24 Tip of a golf club
25 Snack bar
29 Eye
31 Vin classification
32 Hulking beast
33 Live ESPN broadcast every June
36 Go away in the country?
37 Sans-serif typeface
40 Part of a gym routine
41 Many mirages
43 Minus
44 1996 Madonna starring role
47 Birds with deep drumming calls
49 Qty.
50 Figure skater Baiul
54 Southern California's ___ Freeway
56 Give a whuppin'
57 1990s fad game piece
58 China's Three Gorges ___
59 Unforeseen development . . . or a feature seen four times in this puzzle's answers?
62 "That's too bad"
65 Venom, e.g.
66 100+, say
67 Some repurposed cornfields
68 Standing
69 Have a bill, say
70 All thumbs
71 Certain encls.

DOWN

1 Suddenly appears
2 Get mad
3 Get mad
4 Constituent part of Russia bordering Mongolia
5 Restaurant availability
6 Heckling, e.g.
7 Tirade
8 Up the creek
9 Put on
10 Hearst monthly
11 Some caches
12 Allen Ginsberg's "Plutonian ___"
13 The occasional firework
19 :
21 Bit
26 "___ Wiedersehen"
27 City on a lake of the same name
28 Barclays Center squad
30 Essential macromolecule
31 Went furtively
34 Act out
35 Didn't rely solely on memory
37 Repeated title role for Jim Carrey
38 1960 Olympics host
39 Flood
42 Q&A part: Abbr.
45 Like "tabu" or "iglu": Abbr.
46 Horse color
48 "Right away"
51 Tops
52 Green person
53 F.B.I. employees
55 Savory quality
56 Plot point in many a soap opera
60 U.S. college whose campus is less than 1,000 ft. from Ciudad Juárez
61 Meeting places
62 Question that's an anagram of 63-Down
63 Question that's an anagram of 62-Down
64 Review poorly

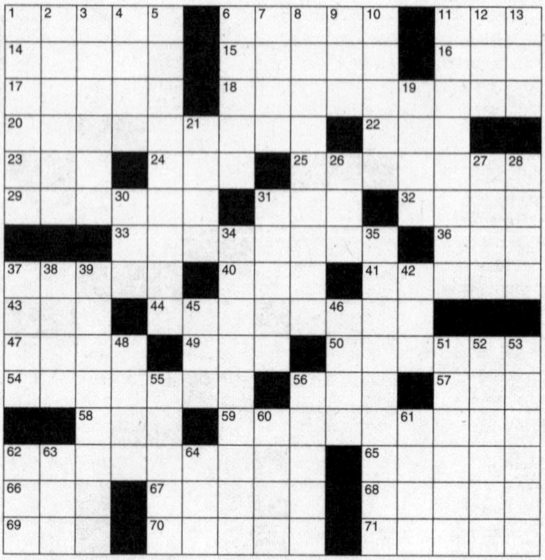

by David Woolf

ACROSS

1 Fritter away
6 Strongman player on "The A-Team"
9 Spanish ___
13 It preceded "Eleven," "Twelve" and "Thirteen" on the big screen
15 Slip in a pot
16 It becomes its own synonym when "cap" is added in front
17 *Speedy shipping option
19 Hollywood's Ken or Lena
20 Have confidence in
21 International airport near Tokyo
23 *Romantic comedy featuring two members of the Brat Pack
26 A person's soul mate
27 Pink-slip
28 Odin sacrificed one for wisdom
29 Percentages and such
30 Like much car chase footage
33 *Going back to square one
39 Hand-played drum
40 Presley's "___ Las Vegas"
41 HBO rival
44 Uncover, poetically
45 Bishop and knight
47 *Recurring soap opera plot device
51 "Hold on, I just might have a good solution . . ."
52 "Care to explain?"
53 Desktop pic
54 Minuet meter . . . or a description of the answers to the starred clues?
59 Converse
60 "___ Mutual Friend"
61 Heavy hitter
62 Life span of a star
63 One end of a rainbow
64 Something to take a nip from

DOWN

1 Came out on top
2 Bridge four-pointer
3 Congress
4 Decorative ink
5 Evasive maneuver
6 Sporty Mazda
7 French king
8 Beat a hasty retreat
9 Native Kiwis
10 Necessitate
11 Like the toves in "Jabberwocky"
12 Half of Congress
14 Brown, in a way
18 Fashion inits.
22 Historical record
23 At the drop of ___
24 Testing stage
25 "Make like a tree and leave!"
26 Gridiron successes, for short
30 Chips in a pot
31 I
32 Where couples may register under assumed names
34 Obnoxious sorts
35 Charlatan, of a sort
36 Smoking cigars, e.g.
37 It becomes its own synonym when "for" is added in front
38 Dorm V.I.P.s
41 Gated water channel
42 Bigwig
43 Checked out
45 Parts of ratchets
46 Reflexive pronoun
48 Ladies' counterparts
49 Position for Cal Ripken Jr.
50 Snappy dresser
55 Young competitor in "The Hunger Games"
56 Mrs. McKinley
57 Booker T.'s backup
58 "Oh, no!"

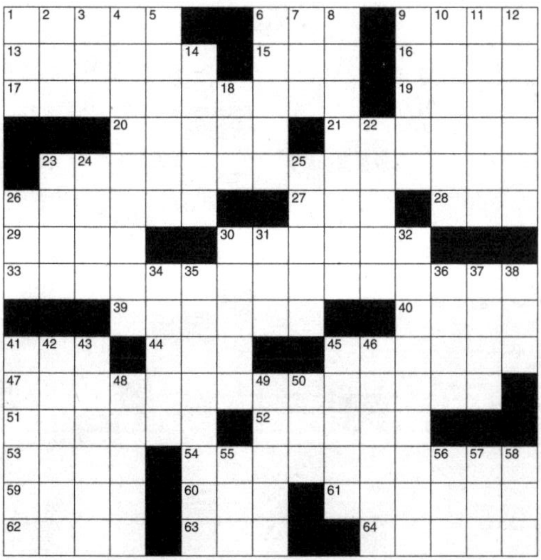

by Alex Boisvert and Jeff Chen

78 MEDIUM

ACROSS

1 Film character who says menacingly "I think you know what the problem is just as well as I do"
4 Abbr. in the Guinness logo
8 Medium size in a lingerie shop
12 Mom's all-American partner
14 Lingerie material
16 Flaw in an argument
18 The Olympic Australis is the largest one in the world
19 Modern form of customer support
20 Stir
23 Leader of four U.S. states
24 –
32 "I don't know the question, but ___ is definitely the answer": Woody Allen
33 Nada
34 "The Washington Post March" figure
35 The Washington Post April figure
36 Button on a DVD player
39 Way up a mountain
40 Shade akin to sand
42 Wing it, in a way
44 Cabinet dept.
45 Relaxing baths
47 Rafter's aid
48 Born
49 –
53 "Here ___!"
54 Tank top relative
55 Least refined
60 Italian bubbly
64 Reach a conclusion by assuming one's conclusion is true
67 Singer Green
68 Thawed out
69 Tiny bit
70 Gets down
71 Ones having issues at work, for short?

DOWN

1 Los Angeles Angels' cap feature
2 Per
3 Sports org. with the Vare Trophy
4 Old Common Market abbr.
5 Luxury hotel perk
6 Do ground-breaking work
7 Give meaning to
8 Author who wrote "Some day you will be old enough to start reading fairy tales again"
9 Course that tests one's limits, informally
10 Pac-12 school
11 12-point
13 Candle scent
15 WSJ competitor
17 "Voulez-vous coucher ___ moi?" (lyric of a 1975 #1 hit)
21 Flabbergast
22 Kind of board
24 –
25 High light?
26 Ones making a big scene?
27 Tore
28 Blarney
29 Castro, por ejemplo
30 Phraseologists' concerns
31 –
37 Stopping point
38 Indians and Red Sox All-Star pitcher Luis
41 Hawaiian instrument, briefly
43 Cracker topper
46 Place to get a wax job?
50 Pulitzer winner James
51 Source of five daily calls
52 "Sweet!," old-style
55 Network where Alex Trebek began his TV career
56 Saxophone, e.g.
57 New ___
58 Town almost destroyed in the D-Day invasion
59 Ahi, but not mahi-mahi
61 Label info
62 Pointy-___
63 Stopping points
65 Young amphibian
66 Grp. known for sliding in the spring

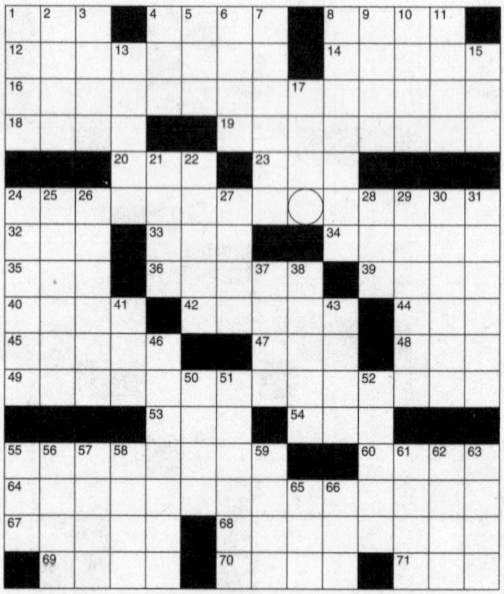

by David Liben-Nowell and Tom Pepper

MEDIUM 79

ACROSS
1 So last year
6 Got one's serve past
10 One of the A's in A.M.A.: Abbr.
14 Flopper in basketball, e.g.
15 Buyer's protection
17 Some lab work
19 Home of Spaceship Earth
20 Rather, informally
21 "Hamlet" soliloquy starter
23 Source of income
27 Fab Four surname
29 Whacked, so to speak
30 Vein find
31 Filch
33 Musician's booking
34 Environmentalist's concern . . . or a hint to the circled letters
40 Front end?
41 Part of an insect's body that holds the legs
43 ___ Z (the works)
46 Way up or down
48 Crop up
49 Like some ad campaigns
52 "Calvin and Hobbes" conveyance
53 Emmy classification
54 "W" is one in Welsh
56 School branch
62 Approximately
63 Starts on baby food, say
64 ___ a one (zero)
65 Moonshine holders
66 Sharpshooter Oakley

DOWN
1 U.S.M.C. one-striper
2 What a doctor may have you say
3 Arcade game played on an incline
4 Motto for a 1-Down, informally
5 ___ the Red
6 Shooting marbles
7 ___-de-sac
8 Have one's fill
9 Rap's Dr. ___
10 Bit of funny business
11 Pie-eyed
12 Return addressee
13 Prove false
16 Invite for coffee, say
18 .net alternative
21 Kitchen meas.
22 Ear-related
24 Largest country in Africa
25 Of the flock
26 Like skinny jeans
28 Dream state
32 "Nick of Time" singer Bonnie
35 Reds or Blues
36 "Got it!"
37 5-Down and cohorts
38 Cast-iron cooker
39 Maneuver with care
42 Marked, as a ballot
43 Builds a new room, say
44 Capital of Albania
45 "Friends, Romans, countrymen . . ." sort of speaker
46 Teatro alla ___
47 Fixes firmly
50 Mani-pedi tool
51 Position: Abbr.
55 Trumpet or guitar effect
57 War on Poverty prez
58 Note in a pot
59 Yank's cousin
60 College, in Down Under slang
61 Minn.-to-Ala. direction

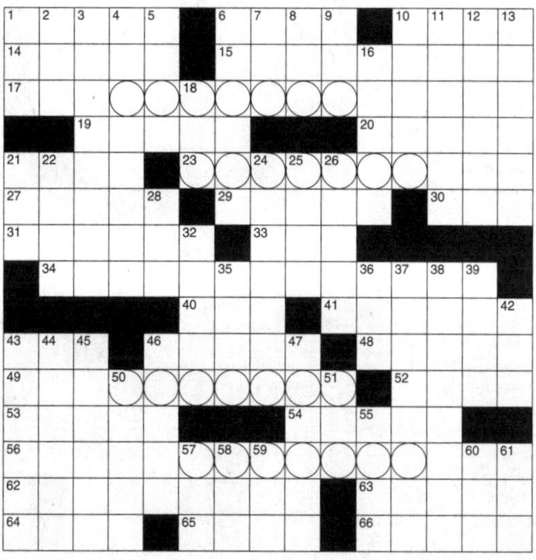

by Andrew Reynolds

80 MEDIUM

ACROSS

1 Elected
6 Big online source for film info
10 "Gotcha, dude"
14 Pep
15 ___ Valley (Utah ski resort)
16 Fallon predecessor
17 Double solitaire?
19 ___ buco
20 Entry points
21 Double space?
23 Light touch
24 "And what ___ rare as a day in June?": Lowell
25 Volkswagen model
26 Surrounded by
28 Leave early, say
30 Give the stink eye
31 Jet for a jet-setter
33 Double take?
38 Mass distribution?
39 Supermodel who married David Bowie
41 War zone, e.g.
44 Benefit
46 Supreme Court justice nominated by Bush
47 Stick with it
49 Zika virus tracker, for short
50 Double life?
53 Noah's escape
54 "Do I ___!"
55 Double back?
57 One of its sources is Lake Tana
58 Champagne name
59 1890s vice president Stevenson
60 "Who ___?"
61 "Who ___?"
62 Self-congratulatory words

DOWN

1 Like London's City Hall
2 Robert Galbraith and J. K. Rowling
3 "Excellent, mon ami"
4 "Die Meistersinger von Nürnberg" heroine
5 Comics troublemaker
6 No-nos in Leviticus 26:1
7 Bay Area's ___ College
8 Crème-crème filler
9 Welsh word that starts a noted college name
10 Cole Porter tune sung by Frank Sinatra and Maurice Chevalier
11 Spaniard granted the right to conquer Florida by Charles V
12 As found
13 Proficient with
18 Attic buildup
22 Activity for some wedding hires
27 Make a scene, say
28 Govt. IDs
29 It might be taken before a trip
31 Jazzman Baker
32 What an otoscope examines
34 Lightly touch, as a shoulder
35 Co. money manager
36 How conflicts are best resolved
37 Nightmare
40 Bit of Blues Brothers attire
41 Asylums
42 Pig featured in a series of children's books
43 On-schedule
44 Knowing all about
45 Like some parking garage rates
47 Current events?
48 5.5-point type
51 One appointed to the Royal Victorian Order
52 Ancestor of a cello
56 Oklahoma city

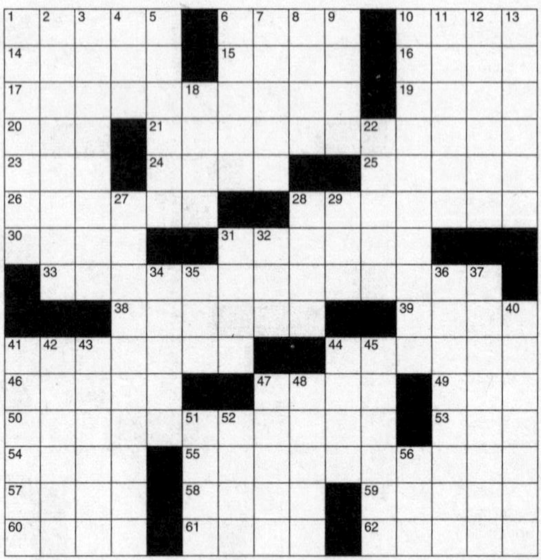

by Ellen Leuschner and Jeff Chen

ACROSS

1 "Sonar"-equipped fliers
5 "Absolutely!"
10 Thrust
14 Latvian capital
15 Creamer of the L.P.G.A.
16 Dinner in a bowl
17 What is "It"?
20 Piece of low-end jewelry?
21 Pugilistic victory, briefly
22 Compete
23 Falcon's home: Abbr.
24 Sitcom whose four main characters are convicted of a crime in the final episode
26 Old TV title role for Raymond Burr
30 Spring's counterpart, tidewise
31 With 43-Across, "What is it?"
33 Proscriptions
36 Photo badges, e.g.
37 Quintets
40 Whom les Trois Mousquetaires served
41 Acquires
43 See 31-Across
45 Grub
48 Like pumpkins during the fall
49 Conical topper
52 ___ Lanka
53 Rainbow, for one
54 Little nipper
55 Timon of "The Lion King," e.g.
59 What is it?
62 Biblical twin described as a "cunning hunter"
63 Pay for
64 Shade darker than eggshell
65 Item of loungewear
66 Classical promenades
67 "How's ___?"

DOWN

1 Outduel, e.g.
2 Ford or Lincoln
3 Part of a canopy
4 One who may finish on a high note
5 Metaphor for easy access
6 Be suspended
7 Guffaw
8 Top-tier
9 Hit home
10 Yenta's "gift"
11 Song lyric before "in the winter when it drizzles" and "in the summer when it sizzles"
12 Take a turn for the worse?
13 Took a hit, in a way
18 Asks for money
19 Extinct
24 Carry out a duty with diligence
25 Groovy
26 "Right on," to a hipster
27 Harassed persistently
28 Chesapeake Bay delicacy
29 Men's studies?
32 Cry after "hot"
34 Taboo
35 Omen
38 Decadent ones are often very rich
39 Binaural
42 Sr.'s challenge
44 Cafeteria headwear
46 Thsi clue has one
47 Redirects, as a train
49 Post or Daily News
50 Juvenile comeback
51 Split up
55 Grp. assigning film ratings
56 ___ brothers, big political donors
57 Indefinable presence
58 Letter-shaped fastener
60 Haul into court
61 "The Revenant" star, to fans

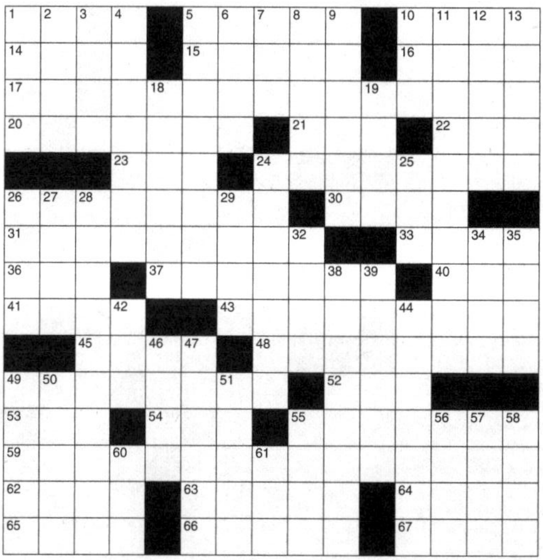

by Timothy Polin

82 MEDIUM

ACROSS

1 Onetime debater with Joe Biden
9 Response to a verbal slam
15 Diner breakfast specification
16 Golden galloper
17 Tests of crews' control?
18 Some tennis strokes
19 You might leave them in stitches, for short
20 [snort]
22 Actress Graff
23 Wings: Lat.
25 Odor-Eaters, e.g.
27 With 48-Across, memorable Al Pacino movie line . . . or a hint for this puzzle's theme
31 Refrain from farming?
32 Role in "Doubt" or "Dead Man Walking"
33 Drench
36 Becomes wearisome
37 Tracks with malware, say
41 Ambitious climbers' mecca
43 "The Racer's Edge" product
45 Ivanovic of women's tennis
46 One making introductions
48 See 27-Across
52 1909 Matisse masterpiece
55 Captain's logs?
56 Follows
57 Secular
59 Alma mater of 30-Down, for short
62 Kanye West's "Yeezus," for one
64 Oktoberfest venue
67 Author ___ Leonard
68 Coal-mining center
69 Knocked out, as an audience
70 2014 Record of the Year winner for "Stay With Me"

DOWN

1 Peeved
2 Not equivocate about
3 Rules, briefly
4 The Altar constellation
5 Boiling, with "up"
6 Spacious and splendid
7 "The Adventures of ___" (Ogden Nash poem)
8 Big Board inits.
9 Some Australian exports
10 Big-picture approach to patient care
11 Many emojis
12 In better condition
13 Concerning
14 Things made in a photo booth
21 Roman emperor who completed the Colosseum
23 Sushi bar offering
24 They may be conceived around Halloween
26 Texting while driving, e.g.
27 Calyx part
28 Suffers
29 Not long ago at all: Abbr.
30 2000 N.B.A. M.V.P. with the Lakers
34 "Back in my day . . ."
35 Hammer extremity
38 Brady bunch, in headlines
39 Bond yield?
40 Big name in foam-based weaponry
42 Evidenced fear, in a way
44 Dallying sort
47 Sch. along the Charles
49 Arrange coverage for
50 Quaker State city subject to lake-effect snow, for short
51 Gesture indicating "How stupid of me!"
52 Like the graphics on an Atari 2600, in brief
53 Level near the bottom of the minors, informally
54 "Scarface" director
58 "___ le roi!" (French Revolution cry)
59 With 61-Down, city named for a Book of Mormon prophet
60 Bad mood
61 See 59-Down
63 Subject of a scrip
65 Dorm V.I.P.s
66 Film buff's channel

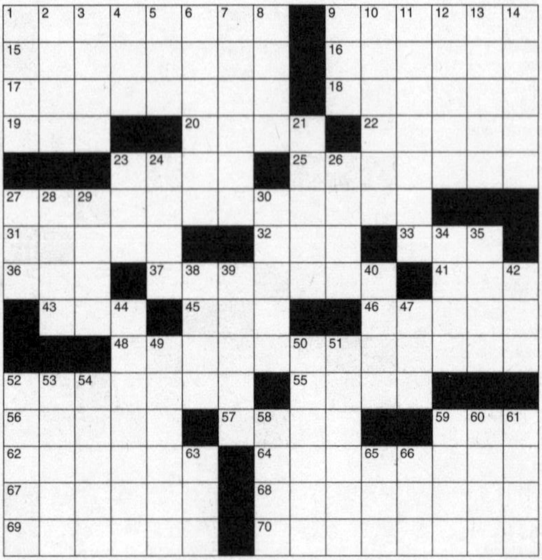

by John Lieb

MEDIUM 83

ACROSS

1 "Oh, yeah . . . ," in a text
4 Prefix with musicology
9 Dogie-bagging rope
14 "Of course!"
15 "Of course!"
16 Sleep clinic concern
17 Oil dispenser on a Food Network show?
20 Egypt's Mubarak
21 Brake plate
22 Ones put on the rack?
23 Lively movement
26 Hasbro board game in which armies conquer territories
28 Genre for "Dueling Banjos"?
33 Vicious, as a fight
36 Modernists, informally
37 Slightly pickled
38 Highlands refusal
39 Armani with a plaque on the Rodeo Drive Walk of Style
41 Vs.
42 Hit the bricks
44 Actress Drescher
45 Cousin of -trix
46 Weasellike animal kept as a fashion accessory?
49 Dope
50 How black holes are packed
54 Massachusetts' Cape ___
56 Fleecy boots
59 Place for a bald-headed baby?
60 Equipment endorsed by Inside Tennis?
64 What someone who is overly verklempt might do
65 Big player on draft day
66 Certain special FX
67 Hairy-chested, say
68 They may be waved at concerts
69 Your, in Paris

DOWN

1 Ancient Roman meeting places
2 Former Fox series set in California
3 Actress Kate of "Grey's Anatomy"
4 Green person, for short
5 "___-Pan" (James Clavell novel that preceded "Shogun")
6 Brooklyn ___, N.Y.
7 CBS military drama
8 "Call on me! I know this!"
9 Give an earful
10 Loan letters
11 Caught unawares
12 Sow
13 Proverbial "wild" things that are sown
18 Other side
19 Seaweed at a sushi bar
24 Pueblo people of New Mexico
25 Something not repeated
27 '80s missile shield plan
29 Former Yankee manager who also served as player-manager of the Mets
30 One of the nine worlds of Norse mythology
31 World Series of Poker channel
32 Class
33 Silver State sch.
34 Mother of Cronus and Rhea
35 Pressuring
39 Comic strip featuring Satchel Pooch and Bucky Katt
40 About
43 Car registration fig.
45 Bibliographical abbr.
47 Eastern mystic
48 Puts into effect
51 Burp
52 Feudal lord
53 Himalayan cryptids
54 Around-the-clock, in a way
55 "The Lion King" lion
57 Nibble (on)
58 Its mascot is Sonic the Hedgehog
61 N.L. East city, on scoreboards
62 Knights of ___, villainous group in "The Force Awakens"
63 "What next?"

1	2	3	■	4	5	6	7	8	■	9	10	11	12	13
14			■	15					■	16				
17			18						19					
20					■	■	21				■	22		
23					24	25	■	■	26		27		■	■
■	■	■	28				29	30					31	32
33	34	35		■	36				■	37				
38			■	39					40		■	41		
42			43		■	44				■	45			
46					47					48		■	■	■
■	■	49				■	■	50				51	52	53
54	55		■	56		57	58	■	■	59				
60			61					62	63					
64					■	65					■	66		
67					■	68					■	69		

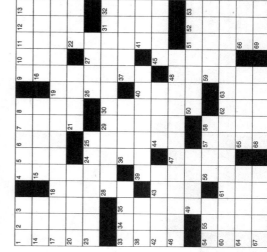

by Tony Orbach

84 MEDIUM

ACROSS

1 Tablecloth material
5 Some spoonfuls
10 Mull (over)
14 "My turn"
15 Space ___
16 Naturalization requirement
17 Mathematician John portrayed in "A Beautiful Mind"
18 Part of a classical education
19 One-named singer born Christa Päffgen
20 Ziegfeld Follies costumer
21 Fowl territory?
23 Societal instability resulting from a breakdown in values
25 He gave Odysseus a bag of winds
28 Like traditional media, to some
29 Original airer of "The Office"
32 Sound from a haunted house
33 CVS rival
36 Cannes condiment
37 Summer amusements . . . or a literal description of three answers in this puzzle
40 Employer whose workers don't discuss their jobs much, in short
42 Top choice in December?
43 Nighttime irregularity
46 ___ Clare, ward in Dickens's "Bleak House"
47 Take the wrong way?
51 Free-for-all
53 Small fry
54 Home of the Big House in college football
58 Piddling
59 Atmosphere
61 Spacious
62 App purchaser
63 Noodle concoction?
64 Home for American alligators
65 Stocking material
66 Abbr. found on some corporate logos
67 Gesture made with the thumb and nose
68 Decryption needs

DOWN

1 Hereditary
2 Site where cuneiform tablets were discovered
3 Made-to-order
4 Transient things
5 Sweet, in Sorrento
6 Hawaiian seafood
7 Radio listener grp.
8 ___ Blair, George Orwell's real name
9 Decaf choice
10 Sarah ___, protagonist of "The Terminator"
11 It usually reveals more than you want
12 Sentence shortener
13 Question suggesting "Never heard of 'em"
22 Brain test, briefly
24 "Oh, really?"
26 OPEC member: Abbr.
27 High-profile gig for a musician, for short
29 He actually said "I really didn't say everything I said"
30 Headquartered
31 Lashes
34 "TRUS___" (2016 political slogan)
35 Checked off the bucket list, say
37 "Care to make it interesting?"
38 "Entourage" actress Mazar
39 SpaceX C.E.O.
40 Stinker
41 Angel's payoff, for short
44 Santa's reindeer, counting Rudolph
45 Rand popular with the Tea Party
48 Newborn attire
49 In a bad way
50 Moves behind?
52 Put-downs
53 Iconic green poison symbol
55 Equine color
56 Laddie
57 Melville's second novel
59 Battle
60 Subjects of some voting laws

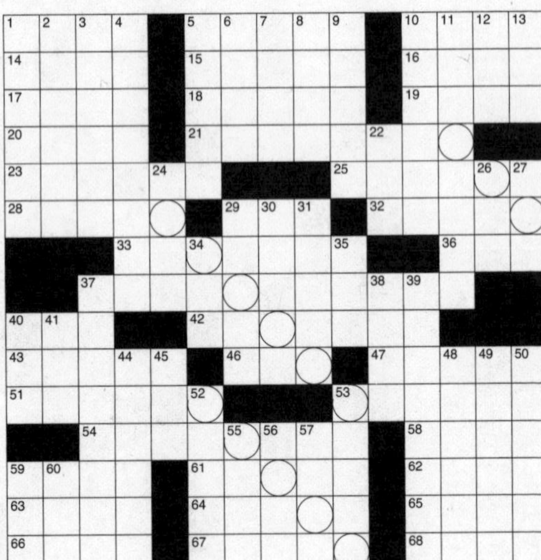

by Jason Flinn

ACROSS

1 Uncommon bills
5 Texas city where Dr Pepper was created
9 Wraiths
15 Reducing wind resistance
16 Hairstyle maintained with a pick
17 Receptacle in a machine
18 Baseball scoring play
20 Rara avis
21 Understand
22 Munched (on)
24 "Layla" musician Clapton
25 Site of an iconic war photo
27 Hockey scoring play
29 Ephron who wrote "When Harry Met Sally"
30 Moment to come, briefly
32 French pronoun
33 Onager, for one
34 Catch the light
36 Makes red in the face
39 Proposal of Woodrow Wilson . . . or what the scoring values of 18-, 27-, 55- and 66-Across total
44 Spotted attending
45 Santa-tracking org.
47 Multi-episode story line
50 Canal zone?
51 Grunt upon hoisting something heavy
54 ___ E. Coyote
55 Basketball scoring play
58 Material that is foreign to the body
60 Pro ___
61 Cocktail recipe phrase
63 A deer, a female deer
64 Question in response to "I am"
66 Football scoring play
68 Real keepers?
69 Mechanical repetition
70 Laments
71 Main course
72 Yankee nickname beginning in 2004
73 Raison d'___

DOWN

1 Identifying, on Facebook
2 Lycanthrope
3 Handel's "Messiah," for one
4 Male delivery
5 Words finger-drawn on a dirty car
6 Not sinking
7 Study all night, say
8 Vigor
9 All set
10 Concealed
11 Word at the bottom of a blog page
12 Dark volcanic rock
13 Loose garb in ancient Rome
14 Little bits
19 Cicero's 601
23 Readily accept
26 Two-faced Roman god
28 Many a Happy Meal toy
31 Neck of the woods
35 Golf course obstacles
37 Aware of
38 Persuades in a deceitful way
40 Place to chat over a hot drink
41 Name in a 2002 scandal
42 Auditioned
43 More pallid
46 Chant at a basketball game
47 Structure that's roughly a triangular prism
48 Enter with much commotion
49 Most adorable
52 Proceeding unthinkingly
53 Like some smiles and humor
56 Mantle or crust
57 Aquarium fish
59 Last in a series
62 D-worthy
65 Bauxite, for aluminum
67 Beats by ___ (audio brand)

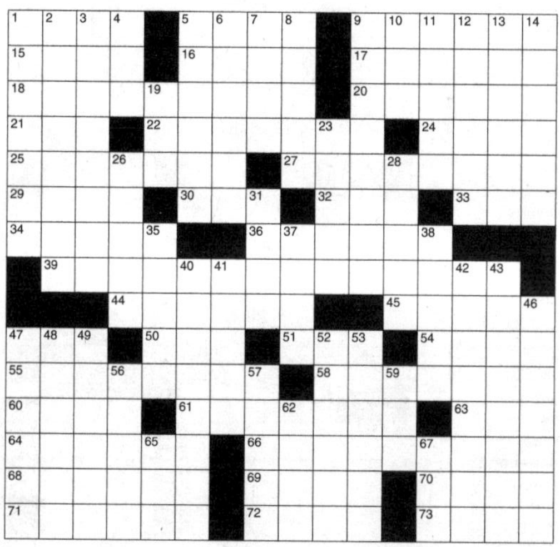

by Tom McCoy

86 MEDIUM

ACROSS

1 Collateral, of a sort
5 "More or less"
8 Handled the last details of, with "up"
14 Mark up
16 Harvest, perhaps
17 One rubbing you the right way?
18 Is overwhelmed
19 Romantic night in Kentucky?
21 Vehicle in "Frozen"
22 Textbook market shorthand
23 Savory and sage
26 Sport-___
28 Venison source
30 Nerd (out)
31 Friend of Buzz in "Toy Story"
34 "Come on, Doris"?
36 Gold of "Entourage"
37 One you might hang with
39 Nevada county with part of Death Valley National Monument
40 Rocky subject?
41 Counterfeit Dodge?
44 Blusterous
46 Relative of -ess
47 Frosting ingredient, often
48 Vitamin World competitor
49 Carlos y Juan Carlos
51 "I thought you had my back!"
53 Decreases
57 Fishing boat at summer camp?
60 Pickens who's a 33-Down
62 Not sold on TV or online
63 Title figures in a Gilbert and Sullivan opera
64 Alternative to Wi-Fi
65 Doesn't let lapse
66 Tempeh base
67 Pharmacy stock, informally

DOWN

1 Innocents
2 Completely
3 Occur subsequently
4 Failure to sneeze?
5 "Hear, hear!"
6 Take home . . . in more ways than one?
7 ___ Greene, character on "The Walking Dead"
8 Harvey ___ College
9 TV personality with the best seller "What I Know for Sure"
10 Marco Rubio, to Jeb Bush, once
11 Booted, say
12 Gazillion years
13 Drunk's woe
15 Graffiti mark
20 Kind of treatment
24 Lengthening shadow?
25 Brilliantly blue
27 Redheads or book lovers, maybe
29 Big name in jewelry
31 Symbol of thinness
32 Hold the floor
33 David or Charles Koch
34 Taken for a fool
35 Wrapped (up)
38 Contribute
42 Escort after a party
43 Gives it another go
45 Student housing in Fairbanks?
48 Nervous and apprehensive
50 Muscle-bone binder
52 Nearing the bell, maybe
54 Carried
55 Multiply
56 Networks: Abbr.
58 Word after hand or zoom
59 Geneviève, for one: Abbr.
60 ___ : Tuesday :: Odin : Wednesday
61 Garden worker?

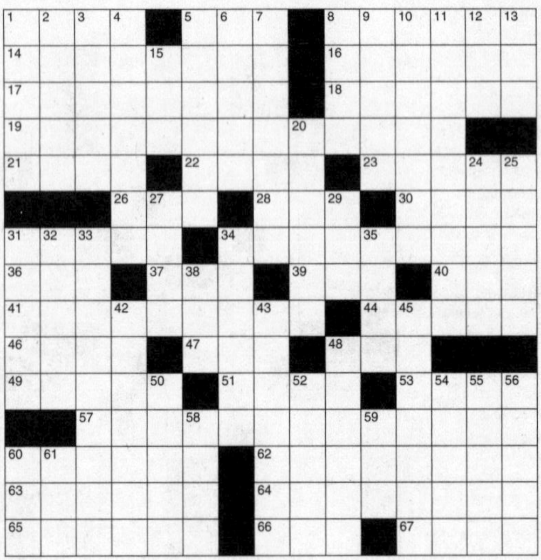

by Alex Bajcz

ACROSS

1 Grand Canyon, notably
6 Muesli morsel
9 Acceded, informally
14 Three-line work
15 Mid-11th century year
16 Still in the running
17 Pen name of the female author of "Wuthering Heights"
19 Tiniest bit
20 Denials
21 Body of agua
22 Rome's Via ___
23 Pen name of the female author of "Out of Africa"
25 Makes hazy
29 Tiny
30 Not getting much rain
31 Bed of roses, so to speak
34 Has a yen (for)
39 Pen name of the female author of "The Cuckoo's Calling"
42 Written contest entry, say
43 Terrier of old whodunits
44 Attorney general parodied by Ferrell
45 It's a "gift"
47 Coarse-toothed tool
49 Pen name of the female author of "Silas Marner"
55 Having new energy
56 Fashion editor Wintour
57 Affirmative
60 Inner self, to Jung
61 Pen name of the female author of True Detective stories
63 Travel guide listings
64 Cryophobe's fear
65 Wispy clouds
66 Cash in Baja
67 Traditional dog name
68 15-Across, e.g.

DOWN

1 "Big Brother" host Julie
2 Prop at a Christmas play
3 Has a bug
4 Boot attachment
5 Five Pillars adherent
6 Last in a series
7 "No problem here"
8 Up to, informally
9 Approached
10 Dior dress style
11 Trellis climbers
12 Party notice that lands in your inbox
13 Possessive spirit
18 Hound variety
22 Go head-to-head
24 Spoke at length about, with "on"
25 Unpainted, say
26 God with a bow
27 "Mine!," in a schoolyard
28 What comes to mind
32 Visibly awed
33 Carrier with a Copenhagen hub
35 Be a kvetch
36 Hotfoots it, old-style
37 Volcano in Catania
38 Gallery event
40 Wimbledon court surface
41 Noble's domain
46 Hill V.I.P.: Abbr.
48 Lake that's the source of the Mississippi
49 Get, as a point
50 Counting-off word
51 Articles that are sometimes prewritten
52 Womanizer
53 Tilter's tool
54 Reference book feature
57 Story you can hardly believe
58 Shade of raw linen
59 Take off the top
61 Word before gun or guitar
62 Pewter, mostly

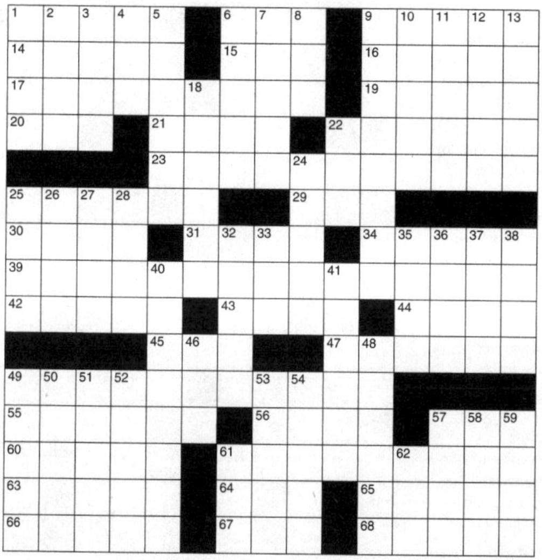

by Jeff Stillman

MEDIUM

ACROSS

1 50s president
6 Rappeller's need
10 Foot, to Flavius
13 Goldfinger's first name
14 French assembly
15 Stand buy
16 "Return of the Jedi" villain
17 See 27-Across
19 Big brass
21 Online identity
22 Like some office furniture
26 Writer Calvino
27 With 17-Across, reference book for a writer
28 Like the heads of many hairbrushes
30 Duke, e.g.: Abbr.
31 Morlock victims, in science fiction
32 Spoilers?
34 London theater district
38 Inventor of roll film
42 Sorts (through)
44 Very light
45 Go out
48 Cleveland Browns great Graham
49 Manhattan eatery since 1927
51 Resentment
53 Subway entrance
55 Teakettle parts
57 Peals
58 Annual department store event
60 Zip
64 Asian holiday
65 Cut off
66 Ones in cocoons
67 Oral hesitations
68 Topiary trees
69 Word on an old gas pump

DOWN

1 Perform
2 Laundry container
3 Hidden means of support?
4 Extinct creature with armored spikes on its back
5 Bingeing
6 Arctic gale
7 Brian of ambient music
8 "Now!"
9 Show real eagerness
10 Persian ruler
11 Artist Monet
12 Power measures, informally
14 Fortitude
18 Sigma follower
20 Rip off
22 Frisbee, e.g.
23 Cry of innocence
24 He, for one: Abbr.
25 Overhang
29 Santa ___
33 Commences
35 Plugs
36 Pond young 'un
37 Katarina ___, two-time Olympic gold-medalist skater
39 Skirt style
40 Seed covering
41 Inits. at 11 Wall Street
43 Contemporary of Wordsworth and Coleridge
45 Attacks from all sides
46 Gable part
47 Think of as the same
49 TV home of "Weekend Update," in brief
50 Slanting
52 Runner of many Apple devices
54 Spats
56 Worry
59 "___ got it"
61 Nascar stat, for short
62 Remit
63 Daughter of Loki

by Kurt Krauss

ACROSS

1 Parks who sparked a boycott
5 City of central Iowa
9 Install, as a bulb, with "in"
14 ___'acte
15 In perfect condition
16 Prom queen's wear
17 Start of a seasonal letter
19 N.B.A. Hall-of-Famer Bird
20 Words from Shakespeare
22 Airing after midnight, say
23 Closemouthed
24 In the sack
27 ___ pressure
28 Words from Socrates
31 Convenience store conveniences
32 Showing no emotion
33 Major employers on reservations
37 Directors' do-overs
39 Crème de la crème
40 All Harrow students
41 Words from Sartre
44 A cygnet is a baby one
48 [Ignore prior marks]
49 Particle in a salt solution
50 Possible response to "Gonna win?"
52 Words from Sinatra
55 Veal cuts
57 They all start with "K" and "W" in the U.S.
58 Reed section
59 James with a posthumous Pulitzer
60 "I'm impressed!"
61 Sculpted body part
62 Speedsters of old autodom
63 Turns right on a horse

DOWN

1 Variety of pasture grass
2 Common soccer draw
3 Horse house
4 Overdue debt
5 Almond-flavored liqueur
6 Sen. Al Franken's state: Abbr.
7 Lays to rest
8 Central Park's "Alice in Wonderland," for one
9 Normandy battle site
10 Panini bread
11 Bibliophile's prize
12 Flub
13 Very, informally
18 W. C. Fields persona
21 Texter's "Didn't need to hear that!"
25 Actress Falco
26 Nonfiction films, for short
29 Meditation sounds
30 Fliers until '03
31 Start to freeze?
33 Musical with Rum Tum Tugger
34 Scads
35 Delivery entrance, perhaps
36 Deuterium and tritium
37 Stick up
38 Halloween mask features
40 Slavery
42 Sis, for example
43 Hot Wheels product
44 Mole's work
45 Prank involving underwear
46 P.D.Q.
47 Executioners' devices
51 No longer used, in a dict.
53 ___ buco
54 Prefix with resin
55 Jail cell sight
56 "Game of Thrones" network

by Pawel Fludzinski

90 MEDIUM

ACROSS

1 Don Draper or Roger Sterling, on an AMC series
6 Club ___
10 You might be honored with one: Abbr.
13 Worthy pursuits
14 It's responsible for controlling a pupil
15 Bar barrier
16 Camera operators, gaffers, etc.
17 1976 Dustin Hoffman thriller
19 More desertlike
20 Courier or Myriad
21 Jumble
22 Stage for Hulk Hogan
24 Object depicted on the cover of Pink Floyd's "The Dark Side of the Moon"
25 Venomous menace
26 Ampersand follower, maybe
27 Soybean snack
29 Senate majority leader before McConnell
31 World music's King Sunny ___
33 See 39-Across
34 What 3M's Scotch is a brand of
38 "___ Parisienne" (Brigitte Bardot comedy)
39 Hole in 33-Across
40 Hanoi holidays
43 ___ market
47 Thurman of "Kill Bill"
49 San Francisco's ___ Valley
50 Ones getting the red-carpet treatment
51 Arrival or departure approximation
54 Cannes film
55 Heedfulness
56 Actress de la Garza of "Law & Order"
57 Rothko's field
59 Winter trail transport
60 One of five in Yahtzee
61 Greek colonnade
62 Penguin variety
63 Start to skid?
64 Responses to some OnStar calls
65 Stand

DOWN

1 Opposed
2 In bad shape
3 Colt carriers
4 Messages often with exclamation points
5 Neighbor of Victoria: Abbr.
6 "America's Got Talent" panelist
7 Buddhist monks wear it
8 TMZ fodder
9 Cool-cucumber center?
10 Mexican bloom
11 Self-interest doctrine
12 Subject of a modern map
13 "Dem's fightin' words!"
18 Agony
20 Antiquers' delights
23 Rental car alternative
24 Subject of a frame job?
28 Cabbage
30 Beat it!
32 Enforcer of the Solid Waste Disposal Act, for short
35 Working without ___
36 Like two angles in a right triangle
37 Sucker holder
41 Filing target
42 Put under
43 Front
44 They've got you covered
45 Helps with the dishes
46 Underwater behemoth
48 Only #1 hit for Boston
52 Mex. misses
53 Bitter ___ (purgative medicine)
55 Foe of Caesar
58 Q followers
59 Encl. to an editor

by James Tuttle

MEDIUM 91

ACROSS

1 DuVernay who directed "Selma"
4 Cause of 1840s–'50s emigration from Ireland
10 "___ difference!"
14 Comfy shoe
15 Spotted wildcat
16 Airline seat part
17 Where the midnight sun can be observed
20 African nation renamed in 1997
21 "As if!"
22 Chills out
23 Diva's problem
25 Daniel who created Friday
27 Place for a trophy case
28 ___ pie (old British dish)
30 Like early audiobooks
34 One out of 100
37 Actress Seehorn of "Better Call Saul"
38 "No need to discuss it"
42 It may be put in a bun
43 Won, as a voting demographic
44 Bitter salad green
46 Decimal base
47 "___ chance!"
50 Singer with the #1 hit "TiK ToK"
53 Nina of jazz
55 Ticked off
58 Great Lakes freighter load, perhaps
60 Grounds for lawsuits
61 Rotisserie League game
64 Pre-cable TV problem
65 Contributes, as to a pool
66 Roll call vote
67 "The Simpsons" bus driver
68 State confidently
69 Most univ. applicants

DOWN

1 Bowled over
2 Internet-based phone provider
3 Kung fu movie genre
4 What 17-Across has, phonetically
5 Georgia Tech's athletic org.
6 Crystal ___
7 Tale of Troy
8 Night, in Nicaragua
9 And more, briefly
10 Souped-up vintage auto
11 Jump shot paths
12 Brewer's ingredient
13 Some glass prostheses
18 Singer Grande, to fans
19 Pitching wedge, for one
24 Poses a danger to
26 What 38-Across has, phonetically
29 Mantra-chanting priest
31 Tuna at sushi bars
32 Word with pig or play
33 Absorb, as a loss
34 Worrisome call at home
35 Only non-U.S. M.L.B. team, on scoreboards
36 ___ cloud (source of comets)
38 Article with no equivalent in Russian
39 Chinese dynasty after the Qin
40 Rescuer's offering
41 Showing sorrow
45 Hindu sacred writing
47 What 61-Across has, phonetically
48 Half a rack, to a hunter
49 Cars since 2006
51 Georgetown athletes
52 "We have the meats" fast-food chain
54 Unruly bunch
55 "In that case . . ."
56 Go on a tirade
57 Macramé feature
59 Stress-free state
62 Place to wear a wrap
63 Elton John title

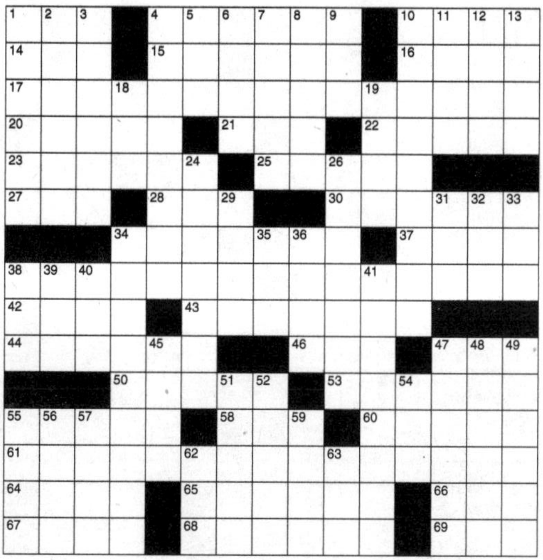

by Zhouqin Burnikel

92 MEDIUM

ACROSS

1 Unlatched, say
5 Pollock painting unit
9 Vitriolic
14 Natural harbor
15 Fluctuate wildly
16 "Muy ___" (Spanish approval)
17 Part 1 of a punny quip about a perp's predicament
20 Chilean-based carrier
21 The "oven" in "have a bun in the oven"
22 Turing test participant
23 Depository deposits
25 Out
28 Quip, part 2
31 Reap
32 Cap
33 Bruno ___ Prize (astrophysics award)
34 Quip, part 3
37 Fall that might cause falls
41 Motorist's aid, for short
42 Emote
46 Quip, part 4
50 ___ de Saint-Exupéry, author of "The Little Prince"
51 Titular queen of Castile in a Handel opera
52 Political leader?
53 Feature of some gardens
56 Tyler of "The Lord of the Rings"
57 End of the quip
61 Bygone name in Chinese politics
62 Gallery on the Thames
63 Proofer's "oops"
64 Supposes
65 One of two Danish kings
66 One who sends things up?

DOWN

1 Ape
2 Daughter of Sweeney Todd in the Sondheim musical
3 Count of Monte Cristo, e.g.
4 Agent, informally
5 Independently
6 Capital of Togo
7 ___ and terminer (criminal court)
8 Ship mates
9 Obliques, e.g.
10 Part of the Maxwell House logo
11 Some sneakers
12 They can be gross
13 Two-part letter
18 Pity
19 Natl. sports org.
24 Totally defeat
26 Rent
27 Boo-___
29 "Few love it unless in themselves," per Lord Chesterfield
30 "It's ___" ("Let's shake on it")
34 "The Bell of ___" (Longfellow poem)
35 "The Facts of Life" actress
36 Was unhappy (with)
37 Like phone numbers at meetups
38 Shortest route around a track
39 One-named Grammy winner for "American Boy," 2008
40 Kind of trip
42 Press room?
43 One of a pair of Monopoly properties
44 Kennedy in-law
45 Nautical command
47 Playwright William
48 Provoke
49 Trading group, e.g.
54 Intense dedication
55 Companion of Butch and Sundance
58 "___ Malala" (2013 best-selling autobiography)
59 Modern prefix with gender
60 Approx. 5 cc

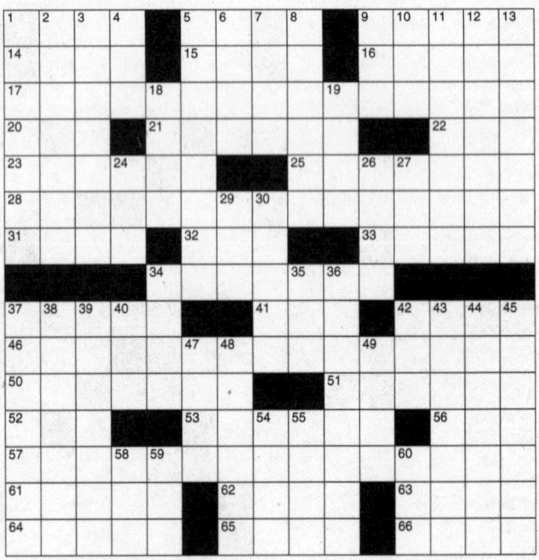

by Morton J. Mendelson

ACROSS

1 Start of a Latin 101 conjugation
4 Eastern Mediterranean port since ancient times
9 "Take Care" rapper, 2012
14 Sessions, e.g.: Abbr.
15 Total
16 "I am ___, hear me roar"
17 Dough in hand, redundantly
19 Clued in
20 Big name in 1950s presidential campaigning
21 Full of shadows
23 Scotch topper
24 Juicy fruit
25 State capital near Lake Tahoe
27 Course reversal
29 Chick's tail?
30 Class with many unknowns: Abbr.
32 Brand with "Old World Style"
34 Klutz's utterance
38 Person who's ready and able to help . . . or a literal description of four occurrences in this puzzle
43 Lead-in to girl
44 Off-base sort?
45 School's end
46 Tomato variety
50 Got under the skin of
52 Gym activity that works the pectorals
56 Quiet place to pray
59 Org. that encourages flossing
60 Many a Wall Street Journal graphic
61 Like much state fair fare
62 Little bud
64 Last one in, say
66 Calendario start
67 Love to pieces
68 Chowder head?
69 ___ Hannah of "Blade Runner"
70 Not so hot
71 Sin

DOWN

1 Acronym on Beyoncé records
2 Gettysburg general
3 Chargers' action
4 First name at Woodstock
5 "I'd like to buy ___, Pat"
6 Spanish steps?
7 ___-de-lis
8 Actress Milano
9 Johnson also known as "The Rock"
10 Ticket info
11 Prized Italian instrument
12 Gold standard
13 "In the practice of tolerance, one's ___ is the best teacher": Dalai Lama
18 Rodgers's partner, in song
22 Sent to the canvas, for short
25 Bonkers, in modern lingo
26 Some "American Greed" subjects, for short
28 Big coffee server
30 1977 album with the hit single "Deacon Blues"
31 Great deal
33 Spanish article
35 Leaning column
36 Mini-spacecraft
37 Bad name for an anger management counselor?
39 Traffic cop, for short?
40 Resealable bottle feature
41 ___ d'oeuvres
42 "Benevolent" fraternity member
47 "Would ya look at that!"
48 Dash abbr.
49 Genesis landing site
51 Get through hard work
52 Sweltered in the sun
53 Minneapolis suburb
54 Third-place finisher in 2000, 2004 and 2008
55 Diminish by degrees
57 Bob with the Silver Bullet Band
58 Yard tool
61 Farm store purchase
63 Wine descriptor
65 TNT part

by Andrew J. Ries

94 MEDIUM

ACROSS

1 Foe of the Ottomans
6 Info for some limo drivers
10 Nursery bagful
14 A white one is said to symbolize "I'm sorry"
15 Shop window sign
16 Like dumb blonde jokes
17 Brother Antonio or Girolamo in music history
18 When shortened, ear swabs
20 2016's "Ghostbusters" and "Ben-Hur"
22 Film chimp
23 Hot
24 "Be that way!"
25 Warriors' league, for short
28 Feature of many an action film, paradoxically
30 Refuse
32 Rolling Stones #1 hit with the line "You're beautiful, but ain't it time we said goodbye?"
35 y, for one
37 Music box music
38 Compact material
39 Second letter before 7-Down
40 Lightly burn
41 Place where things may be burned
42 Put away
43 It's a deadly sin
44 Make a mistake
46 Scottish estate owner
48 ___-country (music genre)
49 Open wide
51 Chicken tikka ___
55 Letter before 7-Down
57 Best
58 When shortened, ski lifts
61 Pindar, for one
62 Small matter?
63 London cricket ground, with "the"
64 Painter's preparation
65 One might ask for them to be cooled
66 Ordering option
67 Grateful?

DOWN

1 Hollywood Boulevard sights
2 "Network" director
3 1836 battle site
4 When shortened, winning symbols
5 "Chi-Raq" director, 2015
6 Titles of lawsuits?: Abbr.
7 Greek letter
8 Out
9 Another plate
10 Skating maneuver
11 When shortened, rocket seal
12 Words With Friends, e.g.
13 Oscars V.I.P.s
19 ___-length
21 Composer who co-created "Oblique Strategies"
24 When shortened, violin feature
26 Hogwash
27 Butterfly attractor
29 Mini-___
31 When shortened, lesser-played songs
32 Sommelier's concern
33 Untried
34 When shortened, topic in sexology
36 Its eastern and western borders are formed entirely by rivers
40 1777 battle site
42 Modern-day harvester
45 Popular boots that originated from surf culture
47 Puck, for one
50 Conductor Järvi
52 Simple-living folk
53 Hallström who directed "The Cider House Rules"
54 Some flutes
56 Alternative to Beneful
57 1993 and 1995's ___ Accords
58 ___ Boston (luxury hotel)
59 Took 9-Down, say
60 Remover of dirt . . . or spreader of dirt?

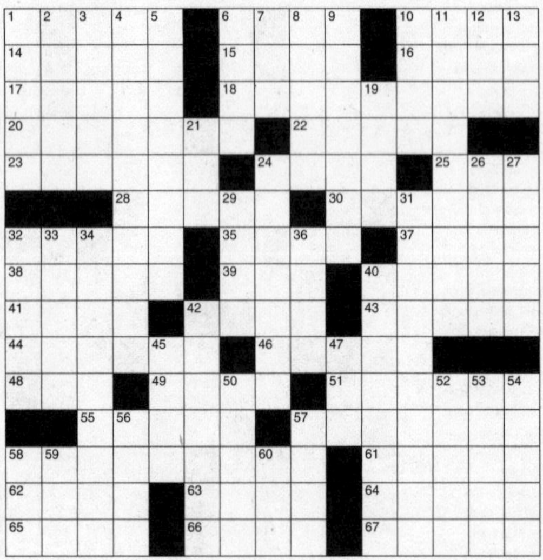

by Andrew Zhou

MEDIUM 95

ACROSS

1 Screwed up big-time
7 Early 10th-century year
11 Fit to be tied
14 Dickinson with a modeling agency
15 Leisure
16 Fire truck accessory
17 Rock's Blue ___ Cult
18 Scott in 1857 news
19 ___ de la Cité
20 Triple Crown stat
21 Eventually
23 Orch. section
24 Supreme Court justice who replaced Stevens
26 U.N. agcy. that promotes "decent work for all women and men"
27 ___ Islands (autonomous part of Denmark)
29 G.O.P. org.
30 Well-wisher's wish
32 Erik of "CHiPs"
34 Gives the slip
35 Ariz.-to-Kan. direction
36 ___-mo replay
37 Odin's realm
41 Muscle builder for Popeye
45 Mark in the intersection of 19-Across and 11-Down
47 Coffeehouse combo, often
48 Lightning Bolt
49 "Footloose" hero ___ McCormack
50 To a degree, informally
52 Denouement
53 Awaited a tongue depressor, maybe
55 Tempe sch.
56 12 meses
57 "You ___?" (butler's line)
58 French waiter
60 E-guffaw
61 Advance slowly
62 Mark in the intersection of 17-Across and 1-Down
63 Part of a financial portfolio, for short
64 Greet's partner
65 "___ Fables"

DOWN

1 One-named singer from Iceland
2 Expose for all to see
3 Midshipmen, after commission
4 Jokester
5 Strand at a ski lodge, maybe
6 Migratory seabird
7 Mark in the intersection of 58-Across and 43-Down
8 Rocky Mountains rodent
9 "Gotcha"
10 Struck (out)
11 Restaurant V.I.P.
12 Frontman of the "Welcome to the Jungle" band
13 Poor grade
22 Mark in the intersection of 56-Across and 38-Down
23 "Elephant Boy" boy
25 Don't just sit there
27 Arsonist, e.g.
28 Alf and Mork, for short
30 The N.C.A.A.'s Aggies, informally
31 DNA strand shape
33 Any airing of "Friends," now
36 Pass, as time
37 Prefix with pressure
38 Opposite of "No way, José!"?
39 What may be in a breakfast bar
40 Pepto-Bismol target
41 Deceptive dexterity
42 Hoopla
43 Neighbor of Aruba
44 Steaming bowlful
46 Champagne's place
50 "Tsk, tsk!"
51 Em and Polly, in literature
53 Mentally together
54 Contents of un lago
56 Boxing's "Louisville Lip"
57 Backboard attachment
59 "Treasure Island" monogram

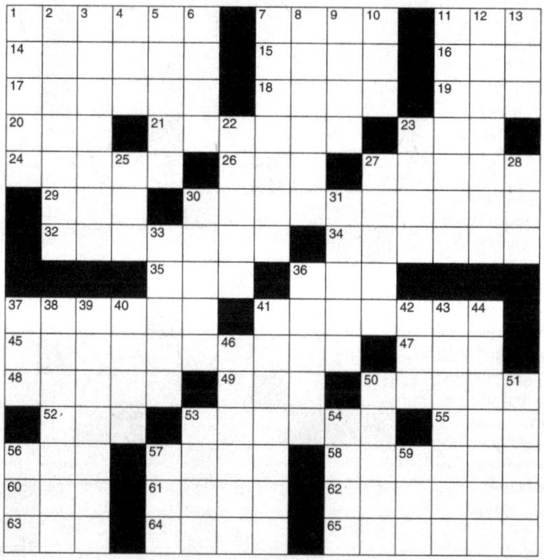

by Wren Schultz

MEDIUM

ACROSS
1 Fool
5 Key of Beethoven's Symphony No. 7: Abbr.
9 Top prizes
14 Brother's place, informally
15 Fictional home that was won in an all-night poker game
16 Band
17 Electro house or dubstep
19 Navajo dwelling
20 Luke's mentor
21 Something often described as "even"
23 Caution to drivers
24 Strong and majestic
27 Something that may be loaded
30 To the point
32 Doesn't have enough
34 Plus
36 Play the siren to
37 TV or radio ad
40 Academy newbie
42 Literary Jaffe
43 Any element in the first column of the periodic table, except hydrogen
45 Turkish moolah
47 Creature that comes ashore to lay eggs
49 Whippersnapper
53 For instance
54 First name in gospel
56 Sound from a fan
57 Proficient
58 Mental flub
60 Roundish
63 Trust
66 Party souvenir
67 Court call
68 Jabber?
69 Pancake
70 "Hercules" spinoff, informally
71 Hold up in traffic?

DOWN
1 Nose nipper
2 Suitable for farming
3 Redeemer
4 Contents of a slow cooker
5 Carrying ___
6 More, to Manuel
7 Radio journalist Shapiro
8 With 48-Down, children's toy . . . or a hint to this puzzle's theme
9 Common quesadilla filler
10 Summer Olympics venue
11 Texter's "Holy cow!"
12 Sched. uncertainty
13 Delivery outcome, sometimes
18 13-Downs, e.g.
22 Playwright Eve
25 Cy Young winner Hershiser
26 Chocolaty spread
27 Knucklehead
28 De-crease
29 European erupter
31 Used, as a desk
33 Like arctic winters
35 Rotini shape
37 Freshness
38 Court stance
39 "Sounds good to me"
41 Jessica of "7th Heaven"
44 Strong feller?
46 Enlightened
48 See 8-Down
50 Home of Gannon Univ.
51 N.B.A. Hall-of-Famer Bob
52 Communication connection
55 Neighbor of Majorca
57 On
59 Opposite of sans
60 Not on
61 ___ d'Or, Quebec
62 Sinatra's wife between Nancy and Mia
64 Spy satellite, so to speak
65 Writer Deighton

by Susan Gelfand

ACROSS

1 Young fellow
6 Contrarian
10 Former Israeli P.M. Barak
14 Beef on the hoof
15 Go like heck
16 Arnold, Ronald or Roland
17 Military vehicle for actor William?
19 Ballroom motions
20 Gibbons, e.g.
21 Part of a comedy routine
22 Strong suit
23 Part of a certain cage
24 Makeup for actor Kevin?
27 So last year
29 Burj Khalifa's home: Abbr.
30 Nevertheless
31 Much of the moon's landscape
35 Department store department
36 Footwear for actor Ted?
38 Product that can maintain a bikini line
40 Tailoring measures
41 She, in Lisbon
42 [That is so disgusting!]
43 Chalupa go-with
47 Cudgel for actor Christopher?
52 Texter's reaction to a joke
53 Playground retort
54 Xbox ___
55 Up to it
56 Not too shabby
57 Equipment for actor Michael?
60 Krabappel of Springfield
61 City ESE of Turin
62 Proselytizer's handout
63 Need a bath badly
64 "Hey, take it easy!"
65 Beefy-T brand

DOWN

1 C's equivalent
2 Perfect place
3 People people
4 Sneakers that come in over a hundred designs
5 Metallurgist's sample
6 Dormered area, maybe
7 "Fantabulous!"
8 Color similar to Crayola's Tumbleweed
9 Bug big-time
10 Supply, as a chair
11 Salon supply
12 A zillion
13 Jumps ship
18 Draft org.
22 Moriarty, to Holmes
24 "Feel the ___" (2016 campaign slogan)
25 Tend to
26 Ottoman title
28 Sign of past trauma
32 Like Mongols
33 Patio grill accessory
34 Two of nine?
35 Badlands sight
36 Feature of a landline, but not a cellphone
37 Trans-Siberian Railway city
38 Practitioner of aromatherapy and astrology, maybe
39 How birthday cake may be served
42 ___ Metro (bygone car)
44 Competitor of The North Face
45 Comforting words
46 "Fore!" and others
48 Big employer in Rochester, N.Y.
49 Classic TV sidekick
50 Where Uttar Pradesh is
51 Onetime title for Carly Fiorina
55 Uttar Pradesh city
57 "The ___ is a ass": Dickens
58 Baseball bat material
59 Ultimate degree

by Sean Dobbin

MEDIUM

ACROSS

1 Powder used to combat moisture
7 Cool, in hip-hop slang
10 Opening part
14 Obtrude
15 Nutritional std.
16 Party that might start after midnight
17 Pair of big jets?
18 "Evolve" artist DiFranco
19 Piece designed to sway
20 Monster of fantasy
21 With the circled letters, investors not involved in the management of their businesses
23 Baby transport
27 Fake blood, e.g.
28 Go unused
29 Crude measurements?
33 Claude who played Sheriff Lobo
34 Source of soft wool
36 Navigational aid
37 Building extension
38 Renaissance ___
39 1920s silver screen star Naldi
40 Juicy ending?
41 Photo finish
42 Woe for newborns (and thus new parents as well)
43 Trattoria dessert
45 Strong and proud
47 Dickens pen name
48 Singer's volume?
49 With the circled letters, large but not often vocal voting bloc
53 ___ courtesy
54 Nobel Prize subj.
55 Preschool break
56 Elbow
60 Summer camp locale
61 Computer file suffix
62 Wilde of TV's "House"
63 Didn't make it
64 Paige, to Jason, in "FoxTrot"
65 Unsay

DOWN

1 Mexican relative
2 Terse, introspective question
3 A D.J. might spin them
4 Salon job
5 Email addresses, sometimes
6 Agave drink
7 Hang
8 "Downton Abbey" maid
9 A legitimate object to attack
10 Swedish money
11 Mane area
12 In the strike zone
13 Hotel reservation specification
22 When tripled, 1970 film about the attack on Pearl Harbor
23 Try to scratch
24 Modern Japanese martial art
25 "Stand by Me" director, 1986
26 Trattoria desserts
29 Just
30 Estevez of the Brat Pack
31 Many a Dream Act beneficiary
32 Sissy of Netflix's "Bloodline"
35 Wasted
38 Publications for and by aficionados
39 7 or below on the pH scale
41 Shrubby wasteland
42 Wii, for one
44 Broadsided, informally
46 Key with four sharps
48 Creates a buzz for
49 Blend
50 Berry advertised as healthful
51 Ridiculously inadequate sort
52 Curbside call
57 F.D.R. program, for short
58 Broadway's ___-Manuel Miranda
59 Do lunch, say

by Damon Gulczynski

ACROSS

1 Kimono closer
4 Luxuries
10 Org. for women taking courses?
14 Enjoyable
15 A Jackson sister
16 Tesla power source: Abbr.
17 Country that's an extremely close American ally, so to speak
20 Bit of name-calling
21 They'll check your bag at the airport, for short
22 Buds in Bordeaux
23 Tiny, informally
24 Special perception
28 ___ embarrassment
30 "Shows you!"
31 Sashimi selection
32 Follows
34 ___ jeans
35 Theater, design, etc.
36 Power source for a subway train
39 M.L.B. Triple Crown category
42 Rejections
43 Billed to be
47 Sea eagle
48 Like monsoon season
49 Meager
50 Unwanted tagalong
55 Concerning
56 Oxymoronic purchase at a blowout sale?
57 Up in the air, as what to air, for short
58 Word with work or window
59 Rant continuation . . . or a hint to this puzzle's theme
63 College in Portland, Ore.
64 Cavalry attack
65 Actress Long
66 Pal of Stan on "South Park"
67 In need of some garage work
68 Measure of econ. strength

DOWN

1 In the wrong place at the wrong time?
2 Permanent, as bookshelves
3 Pervades
4 No-___ zone
5 Travels à la Huckleberry Finn
6 Formal response to "Who goes there?"
7 Title Seuss character, with "the"
8 Fleur-de-___
9 Used a rocker, e.g.
10 "I can do that for you"
11 Easier to see
12 Braces oneself
13 One-hit wonder?
18 Auditions
19 Boy Scout uniform part
25 Avenger with a hammer
26 Mideast group
27 He won the 1994 U.S. Open in a 20-hole playoff
29 "Bah!"
33 Muscle power
34 Scrip writers
35 Like a home purchase without financing
37 Hyman ___, main antagonist in "The Godfather Part II"
38 Android alternative
39 Red card issuer, for short
40 Pop diva Spears
41 Nonbeliever
44 Debonair
45 Late justice Scalia
46 Temporary solution
48 Not just if
51 Quid pro quo
52 Allen who led the Green Mountain Boys
53 He once asked "How far down can a thumb go?"
54 Elephantine
59 Couples cruise ship?
60 Condition affecting TV's Monk, informally
61 Not just a
62 Politico Cruz

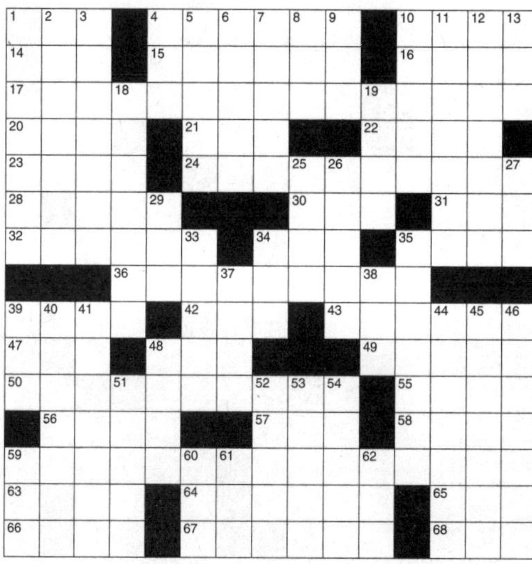

by Jason Flinn

100 MEDIUM

ACROSS

1 *Pitiers
6 *Cubit
10 1/
13 Black winds
14 More than giggle
15 Abs and such
16 *Bite down, in a way
18 Places for naps?
19 Total revolution
20 About
21 Much
22 Southwestern home
24 Cool air?
26 Tarantula-eating animal
28 God, in the Torah
30 Nerve center
31 Dark films, informally
33 Service jobs
37 Alma-___, Kazakhstan
38 Word of logic
39 Gin cocktail
40 Some atom smashers, briefly
42 Purple shade
44 Target of a strip search?
45 2016 Key and Peele action comedy
46 Fasten on
47 Goose: Fr.
48 Jargons
50 "Crashing the Party" author, 2002
52 Eat in excess
55 "Well!"
56 Put-down in an argument
57 Flirt
60 One working at home, for short
62 Actor whose last name is a 41-Down of his first name, after a D is changed to an N
63 *Polite star?
66 20 quires
67 Designer for the Ziegfeld Follies
68 Milton of comedy
69 Show imperfection
70 *Sitting figures, maybe
71 *Give a permit to, say

DOWN

1 Ending for martyr
2 Ancient Greek coin
3 *Lolita's workplace, in song
4 *Stick it to
5 What's funded by FICA, for short
6 Empath on the U.S.S. Enterprise
7 What comes before honor?
8 Southwestern spreads
9 Make a father of
10 Work measure
11 Rival of ancient Sparta
12 *Avian digits
15 *Britain's location
17 Record label for Miley Cyrus and Kelly Clarkson
23 *Source of gravity
25 *Exit payments
26 Snooker accessory
27 Convex navel
28 Notorious bailed-out insurance co.
29 "Move on!" . . . or how to decipher the 16 starred clues
32 Words of logic
34 *Bar order requiring celerity
35 Goosebumps-inducing
36 Part of a long drive?
39 Instinctual
41 *Suite for use?
43 The French?
46 Needle holder
49 Prepared
51 *Mojito, for one
52 *What visitors minimize
53 Gulf vessel
54 Weather forecasting aid
55 Apology opener
58 Indicate that one needs a hand?
59 Old 9-mm.
61 Influence
64 Stephen Colbert's network
65 "Didn't I tell you?!"

by Timothy Polin

ACROSS

1 Yoda, e.g.
11 Communication problem?
15 Last of a series of nicknames
16 Zero
17 Billy Crystal's role in "The Princess Bride"
18 Enigma machine decoder Turing
19 It's not a welcome sign
20 Facebook and others
21 Primary funding sources, briefly
22 Facebook, for one
23 Org. whose symbol is an eagle atop a key
24 How garden vegetables may be planted
26 Upset
28 Manicure destroyer
29 Hot Wheels garages?
33 Rhoda's TV mom
34 Emerald ___ borer
37 Expert savers
38 Constitution Hall grp.
39 Marathon champ Pippig
40 Mesozoic Era period
42 Home of Queen Margrethe II
44 Rank below marquis
47 "Let's do it!"
48 Sch. whose first building was Dallas Hall
51 Matches, at a table
53 "Caravan of Courage: An ___ Adventure" (1984 "Star Wars" spinoff)
54 Some Siouans
55 Bayh of Indiana politics
56 Flock gathering place
57 Group getting its kicks?
59 Rep
60 "I could use some help here . . ."
61 First name in architecture
62 Place to test the water

DOWN

1 Harry Potter's father
2 Alchemist's concoction
3 Frito-Lay chip
4 "Bleah!"
5 El Capitan platform
6 Literary hero whose name is Turkish for "lion"
7 Parts of a flight
8 2012 Republican National Convention host
9 Connection concerns, for short
10 "Toy Story" dino
11 Show impatience with
12 Developing company?
13 Wrapper that's hard to remove?
14 It's tailored to guys
24 Drinks with domed lids
25 Interest for a cryptozoologist
27 Impasse
28 Quadrant separator
30 "___ serious?"
31 Lab report?
32 Pay termination?
34 Nielsens measure
35 Fancy glasses
36 Malady with many "remedies"
41 Legal precedents
43 Get by
45 Awaken
46 Get support from
48 Photosynthesis opening
49 Interest of a mycologist
50 Quotidian
52 Old dummy
54 "Wait, I know that!"
57 Some savers' assets
58 Main hub for Virgin America, for short

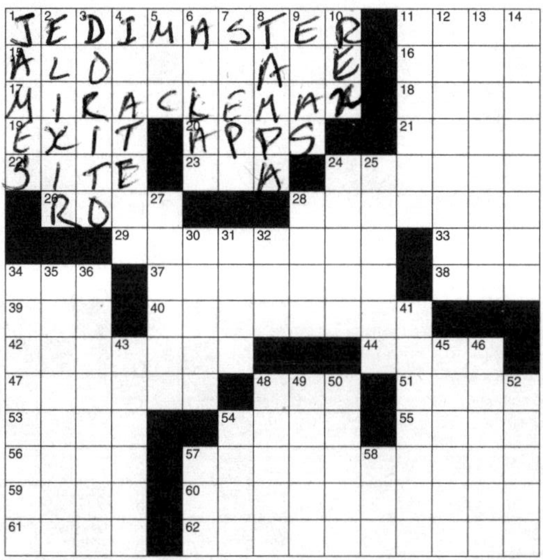

by Robyn Weintraub

102 HARD

ACROSS

1 Eighty-sixes
7 Rhetorical creation
15 Green
16 First Palme d'Or-winning film directed by a woman (1993)
17 "That thought already occurred to me"
19 Let fate decide, say
20 Subatomic particles with zero spin
21 Kind of cabbage
22 Pillory
26 Pump option, for short
27 Marinara sauce ingredients
32 Structures with excellent insulation
34 Telemarketing tactic
36 Try to find oneself?
38 Warming
39 David Fincher thriller of 2014
41 Had a list
42 Bid on a hand unsuited for suit play, maybe
43 Cusk-___ (deepest living fish, at 27,000+ feet)
45 Rockets
46 Leaders in robes
48 Screens
53 Onetime Fandango competitor
58 One with a long stretch to go?
60 Blaring
61 Fisher for compliments on one's dress?
62 "Les Misérables" extra
63 Managed

DOWN

1 Infatuated, old-style
2 Italian city where Pliny the Elder and Younger were born
3 Matrix specifications
4 "Sob"
5 Type of mobile phone plan
6 Take to living together, with "up"
7 Austrian philosopher Rudolf
8 "Phew!"
9 One might turn on it
10 Per
11 Modern flight amenity
12 Main ingredient of rémoulade
13 Composer of many limericks, for short
14 "À ___ la Liberté" (1931 René Clair film)
18 Period of a revolution?
22 San ___
23 Urge
24 It's all the same
25 Einstein-___ bridge (wormhole)
27 Game's turning point?
28 Brand of sponge
29 Cousin of a skate
30 Neuter
31 Places for runners
33 First word in many temple names
35 Something odd in roulette?
37 Pricing model for many apps
40 Newspaper name that becomes a beverage if you insert an "a" after its fifth letter
44 "___ a little!"
47 State fair attractions
48 Uphill climb, say
49 Drone's place
50 Breaking a comb, in Japan, e.g.
51 "I agree," in slang
52 Toni Morrison novel
54 Menu bar heading
55 Plot feature in "Hansel and Gretel"
56 Old brand in the shaving aisle
57 Puzzle designer Rubik
59 Young women's grp.

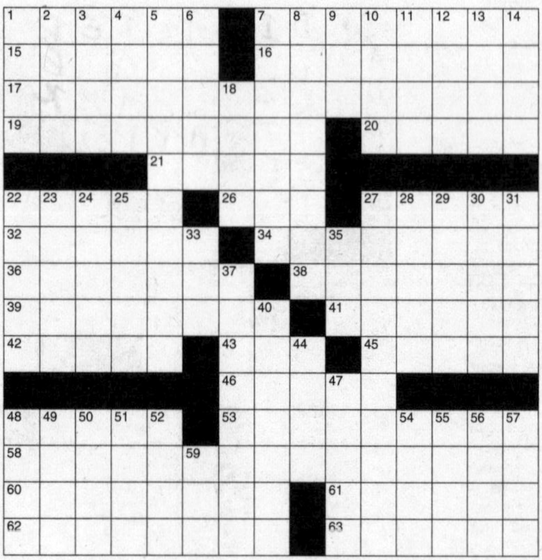

by Julian Lim

ACROSS

1 Connections
4 Connections to the sternum
8 Not assured at all
13 "You can figure as well as I can"
16 Treasure
17 Cream song with the lyric "Dance floor is like the sea, / Ceiling is the sky"
18 Things that may be compressed
19 Excluded category in the Paleo diet
20 Little treasure
21 Now
22 Kind of wave
23 Wasabi go-with in sushi meals
24 List heading
25 People who are in them are out, in brief
26 Shavit with the 2013 best seller "My Promised Land"
27 Where Spike Lee earned his M.F.A.
30 Little: Fr.
31 Not identifying with one's assigned sex
34 1851 Sojourner Truth speech
35 Online addresses, in part
36 "Ur hilarious!"
37 Bit of evasion
38 Still
39 Two or three sets, say
42 Where the Taj Mahotsav festival is held
44 Either director of "Inside Llewyn Davis"
46 Part of MSG
47 Fit
49 Info in a Yelp listing: Abbr.
50 Either half of a 1973 "duel"
51 Lacked options
52 Ask
54 Tribe whose name means "long tail"
55 Dessert so-called for its portions of flour, butter, eggs and sugar
56 Purchase at a golf pro shop
57 Purchases at a golf pro shop
58 Flushed

DOWN

1 "Don't you doubt me!"
2 "You cheated!"
3 Round containers?
4 Bet (on)
5 Subj. of many antiglobalization protests
6 Threat of a strike, in labor negotiations
7 Lead
8 Birdbrained
9 Birdbrain
10 Typical "S.N.L." start
11 Something you can control the volume with?
12 "Me?" follower
14 "___, boy!"
15 Terse and unadorned, as writing
23 Part of MGM's motto
26 "Babalú" bandleader
28 Ones ranking above knaves
29 Not realized
31 Fashion mogul Gunn
32 ___ Marcos, Tex.
33 Some "CSI" figs.
34 App with over 200 free stations
35 Place to play with toys
36 Things that might be batted at a ball
39 Approach
40 Something not many people laugh at
41 Blew it
43 Floral symbol of patience
45 ". . . but I could be wrong"
46 Comedian Maron
48 Superlatively
50 Contends (for)
53 Clément Marot poem "A ___ Damoyselle Malade"

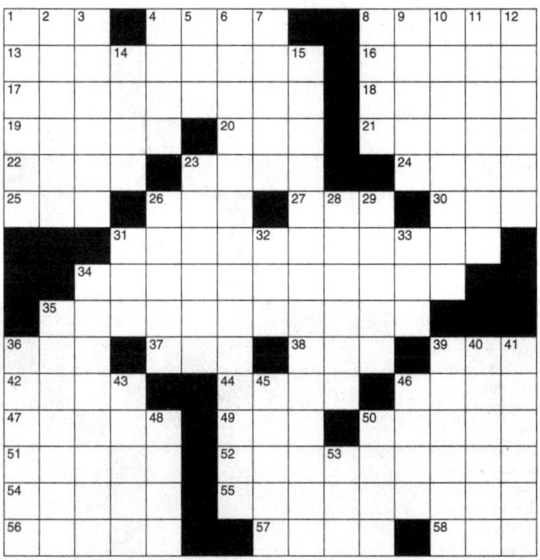

by Natan Last

104 HARD

ACROSS

1 Something that might be built around a police station
8 Hen tracks
15 Came aboard, in a way
16 Long-running Joel McHale show on E!
17 Not free
18 Seedy place
19 Bengali who won the 1913 Literature Nobel
20 Small glass disk used as an ornament in a stained-glass window
21 Melted munchie
22 Kind of bean
23 Follower of a team
24 Rear
25 Source of anago sushi
27 Golf units: Abbr.
28 Roughly half of all binary code
29 "Friendly staff" or "For a limited time only"
31 Swallowing worry in an old wives' tale
36 Potential libel defendant
37 Next ___
38 Latin trio leader
41 No-brainers?
42 Call from the lobby, perhaps
43 "Utopia" writer, 1516
45 "___ thou love me?": Juliet
46 Completely block
47 "The difference between ordinary and extraordinary," per Vladimir Horowitz
49 Steve Buscemi's role in "Reservoir Dogs"
50 Reveal
51 Triple-platinum Lady Gaga hit of 2011
52 Longtime fitness guru Jack
53 Keep close relations?
54 Part of a physical
55 Common dorm room decorations

DOWN

1 Words of explanation
2 Something sweet potatoes provide
3 Brightly colored marine fish
4 Three albums bound together, e.g.
5 Hero-worship, say
6 Jazz pianist Allison
7 Raid target
8 Forte
9 Directive in tennis after odd-numbered games
10 On a pension: Abbr.
11 Lent symbols
12 Unclear, as thinking
13 Put off guard
14 Blender settings
20 Goes without a leash
22 A child can have a blast with it
25 People ruled by an elective monarchy
26 ___ al Khaymah (one of U.A.E.'s seven emirates)
30 Isolate
32 Go head-to-head with?
33 Doctor's patient, e.g.
34 Create a tunnel beneath
35 "The Brady Bunch" bunch
38 Shot glass?
39 Béchamel sauce with Gruyère added
40 Font of knowledge
44 Brilliance
46 Easily outscores
48 What calisthenics improve
49 One up front?
51 High-pitched cry

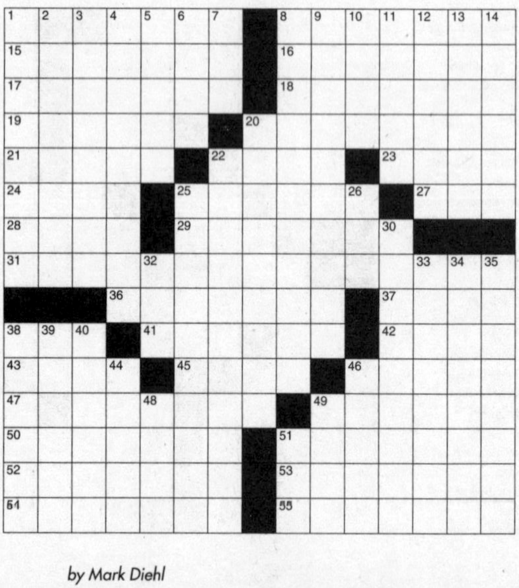

by Mark Diehl

ACROSS

1 Hit 1981 Broadway musical made into a 2006 film
11 Like five-star accommodations
15 Pet project for a 14-Down
16 Regarding
17 Acts in some rituals
18 Deal with a huge catch
19 One-named New Ager
20 One who might say "Brace yourself!," in brief?
21 "Don't ___!" (parental admonition)
22 Mag crowning a "Bachelor of the Year"
24 Plot element?
25 Bogus, to Brits
27 What Indiana University's superimposed "I" and "U" looks like
28 Sioux City-to-Fort Collins dir.
29 Place
30 Bounty work?
33 Scare
35 Treaty of Rome creation, for short
36 Find x, say
37 Aid in collecting evidence
40 It forms part of the Polish/German border
41 Burgundy season
42 Professional fixer
43 Hawkeye rival, briefly
45 Cheesemaking need
47 ___ Brava, Spain
48 Old Peloponnesian power
49 Label a bomb
50 "I'm at your disposal"
54 Slender
55 Desk accessory
57 Geological units
58 Make one's head spin?
59 Bit at the bottom
60 Hit 2005 Broadway musical made into a 2014 film

DOWN

1 Time to strike
2 First name in gossip
3 ___ Krenz, last Communist leader of East Germany
4 "Henry V" battle setting
5 Boris or Natasha, to Fearless Leader
6 Contract
7 Statement after a valiant attempt
8 Common concerto closer
9 Stock to be split?
10 Ceremonially gowned grp.
11 Meal, in Italy
12 Who wrote "There is no sin except stupidity"
13 Goes from the top
14 One with a lot to think about
21 23-Down travelers
23 See 21-Down
24 Old geographical inits.
25 Possibility considered after an air accident
26 Combustion contraption
27 Noted kidnappee of 1613
29 Slashed
31 Put in stitches
32 Guessed
34 Romeo's repertoire
38 What a birdie flies over
39 Take all the dishes from
44 Solid
46 Request to leave out for takeout?
47 Bring all the dishes to
49 Father of the mariée
51 Cosmetician Laszlo
52 Gray of R&B
53 Things opened in the morning
55 "All the way with ___" ('64 slogan)
56 Scratch

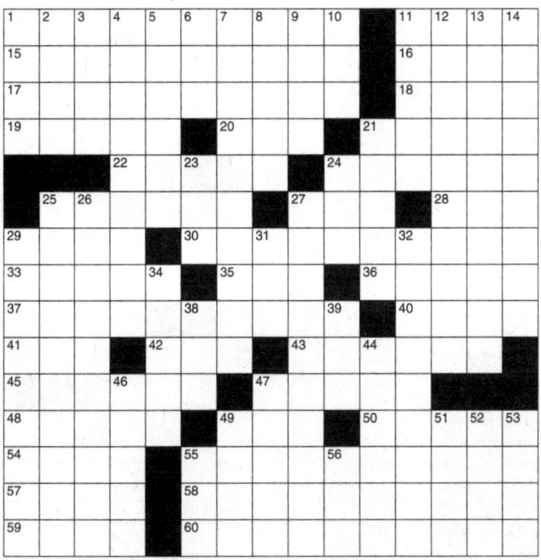

by Peter A. Collins

106 HARD

ACROSS

1 Center of a defense
16 One saying "We can do it!"
17 Bavarian region that the Danube passes through
18 Brunch treat with egg and potatoes
19 Girl's name that becomes a contraction when its first and last letters are switched
20 "Yes, ___"
21 It goes with the flow
22 Caps preceder
23 What's what in Italy?
26 Org. that tracks baby name popularity
28 Briny
29 Give a dirty look
32 Menu promise
34 Contacts in an emergency
37 Subject of a museum in Richmond, Va., for short
40 Things a bartender strains to make
43 Hush-hush org.
44 Hush-hush org.
47 Rural call
48 Actress Benaderet who voiced Betty Rubble
50 Take up and hold, chemically
52 "Sick"
54 Raise the volume?
55 Teddy, e.g.
60 Was completely honest
61 Explain further
62 Some support for local schools

DOWN

1 Has faith
2 Busy
3 Wikipedia option
4 College near Albany, N.Y.
5 Yesterday, in Italy
6 Line of additives
7 Ruler's title from which the word "chess" is derived
8 Ultimate object, to Aristotle
9 Popular cologne that shares its name with a literary character
10 Chemistry concentrations
11 "___ is whatever distracts": Kafka
12 Founder of Egypt's first dynasty
13 Belief in a strong central government
14 Irks
15 Marker in the woods
23 Run
24 Malediction
25 Opposite of fast
27 Santa ___
30 Two semesters abroad, maybe
31 Boy's name repeated in a nursery rhyme
33 ___ whim
35 Wunderbar
36 Cadenza maker
37 Stores on a farm
38 Not voiced, as the first "d" in "Wednesday"
39 Bach piece
41 Like Catalonia
42 Relating to the moon
45 Ex ___ (as a favor, in law)
46 Ones getting passed in a race
49 Alternative form of a gene
51 European hotel fixture
53 Inroads
54 Conference site
56 Stick fast
57 What's yours in Montréal?
58 Condoleezza Rice and Martin Luther King Jr., for two
59 "2012" actress Amanda

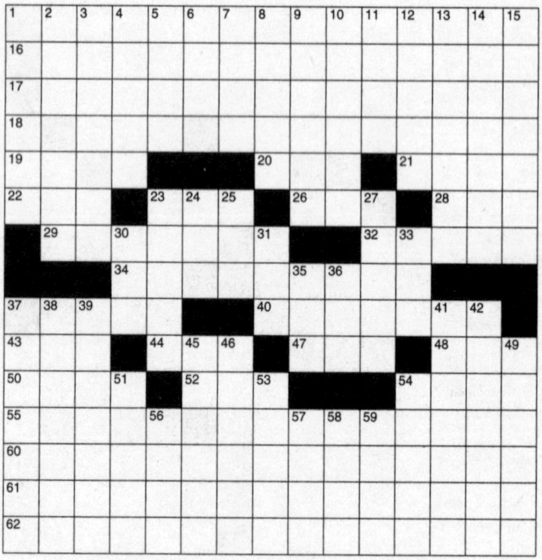

by Jason Flinn

HARD 107

ACROSS
1 Little man
5 Less likely to be caught
15 Dueler's option
16 Washington city famous for its sweet onions
17 Virginia and Truckee Railroad terminus
18 Grave words
19 Keeps from backing up
21 Disappointed outburst
22 Spring's opposite
23 Number of letters
27 Women who might share the same surname
30 Net game?
31 Pet sound
34 Administrative title
35 Man in black, perhaps
36 Novelist Jaffe
37 Dimwit
38 Rule of order?
40 Lincoln signed it into law in 1862
41 Like some deliveries
43 "I forbid," to Caesar
44 ___ Sea (the "Sea of Islands")
45 Collections of episodes
48 Cab supplier
53 Part of a pod
54 Chlorofluorocarbons damage it
55 Vassal's reward
56 Shot blockers
57 Lose vividness

DOWN
1 Major quinoa exporter
2 Boot hills?
3 Carol king
4 Taxonomic terms, for instance
5 Big gulp
6 Tropical acquisitions, maybe
7 Classic vineyard tree
8 Cask beverage
9 Fly the coop
10 Smallest prime
11 School attended by Churchill
12 Old war story
13 Give a lift to
14 Merlin Olsen's team
20 Pro-am tourney, often
23 "Der Judenstaat" movement
24 Laser alternative
25 What parents might prompt kids to say
26 Exec's perk
27 Tom Collins ingredient
28 Handle again?
29 Eight-footer?
31 Suspensions of activity
32 Nestled
33 Steam engine pioneer James
36 Leaves, as in a western
38 Multiplicity
39 Broad bean
40 Mount St. ___
41 Won thing
42 Talked ad nauseam
44 Not on base?
45 Future reporter
46 Needs to make a retraction
47 On base
49 Dry, on Champagne bottles
50 "Rockaria!" band, briefly
51 Place to go, for short
52 Strong base

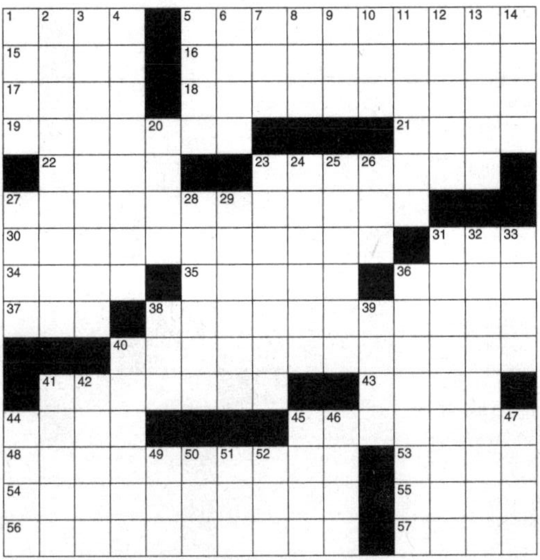

by Patrick Berry

108 HARD

ACROSS

1 Drop-in shot?
10 Button-down
15 Emmy-winning sitcom actor of 1974 and '78
16 Reading volume
17 Twinings product
18 Some voices
19 Highest peak in the Philippines: Abbr.
20 Locale of the Falkland Isls.
21 Exercise position that strengthens the abs
22 Sessions of Congress
23 Like a Grand Inquisitor
25 Force in W.W. I and II
26 ___ jolie
27 Something paid by a hypocrite
30 Sickly sweet sentiment
31 Spurn
32 Personal problems
36 Breaks one's word?
37 Got less dense
39 Prefix with design
40 Kind of team
42 It may be quarter-sized
46 Mean fig.
47 Cone filler
48 It has a solo near the end of "An American in Paris"
49 Swallows things?
52 What nobody can stand to make?
53 Like some unwanted deposits
54 Bobby who wrote "Route 66"
55 At the beginning
57 Soft and flexible
58 She played Natasha in 2000's "The Adventures of Rocky and Bullwinkle"
59 Skirts
60 Stress test apparatus

DOWN

1 Cause
2 Schnoz
3 Shaped like Saturn
4 Recurrent themes
5 Vintner's prefix
6 Really important
7 It's superior to Superior
8 Rendezvous
9 Unsupported?
10 Come-on comeuppance
11 One holding notes
12 "You go, sister!"
13 Wryly amusing
14 Stationery store stock
23 Sales specialists
24 You can't focus when this is on
28 Lost wheels, maybe
29 Flight pattern
30 Something passed down the line
32 "No-o-o-o!"
33 Had a chilling effect?
34 Monotonous
35 Lufthansa connection?
38 Herald
39 Activity for running mates?
41 FedEx employee, at times
42 Center of a square, maybe
43 Allan-a-Dale, e.g.
44 Dense
45 Julie with two Tonys for "The Lion King"
50 Swagger, slangily
51 1974 film with three stars in its title
53 Toothbrush or mattress specification
56 Sci-fi character who takes the red pill rather than the blue one

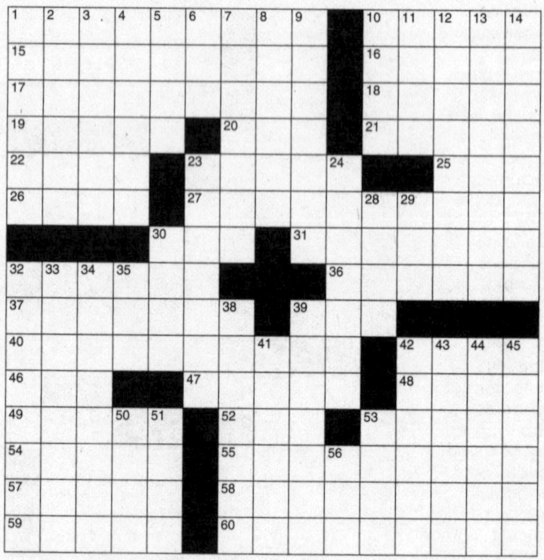

by Sean Dobbin

ACROSS

1 Viking girl in "How to Train Your Dragon"
7 Intimates
13 Comics tyke
15 Starling of book and film
16 Epic number
18 So-called "fifth qtrs."
19 Postwar German nickname
20 Kenan's sitcom partner
21 Next
23 Irrelevant info
24 Trinidad o Tobago
25 Shot putters' needs?
26 Squash
27 Unleashes (on)
28 Its main characters go to hell
31 ___ Green, 2006 Bond girl
32 Chris who sang "The Road to Hell," 1989
33 Tools with swiveling blades
40 Directed
41 Fantasy sports option
42 Like some additions and editions
44 With 36-Down, bit of clothes mending
45 Like drafts
46 Emphatic type: Abbr.
47 Lance on a bench
48 Snowflake or crystal shape
50 Outer limit
51 Functioning again
54 Like Charlie Brown's kite, ultimately
55 Large game bass
56 Great-aunt in "David Copperfield"
57 Saws

DOWN

1 Dandy wear
2 Enveloped
3 Byzantine art bit
4 Pensioned: Abbr.
5 Light music source?
6 Appealing figure?
7 Rice elbows, e.g.
8 Facility
9 Lilt bit
10 Registers
11 Big name in car parts
12 Automotive models S and X
14 For three, to Frédéric
15 Chuck who advised Nixon
17 French-speaking land where John James Audubon was born
22 Fashion designer Lepore
24 Bar-Ilan University student, e.g.
29 Power inits. beginning in 1933
30 "An ___ held by the tail is not yet caught" (old proverb)
33 It's named for its five carbon atoms
34 Old sandlot game
35 Baroque
36 See 44-Across
37 Internet hookups?
38 Fairly clean, so to speak
39 Comic book writer with a National Medal of Arts
40 Winter wear resembling overalls
43 Graybeards
48 Boot
49 Add superfluous stuff to
52 Some chess pieces: Abbr.
53 Period of veinticuatro horas

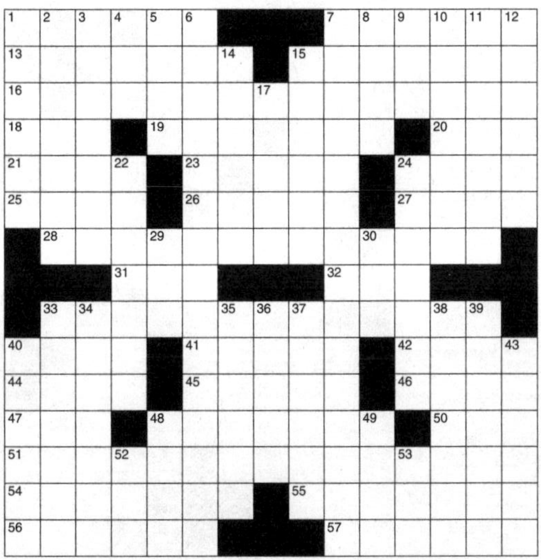

by Paula Gamache

110 HARD

ACROSS

1 "This is the life!"
8 Realize
11 Canal problems?
13 Like some plane exits
14 It keeps things on track
16 Rightmost column of the periodic table, e.g.
17 French pronoun
18 Supply-side policies tied to a political era
20 ___ bath
22 "Ish"
23 Corner
25 Old things that are new again
26 Not given, say
28 Surround
29 Instruction in many a steak recipe
31 Vasco da ___
32 Shipping platform
34 San ___
36 Real-life New York hospital sometimes seen on "Law & Order: SVU"
38 ___ Stark, half brother of Jon Snow on "Game of Thrones"
40 Subway car during rush hour, seemingly
42 Check
44 Marvel superhero
46 Beam
47 Squeezing
48 "Wheel of Fortune" penalty
50 Mythological subject for Leonardo, Correggio and Rubens
51 "Oh, that's brilliant!"
52 Tax
53 Sawbucks

DOWN

1 Shield decorated with the head of a Gorgon
2 Take to the police station
3 British port from which John Cabot sailed to the New World in 1497
4 "There's a good ___"
5 Decorator with good taste?
6 Donkey's mate
7 Salty gulp
8 "Absolutely out of the question!"
9 Pitches
10 Wife in John le Carré's "The Constant Gardener"
12 John Hancock, notably
13 Snack brand since 1975
15 Freight
16 Very light, delicate material
19 Sprint Cup awarder
21 Player of a green alien in "Guardians of the Galaxy" and a blue alien in "Avatar"
24 Passing sounds?
27 Actors, to agents
30 Climax of a TV makeover
32 Betrayal
33 City called "The Old Pueblo"
35 Become noticeable in an unpleasant way
36 Carnival person
37 Falls flat on one's face
39 Word with standard or water
40 Great Lakes fish
41 Certain heiress
43 Repetitive sorts
45 French city once held by William the Conqueror
49 Big natural resource in Malaysia

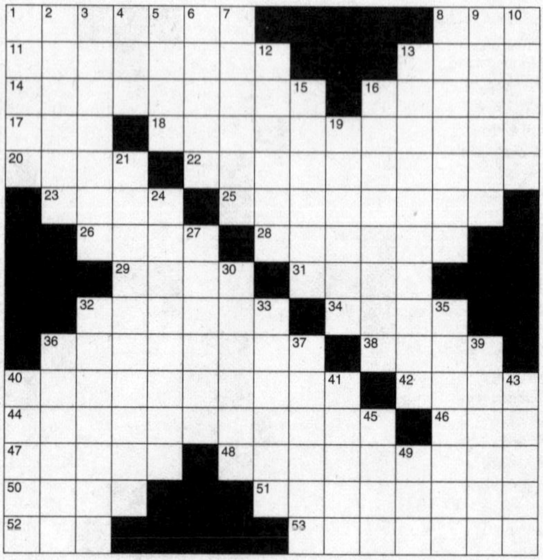

by Kameron Austin Collins

ACROSS

1 Shout when there's no cause for alarm?
5 2008 R&B Grammy winner for "Growing Pains"
10 Throw
14 Little opening?
15 Peripheral
16 Like many flu sufferers
17 Taking some heat?
19 Heat meas. that also names a major L.A. TV station
20 Request at a ticket window
21 Really get to
22 Bit of vaquero gear
23 Product boasting "a unique blend of 23 flavors"
25 Dungeons & Dragons race
26 University of Cincinnati squad
27 Replies from con men?
28 Norman who wrote "A River Runs Through It"
29 Smidge
30 Resident
31 Ed promoter
34 Green-glazed Chinese porcelain
35 Attorney general under Bush 41
36 Not fit for Passover
38 "Miss Julie" composer
39 Like literati
40 Networking aid
41 Opposite of division
42 It's similar to pale lager
44 Going ___
45 Possible purse pooches
46 Provide design details for
47 Comparatively corrupt
48 Send packing
49 "One World" musician John
50 Mancala playing piece
51 Fiddle (with)

DOWN

1 Full of sauce
2 The Ainapo Trail is on its slope
3 Rattled
4 Entrees from the frozen food department
5 Lisa of "The Cosby Show"
6 Selene's Roman counterpart
7 Relative of "Without a doubt" in a Magic 8 Ball
8 Powerful foe of the Man of Steel
9 Watt-second fraction
10 Battery container?
11 Come to terms with
12 They often follow showers
13 Shortest-serving U.S. vice president (31 days)
18 Interjection of dejection
21 Tart flavor
24 Primp
26 Vehicle that's loaded in a Harry Belafonte hit
28 Highlight for some hockey fans
30 For-profit university with dozens of U.S. campuses
31 What a reverse stock split increases
32 Like much of northern Siberia
33 Chair pair
34 Prestigious Pasadena institution
35 A rut often leads to it
36 Delaware Valley tribe
37 Groups of power brokers
38 Change
39 Oktoberfest fare
40 Embarrassing sound in a lecture hall
43 Start for seas or seasons
45 Atlanta-based media inits.

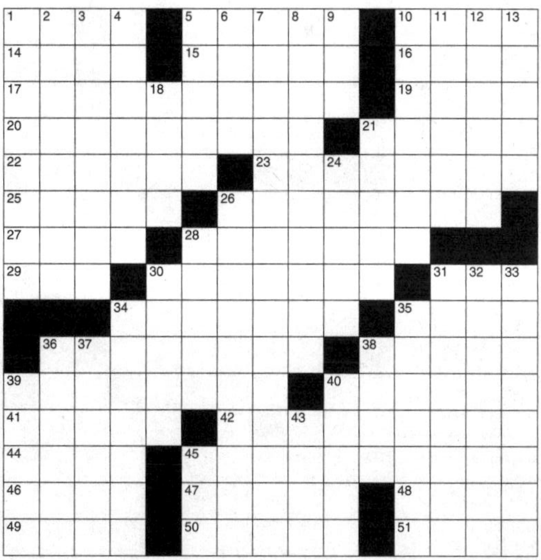

by David Phillips

112 HARD

ACROSS

1 One of a trio in a children's story
9 Bar order after a very hard day, maybe
15 Lacking any sides
16 Puffin relative
17 Haggard
18 Prize at the top of a maypole
19 Mixing and matching?
21 Start of many a dance routine
22 Suffix with market
23 Large fern
25 Renegade and Renaissance, to the Secret Service
29 Things bench players need?
30 Pandemonium
31 Sackers in the sack of Rome, A.D. 410
34 Think tank, e.g.: Abbr.
35 Spent
36 Hotel amenity
37 Treats as in "South Park" or "Doonesbury"
39 Drift
40 During
41 Viciously criticizes, informally
42 Clothing company whose mail-order catalog debuted in 1905
44 It lacks letters on a telephone keypad
45 ___ cannon (sci-fi weapon)
46 Trattoria entree
52 Saggy and crinkled
54 Following the beat?
55 Fidelity competitor
56 Toddler's handful
57 Spy group
58 Green-light

DOWN

1 Traps and yaps
2 Like some rabbit ears
3 Certain dam
4 Worrisome marks in high school?
5 Source of buyer's remorse
6 Whittles away
7 Battling
8 Torn
9 Huge stock purchase at the start of a day's trading
10 Shorts popular in the 1920s and '30s
11 It might be picked for a song
12 "The Great" magician whose signature trick was the "floating light bulb"
13 River of myth where one drinks to forget
14 ___ Edwards, John Wayne's role in "The Searchers," 1956
20 Birds in hieroglyphics
24 Cask maker
25 Eastern ties
26 Eric of "Hulk"
27 Dry sorts
28 What isn't working?
29 Lab vessel
31 Hungarian hunting dog
32 Tough
33 Some photog purchases
35 Innocent
38 Ancient collection of Sanskrit hymns
39 Rehabilitative effort
41 Quick
42 Dog command
43 ___-Novo (capital on the Gulf of Guinea)
44 "___ cum pretio" ("Everything has its price")
47 Parenthetical figure, often
48 Hot compress target, perhaps
49 Parenthetical figures?
50 Vulgarian
51 Brand with a Gravy Cravers line
53 Announcement carriers, for short

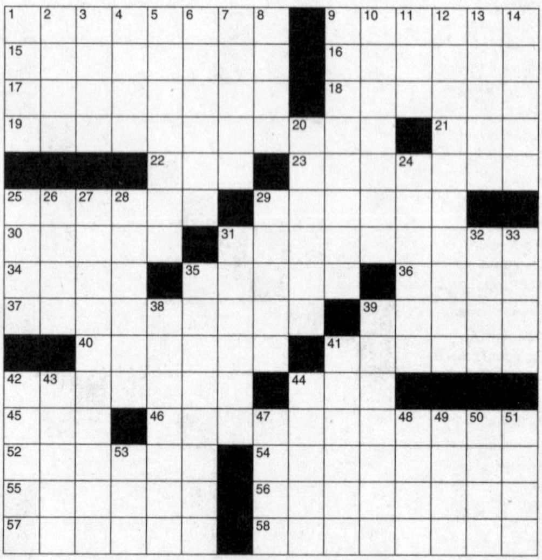

by Samuel A. Donaldson and Brad Wilber

ACROSS
1 Stare in astonishment
5 Horatian or Keatsian
9 Clean freak of sitcomdom
14 Long
15 Dance that might give you a lift?
16 Campbell on a catwalk
17 Setting for fans
20 Fortune 100 company whose name starts with a silent letter
21 Part of le Parlement français
22 Judgmental sound
23 Chicago exchange, in brief
25 First name on a B-29
27 Jonathan Swift satire
33 Dent or crack
34 Frank narrative
35 Balloon-carried probe
36 Prior: Abbr.
38 Circumvent
40 Zip
41 System in which 33 and 63 are "!" and "?"
43 Southern alma mater of Newt Gingrich
45 Category
46 Actress who starred in "The Fault in Our Stars," 2014
49 Snack brand since 1967
50 Luau staples, for short
51 Threepio's first master
53 Some cat sounds?
56 Certain absentee voter, for short
59 2012 Best Actress nominee for "Zero Dark Thirty"
62 Opposite of afore
63 With 67-Across, attachment to a string instrument
64 Shade similar to camel
65 Classic car company co-founder
66 City on der Rhein
67 See 63-Across

DOWN
1 Mad
2 Plot piece
3 Question upon completing an argument
4 Like many farm animals
5 Sister brand of Alpha-Bits
6 Sleuths connect them
7 "Of wrath," in a hymn title
8 John Steinbeck novel
9 De-clogs
10 Shetlands turndown
11 Crawl
12 They might work at a revival, for short
13 Chance
18 Took a 13-Down
19 "Hawaii Five-O" nickname
24 Collectors of DNA, prints, etc.
26 Avian symbol of Ontario
27 Grp. behind the Oscars
28 Reed section?
29 Nonplussed
30 Amazon offering
31 Nonplus
32 Unsafe, as a boat
37 Number on a grandfather clock
39 Drop ___
42 "It's probably a trick, but tell me"
44 They join teams
47 Wire transfer?: Abbr.
48 Role for which Michael C. Hall got five straight Emmy nominations
51 Cracked
52 Mount near the Dead Sea
54 37-Down, to Diego
55 Doctor seen by millions
57 Hauteur
58 Hardware bit
60 U.S. Army E-7
61 "___ Vickers," Sinclair Lewis novel

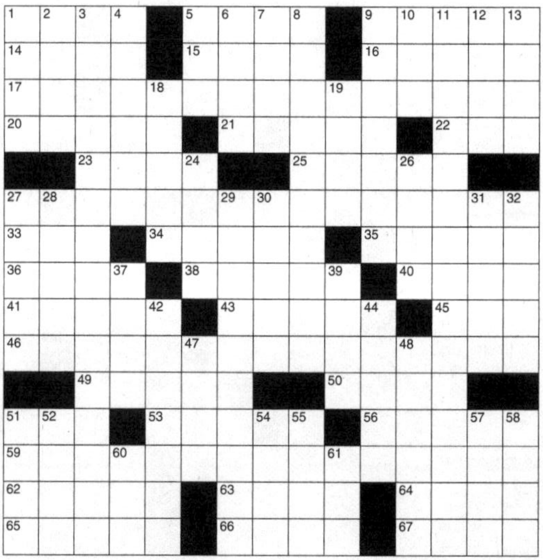

by Mary Lou Guizzo

114 HARD

ACROSS
1 Make look old, in a way
9 Whiz at multiplication?
15 Nail
16 Nail, e.g.
17 Subject of the 2015 film "Sicario"
18 Relative of Rex
19 Stopover point
20 So-called "Commander of the Faithful"
21 Net support
22 Text qualifier
23 "Success is counted sweetest / By those who ___ succeed": Emily Dickinson
25 Duran Duran frontman Simon
27 Fast-talking
28 Five-time N.B.A. All-Star Pau ___
30 Top class: Abbr.
31 Clipper features
32 It may be held at arm's length
35 Ubiquitous label
36 Couple of star-crossed lovers?
37 Name of eight counties in the central and eastern U.S.
38 What some pockets are filled with
39 W.W. I battle site at which the tank was introduced
43 Spots to hide?
44 Fix
46 Deicing formula
47 Pitch
48 Big name in headphones
49 Pretentious query
51 Battery device?
52 2004 film with the tagline "One man saw it coming"
54 Friendly query
56 Rises
57 "Apparently I snore so loudly that it scares everybody in the car I'm driving," e.g.
58 Piano
59 Locale of the ancient kingdom of Navarre

DOWN
1 Summer job?
2 Lens cover
3 Its icon contains a pair of quavers
4 Follow closely
5 About 60% of a tot's body, to a tot
6 Even a smidgen
7 Pilot's opposite
8 Drones and such
9 ___ Square, center of Tel Aviv
10 Smidgen
11 Cousin of FYI
12 Transept setting
13 Low-fat dessert
14 Pounds
21 "The Bachelor" high point
24 Cash in the music business
26 "You want to fight?!"
27 Prepares to pass, perhaps
29 Natural projection
31 Places to wallow
33 Redolent ring
34 Unlikely to make advances
35 Clear auto option
36 Swiss treaty city
37 Dyes with wax
40 Kind of biology
41 Big name in computer security
42 Kindergarten brand
44 Like craft fairs
45 Shell occupant
48 Filmdom's Chucky, for one
50 Man, but not woman
53 Counter letters
54 Small vault
55 Mao colleague ___ Biao

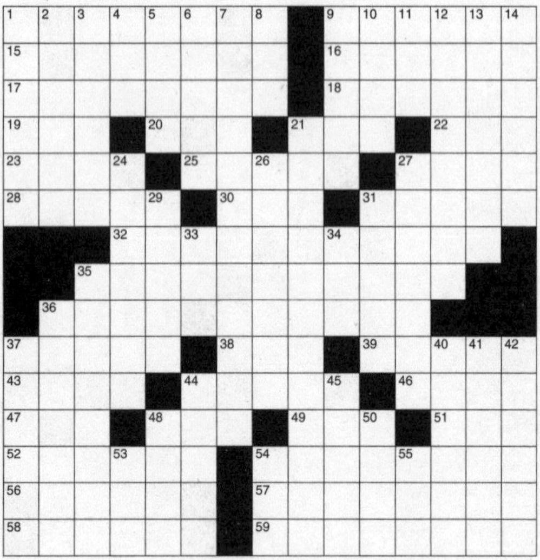

by David Steinberg

ACROSS

1 One inclined to patronize a farmer's market
9 Cetacean's closest relative
14 Ready for a road trip, say
15 Old epic recounting wanderings
16 Ones who don't take a seat?
17 With precision
18 Reply of feigned surprise
19 It leads to early advancement
20 Bombshell
21 Longtime Princess Royal
23 Bega with the hit "Mambo No. 5"
24 "Wrath of the Titans" antagonist
25 Region around a star "just right" for habitable planets
30 Like some jet refuelings
31 "Sometimes a Great Notion" novelist, 1964
32 Puerto Rico is on it year-round, for short
35 Little bit
36 Subject of a museum in Louisville, Ky.
38 24/7/365 facilities
39 Alternative to chinos
41 Moving like 43-Down
44 Have a bawl
48 Words of confidence
49 "I knew a man Bojangles and ___ dance for you . . ." (1968 song lyric)
50 They're not refined
52 Naval hero with five U.S. counties named for him
54 Asset in climbing the corp. ladder
57 Big ___
58 Means of getting the word out?
59 When many fans come out
61 Beverage brand with three leaves in its logo
62 Used car selling point
63 Long hoops shots
64 Presenter of many listicles

DOWN

1 A baby one is called a cria
2 Major Taiwanese export
3 House of cards?
4 Bother
5 Hop, skip or jump
6 Jazz singer whose surname came from pig Latin
7 Tolkien character
8 They're longer than singles, briefly
9 Give attention
10 Flabbergasted
11 Appropriately named Reds legend
12 Brew named for a Czech city
13 Long, trying trips
15 Aimée of film
20 "Knock yourself out"
22 Cabinetry material
23 Rule, in Rennes
26 Possible response to "Huh-uh!"
27 Mount with the Cave of Zeus
28 September honoree
29 Potato ___
32 The discovery of penicillin, e.g.
33 Casting director?
34 Act the judge
37 Cover for someone, say
40 Bourbons, e.g.
42 Time magazine's "scholarly Everest," for short
43 Oil or honey
45 2009 and '13 sci-fi role for Zoë Saldana
46 Refined
47 Boob tube
51 Bergen dummy
53 Butt end?
54 Where to look for starters
55 "Love Is Just a Four-Letter Word" singer
56 Complete
59 Play ___ (be disruptive)
60 Conservation org. with a panda logo

by Brandon Hensley

116 HARD

ACROSS

1 "Yes, I already know her"
6 Put off
10 Foundation piece
14 Neocon's target of derision
16 Prepare for a later showing, maybe
17 Buttinsky
18 Major name in cards
19 Satisfied
20 Pro sports figures
22 Pumas alternative
23 Wavy fabric pattern
26 Got into a stew?
27 Part of STEM, for short
28 [All of a sudden!]
29 Major in the future, perhaps
31 Broke down, in a way
34 Charm City landmark
35 Arbiter of 1980s TV
36 Gardens of Babur city
37 Hectically
38 Mountains have grown over them
42 Well-connected people
43 One dealing in space and time
45 Setting for Ansel Adams
46 Tony Blair's period as British P.M., e.g.
48 Critical assignment
49 Gorge oneself with, facetiously
50 Quaff at the Three Broomsticks inn
54 Wipe the floor with
55 "Something seems off . . ."
56 Legend of climbing expeditions
57 "The ability to describe others as they see themselves," per Lincoln
58 Possible "OMG!" follow-up

DOWN

1 Beats someone in
2 Develop
3 "Navicella" at St. Peter's, for one
4 "Love of My Life (An Ode to Hip Hop)" Grammy winner
5 B and O, e.g.
6 In the pros?
7 Aviary cry
8 One of two slices of pizza?
9 Miss, e.g.
10 Van Gundy of the N.B.A.
11 Sweet, tangy drinks
12 Directed elsewhere
13 Complete works, maybe
15 Modicum
21 Clichéd company slogan
23 Attacked
24 Something Rihanna and Madonna each have
25 "I Wanna Be Your Dog" vocalist
28 Warn of
30 Browser feature
32 "Good to hear"
33 Malodorous
34 One with the motto "Do Your Best"
35 Woman of mystery?
36 Noted jazz trombonist's nickname
39 Some pups
40 Negotiation's terse conclusion
41 Like many convertibles
44 Gas pump option
45 Puts away, as a banner
47 Set against
48 Krusty's sidekick on "The Simpsons"
51 "Royal Pains" network
52 Showtime affiliate
53 Occasion for gifting red envelopes

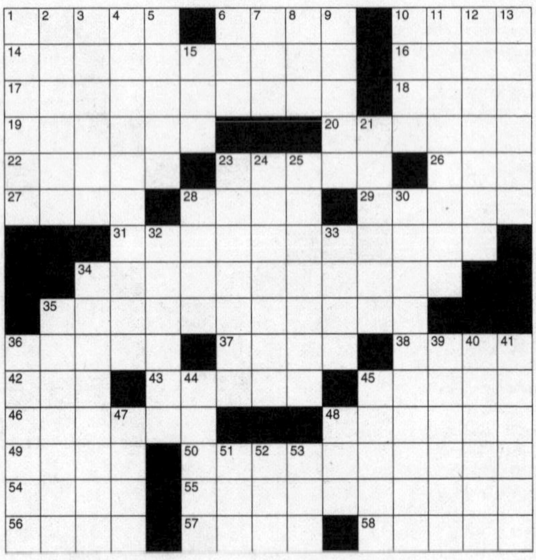

by Peter Wentz

ACROSS
1 Order
5 ___ palm
9 It's made with syrup
13 Town near Ireland's Shannon Airport
15 A caller may be on this
16 Track type
17 & 18 Italian-born composer
19 Something a scow lacks
20 It's often hooked
21 Carlos the Jackal, for one
23 Start of a Beatles refrain
25 Eastern titles
26 ___ loss
27 Bars in cars
29 "A ___ champion never handled sword": "Henry VI, Part I"
31 "Understood"
33 Danny's love in "Ocean's Eleven"
34 & 35 German-born composer
38 Man's name that spells a fruit backward
41 Class lists?
44 Takes one's sweet time
48 Kind of car or class
50 2014 Oscar winner for Best Foreign Language Film
51 Space cadet's need?
53 Prompt
54 His first tweet ended "I bless all of you from my heart"
57 What the lowing herd wind slowly o'er, in verse
58 For the calorie-conscious
59 & 60 Austrian-born composer
61 N.B.A. coach Spoelstra
62 Put on
63 Spiny shrub
64 Without
65 Ligurian Sea feeder
66 North Sea feeder

DOWN
1 "Austin Powers" villain
2 Out of this world?
3 Longtime grandmotherly "General Hospital" actress
4 Short-beaked bird
5 "Aren't you forgetting something?"
6 Jumble behind a computer desk
7 Hazel relatives
8 "Cool, man!"
9 Popular 9-Across
10 Gorged
11 Shakespeare character who says "I dare damnation"
12 Paying close attention
14 Retirement party, e.g.
18 Without
22 Tour grp.
24 "Happy Days" malt shop owner
28 File certain papers
30 "View From the U.N." memoirist
32 Hosp. staffers
35 Cry that's often doubled
36 Place for a bust
37 Doubling up?
38 Food
39 Port alternative
40 "Sign me up!"
42 Heating equipment
43 Put completely (in)
45 TV option, for short
46 Engineer Gray who co-founded Western Electric
47 Aid
49 Shepard's role in "The Right Stuff"
52 ___ Allen Express (Amtrak train in the Northeast)
55 Horror movie sounds
56 Letter ender
60 "Whew!"

by Jacob Stulberg

118 HARD

ACROSS

1 Lives the dream
10 Taken alone
15 It has you covered
16 Longtime comic strip queen
17 Single-speed two-wheeler
18 Hip-hop artist Kendrick ___
19 Basket weave?
20 Still in the box, perhaps
21 It may cover all the bases
22 Audio engineer's concern
24 Taco stand add-on, in brief
26 Salt sack?
27 Teflon, e.g.
29 The way it is
31 Alley-oop starter
33 Screw feature
34 Old TV channel that aired XFL games
35 People's Sexiest Man Alive of 2001
39 Language in which "thank you" is "grazzi"
41 Ruling body?
42 Homer's "bulwark of the Achaeans"
44 Girl's name that sounds like a letter
45 Facebook-checking fixation, e.g.
48 Come back
52 Approach
53 List in a 36-Down: Abbr.
55 Part of many an emoticon
56 Stamped
57 Cultivation aids
59 Wax source
60 Rotten
62 Half-wits
64 Master of the King's Music under George V
65 Cry after "Freeze!" on a 1980s TV show
66 Loses momentum
67 Proverbial tools for wrongdoing

DOWN

1 Defendant in a 1963 obscenity trial
2 Severally
3 Pie wedges in Trivial Pursuit, e.g.
4 Tyrant Amin
5 Be thick (with)
6 Hotshot
7 Third grade?
8 Orders
9 Sri Lanka-to-Singapore dir.
10 Hang (around)
11 Lifts a lot
12 "All Quiet on the Western Front" novelist
13 Brand-new outfits
14 Bit of Secret Service gear
23 Gallery fill
25 Chill, so to speak
26 Murder mystery staple
28 Little-known
30 Vile sort
32 ___ Fresh (Tex-Mex chain)
35 What toothpaste goes on
36 Lessor's log
37 "Run along now!"
38 Babe watcher, maybe
40 Many an Instagram user
43 ___ process (sternum part)
46 Bit from "Poor Richard's Almanack"
47 Like many Second Viennese School works
49 Posthumous Rock and Roll Hall of Fame inductee of 2014
50 Bargain bin buy at a record store
51 Big Cup brand
54 Dreaded classroom note
58 ___-poo (designer dog)
61 Alumni data: Abbr.
62 Fitness mag stat
63 Stowe heroine

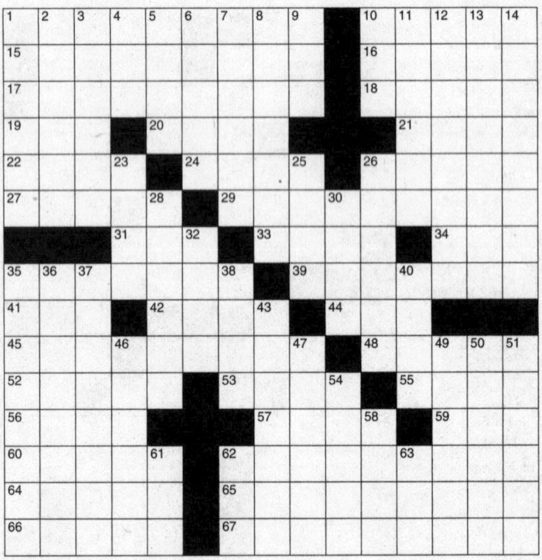

by James Mulhern

HARD 119

ACROSS

1 1991 Scorsese/De Niro collaboration
9 Something exciting to play with
15 Fragile fabric made from certain plant fibers
16 Tough leather
17 Amscrayed
18 One getting lots of take-out orders?
19 Edward VII or VIII, in India: Abbr.
20 ___ nullius (no one's property)
21 Pioneering labor leader Samuel
22 Was suddenly successful
24 Nullius ___ (of no legal force)
25 Like NSFW links
26 Kennedy and Bush 41, but no other U.S. presidents
28 Chuck
29 "Mum's the word"
31 Little, in Lockerbie
32 Cross collections, e.g.
33 Roughneck's workplace
35 It's in the far northwest
37 Product of Greek culture?
38 Moderately dry
39 True
40 Splitting words
41 "Mr. ___" (Styx hit)
42 Blow hole?
45 Winner's prize on "RuPaul's Drag U"
46 Gap fillers, of sorts
47 "My response was . . . ," informally
48 "Grey's Anatomy" actress with five straight Emmy nominations
50 Hands on deck
51 Hand wringer's cry
52 Flip
53 Bridge tolls, e.g.

DOWN

1 They might spook spelunkers
2 Where the San Antonio Spurs used to play
3 Blowhard
4 Job ad inits.
5 Broccoli bit
6 Like pain after treatment, often
7 Nails
8 Stop sign?
9 Unwanted attention
10 Checks out
11 Adds with a whisk
12 Makeshift coaster, maybe
13 Reason to hold your nose
14 Gen ___ (millennials)
21 Yellow-flowered plant producing a sticky resin
23 Chicago Fire's sports org.
24 Noisy recreation vehicles
26 Blanket
27 "Uh-huh, I believe THAT"
29 "Hold your horses"
30 Forgo a night out
32 His wife and sons were Depression-era criminals
34 Couple taken out on a rainy day
36 2/2, to Toscanini
37 Key-ring ornament
39 Demolition cleanup machine
41 ___ Barber, five-time Pro Bowler from the Tampa Bay Buccaneers
42 Like some legal decrees
43 Owl's hoot, to some
44 Pomeranian, e.g.
45 Cross words
48 Trifle
49 Org. in the gulf war's Operation Granby

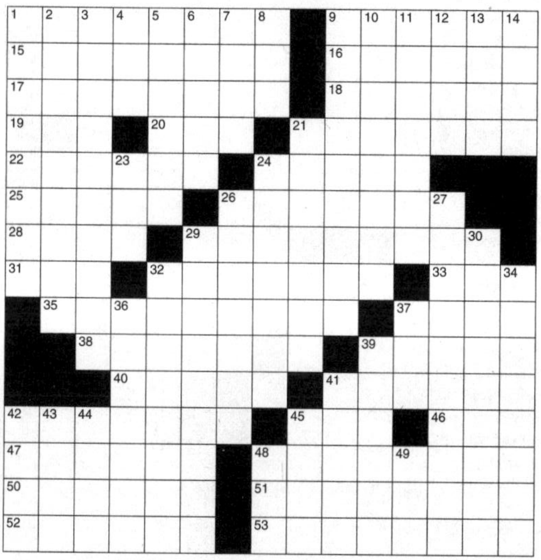

by Paula Gamache

120 HARD

ACROSS

1 Anchor line
11 Dinner serving in the Prodigal Son parable
15 Be set
16 Stick in the refrigerator
17 Without stopping
18 Trade rights, say
19 Hunger
20 Granted access
21 Up to the ___
22 Dwarf planet discovered in 2005
24 Bit of vaquero gear
26 Hunger
27 Gets back (to)
29 Will with parts
31 Infant's attachment?
32 Aural "OMG!"
34 "Child's play!"
36 Concoct
40 Shows aging, in a way
41 Many a Rolling Stone cover subject
43 Senate greeting
44 Online qualification
45 Set in motion
47 Expect
51 Servings with tandoori chicken
53 Did a farrier's work on
55 ___ wave
56 Tough problem
57 It "hath put a spirit of youth in every thing," per Shakespeare
59 Something a U.P.S. driver has: Abbr.
60 ___ Valley, Calif.
61 Book with profiles of many famous people?
63 Shadow
64 Coco Chanel, par exemple
65 Historically
66 Words before crashing?

DOWN

1 "Casey at the Bat" writer
2 No fans
3 Czar known for his mental instability
4 Frites seasoning
5 Hill climber of note
6 Say
7 Does in
8 Florida community with a portmanteau name
9 What makes you you
10 Bomberman console, briefly
11 ___ Brava (Spanish resort area)
12 "Ocean's Thirteen" co-star
13 Dog checker?
14 Permanently
23 Dog command
25 Confounded
28 Rigs
30 Crumbly Mideastern dessert
33 "Mad props!"
35 A host
36 Toasts
37 Language in which "hello" is "buna ziua"
38 Like some forecasts
39 Virginia tribe
42 One spotted in tall grass
46 Base of a follicle
48 Website for budget travelers
49 Connected (with)
50 Crawled (with)
52 Metro entrance
54 Sponge
58 Product from une vache
61 Beautician employer
62 "The Wolf of Wall Street" star, familiarly

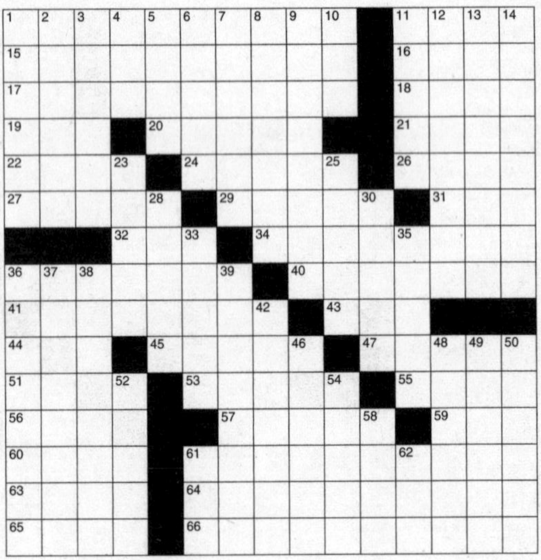

by Julian Lim

ACROSS

1 King or queen
4 Record six-time N.B.A. M.V.P.
15 Northeast sch. in the Liberty League
16 Rather caricatured
17 Understanding responses
18 One involved in a pyramid scheme?
19 Broke down, say
21 End of a Hemingway title
22 Fleck on the banjo
23 Atlanta train system
25 Drink often served chilled
27 Bert's sister in children's literature
28 Dandy headpieces
31 Catch
33 Excessively harsh
35 Philadelphia train system
39 Trio in Greek myth
40 New Deal org.
41 Pope John Paul II's first name
42 Was out
43 Aida in "Aida," e.g.
45 Go preceder
47 Unsightly spots
48 Country music's ___ Brown Band
51 Digs
53 Early customer of Boeing
54 Old Testament kingdom
56 Like the cities Yazd and Shiraz
59 Transport method usually used in the winter
61 One who can see right through you?
64 Author Chinua Achebe, by birth
65 Back-to-back hits
66 "Kate Plus 8" airer
67 Harmless slitherer
68 See 63-Down

DOWN

1 Something that's knitted
2 Here today, gone tomorrow
3 Quite different
4 Latin grammar case: Abbr.
5 Country with the King Hamad Highway
6 Trio abroad
7 Shoshone relatives
8 Player of Cleopatra in "Two Nights With Cleopatra"
9 Who had a #1 hit with "Toot Toot Tootsie (Goo'bye)"
10 Suffix with meth-
11 Spill everything
12 Politico with the 2007 autobiography "Promises to Keep"
13 "The Jungle Book" wolf
14 Put back on
20 Muscle used in bench-pressing
24 Simple dance
26 Things that may be blown
28 Some email pics
29 Photographic memory or perfect pitch, e.g.
30 Master
32 Cincinnati athlete
34 NASA part: Abbr.
36 Outlaws
37 Not too awful
38 Consumables often described with a percentage
44 Comic who said "I open my eyes, remember who I am, what I'm like, and I just go 'Ugh' "
46 Worker on London's Savile Row
48 Weightlessness
49 1943 Churchill conference site
50 Computer programmer
52 Dives
55 Useful thing to keep on hand?
57 "Janie's Got ___" (1989 Aerosmith hit)
58 First in a historical trio
60 Almond ___ (candy)
62 Be short
63 With 68-Across, end of a Hemingway title

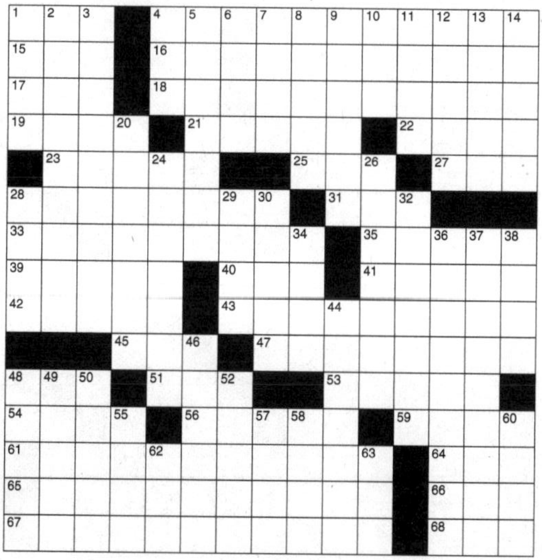

by Evans Clinchy

122 HARD

ACROSS

1 Like a drumhead
5 "Forget about it!"
15 Former education secretary Duncan
16 What may hold a body of evidence?
17 Tie securely
18 1970 #1 hit with the lyric "Just call my name"
19 She played Phyllis on TV's "Phyllis"
21 Film director ___ C. Kenton
22 No-goodnik
23 With 33-Down, same old offerings
24 Heavy duty
25 Spock, e.g.: Abbr.
26 One speaking the language Plautdietsch
28 Dictatorial dispatcher on "Taxi"
29 Unfortunate
30 Encyclopedic
31 Dictatorial type
32 "Murder, Inc." Oscar nominee
34 Husky food?
37 Overseas court figure
38 Bush native to the South
41 Santa ___
42 Get down to nothing?
44 Gym bunnies work on them
45 Animal shelter
46 Party divider
47 "Engineered for life" corp.
48 "Wow"-producing look
49 Lack of punch
50 Olivia de Havilland's Best Actress film, 1949
53 Trusting someone you don't know, e.g.
54 Present reality
55 ___ ether
56 Try to win hands down?
57 Gainsay

DOWN

1 Choices in the baby department
2 Body undergoing desertification
3 Ill-conceived
4 Capital in 1979–80 headlines
5 Lead-in to "Los Angeles" or "New Orleans"
6 Magic, on a sports ticker
7 Quiet after the storm, maybe
8 Stain
9 Reacts to a bombshell
10 Sevilla-to-Granada direction
11 Level in an org.
12 A head might go over the top of it
13 Coming in waves?
14 Really embarrassed, maybe
20 Song played at Staples Center after every Lakers victory
24 Department in Picardy
25 Crown
27 "Great" sleuth of kid-lit
28 Jimmy Carter's mother
31 Weight allowance
32 Consoling gestures
33 See 23-Across
34 "Bewitched" witch
35 Barfly's request
36 Spring break preceder, often
38 Pale yellow
39 20th-century novelist who shared first and middle names with poet Emerson
40 With very little hope
42 Theater stage
43 Like theater seating
45 "Leavin' on Your Mind" singer, 1963
48 Stuff in a backpack
49 ___ speak
51 Give the ax?
52 What la Tierra orbits

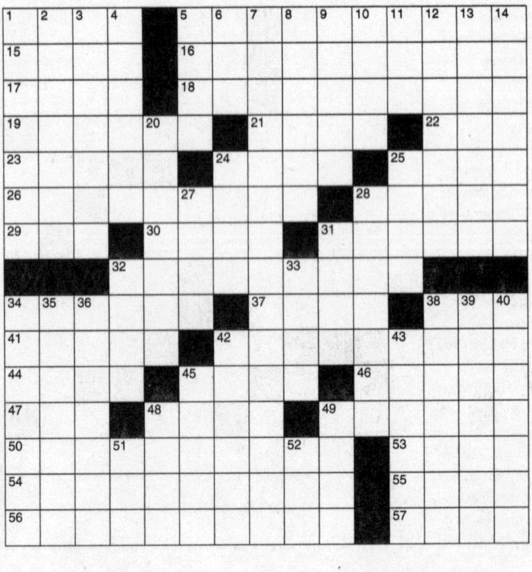

by Roland Huget

HARD **123**

ACROSS

1 Phylicia of stage and screen
7 Reduce to tears?
15 Some highway conveniences
17 Unwelcome war report
18 French force
19 Back tracks?
20 ___-relief
21 Blood letters
22 Green org.?
25 Deem to be dumb
31 Quaint means of manipulation
32 Common instruments in jazz combos
33 Cyclist in peak condition?
34 Fine source of humor, with "the"?
35 This was once "art"
36 U.P.S. unit: Abbr.
37 It may come with a price to pay
40 Cousin of a frittata
44 Major tributary of the Missouri
46 Tamarack trees
50 Didn't stand firm in negotiations
51 "Fish Magic" artist
52 Get beaten by

DOWN

1 Aid for clean living
2 Hyundai luxury sedan
3 Blasts inboxes
4 Billionaire, for one
5 "___ sow . . ."
6 Award since W.W. I
7 Outcome in Eden
8 His: Fr.
9 Dressed
10 Glamour rival
11 Bad singers?
12 "Star Wars" saga nickname
13 Driver's aid
14 What makes a top stop?
16 Grammy-nominated blues guitarist in the Louisiana Music Hall of Fame
21 Husky cousins
22 Punt propeller, e.g.
23 Says, informally
24 ___ Toy Barn ("Toy Story 2" locale)
25 Alloy of tin and lead
26 Just slightly
27 Order to a sommelier, maybe
28 Bow out
29 Not out, but not necessarily up
30 Doctors
31 Debussy contemporary
32 1922 Physics Nobelist
33 1959 Kingston Trio hit
37 Explorer alternative
38 Star seeker?
39 Canvas primer
40 City northeast of Kiev
41 Head Stone
42 Biol. branch
43 The New Yorker film critic Anthony
44 +/–
45 Biol. and others
46 Concert piece
47 Kid's cry
48 College final?
49 It's sometimes shown in the corner of a TV screen, for short

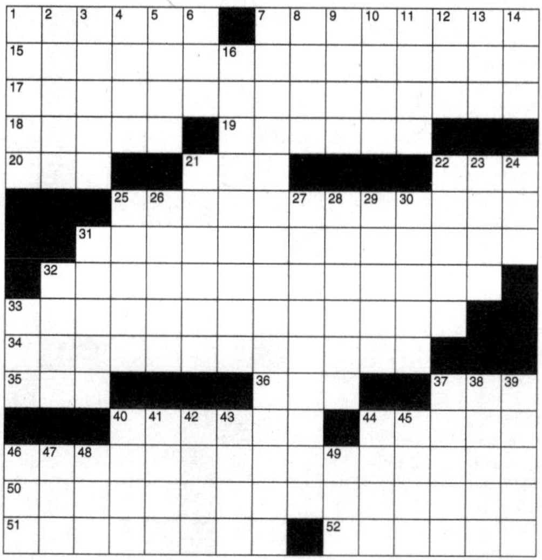

by Martin Ashwood-Smith

124 HARD

ACROSS

1 Spreads
9 Shipping quantity
14 Old-fashioned affair à la "Oklahoma!"
16 Big scrap
17 "Tonight Show" bandleader with a signature 'fro
18 Ancient manuscript
19 Jimmy
20 Something a mother wears
21 Works on the strip?
22 The world's largest one is in South Korea, the second-largest in Sweden
24 See to
25 Sound of moving water
26 Pushes to the limit
28 Joint issue
30 Bush junior?
31 "Hell, yeah!"
35 Kind of
37 "Hang on, hang on"
38 Office drudge
40 Something off the wall?
41 Oakland's Bill ___ Climate Lab
42 Dummies
46 Up
48 Not be free
51 Grateful Dead bassist Phil
52 Robert of "The Girl Who Knew Too Much"
53 One of the 12 tribes of Israel
55 Big inits. in podcasting
56 Termagant
58 Once-popular free computer download
60 Sagal of "Married . . . With Children"
61 #1 going in
62 Twos in the news
63 All but the outer columns, typically

DOWN

1 Where dogs may be put in the backyard
2 Golden Globe winner for "The Wrestler"
3 Bright yellow bouquet
4 Jerk
5 "The fool ___ think he is wise": Shak.
6 Acclaim
7 Personification of Turkey's Weeping Rock
8 Piggy bank contents
9 Canyon maker
10 Keep lubed, say
11 Source of the word "saga"
12 Targets on a hunt
13 Once-common Times Square establishment
15 Bummers
23 Horror movie locale
25 Aforementioned
27 Dome of the Rock, e.g.
29 "Eeep!"
32 Get together
33 Not having many different parts?
34 Alpine region
35 Target of a trap-neuter-return program
36 Vial that a villain might withhold
38 Make a flying jump in the winter
39 Morale booster on base
43 "No problemo"
44 Keen-eyed fisher
45 Does a virtuoso guitar solo, slangily
47 Home of the real-life House of the Seven Gables
49 Condition
50 Like the answer "No."
54 Fetor
57 Start to function?
59 One of the 63-Across: Abbr.

by Josh Knapp

HARD 125

ACROSS

1 Subcompact
8 Subject to an air attack
14 Well-known, now
16 Big name in guitars
17 Put on a pedestal
18 Lock horns
19 Fall foliage color
20 "Girl With a Hoop" painter
22 Banff wildlife
23 First name in cosmetics
25 Common waiting room viewing
26 Fictional race of the distant future
27 Picasso masterpiece with a French title
30 Cousin of a blintz
31 "Hotel Impossible" airer
34 P.M. who won the 1957 Nobel Peace Prize
35 Miraculous solutions
36 Friends, in slang
37 Sir William ___, so-called "Father of Modern Medicine"
38 Runs off at the mouth
39 Guitar-making wood
40 Post-tragedy comment
45 Common question after a name is dropped
46 Salad base
49 ___ war
50 Like some warfare
52 Decision debated for decades
54 Worrisome engine sound
55 Fret about
56 Corsairs and Rangers of the 1950s
57 Things in keys

DOWN

1 Op art pattern
2 It flows for nearly 2,000 miles in Asia
3 Big mushroom producer, in brief
4 "___ war": F.D.R.
5 Frame from a drawer
6 "Jake and ___" (comedy web series)
7 Give a dynamite finish?
8 Form of civil disobedience
9 It's a lift
10 Bled
11 Kings' supporters
12 Dropped like a jaw
13 Book before Daniel
15 Office drones
21 Amoeba feature
24 Gives a lift
26 Lubitsch of old Hollywood
28 State
29 Denoting the style in which one might consider this clue to be written
30 Sympathetic sorts
31 Gets from A to B instantly
32 Says one can make it, say
33 Well
34 Be in store
35 Means of obtaining private information
39 Name in many van Gogh titles
41 "Incredible!"
42 Italian wine
43 Guitar-making wood
44 Ones preparing Easter eggs
46 Presumption
47 "___ problem"
48 In public
51 Ending with Manhattan
53 Bugs on the road

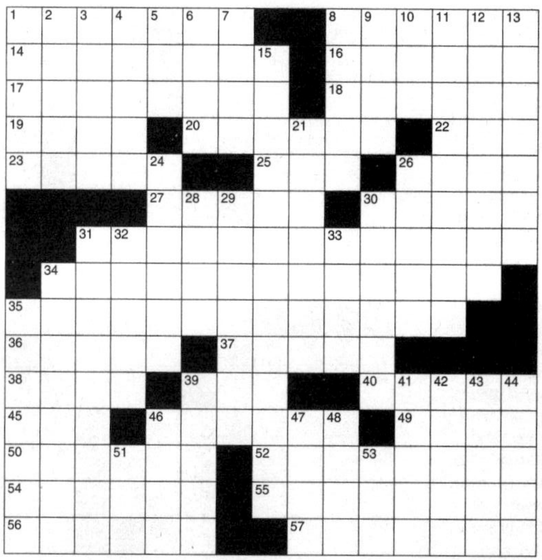

by Michael Wiesenberg

126 HARD

ACROSS

1 Patron for the desperate
7 Ones seeking maximum exposure?
14 ___ blanc (wine variety)
15 Couples' soft spot?
16 Threw
17 A priest, not a beast
18 "The Magpie" and "Grainstack"
19 Bounder
20 Not much, in recipes
21 Early second-millennium year
22 Brushed instrument
23 Vulgarian
24 Stocking stuffer
26 Brace
27 Extremely green
30 "Save Me the Waltz" novelist, 1932
35 2014 U.S. Women's Open winner
36 Band options
40 "And . . . ___!"
41 Enraptured
42 Comedian Marc who recorded a memorable podcast with President Obama
44 Some PCs
45 Bench warmer?
46 Tender
48 Set
49 Green Lantern's archenemy
50 Surrounded, old-style
51 Yet to be imagined
52 Twerp
53 QBs, at times
54 Rush relatives

DOWN

1 Bathos
2 Presidential first name
3 "The Land of Painted Caves" author, 2011
4 Not yet available, as a stock
5 "And how ___ the wise man? as the fool": Ecclesiastes 2:16
6 Modern synonym for 5-Down
7 Aliens
8 Pigmented layer
9 Some PCs
10 Christmas or Easter, for example
11 Main passage
12 Good name for a girl who procrastinates?
13 Like heists and operas
15 Getting totally confused, idiomatically
21 Mojos
24 Eastern mystics
25 Point of view
28 Croque-monsieur ingredient
29 Set
31 Came back strong
32 1978 Robert Altman comedy with Desi Arnaz Jr. and Carol Burnett
33 Department store department
34 Global warming periods?
36 Charges
37 Berth site
38 Fans of pharaohs?
39 Ones with a lot of down time?
43 Long time follower?
45 Who's "got a gun" in a 1989 Aerosmith hit
47 Common newspaper name
48 Chops

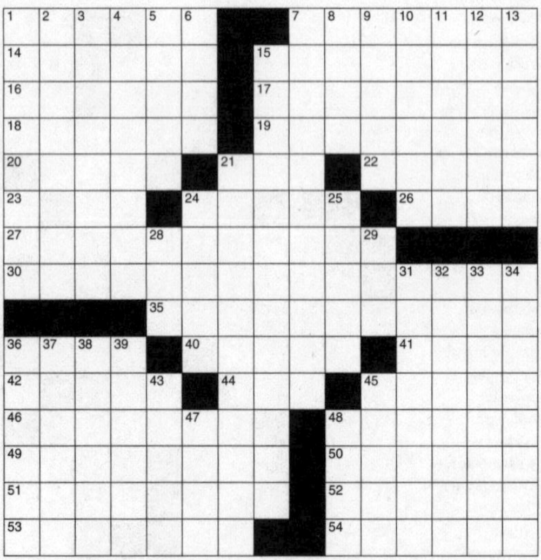

by Byron Walden

ACROSS

1 Far and away one's favorite writer?
7 Mellow R&B track
14 Fly
15 Primitive and backward
16 Items with decorative scrolls
17 Slice from a book?
18 Pay homage, in a way
19 "___ off!" (phrase of homage)
20 Scratches (out)
21 French border region
23 One on the trail, for short
24 Room in Clue
27 20-20 and others
28 Bungling
31 There's one for Best New American Play
32 Extreme
34 500-pound bird hunted to extinction
35 Film character who said "Look, I ain't in this for your revolution, and I'm not in it for you, Princess"
37 A, B or C, but not X, Y or Z
39 ___ caution
40 Knee jerk, e.g.
42 Head shop buy
43 Unite
45 Hue
46 "Woe ___ them that call evil good": Isaiah
47 "The Lost Tapes" rapper
48 Took care of, as guests
50 Z's : sleep :: wavy lines : ___
52 ___ Préval, twice-elected president of Haiti
53 Crude Halloween costume
57 "Drink" for the overly critical
59 Crèche setting
60 Schiller work set to music by Beethoven
61 Little rock
62 Symbol of modern communication
63 Out of retirement?

DOWN

1 Stuff
2 Flush
3 Water source for 11 countries
4 Some blonds
5 Snorkeling mecca
6 ___ Echos (French daily)
7 Pink property
8 Cuts (off)
9 Light air, on the Beaufort scale
10 "It's our time to go!"
11 "Glengarry Glen Ross" co-star, 1992
12 Chill in bed?
13 Pro team with blue-and-orange jerseys
15 Orthodontic device
19 Supposed morning remedy
22 Dusty, fusty or musty
23 British P.M. before and after Addington
24 Blah
25 Lower
26 Statements for the record
29 Aim
30 Steps in a ballroom
33 Puts the kibosh on
36 Underground rock bands?
38 Where Etihad Airways is headquartered
41 ___ Tunes
44 One of the knights of the Round Table
49 Acid/alcohol compound
50 Excited pupil's shout
51 Art genre for Man Ray
52 Punjabi chief
54 Weakens
55 W competitor
56 ___ Vogue magazine
58 Go to waste
59 Day ___

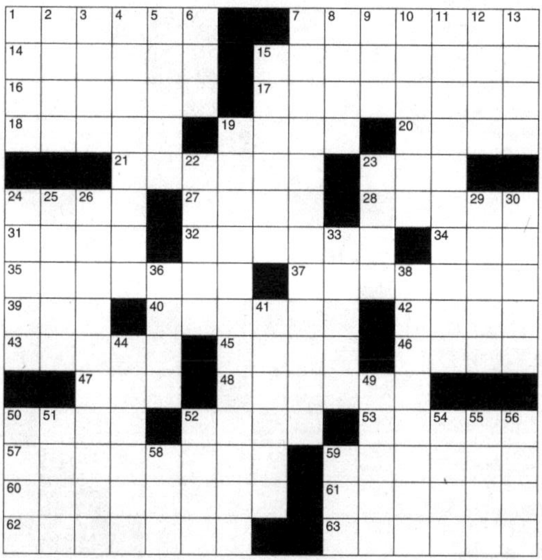

by Ian Livengood

128 HARD

ACROSS

1 Produces heat?
6 Isn't fooling
13 Contents of a bag behind a mound
14 What some women are waist-high in
15 "The Coming of Arthur," e.g.
16 Fictional dog owned by the Winslow family
17 Be of the opinion
18 Fajitas and such
19 Winter hours in Kan.
20 Big dip
22 Gig composition
23 One with a supporting role
24 "Hop-Frog" author, for short
25 Suburb of San Diego
26 "___ Mistress" (1982 horror film)
27 Latin word usually shortened to "c."
28 Rough, loosely woven fabric
29 Crooner with the 1978 platinum album "You Light Up My Life"
30 Groups usually of 13
31 Unhealthily light
32 Grandparents, often
33 Hip attachment?
34 Mechanism for making things disappear in "1984"
38 Fraternal patriotic org.
39 Guards on the gridiron
40 Final menu option, maybe
41 Like conspirators
43 Street with an office
44 458 and 488 on the road
45 Listing
46 Up a tree
47 Arthur Ashe Courage Award and others

DOWN

1 Sight after a blizzard
2 What calves may get caught in
3 Hitherto
4 Pioneering woman in American literature?
5 Staple for sketches, for short
6 Many a West Jordan resident
7 Irish revolutionary Robert
8 Brand of lemon dish liquid
9 Jimbo's sidekick on "South Park"
10 Williams-Sonoma line
11 Calligrapher's grinding mortar
12 Frightful little suckers
14 You can't go over them
16 Petrifying figure
18 Certain home subcontractors
21 Alternative to chow fun
22 Elegant surroundings for kings and queens?
24 Bistro
25 1995 top 10 hit for Hootie & the Blowfish
26 Life ___
27 One of a pair that clicks
28 Whirlybird whirlers
29 Clusters of mountains
30 Noted 1950s backup band
32 Bereft
34 The "me" in "Roger & Me"
35 Yellow-flowered primrose
36 Drug company founder of 1876
37 Any of les Nations Unies
39 Latte option
42 Get ready to fight, maybe
43 "Lost" actor Daniel ___ Kim

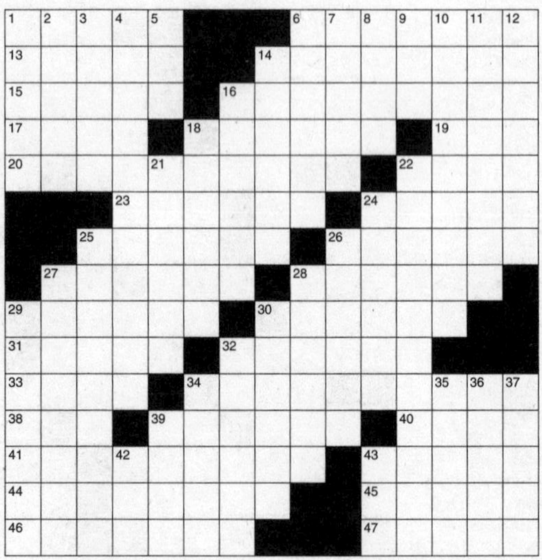

by Damon Gulczynski

HARD 129

ACROSS

1 Sister brand of Scope
6 Like blackjack hands with an ace counted as 11
10 Feature of a modern zoo
14 Athlete who uses steroids
15 Decorative enamelware
17 With 34-, 40- and 60-Across, a somber message for our loyal fans
19 Led astray
20 Agrostologists' study
21 Bud
22 "Whoopee!"
23 Letters before Kitty Hawk
26 Feet, in slang
29 Fruit with yellow skin
34 See 17-Across
37 The Gaels of collegiate sports
38 Actress Issa ___ of "The Misadventures of Awkward Black Girl"
39 Shield from the elements
40 See 17-Across
45 Make less flat
46 You might put stock in it
47 Gloaming, to a sonneteer
48 2 letters
50 Pennsylvania and others: Abbr.
52 Inability to sense smells
56 Vigorous reprimand
60 See 17-Across
62 Large marine fish tanks
63 Cardio option
64 "___ Darkness Fall" (L. Sprague de Camp novel)
65 Chew (out)
66 Collects a DNA sample from, say

DOWN

1 Parimutuel calculation
2 Marquis de Sade, e.g.
3 Made like
4 Pause
5 Fancy fabric
6 Long-range guided missile
7 "___ New Hampshire" (state song)
8 Not clear
9 Closet organizer
10 Comfy footwear
11 Responsibility
12 Play money?
13 1980 Oscar nominee directed by Roman Polanski
16 Patronize, as a hotel
18 Later in the text
23 Capital of the Roman province of Africa
24 Coast
25 "Sí" man?
27 Sandwich topped with tzatziki sauce
28 Goes up, up, up
30 ___ bath
31 Blow away
32 Comedian who married Joyce Mathews in 1941, divorced her in 1947 and married her again in 1949 "because she reminded me of my first wife"
33 Winter X Games host city
35 Curiosity org.
36 Overhaul
41 Thing with a filament
42 Online course
43 Holiday a month before Passover
44 Pulls out
49 Military group
51 Drinker's bender?
52 Taking unauthorized R&R
53 "Good going!"
54 Shouts of support
55 Crib part
56 Go here and there
57 Bay or gray follower
58 His .366 lifetime batting average is the best ever
59 Yahtzee category
61 Quinceañera invitee

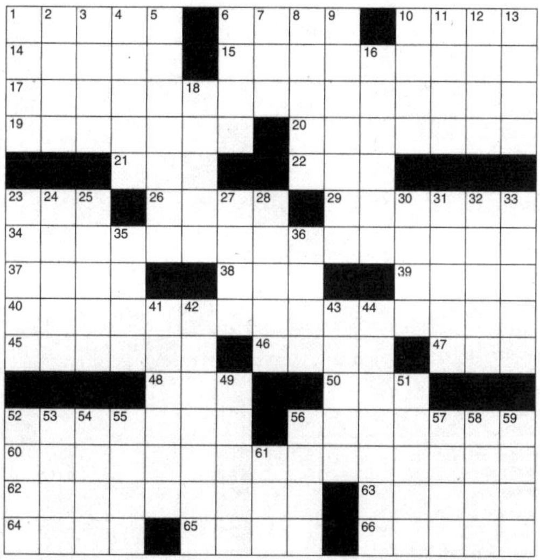

by Peter Gordon

130 HARD

ACROSS

1 Like Michael Strahan of "Live! With Kelly and Michael"
11 Market IDs
15 Mattie Silver's love, in fiction
16 Certain siege defense
17 Trader Joe's competitor
18 Little sweater
19 What you might have for bad eyesight
20 Cross with
22 1950s gym event
23 Flavoring for springerle biscuits and cookies
25 San Diego Zoo's ___ Cam
26 Grp. headquartered in Ramallah
27 Service branch disbanded in 1978, briefly
28 Meet component
30 Strongly urge
32 "41"
34 "Madam Secretary" star
35 Item on many a patio
38 The Georgia Peach or the Sultan of Swat, e.g.
40 "Sir, you are no gentleman" speaker
41 Member of the grammar police, e.g.
43 Bugs
45 Miss from Metz: Abbr.
46 Be all wet
49 Crib note?
50 Toaster, at times
52 Not focused
54 Company division
55 Want
57 "Being ___" (2015 documentary featuring many wipeouts)
58 Name on 2012 campaign posters
60 Metal staple
62 Completely, after "in"
63 Bridal shop service
64 Puzzle (out)
65 Gondola settings

DOWN

1 Showy trinket
2 Figure on many ancient Greek coins
3 Pronunciation-related
4 Things voyagers bring home
5 First of all
6 Takes out
7 Navy vessel
8 Shouts of victory
9 Port in Lower Saxony
10 Bastille prisoner of 1784–89
11 Person staying near home
12 Discount
13 The "you" in the Neil Diamond lyric "Reachin' out, touchin' me, touchin' you"
14 "Hurry!"
21 Wristwatches may make them
24 Erudite
29 Remnant in a 35-Across
31 2015 Rock and Roll Hall of Fame inductee
32 Excludes
33 Kind of day
35 Where Arithmancy is an elective
36 "No need to shout!"
37 Houseware purchases that may have suction cups
39 Crony
42 Some commencement dignitaries
44 "w"-like letters in foreign writing
46 French erudition
47 Animal revered by ancient Peruvians
48 Détour markers
51 Contents of a do-it-yourselfer's gun
53 Sauce traditionally made in a mortar
56 Word in many punny Bugs Bunny titles
59 Some R.S.V.P.s
61 Hall figures, for short

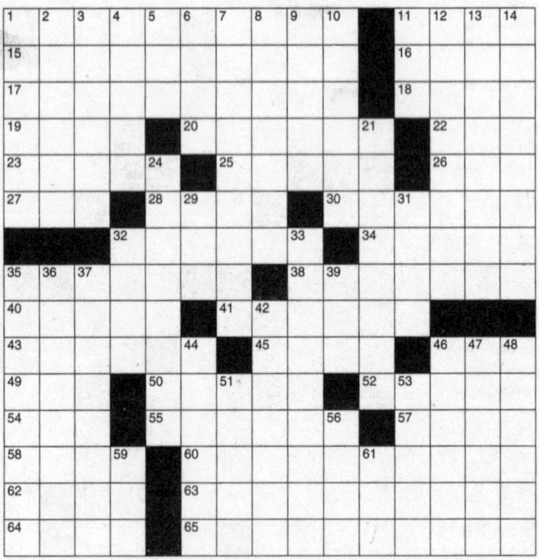

by Doug Peterson and Brad Wilber

ACROSS

1 Blue period?
7 Pet that needs a sitter?
13 Best Actor Oscar nominee for "The Lion in Winter"
14 Oriental blossom
15 Sartre's first novel
16 What you might get a distorted picture from?
17 Tee off
18 Detective fiction author Paretsky
19 Fragrance created by Fabergé
20 Scoring low on the excite-o-meter
21 Rarely missed stroke
23 Fore-and-aft-rigged vessel
24 Country ___ & Suites
26 Fictional biographer
28 "___ Will Be Loved" (Maroon 5 hit)
29 Restaurant critic who lent his name to a brand at the supermarket
32 Show authority?
34 Lightens up, say
36 Service station offering
39 "Beauty and the Beast" lyricist Howard
40 Macabre
42 Obedience school command
44 Foundry supply
46 Rolled item
47 Tribal title
48 Scorecard figures
49 Unpaid interest?
51 Ontario town across from Buffalo
53 Electrify
54 Club that "even God can't hit," according to Lee Trevino
55 It's not common knowledge
56 Worker at a station
57 Dirty

DOWN

1 "Hasn't scratched yet!" product
2 Concluded
3 Ring for dessert
4 Pharmacological amount
5 Bright-eyed
6 Parliamentary vote
7 Horne of "The Lady and Her Music"
8 "I can finally relax!"
9 Nonhuman explorer
10 Woos
11 "This being the case . . ."
12 Get a mouthful?
14 Side lights?
16 Grammy-nominated rock band for "Epic"
18 Setting of many pirate stories
22 Stirs
23 Gave a leg up to?
25 Fly in the ointment
27 At one's disposal
30 Renaissance Faire garment
31 Reputed
33 One who gets no credit?
35 Salt Lake City daily
36 Demand
37 FaceTime device
38 Raised
41 Security system component
43 Shenanigan
45 Gather together for stitching
48 Kind of plane
50 1977 horror film set in Newfoundland
52 Timeline segment
53 Listing on a Rolodex

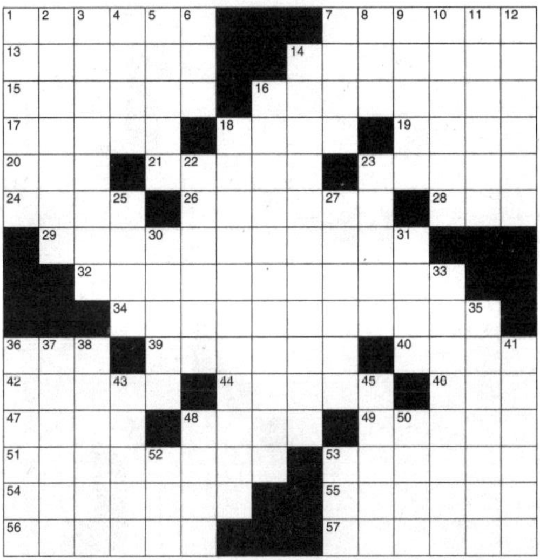

by Patrick Berry

132 HARD

ACROSS

1 Steven who co-created TV's "Sherlock"
7 Remote possibilities
15 Fat fingers?
17 Get the word out, maybe?
18 Big name in fast food
19 Better than, with "a"
20 School group working in harmony?
22 Unspecified power
23 Something to shuck
24 Something to shuck
25 Kind of sauce
27 Thought starter
28 Three-piece
29 It's no surprise
30 "The Paper Chase" novelist
33 Stock report?
34 It has layers upon layers
36 Sitcom on which Stephen Hawking and Buzz Aldrin have appeared
39 "The Color Purple" role
40 Lee making a scene
41 Wilber who founded a fast-food chain
42 Whopper server?
43 "Monsters, Inc." employees
45 Alternatives to clubs
46 Old Lutheran movement
47 Range of sizes, briefly
50 Member of comicdom's S.H.I.E.L.D.: Abbr.
51 Disturber of the peace
52 Exhibit, e.g.
54 Some brewskis
57 "The Naked Maja" and such
58 IHOP option
59 Whitehouse in D.C., e.g.
60 It may be out for blood
61 Hold with both arms, say

DOWN

1 Command in Excel
2 Fort town in the Second Seminole War
3 Circular
4 Clifford Irving's "Autobiography of Howard Hughes," e.g.
5 Sky line
6 Unwelcome Internet activity
7 Six L's
8 One who wasn't high-class, per a 1956 hit
9 Probably gonna, more formally
10 When doubled, a taunt
11 Home to Bellevue U.
12 250-year span in Japan's history
13 California city for which element #116 was named
14 Tick off
16 Slight blemish
21 It may grow between buds
26 Draw out
27 They can't be saved
28 ___ Ragg, Sweeney Todd's assistant
29 "That's O.K., everything's fine"
30 Like Advil or Motrin, for short
31 It's a hard act to follow
32 Took down a peg
35 Dec. 31
37 Medieval steel helmets with visors
38 Alter ego of "Batman" villainess Lorelei Circe
44 Tears apart
45 Mongolian for "hero"
46 Focus of some high-profile 1970s lawsuits
47 Dithers
48 Marilyn of the 5th Dimension
49 Watch's partner
51 Ending for evil or wrong
53 Stand-in for the unnamed
55 Inc. cousin
56 French possessive

by David Phillips

HARD 133

ACROSS

1 Artificial eyelashes, informally
8 Things with round numbers?
15 Reply to a pushy person
16 Far out?
17 Not flirting with your friend's girlfriend, e.g.
18 Gets crushed by, say
19 "Cats" monogram
20 Peaceful protests
22 Athletic great whose name and jersey number rhyme
23 I Samuel preceder
25 Point ___, Calif.
26 Problem on a record
27 Really get to
29 Yankee opposer
30 Color whose name is French for "mole"
31 It may represent November
33 Quit
35 Seat of Oklahoma's Garfield County
37 They surround lenses
38 Friend on "Friends"
42 Zip, as a Ziploc, say
46 Angel hair toppers?
47 Shout while shaking a pompom
49 Friend of Buckwheat
50 Give out
51 The band fun. and others
53 Look through?
54 Ring letters
55 "Take it easy, bro!"
57 "Odi et ___" (Catullus poem)
58 Beyond the requirement
60 Electronic music genre
62 Bogey
63 Pouring poison into a stream, e.g.
64 Answer to "Capisce?"
65 Spicy cuisine

DOWN

1 Plant seen on the Sistine Chapel ceiling
2 In an ordinary fashion
3 Shower clothes
4 Quotation qualifier
5 Teenage dream?
6 "Star Wars" moon
7 In any way
8 Certain pop music fan of the 2010s
9 Cellular transmitters
10 Bygone sportscaster Hodges
11 ___ Styles, lead character in "Boyz N the Hood"
12 Screwdriver selection
13 Gotham building-climbing tool
14 Expressed derision
21 Sized up
24 One low on dough
26 Big wind
28 Keeps a watch on
30 Kept a watch on?
32 Bagel
34 "Right honourable" sort
36 Behind
38 Treat for a dog
39 Treat for a dog
40 Things you can assume
41 Skate park fixture
43 All over the place
44 California's so-called "Island City"
45 Make public
48 Poker variant
51 Low par
52 Angel hair topper
55 Quicken Loans Arena cagers
56 ___ One (2013 release)
59 Pounded paste
61 Zymurgy, e.g.: Abbr.

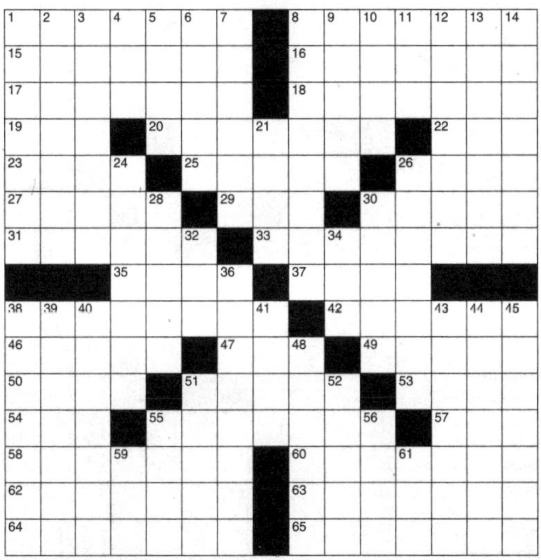

by David Steinberg

134 HARD

ACROSS

1 Edible Asian sprout
12 Something found naturally in tomatoes and potatoes
15 "Like, are you serious?!"
16 Top of an outfit?
17 Furniture item with a rounded back
18 Head
19 Winter coat
20 Seek to explain, in a way
22 Some of them are devoted to gangsters
25 Not close
26 Bob ___, leader of Canada's Liberal Party before Justin Trudeau
27 Org. in the documentary "Citizenfour"
28 They clear spots
31 Jerks
33 Expired
35 Misunderstand
40 One taking the big view, medically
41 Bond producer
42 Top of the British judicial system?
45 "This is ___"
47 "Your table will be ready in five minutes," possibly
48 Tess's lover in "Tess of the D'Urbervilles"
49 Orange snacks
51 Something that may be jam-packed
55 Stopped winging it?
56 Bolster
57 Distant ancestor
61 Information after "Je m'appelle . . ."
62 Car engine component
63 ___-Chapelle
64 Much-joked-about cafeteria offering

DOWN

1 Seafood shack item
2 Quack stopper, for short
3 Christmas superlative
4 Relating to element #56
5 Patrick Stewart's adaptation of "A Christmas Carol," e.g.
6 More after more?
7 Tick
8 Routine responses
9 Pearl Buck heroine
10 Massachusetts' ___ College
11 Hardly a vet
12 Place to get a brew in more than 11,000 U.S. locations
13 Alaska Airlines hub
14 They're history
21 It might help you on your return
22 Assault, as a commanding officer
23 ___ 10
24 Pincered creature
28 How much to be above, as they say
29 Teacher at Oxford
30 Only actor to appear in all eight "American Pie" films
32 Magnum opus of Spinoza
34 ___ subtilior (musical style)
36 Country's ___ Young Band
37 Doctor of book and screen
38 It's found on the side of a highway
39 Passing requirements
42 Ancient Greeks, e.g.
43 Broadway Billy
44 Software text page
46 Warmer, in a way
49 Southeastern European
50 Cold medicine brand
52 Level
53 Sir ___ Ive, designer of the iPad, iPod, iPhone and iMac
54 Qts. and gals.
58 Stretch (out)
59 A.C.C. school
60 Good to go

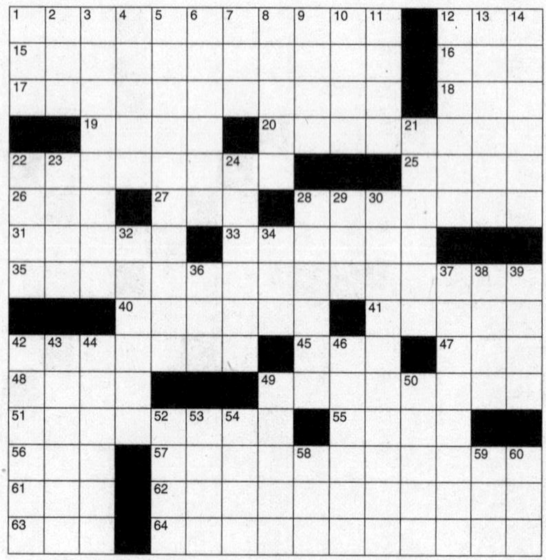

by Andrew Zhou

HARD 135

ACROSS

1 Too-clever-by-half type
12 Important school fig.
15 Taunt to a head-turner
16 Head-butter
17 Make an Amazon visit, say
18 Thoughtful gift?
19 Lady, for one
20 What a pacer may be experiencing
22 Project Mercury primate
23 Still red, say
25 Flier not found in 49 states
26 Conform to the party line?
27 Salon job, for short
29 Hallmark occasion
33 Chinese Fireball or Norwegian Ridgeback, in Harry Potter
35 Reproductive couple
36 Sharp shooter?
37 Music style featuring accordions
38 They play by themselves
39 Co-star of TV's "thirtysomething"
40 Trickery
41 A unit
43 Years abroad
44 Moose predator
48 Broad in tastes
50 Like silt vis-à-vis sand
51 Years ___
52 "Have some fun!"
55 Fox coverage that may be controversial?
56 What shoulders are often used for
57 Some M.I.T. deg. holders
58 It has many cells

DOWN

1 Hit, old-style
2 Sausalito's county
3 Increase
4 Casting needs
5 Roller on a carriageway
6 ___-hoo
7 Many a Weird Al Yankovic title
8 Cause of a rash response?
9 "Got me"
10 Pick up, as ice cubes
11 Crocheter's purchase
12 Title food in children's literature
13 Crashed
14 Tour gear
21 Relative of Sinhalese
23 Event with goat tying
24 Santa ___ (weather phenomena)
26 Tony
28 Holiday spots?
29 Doofus
30 Lions, Tigers and Bears play in it
31 Cold remedies?
32 Depression shared by soldiers
33 Hills' counterparts
34 Amazonas and Nilo
36 Certain plea, for short
38 Not faking it
40 Legal release
42 Bad things to find in theories
44 Singer's concern
45 Let loose
46 Row with many people
47 "Give it ___!"
48 Monk's on "Seinfeld," e.g.
49 Definitely not step lively
50 Bass parts
53 Turkish chief
54 Set the pace

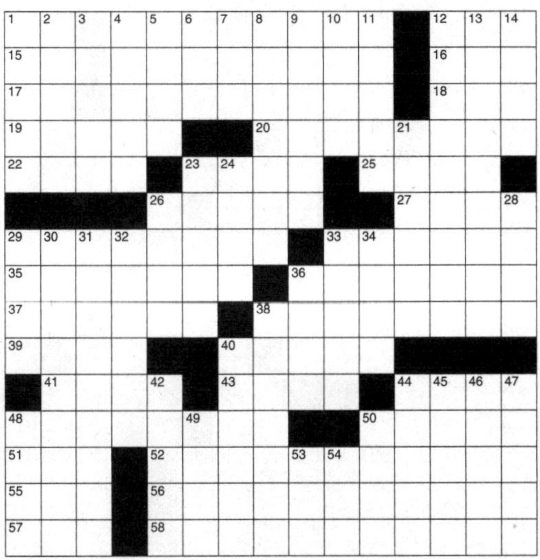

by Robyn Weintraub

136 HARD

ACROSS

1 Give up out of frustration, in slang
9 Person with pressing things to do?
15 [Shrug]
16 Very much
17 Exile
18 Blogging site owned by Yahoo
19 Lose support
20 Look inside
22 "The Glass Bead Game" author
23 10/15, e.g.
25 Table material
27 Garbage
29 Acronym in 1990s news
30 Ingredient in a Dark 'n' Stormy
33 1936 novel family
36 Wander around Hollywood, maybe
38 Banded status symbols
40 Paris suburb that holds the tombs of numerous Fr. monarchs
41 Ideal height for some contact
43 Counterintelligence grp. in 007 novels
44 Partners of 58-Across
45 "CSI" setting
47 Intl. org. that was the first to land a probe on a comet (2014)
48 Cheese dish
50 Novel character with "a comfortable home and happy disposition"
53 Some party wear
56 Shop item
58 Partners of 44-Across
59 "Aladdin" setting
61 Chocolaty treats introduced in 1932
63 Piece of den furniture
64 Relationship in many a Seth Rogen film
65 Sitcom character whose dancing is described as "a full-body dry heave"
66 Frowned-upon construction material

DOWN

1 Portia de ___ (Ellen DeGeneres's wife)
2 In the future
3 Some home remedies
4 Hall of fame on TV
5 Learning center
6 Like all contestants on "The Bachelor"
7 How soda may be sold
8 Highlanders, e.g.
9 Astronomers' std.
10 Parent's reproof
11 Citi Field icon
12 Winners at the Battle of Chickasaw Bayou, for short
13 "___ well"
14 Pericles' domain, in Shakespeare
21 Lots
24 The New Yorker cartoonist Edward
26 Need for sabermetricians
28 Panama Papers revelation
30 Went unchecked
31 Tomb Raider weaponry
32 Go together
33 Self-described "Family City U.S.A."
34 College athlete wearing blue and gray
35 End
37 One of the 12 gifts of Christmas
39 Jason of "How I Met Your Mother"
42 1987 #1 hit with the lyric "Soy capitán, soy capitán"
46 Things played on the floor
48 Black hat wearer
49 Pound
51 ___ Island, Fla.
52 Yo-yos
53 "The Twilight Zone" episode, usually
54 Like some arguments
55 City captured during the Six-Day War
57 "A Series of Unfortunate Events" villainess
60 Word that sounds like a letter of the alphabet that's not in it
62 Results of some four-year programs, for short

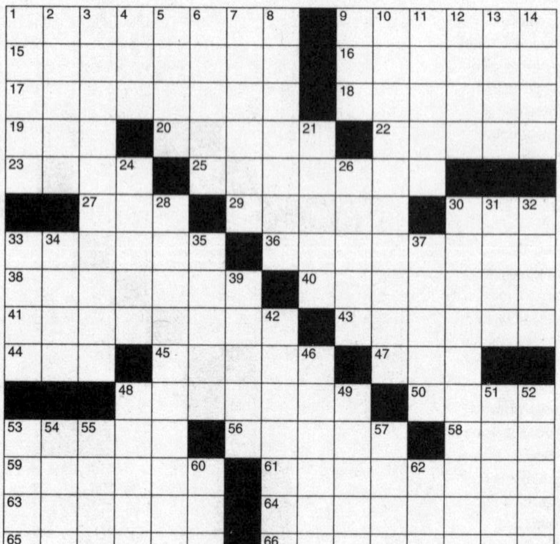

by Paolo Pasco

HARD 137

ACROSS

1 Graveyard hour
7 Dark as dark can be
15 Nova Scotia, once
16 Not excessively
17 A ghostwriter isn't given one
18 Ball
19 Haggis ingredient
20 "What's hangin'?"
21 It comes to a head
22 Ursule, e.g.: Abbr.
23 Means of tracking wildlife
26 Old radio dummy
27 Squeaker in a cage
30 City on the Oka River
31 Arles article
32 Lucky strike
35 Result of holding or hooking
37 Shot-putter's activity
39 Latin word on a diploma
40 Dedicated to
41 Conclusion lead-in
42 Tropical smoothie flavor
45 Double-dipping, e.g.
48 Answering to
49 ___ Balls
50 Healing helper
51 Show that's earned more than 40 Emmys, in brief
52 Lack of anxiety
54 Spreadsheet function
56 Sonnet-ending unit
58 72 of its 108 lines end in "-ore" sounds
59 "The Evangelist" of Christianity
60 Book that doesn't require much time or thought
61 "But still . . ."

DOWN

1 Dynamite
2 Hostile looks
3 A 99¢ burger may be on it
4 "Desperate Housewives" housewife
5 Slangy "True, no?"
6 Questel who voiced Olive Oyl
7 Fitting gifts for puzzle enthusiasts?
8 "Uncle!"
9 Too much, to Marcel
10 See 38-Down
11 Valentino type
12 Fourth-wall breaker
13 Star on the horizon?
14 Work digitally?
22 Fill time at an airport, say
24 Symbols of change, in math
25 Shot from behind the arc, informally
26 Shot putter's supply?
28 Grist for a war of words?
29 Ageless, ages ago
33 It often catches an infection
34 Rail heads
36 "OMG, I'm cracking up!"
37 Place for a stove light
38 With 10-Down, turn in
40 First country in the world with universal suffrage (1906)
43 Product of natural outdoor steeping
44 Onetime motel come-on
45 Refinement
46 Warm welcome?
47 Snoozers
51 Relief pitcher's success
53 Pistolet ou canon
55 "God, home and country" org.
56 Literary monogram
57 Fight call, for short

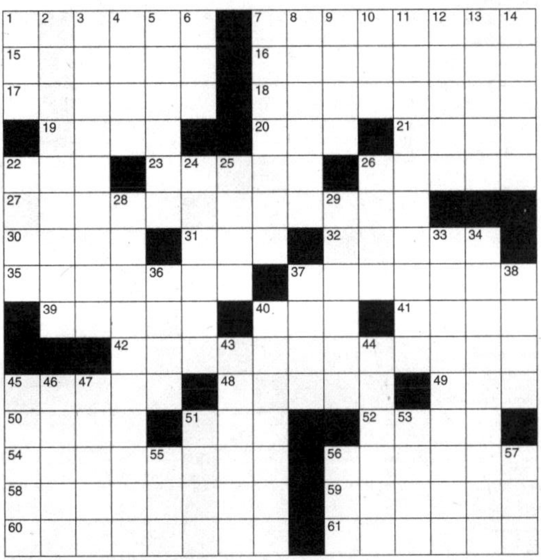

by Andrew Kingsley

138 HARD

ACROSS

1 Result of a bad trip
10 Signs of life
15 Paper pusher?
16 What some people do to vows
17 1998 Spike Lee film
18 Sunflowerlike flower
19 Royal name in ancient Egypt
20 The Rosetta Stone, for one
21 Engineer's home, for short
22 "I'm not buying it"
24 Small vault
25 Caribbean port
28 Choices, choices
29 Pantheon member
30 They cast no votes
32 Key employer in England?
34 Woodworker's device, informally
37 Advance men?
38 "The Miseducation of ___ Hill" (1998 Grammy-winning album)
39 Allen of Hollywood
40 Moscato bianco grape product
41 Ring
43 City across the border from Eilat
47 Max. 3,333,360, in Pac-Man
48 Game also called Five in a Row
50 What three of California's four largest cities share
51 Common name for a chimp
53 Doing mean work?
56 Very loud
57 Light
58 Teacher's implementation
59 Affected by wind or water, say
60 Massage
61 Upset

DOWN

1 Key that's oxymoronic at school?
2 At the original speed, musically
3 Entrap
4 "A Yank at ___" (Mickey Rooney film)
5 Substance
6 Gain access, in a way
7 Body-related
8 Fearsome foes
9 Bone-boring tool
10 Stopped lying
11 Almost up
12 Desk feature
13 Grammy-winning LL Cool J song that starts "I've been watching you from afar for as long as I can remember"
14 They clean up well
23 Longtime Indiana senator defeated in 2012
26 Mediterranean vacation spot
27 "Men always hate most what they ___ most": H. L. Mencken
29 Public figure?
31 "Whatever Lola Wants," e.g.
33 No longer tied up, say
34 Raucous card game
35 Really must go
36 Best at play
37 Alternators in some internal-combustion engines
39 Acts of a scalawag
42 Put down
44 The Golden Horde, e.g.
45 War cry
46 First name in European politics
48 Ran through
49 Get a handle on
52 Herbal stress reliever from Polynesia
54 "___ Baby" (song from "Hair")
55 Unappealing bowlful

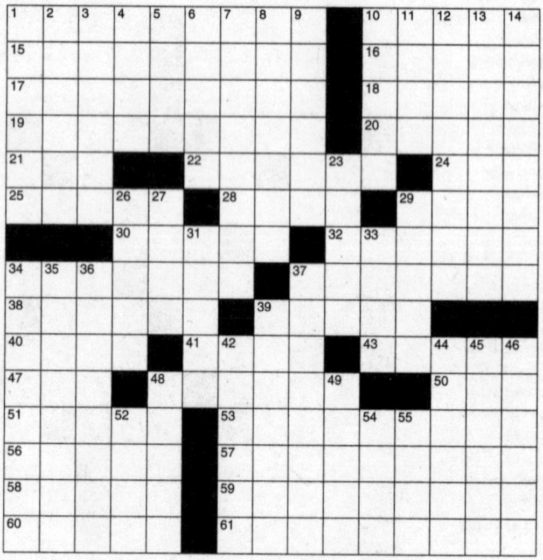

by Mark Diehl

HARD 139

ACROSS
1 Holder of many titles
12 Show with the record for most Emmys won in a single year (12)
14 Encountered trouble
16 Snags
17 What a star may represent
18 Non-Rx
19 Rx abbr.
20 Locales for deep investigations?
25 "We should get going"
29 Home to the naturally pink Lake Retba
30 Attended as an observer
31 It's spanned by the Ponte Santa Trinita
32 Army ___
33 Allison Janney's role on "The West Wing"
36 Architect/sculptor with an eponymous New York museum
40 Control and make use of
41 Big name in late-night
42 Topkapi Palace resident
43 Choler
44 Deadline in a western
49 Anticipate
53 Turn lemons into lemonade, so to speak
55 Countercharge
56 Help someone

DOWN
1 M.R.I. alternative
2 "The Zone of Interest" author, 2014
3 Seat of Washoe County
4 Spoil, with "on"
5 Some successful Wharton grads, for short
6 Sports person: Abbr.
7 G
8 They may be graphic
9 Some temperatures
10 Go ___ length
11 Bronze
12 Relative of a soul patch
13 Commences
14 Luster
15 Transcribe
21 Get into one's head
22 Tally
23 Mamie Eisenhower hairstyle
24 Grinds
25 Info in a 1-Across
26 Means of divination
27 Put on
28 Showed great happiness
33 It might be yawning
34 Luxury car name since 1935
35 Started, as a generator
37 Lingerie material
38 Speedball component
39 Like atoms with full outer shells
45 Miami Beach architectural style, informally
46 ___ vez (again: Sp.)
47 Clay, for one
48 Friend of Bubbles, in an animated film
49 Hang
50 Focus of some prep books
51 Battle of ___ (1943 U.S./Japanese conflict)
52 Rouge alternative
54 Thumbnail item

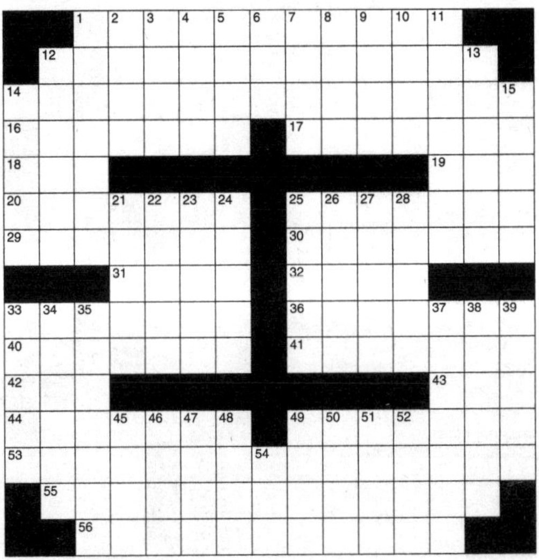

by Julian Lim

140 HARD

ACROSS

1 Small, slim daggers
9 Apple variety
15 Single from Springsteen's "Born in the U.S.A."
16 Major protest
17 Many a Harpo Marx joke
18 Extremely fast?
19 Dip ___ in
20 Get the lead out?
22 "Poor little" one in Coleridge's "To a Young Ass"
23 Automatic, for one
25 Like Egypt
26 Jerks
27 They're followed on message boards
30 "Hmm"
32 Writer who gave his name to an annual award
33 Many vacationers bring them home
34 Question before a personal update
40 Something depicted for goodness' sake?
41 With 48-Across, enters stealthily
42 One-knee plea
46 Entertains at bedtime
47 Color of McCartney's "Sgt. Pepper" uniform
48 See 41-Across
50 Belt line?
51 Sharp's opposite
52 Sharp's handful
54 Captain of fiction
57 Like corduroy
59 Cheese choice
61 As a replacement
62 Simplest sort of deal
63 Insistent retort
64 A good cure for it is sleep, per W. C. Fields

DOWN

1 Where Fermi studied
2 Cut out
3 Place to be avoided
4 Not learned
5 Like a boat's cockpit, usually
6 Drilling sites
7 Plays with emotions?
8 Rocker with the 1976 album "Live Bullet"
9 "I wish *I* had that"
10 On point
11 Common use for pipe cleaners
12 Like tea bags
13 Plunder
14 Words that may elicit a worried gulp
21 Show title shown on a license plate
24 Like much of the Everglades
27 Way up at a ski resort
28 Primary loser to J.F.K. in 1960
29 Longtime nickname in comics
31 Certain sandal
33 First word of Frost's "The Road Not Taken"
35 "Neapolitan Novels" author Ferrante
36 Pleasure principle
37 Frequent chant in 2008
38 Go for it, with "in"
39 Grp. doing private shows?
42 Home of the soccer team that FIFA named the Club of the Century
43 Mother-or-son Philippine president
44 Bit of gang warfare
45 Some wedding parties
46 Hall-of-Fame N.B.A. player known as "The Worm"
49 One of the singing Braxton sisters
53 Mtg.
55 Where Bambara is widely spoken
56 Fit for service
58 Experts in power: Abbr.
60 Symbol of charge density

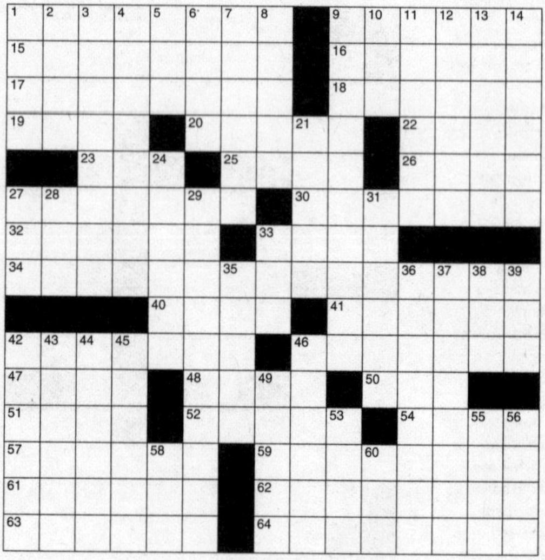

by Kyle Mahowald

HARD 141

ACROSS

1 Bedroom set piece?
14 Band with the 2012 double-platinum album "Night Visions"
16 Celebrity with the fashion line "V."
18 Internet issue
19 Hacking it
20 One tailed in the sewers
21 Want
22 Flares
24 "___ on my bed my limbs I lay" (line from Coleridge)
25 Fill with horror
27 It has a good resolution
28 Lose energy
31 "Di quella pira," e.g.
32 Tigerlike
34 "___ life belongs to those who live in the present": Wittgenstein
36 Chinese province where a spicy cuisine originated
37 Swear
38 Fitness center?
39 Half of a couple
40 Doesn't shut up
41 Targets of President Taft
43 Big maker of 27-Acrosses
44 Souvenir item
46 Unlikely swinger
50 Org. with a name registration
51 Captain ___ (DC Comics superhero)
52 Lacking subtlety, say
53 Extra sauce order?
57 Match.com competitors
58 Jibber-jabbers

DOWN

1 Jeremy of "Entourage"
2 Leave speechless
3 Girl with a gun in an Aerosmith hit
4 What a chair covers
5 ___ en scène
6 Puzzle hunt?: Abbr.
7 "___ dear . . ."
8 Big name in energy bars and smoothies
9 Like some councils
10 It may be running
11 Checks out
12 "J'accuse!" reply
13 Punch line instrument
15 Little something for the road?
17 Piano-playing Cat
22 Sardine relative
23 Beach mold
26 Slams
27 Snarky syllable
28 Distillery eponym Joseph
29 Mud spot?
30 Wreak vengeance on
32 "That's a ___!"
33 Celebrity whose name sounds like a drink
35 Thing, at bar
36 Bad way to turn
38 ___ Peninsula (2014 crisis site)
41 Some beachwear
42 Neat
44 Source of the words "curry" and "pariah"
45 Perform poorly
47 Apply, as Bengay
48 Lies around
49 Chuckleheads
52 Takes in
54 H
55 Opposite of hence
56 Place of corruption

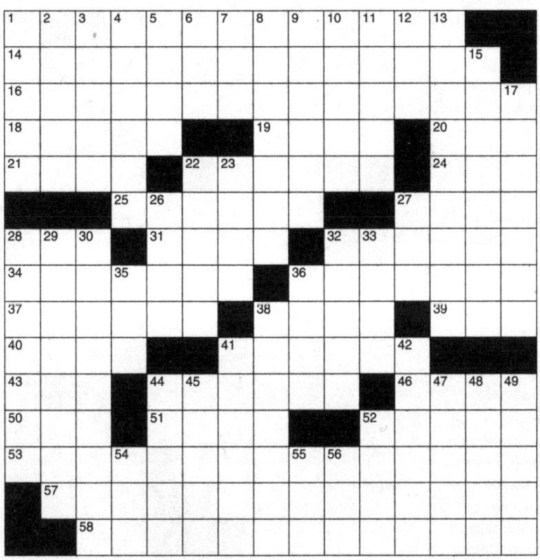

by David Phillips and David Steinberg

142 HARD

ACROSS

1 Colorful carnival offerings
9 Off-key
13 Farm-to-table advocate
14 What's now yours
15 Words recited before "gratia plena, Dominus tecum"
16 Put one's nose to the grindstone
17 Moldable kitchen stuff
18 Like President Paul Kagame
19 Actress Singer of "Footloose" and TV's "Fame"
20 Skipper whose #6 was retired in 2014
21 Where many nuts are housed
24 "The Mod Squad" role
25 Drifted off
26 Supermodel Wek
27 Terminal giant, once
30 Cutting-edge device named for its versatility
32 Grp. with many missionaries
33 Tightener of locks
35 Bucks, e.g.
37 Golf takeback, maybe
38 Crusades, e.g.
40 Like some food and flattery
42 Promote to annoyance
44 Piano bar?
45 Criticized
48 Hard up
49 Cooler person to live with?
50 Charon's passengers
51 Language of the Twelve Tables
52 Revival V.I.P.s, perhaps
53 They corral kids

DOWN

1 Some industrial waste
2 Cutting-edge
3 Its name comes from Nahuatl for "jaguar"
4 Z28 and ZL1
5 They're often standing when the curtains are lowered
6 Sushi wrapper
7 Mayo's place
8 Arabian ___
9 Polish giant, once
10 Part of a rig
11 Like runs caused by errors
12 Hillbilly sorts
14 Flawlessly
16 Lures with music
18 Optimistic
20 Setting of "The Sun Also Rises" and "Some Like It Hot"
22 Spanglish or Franglais component
23 Plant poisonous to cattle
27 "Cross my heart"
28 Material used in apitherapy
29 Shelled shill
31 By the book
34 Tidbits
36 Store locator, maybe
39 Move like a tornado
41 Union jack?
43 Pickup line?
45 Hew
46 He played the U.S. president in "Canadian Bacon," 1995
47 Fox network?
49 24-Across, for one

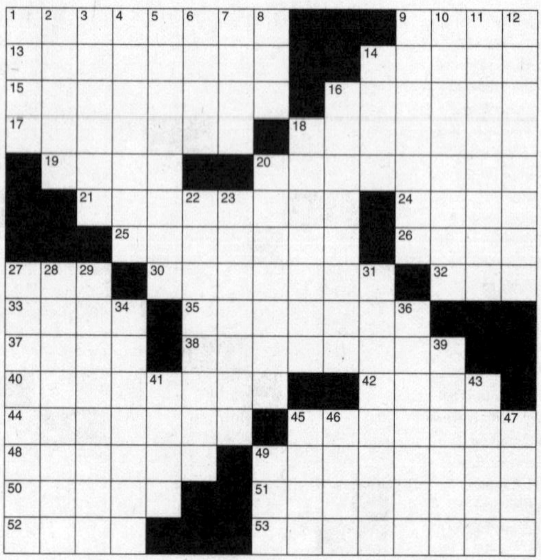

by Jeff Chen

ACROSS

1 "I hear you"
10 Flub
15 Smell-O-Vision competitor of 1950s cinema
16 Sound of an everyday explosion
17 Order-flouting protester
18 Butler who was expelled from West Point
19 It welcomes compliments
20 Evil Queen's disguise in "Snow White and Seven Dwarfs"
21 Pops up
23 Decked out
25 Accouterment for a diva
26 Isle named for a Gaelic goddess
27 Opposing group
28 Best Actress winner for "Klute"
30 Narrow waterway
31 Male offspring, in Munich
32 1992 Olympic figure skating silver medalist
33 Good place to vent
35 Restaurant breakfast innovation of 1971
38 Alternatives to Bartletts
40 Mate 4 life?
41 Many a charity run
44 Paltry amount
45 Squinting cartoon character
47 Add with a beater
48 Curly-tailed dogs
50 Office page?
51 World's second-largest retailer
52 Hit the roof
54 Esquire's target audience
55 Advent time: Abbr.
56 Tiny hairs
57 Item in the lobby of a country inn
60 Peterhof Palace personages
61 11-Down, e.g.
62 Kids' classic that opens "His mother was ugly and his father was ugly"
63 Prized

DOWN

1 Noble at the end of a table?
2 Sauce seasoning
3 Attack viciously
4 Prey for a dingo
5 Roseola symptoms
6 Where the rubber meets the road
7 Chill (with)
8 Renoir vis-à-vis Monet
9 Go up against
10 Lead-in to bones or knuckles
11 Canyon colour
12 Approachable, unglamorous sort
13 Algonquin Round Table, e.g.
14 Pressure cooker
22 Big name in financial fraud
24 "Correct!"
25 Music player for a break dancer
28 Org. with scam alerts
29 "Ariadne ___ Naxos"
32 Comforting words to a worried loved one
34 South American monkeys
36 Impulse buy at a checkout counter
37 "The Day the Earth Stood Still" craft
38 Parts
39 Foster
42 "Impressive!"
43 Bad-mouthed
46 Many an infomercial offering
47 Three in a quarter
49 Burj Khalifa feature
51 Jai alai basket
53 Mission
54 Piddling
58 Former Mideast org.
59 Grill measure, in brief

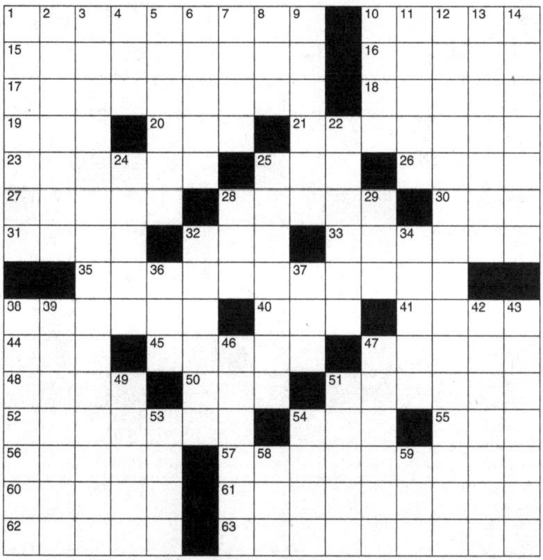

by Kristian House

144 HARD

ACROSS

1 Pockets
16 Fictional character with a ring of power
17 Got back on the horse
18 One who's always positive
19 Cloture voter: Abbr.
20 2016 Republican convention site: Abbr.
21 Cause of a certain dramatic departure
22 "You could've left some of that out"
24 Eastern sovereign
27 Mr. ___, protagonist in Wilde's "The Canterville Ghost"
31 "Gotcha," in old lingo
33 Massage deeply
35 She battled Lucy in "Kill Bill: Volume 1"
36 Finish better than fourth
37 Presidential moniker on "The West Wing"
38 Stuffs one's face with
40 It has base pairs
41 Sistine Chapel setting
43 Totally rules
44 Accepts as true
46 L'___ de droit (the rule of law)
48 Stan's employer on "American Dad!"
49 "I forget the words" sounds
51 Amsterdam of l'Océan Indien, e.g.
53 Old French narrative poem
56 Was kind and generous
62 Handy sofa item
63 "Why should I?!"
64 Film come-on

DOWN

1 They may be on the house: Abbr.
2 Start of a lament
3 Rest period
4 The presidency, notably
5 Standard
6 Potpourri part
7 Less of a dream
8 Anne Sexton's palindrome-inspired poem "Rats Live ___ Evil Star"
9 Fall heavily
10 Retro do
11 "___ Steps" (best-selling religious novel)
12 Accelerando or ritardando negator
13 Girl's name that's a homophone of a cloth
14 Dyne-centimeters
15 Impudent twerp
23 One denoted by a cross on the Vietnam Veterans Memorial, for short
25 Thunderdome, e.g.
26 Zone, so to speak
28 Southern home of Stillman College
29 "Nothing's broken"
30 Lacking
31 It gets clicks for flicks
32 Ordering aid
34 Stuff down the throat of
37 Exec's perk
39 "Boy, ___!"
42 Utah, once
45 Middle Passage transport
47 Like peers
50 They may cut a sentence short
52 Player of the villain in "The Man Who Knew Too Much"
54 Los ___, Calif.
55 T.S.A. request: Abbr.
56 Clasps
57 Pick ___ (fault-find)
58 Tantrum thrower
59 Not worth ___
60 Partner in mapmaking
61 Onetime big inits. in car financing

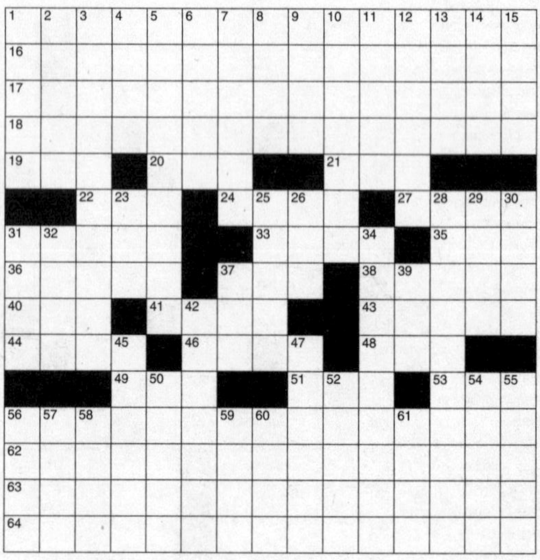

by Jason Flinn

HARD 145

ACROSS
1 Anagrams
10 Spoke hesitantly
15 "Who the hell does he think he is?!"
16 Like basil leaves
17 Italian for "sleeves"
18 Phylum, order or genus
19 Don ___, 1956 World Series M.V.P.
20 Comportments
21 "Bluebeard's Castle" composer
24 Drives
26 Letters in some church names
27 Half-cup measures
29 Kind of classic rock?
32 Coin of Iran
34 Attraction temporarily shut down and partly moved to Siberia during W.W. II
36 Eye
37 Longtime "All My Children" role
38 Mazar of "Entourage"
39 Rule in a kids' outdoor game
41 Lead
42 Old atlas inits.
43 Cameos, for example
44 Like Bernie Sanders, before 2015: Abbr.
45 Turned up
47 Mountain bike features
50 Swell
52 Swell
55 Capital near Lake Titicaca
56 First novel of the Great Plains trilogy
60 "Smart" guy
61 Lead singer for the Cars
62 Hybrid woman-bird monster
63 The "thee" in Shakespeare's line "But I do love thee! and when I love thee not, / Chaos is come again"

DOWN
1 Personal ad designation
2 Chinese tea
3 Published
4 Not straight up
5 Gambling mecca
6 Single-named musical artist
7 Do-overs
8 Single-named artist
9 They're marked with X's
10 Total wreck
11 Benefit
12 Uses flowery language
13 Kind of blue that's close to green
14 Animal shelters
21 Magna Carta drafters
22 Title trio in a 1986 comedy
23 One unlikely to punk out
25 Aids in raising arms?
27 Onetime political leader with a museum in Grand Rapids, Mich.
28 How beer at a cookout might be kept
30 Protect from an overflow, in a way
31 Alternatives to 'Vettes
33 Bucolic setting
34 Simon of Duran Duran
35 Goals of some drives, for short
40 Nine-time Hart Memorial Trophy winner
46 Image Awards grp.
47 Wasn't overturned
48 Starting now
49 Early hour
50 Not so hot
51 When repeated, part of Van Morrison's "Brown Eyed Girl"
53 Cap-___ (from head to toe)
54 Motor problems
57 That: Sp.
58 Kylo ___ of "Star Wars"
59 Mighty Mighty Bosstones genre

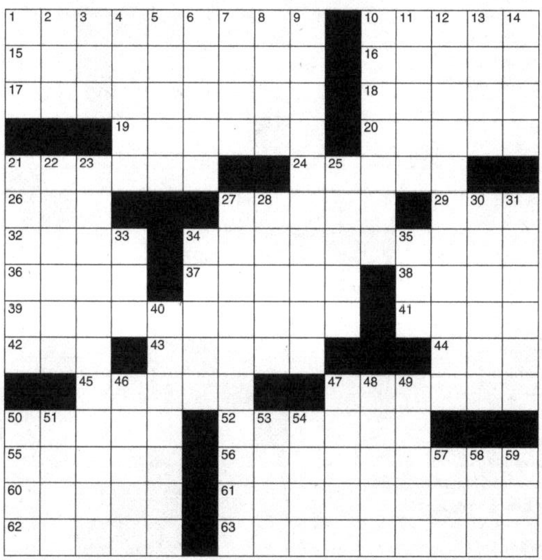

by Damon Gulczynski

146 HARD

ACROSS

1 Case closer
7 French frozen desserts
13 Entangle
15 Fruit
16 Like taxes and fines
18 Doing time
19 Sound effect in the comic "B.C."
20 Decorative skewer for serving hors d'oeuvres
22 VW Golf hatchback
23 11-Down sort
25 Manfred succeeded him as baseball commissioner in 2015
26 Spot at an airport
27 "Get ___!"
29 South of Brazil?
30 Shut down
31 1999 parody featuring the starship Protector
34 What 28 states are
35 Rap
36 Some 40th-birthday gag gifts
37 N.F.L. coach Rivera
38 Spruced up
42 Capital of Washington?
43 "___ thou no poison mix'd . . . ?": "Romeo and Juliet"
45 ___ Bottling Company (Cleveland fixture for over 85 years)
46 "___ expected . . ."
47 Beverage made with petals
49 When Mex. celebrates Independence Day
50 Distraught
52 Spills inadvertently
54 Title brat of kid-lit
55 Go back over
56 Opposite of took off
57 "Gotcha"

DOWN

1 Miss Hungary of 1936, familiarly
2 One way to break out
3 The marrying kind?
4 Marital lead-in
5 Second wife of Einstein
6 Shows signs of aging
7 "Morning Mood" composer
8 Time of self-sacrifice
9 Lummox
10 Feature of many decorative vases
11 High-and-mighty
12 IBM logo feature
14 He said "You kind of live and die by the serve"
17 Provider of more bells and whistles
21 1960s sitcom matriarch
24 Lummoxes
26 Bit of fraternity party detritus
28 Things to blaze
30 Keep informed
32 Head overseas?
33 Play starters, for short
34 Pitching aid
35 [Spoiler alert!] He dies in "The Force Awakens"
36 Like many cheeses and tablets
39 Sights at a Supercharger
40 What gets broken at a mixer
41 "Hot dog!"
43 Wasn't sure, say
44 Heads overseas?
47 Smoke screen
48 Repeated words in a multiple-count verdict reading
51 "Little Birds" author
53 Title meaning "majesty"

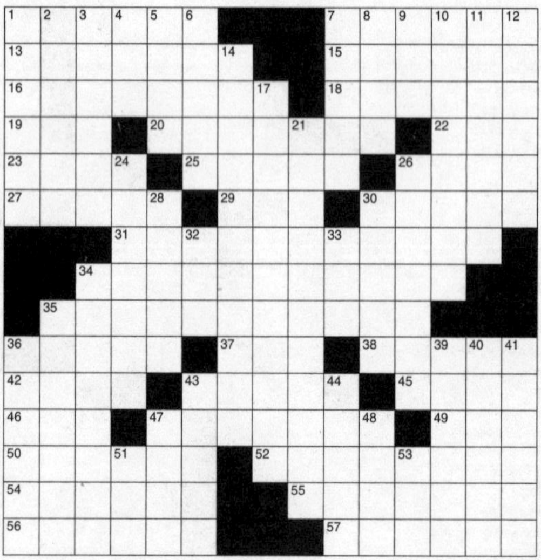

by Frederick J. Healy

HARD 147

ACROSS

1 Singer with the 1977 hit "Lido Shuffle"
7 Things with roots
13 House of Tybalt and Juliet
15 "Under the Lilacs" writer, 1878
16 Eastern border of Manhattan's Tompkins Square Park
17 Staple of Caribbean music
18 Car mentioned in "Hotel California," informally
20 Eponymous bacteriologist Julius
21 Nickname for Francisco
22 The so-called "sunny side"
24 Cold-shoulder
25 Many a circus feat
27 7-Eleven, e.g.
29 Steven Van Zandt's role on "The Sopranos," informally
30 Constantly adjusting one's glasses, e.g.
32 Back on track?
34 Who said "There is nothing more deceptive than an obvious fact"
38 Wing man?
39 1977 reggae classic
40 So-so
41 Concert stage effect
42 Polemologists study them
44 Wiriness
48 Same-sex household?
50 "I deny all that!"
52 Artist Thomas ___, founder of the Hudson River School
53 Bowls are seen in them
55 Harebrained
57 Creative classroom
59 Put one's foot down, in a way
60 "Right-o"
61 Rock candy, essentially
62 Give one's blessing
63 Lounging spot

DOWN

1 Little rascals
2 But
3 Illuminating comment
4 Something a politician proposes that takes heat?
5 Archivist's supply
6 Slummy
7 Who sings "As Time Goes By" in "Casablanca"
8 Thunderous noise
9 End of many a farm name
10 Execrable
11 2000s retro Chrysler
12 Kind of steel
14 Building bar with one flange
19 Sign at a concession stand
23 Katharine ___, onetime publisher of the Washington Post
26 So far, informally
28 Hits on the side . . . or cuts from the back
31 Agemate
33 Andrew Jackson nickname
34 Jaywalkers, e.g.
35 Payments to speakers, say
36 With beauty and class
37 Common character in Dungeons & Dragons
43 Low class
45 Casual response to "Thanks"
46 Title six-year-old of literature
47 Made damp
49 Where to watch the Beeb
51 Cousin of "Skoal!"
54 "The 120 Days of Sodom" author
56 Colombian crop
58 Team on which Larry Bird played, on scoreboards

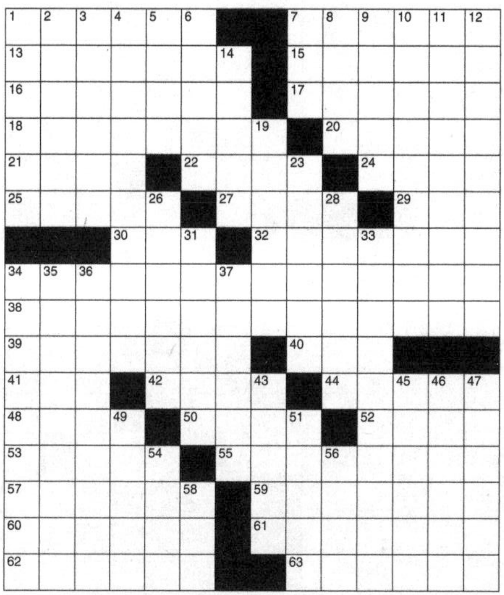

by Josh Knapp

148 HARD

ACROSS

1 Growing group
12 Extremely, in modern lingo
15 Hollywood star whose grandfather was the Cuban patriot José Martí
16 Home of the city and county of Waterford: Abbr.
17 1980s electronic innovation from Detroit
18 Sprint Cup Series sponsor
19 Steamed
20 Many an attendance fig.
21 Basketball Hall-of-Famer Dan
23 Opera genre for "Tosca" and "Pagliacci"
25 Green curtains?
27 Cartoon crony of Fancy-Fancy and Choo-Choo
29 Mine entrance
30 Hooked projection on a bird feather
34 Drizzling clouds
36 New York city near the Pennsylvania border
37 ___ Season Tip-Off (annual hoops event)
39 "Hurray!"
40 Thwart
42 Like seven of the 12 presidents between 1869 and 1923
44 Part of E.M.S.: Abbr.
45 Conditional construct in computer programming
47 Clark Gable film that was a remake of his "Red Dust"
49 Personal info such as education and work history
54 Like Homer Simpson or Herman Munster
55 Big D campus
57 Novarro who played Ben-Hur
58 E.M.S. offering
59 Hydrophilic
62 Prefix with -lithic
63 Ones using slides
64 Doubly hyphenated ID
65 Half-volley in tennis, e.g.

DOWN

1 When "Double, double toil and trouble" is chanted in "Macbeth"
2 Largest employer in the Midwest's Quad Cities, for short
3 NATO alphabet letter
4 Actress Christine
5 Lily Tomlin character with a headset
6 Show sign
7 Burst, in a way
8 Birds whose eggs are incubated by males
9 AriZona competitor
10 Half of hex-
11 Prefix with linguistics
12 Pride of Moscow?
13 One making People look good?
14 Ozone layer issue
22 Seal of office for some pharaohs
24 Bit of footwear, for short
26 Price abbr.
28 Awards that have had a Healthcare category since 2009
30 Unconventional sorts
31 Tender towards one's exes?
32 Failed to honor
33 Defendant's complaint
35 Good deal
38 Area with lawns and picket fences, informally
41 Follower of 50-Down
43 Super Bowl whose pregame show honored the Apollo astronauts
46 Unappreciated by
48 Series often seen with S's on the ends
50 '60s president
51 Some drivers with "slow-moving vehicle" reflectors
52 Sidekick of film and TV
53 Common Allen wrench?
56 Ice Bucket Challenge, e.g.
60 N.L. West team, on scoreboards
61 Start of many California place names

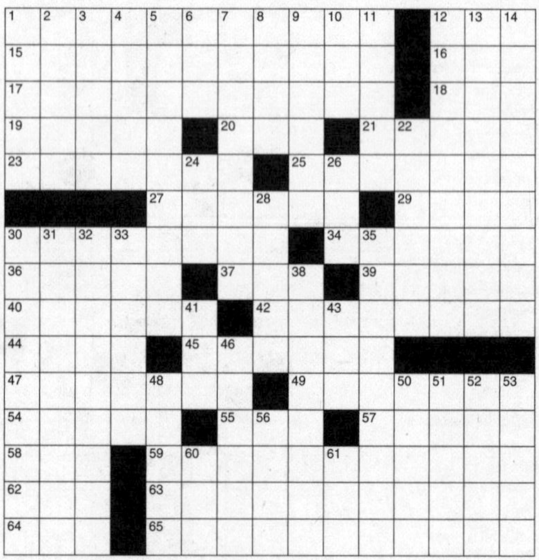

by Byron Walden and Brad Wilber

ACROSS

1 Popular website with virtual animals
8 Met for a party?
16 Film villain who says "Your feeble skills are no match for the power of the dark side"
18 Classic conflict
19 Confederate
20 Bold way to solve a crossword
21 Some AOL exchanges
22 Like teddies, often
23 Source of some leather
25 Wheel that runs?
26 Rat-___
27 Feckless
28 Beau
29 Tough to get ahold of
30 Boots one
31 Anytown, U.S.A., sign
32 Something hot
34 "___ on Fire" (2012 Alicia Keys hit)
35 Executor's charge
38 Camp invader
40 Bellwether's "belles"
44 Carried
45 Put on hold
46 Get-out-of-jail aid, maybe
47 Go without saying?
48 Route through the boondocks
49 Protein-rich paste
50 ___ Tamid (synagogue lamp)
51 Raiser of horses?
52 Like some cakes
53 Classic R&B hit about a returning lover
57 It has multiple clauses
58 Honey
59 Post-Impressionist Seurat

DOWN

1 Very distant clouds
2 Issue
3 Like spectroscopes and microscopes
4 Dictatorial boss
5 Director ___ C. Kenton
6 Prominent feature of a sloth
7 Sign adored by angels
8 Brief refreshers
9 "The Green Hornet" trumpeter
10 Stand on its head
11 Holder of spirits
12 Literally, "land of the sun"
13 Second club used on a par 4 hole, maybe
14 Adams and Jefferson, e.g.
15 Final order of things?
17 Big name in drugs
23 Feudal lord
24 Memo starter
25 Beer-and-whiskey cocktail
28 ". . . let slip the dogs of ___": Shak.
31 Stuck
33 Grabbed something
34 Black-tie event
35 Vernacular much debated in the 1990s
36 By hook or by crook
37 Ancient Greek craft
38 Island north of Antigua
39 Tablet contents, perhaps
41 Not yet admitted
42 Heart
43 They hold water
45 Power in old films
48 Purchase in large quantity
51 Medium gait
52 Twice quattuor
54 Wild way to go
55 Bit of blood-typing shorthand
56 21st word of the Pledge of Allegiance

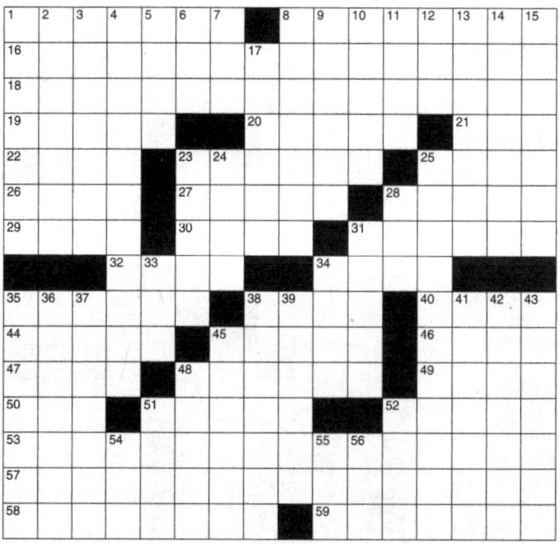

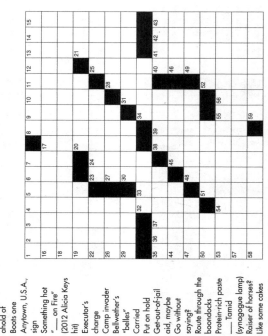

by David Steinberg

150 HARD

ACROSS

1 Ones hanging around a deli?
8 One face in the crowd?
13 Poison also called white arsenic
14 French siege site of 1597
16 Children's song about avian anatomy
17 Lot
18 Barrel holder
19 Something held at arm's length
21 Neighbor of Windsor Castle
23 Priceline possibilities
24 I have, to Henri
25 Converts to pastureland, say
29 Nature
30 Equal: Prefix
31 Post-stunt provocation
34 Ill-fated, old-style
37 Aims
38 After the fact
39 Grub for a grub
40 Zebu feature
41 One might start working on Black Friday
46 Debatable ability
47 Really go up
49 Aye's opposite, poetically
50 "Hear me out"
55 Whacking tool
56 Way cool, in modern lingo
57 Like lingerie
59 James who edited the O.E.D.
60 Bare-bones
61 Bobby who co-founded the Black Panthers
62 Like some unions

DOWN

1 Toast, e.g.
2 Untold
3 Where Shaq won the Adolph Rupp Trophy
4 Two of them are worth a sawbuck
5 Winning move
6 Involving multiple states: Abbr.
7 Deem appropriate
8 Stir
9 Off
10 Tilt
11 Home brewing vessel
12 About 2% of the Hope Diamond
13 Was spitting nails
15 One of the Leewards
20 Establish gradually
22 Tropicana label specification
26 Hardly seen, to Seneca
27 Way back then, way back when
28 Certain Internet diagram
29 Fatsis who wrote the best-selling "Word Freak"
32 Student taking Civil Procedure, most likely
33 Some car wash grps.
34 "The vice of a few intelligent people," per Voltaire
35 Alternative to quinoa
36 Sancho Panza, to Don Quixote
42 Third-ever Best Actor Oscar winner
43 Nix
44 Source of resentment in the Colonies in the 1770s
45 Soviet co-op
47 Monkshood flower's "hood"
48 Baroque window
51 Dunn formerly of "S.N.L."
52 "Annette Sings ___" (1960 pop album)
53 Couple
54 Elephantine Island is in it
58 Mayo, for one

by Andrew Kingsley

Answers

1

O	G	L	E	S	■	C	S	I	■	W	R	U	N	G
F	L	O	A	T	■	R	O	O	■	E	A	S	Y	A
F	A	N	T	A	■	A	C	T	I	N	G	O	U	T
E	R	G	■	N	Y	G	I	A	N	T	S	■	■	■
D	E	S	A	D	E	■	A	S	T	O	■	F	O	X
■	■	T	R	O	W	E	L	■	R	V	P	A	R	K
■	J	E	A	N	■	A	L	A	■	E	L	L	I	E
C	O	M	B	O	■	S	U	P	■	R	O	L	O	S
A	D	M	I	N	■	T	B	S	■	T	W	I	N	■
P	I	E	C	E	D	■	R	E	D	H	E	N	■	■
T	E	D	■	S	U	Z	I	■	H	E	D	G	E	D
■	■	■	S	H	O	W	C	A	S	E	■	D	W	I
S	T	A	T	E	S	E	A	L	■	D	R	O	O	P
P	O	D	I	A	■	I	N	S	■	G	A	W	K	S
A	W	A	R	D	■	G	T	O	■	E	E	N	S	Y

2

O	B	A	M	A	■	C	A	T	T	■	P	O	S	H
T	A	R	O	T	■	A	M	O	S	■	I	T	T	Y
I	N	T	H	E	D	R	I	N	K	■	T	E	R	P
S	A	S	S	■	I	O	N	E	■	M	C	R	A	E
■	■	■	■	M	E	M	O	R	Y	C	H	I	P	S
I	G	O	T	I	T	■	■	■	U	S	E	■	■	■
N	E	P	A	L	■	T	U	N	A	■	S	W	A	T
K	N	U	C	K	L	E	S	A	N	D	W	I	C	H
S	O	S	O	■	A	D	A	M	■	Y	O	S	H	I
■	■	■	T	R	I	■	■	■	S	N	O	P	E	S
S	M	A	R	T	C	O	O	K	I	E	■	■	■	■
H	A	G	U	E	■	C	R	A	G	■	B	O	N	A
E	R	I	C	■	L	U	N	C	H	B	O	X	E	S
M	I	N	K	■	A	L	O	E	■	T	W	E	R	K
P	E	G	S	■	P	I	T	Y	■	W	E	N	D	S

3

D	O	O	R	S	■	A	J	A	R	■	E	T	N	A
I	M	H	I	T	■	R	A	G	U	■	A	H	E	M
V	A	M	P	I	R	E	B	A	T	■	R	A	R	E
A	N	Y	O	N	E	■	S	T	A	L	L	I	O	N
■	■	■	P	E	A	S	■	E	B	A	Y	■	■	■
F	A	V	E	■	D	O	E	■	A	T	O	A	S	T
O	R	O	N	O	■	D	R	A	G	O	N	F	L	Y
N	I	L	■	N	O	O	N	D	A	Y	■	L	A	P
D	E	V	I	L	F	I	S	H	■	A	B	A	T	E
A	L	O	T	O	F	■	T	O	W	■	A	C	E	S
■	■	■	S	A	N	S	■	C	H	E	R	■	■	■
B	E	A	T	N	I	K	S	■	A	P	O	L	L	O
A	C	T	I	■	G	I	A	N	T	S	Q	U	I	D
W	H	O	M	■	H	E	M	I	■	O	U	T	E	D
L	O	B	E	■	T	R	E	X	■	N	E	E	D	S

4

A	L	O	H	A	■	M	O	S	S	■	I	K	E	A
L	U	N	A	R	■	O	H	N	O	■	P	E	R	U
A	R	T	I	F	I	C	I	A	L	C	H	A	R	T
S	K	O	R	■	S	H	O	P	■	H	O	N	O	R
■	■	■	G	A	L	A	■	■	W	I	N	E	R	Y
C	H	E	E	S	E	S	O	F	I	N	E	■	■	■
R	O	L	L	S	■	■	W	O	K	■	S	T	O	P
A	L	L	■	T	A	B	L	O	I	D	■	R	O	O
G	E	E	Z	■	N	Y	E	■	■	I	S	U	Z	U
■	■	■	I	M	O	U	T	O	F	C	H	E	E	R
M	U	S	L	I	N	■	■	F	L	E	A	■	■	■
U	N	C	L	E	■	C	A	F	E	■	M	Y	R	A
C	H	A	I	N	S	U	N	D	E	R	W	E	A	R
H	I	L	O	■	A	R	E	A	■	N	O	T	M	E
O	P	E	N	■	D	E	W	Y	■	S	W	I	S	S

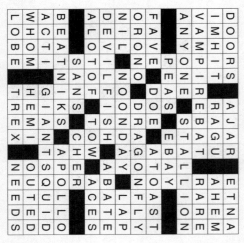

5

R	A	T	I	O	■	C	A	I	T	■	A	D	A	M
P	L	A	N	K	■	R	I	D	E	■	R	E	N	O
M	A	I	N	C	O	U	R	S	E	■	T	A	G	S
■	■	■	■	O	D	E	S	■	■	A	D	D	L	E
L	I	B	E	R	A	L	■	P	A	G	E	B	O	Y
O	L	E	A	R	Y	■	S	E	N	E	C	A	■	■
S	A	N	T	A	■	C	A	A	N	■	O	T	T	O
E	N	C	■	L	A	S	T	L	A	P	■	T	E	X
S	A	H	L	■	C	P	U	S	■	I	R	E	N	E
■	■	W	A	L	L	O	P	■	D	E	F	R	A	Y
S	W	A	P	O	U	T	■	L	U	C	K	Y	M	E
T	A	R	T	S	■	■	S	A	S	H	■	■	■	■
A	T	M	O	■	N	O	N	S	T	A	R	T	E	R
K	E	E	P	■	F	L	U	S	■	R	A	I	N	Y
E	R	R	S	■	L	E	G	O	■	T	H	E	S	E

6

C	L	O	G	■	A	Q	A	B	A	■	D	E	S	C
A	E	R	O	■	V	O	C	A	B	■	R	E	B	A
V	I	E	T	N	A	M	E	R	A	■	A	R	A	L
■	■	■	H	I	S	■	■	B	A	D	G	I	R	L
A	N	T	I	C	■	T	A	R	■	U	S	E	R	S
B	A	R	C	E	L	O	N	A	M	E	T	R	O	■
R	I	O	■	■	A	G	E	■	R	T	E	■	■	■
A	R	I	Z	O	N	A	M	E	M	O	R	I	A	L
■	■	■	I	N	K	■	O	V	O	■	■	D	R	E
■	C	A	P	T	A	I	N	A	M	E	R	I	C	A
W	A	L	D	O	■	O	E	N	■	S	W	O	O	P
O	N	E	R	E	E	D	■	■	I	M	A	■	■	■
R	O	T	I	■	M	I	D	D	L	E	N	A	M	E
S	L	A	V	■	A	N	N	U	L	■	D	O	U	G
T	A	P	E	■	J	E	A	N	S	■	A	L	S	O

7

H	O	P	■	T	A	M	A	L	E	■	R	O	A	R
A	N	I	■	S	P	I	N	A	L	■	E	D	G	E
H	U	N	■	P	A	R	T	Y	F	A	V	O	R	S
A	S	K	S	■	T	E	E	S	■	B	E	R	E	T
■	■	F	I	D	O	■	■	■	C	U	R	S	E	S
P	I	L	L	O	W	F	I	G	H	T	S	■	■	■
S	N	O	O	T	■	A	F	R	O	■	E	P	O	S
I	C	Y	■	H	E	R	O	I	C	S	■	E	W	E
S	A	D	A	■	M	O	L	E	■	O	C	T	E	T
■	■	■	P	O	U	N	D	F	O	O	L	I	S	H
R	E	A	R	M	S	■	■	■	U	N	I	T	■	■
A	R	S	O	N	■	A	U	N	T	■	P	F	F	T
P	O	P	P	I	N	F	R	E	S	H	■	O	A	R
I	D	E	O	■	B	A	D	G	E	R	■	U	Z	I
D	E	N	S	■	C	R	U	S	T	S	■	R	E	P

8

B	L	I	S	S	■	■	A	G	A	R	■	S	P	A
A	A	R	O	N	■	S	C	O	R	E	■	T	E	L
T	M	O	B	I	L	E	H	O	M	E	■	I	K	E
H	E	N	■	P	I	N	E	D	■	D	O	N	O	R
■	■	■	L	E	A	S	■	T	H	I	C	K	E	T
T	S	Q	U	A	R	E	R	O	O	T	S	■	■	■
R	O	U	S	T	■	■	E	G	O	S	■	C	A	M
O	M	I	T	■	S	A	B	O	T	■	C	O	D	A
Y	E	T	■	N	I	L	E	■	■	L	A	S	E	R
■	■	■	T	B	A	L	L	B	E	A	R	I	N	G
M	I	S	N	A	M	E	■	I	T	S	Y	■	■	■
E	M	I	T	S	■	G	A	M	U	T	■	B	I	O
L	O	L	■	T	T	O	P	B	I	L	L	I	N	G
T	U	T	■	A	I	R	T	O	■	E	I	G	E	R
S	T	Y	■	R	A	Y	S	■	■	G	L	A	Z	E

9

G	I	F	S	■	E	B	B	E	D	■	O	P	E	L
O	R	E	O	■	S	A	U	N	A	■	K	A	N	E
B	O	U	L	D	E	R	D	A	M	■	O	P	T	S
I	N	D	I	E	■	■	S	M	A	C	K	E	R	S
■	■	■	D	A	D	S	■	E	T	A	■	R	E	O
A	S	K	■	R	O	C	K	L	O	B	S	T	E	R
W	I	N	G	S	P	A	N	■	■	S	I	R	■	■
E	C	O	L	■	E	R	I	C	A	■	F	A	I	R
■	■	W	O	O	■	■	F	O	R	A	T	I	M	E
P	E	B	B	L	E	B	E	A	C	H	■	L	O	X
E	L	Y	■	E	R	E	■	T	H	O	R	■	■	■
L	O	N	E	S	O	M	E	■	■	R	A	I	S	E
O	P	A	L	■	D	U	S	T	J	A	C	K	E	T
S	E	M	I	■	E	S	T	E	R	■	K	E	N	T
I	D	E	S	■	D	E	A	N	S	■	S	A	D	E

10

L	O	N	G	■	B	A	R	E	D	■	■	E	B	A	Y
O	B	O	E	■	E	M	O	T	E	S	■	L	I	R	A
F	A	R	M	A	N	I	M	A	L	S	■	S	T	I	R
A	M	T	■	L	E	D	A	■	A	T	E	■	T	A	D
T	A	E	B	O	■	S	N	O	W	A	N	G	E	L	S
■	■	■	O	M	I	T	■	P	A	R	L	O	R	■	■
M	U	S	C	A	T	■	P	E	R	■	■	O	E	D	S
I	N	T	E	R	I	O	R	D	E	S	I	G	N	E	R
R	E	E	L	■	■	S	E	S	■	T	O	L	D	Y	A
■	■	A	L	S	A	C	E	■	R	U	N	E	■	■	■
R	A	D	I	O	R	A	N	G	E	■	I	D	S	A	Y
A	M	Y	■	S	Y	R	■	I	S	L	A	■	A	A	A
D	O	J	O	■	A	N	K	L	E	I	N	J	U	R	Y
A	R	O	D	■	N	O	O	D	L	E	■	A	T	O	M
R	E	B	S	■	■	D	I	A	L	S	■	G	E	N	E

11

P	I	T	A		C	Z	A	R		C	A	N	D	O
A	T	O	M		H	O	B	O		A	D	I	E	U
R	E	N	E	G	A	D	E	S		D	A	N	E	S
	M	I	N	O	R	I	T	Y	R	E	P	O	R	T
				A	G	A			A	N	T			
P	Y	R	O	T	E	C	H	N	I	C		A	K	A
R	O	A	D	S			E	A	S	E	M	E	N	T
O	U	Z	O		S	H	A	P	E		A	S	E	A
O	V	E	R	S	E	E	R			K	N	O	L	L
F	E	D		P	A	R	T	Y	P	E	O	P	L	E
			S	A	M			E	O	N				
P	O	E	T	R	Y	I	N	M	O	T	I	O	N	
S	A	V	O	R		M	A	E	L	S	T	R	O	M
S	T	E	N	O		P	I	N	E		C	E	D	E
T	H	R	E	W		S	L	I	D		H	O	S	T

12

G	E	A	R		R	A	C	K		B	E	T	C	H	A
U	T	N	E		I	C	E	E		A	V	A	L	O	N
L	C	D	S		C	A	R	P	E	D	A	B	O	U	T
P	E	R	C	H	E	D	A	T	O	P			U	R	I
S	T	E	A	M	S			I	N	R	A	G	S		
	C	A	N	O	E	I	S	T	S		P	I	E	C	E
					E	M	I	R		T	E	N	A	N	T
F	L	O	U	N	D	E	R	E	D	A	R	O	U	N	D
D	E	L	V	E	S		G	A	S	X					
R	O	D	E	O		S	A	L	T	D	O	M	E	S	
		M	A	N	U	A	L			O	R	O	M	E	O
E	C	O			S	K	A	T	E	D	A	L	O	N	G
G	O	N	E	F	I	S	H	I	N	G		A	P	A	L
O	N	E	P	I	N		A	N	N	E		R	O	T	E
S	K	Y	I	N	G		D	Y	E	S		S	P	E	D

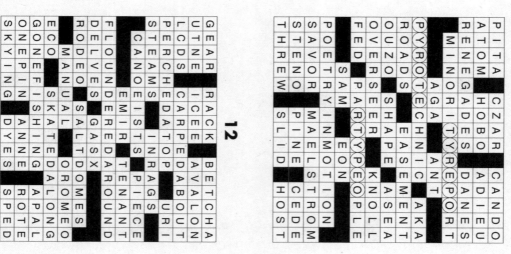

13

L	E	F	T	■	A	L	S	O	■	■	A	B	C	S
I	R	I	S	■	N	O	K	I	A	■	T	O	O	L
M	A	S	K	E	D	B	A	L	L	■	T	O	N	E
A	S	H	■	A	R	E	■	S	T	A	I	N	E	D
■	■	S	T	R	E	S	S	■	A	L	L	E	Y	S
M	A	T	E	S	■	■	K	A	R	M	A	■	■	■
A	V	I	D	■	T	H	E	N	B	A	■	F	O	E
M	I	C	■	C	H	E	W	T	O	Y	■	U	V	A
A	S	K	■	H	E	R	E	S	Y	■	O	N	E	S
■	■	■	D	I	N	E	R	■	■	N	A	N	N	Y
S	H	R	I	N	E	■	S	A	F	E	T	Y	■	■
L	E	O	N	A	R	D	■	N	E	W	■	B	O	B
E	A	V	E	■	V	E	L	V	E	T	R	O	P	E
E	V	E	R	■	E	M	A	I	L	■	O	N	U	S
P	E	S	O	■	■	O	W	L	S	■	W	E	S	T

14

Y	U	K	S	■	I	T	O	N	■	S	I	L	K	S
A	B	I	T	■	P	A	C	E	■	C	H	A	I	N
N	E	L	L	■	O	R	C	A	■	H	E	N	N	A
G	R	O	U	N	D	O	U	T	S	■	A	C	D	C
■	■	■	C	O	N	T	R	O	L	F	R	E	A	K
L	A	D	I	D	A	■	■	■	Y	A	Y	■	■	■
A	U	R	A	■	N	E	W	T	■	D	A	V	I	D
M	T	A	■	T	O	T	A	S	T	E	■	E	L	K
B	O	W	I	E	■	A	N	K	A	■	N	E	I	N
■	■	■	M	A	O	■	■	■	B	L	U	R	A	Y
M	A	J	O	R	P	R	O	B	L	E	M	■	■	■
I	D	E	D	■	T	O	M	F	O	O	L	E	R	Y
N	O	L	I	E	■	C	A	L	I	■	O	B	O	E
D	P	L	U	S	■	C	H	A	D	■	C	A	M	O
S	T	O	M	P	■	O	A	T	S	■	K	N	E	W

15

A	M	F	M	■	N	O	T	E	■	O	F	T	E	N
C	O	R	A	■	E	R	I	E	■	C	A	R	V	E
C	O	E	D	■	W	A	L	L	S	T	R	E	E	T
E	S	E	■	P	E	L	T	■	H	O	M	E	R	S
S	H	O	A	L	S	■	■	B	U	B	■	■	■	■
S	U	N	S	E	T	B	O	U	L	E	V	A	R	D
■	■	B	S	A	■	O	P	T	■	R	I	L	E	Y
L	U	A	U	■	■	B	E	T	■	■	E	L	S	E
E	R	I	C	H	■	B	R	O	■	E	I	N	■	■
M	U	L	H	O	L	L	A	N	D	D	R	I	V	E
■	■	■	■	F	E	E	■	■	A	D	A	G	E	S
A	D	R	I	F	T	■	M	Y	M	Y	■	H	S	T
R	O	A	D	M	O	V	I	E	S	■	A	T	T	A
A	P	N	E	A	■	I	S	L	E	■	B	E	A	T
B	E	G	A	N	■	P	O	L	L	■	E	R	L	E

16

P	L	A	N	E	■	S	K	Y	■	B	R	A	W	L
C	O	R	E	A	■	Y	O	U	■	L	A	V	I	E
S	O	F	T	G	■	N	O	G	■	O	P	A	L	S
■	■	■	F	L	O	C	K	O	F	B	I	R	D	S
T	O	I	L	E	R	■	S	S	R	■	D	I	C	E
M	O	L	I	T	O	R	■	■	O	I	L	C	A	N
C	H	E	X	■	N	A	R	C	■	N	Y	E	T	S
■	■	■	■	H	O	R	I	Z	O	N	■	■	■	■
H	T	E	S	T	■	E	D	A	M	■	M	E	M	O
I	R	A	I	S	E	■	■	R	A	M	A	D	A	N
P	A	R	T	■	S	P	A	■	N	O	C	U	T	S
S	C	H	O	O	L	O	F	F	I	S	H	■	■	■
T	H	A	N	K	■	N	I	L	■	A	T	O	N	E
E	E	R	I	E	■	D	R	E	■	I	W	E	R	E
R	A	T	T	Y	■	S	E	A	■	C	O	R	A	L

17

F	R	O	M	■	I	D	O	L	■	L	A	N	D	S
B	A	K	E	■	M	A	J	A	■	O	R	I	O	N
I	T	S	Y	B	I	T	S	Y	■	M	E	T	R	O
■	■	■	E	L	S	A	■	L	A	B	■	T	K	O
M	A	C	R	O	S	■	C	A	T	A	L	Y	S	T
A	V	A	■	T	Y	R	A	■	P	R	I	G	■	■
P	O	P	S	■	O	A	R	S	■	D	E	R	N	■
S	W	I	M	S	U	I	T	E	D	I	T	I	O	N
■	S	T	U	N	■	D	R	N	O	■	O	T	T	O
■	■	A	R	I	A	■	I	D	E	A	■	T	M	I
G	O	L	F	C	L	A	P	■	S	L	A	Y	E	R
A	C	C	■	K	I	M	■	E	G	O	S	■	■	■
S	T	I	L	E	■	I	T	C	O	U	P	L	E	S
P	E	T	E	R	■	S	O	H	O	■	C	O	V	E
S	T	Y	E	S	■	H	O	O	D	■	A	L	E	X

18

T	A	L	C	■	H	A	Z	Y	■	A	P	O	L	O
O	D	I	N	■	A	G	U	E	■	V	I	D	A	L
B	O	M	B	S	H	E	L	L	■	A	R	O	S	E
E	R	E	C	T	■	■	U	P	S	T	A	R	T	S
Y	E	S	■	R	A	H	■	S	E	A	T	■	■	■
■	■	■	R	E	S	E	T	■	W	R	E	C	K	S
T	I	M	E	S	H	A	R	E	S	■	S	H	I	A
R	O	A	D	S	■	T	I	M	■	S	H	I	N	S
I	T	C	H	■	C	H	O	P	S	T	I	C	K	S
M	A	K	E	D	O	■	S	T	R	A	P	■	■	■
■	■	■	R	O	O	F	■	Y	O	N	■	J	A	B
B	E	A	R	S	K	I	N	■	■	C	R	U	D	E
A	T	R	I	A	■	E	Y	E	S	H	A	D	E	S
S	T	I	N	G	■	N	A	P	A	■	K	E	P	T
H	E	D	G	E	■	D	D	A	Y	■	E	A	T	S

19

P	O	L	K	■	A	M	T	S	■	B	E	L	I	E	D
O	V	E	N	■	P	O	R	K	■	E	V	O	L	V	E
I	A	G	O	■	P	L	A	Y	■	R	E	U	S	E	S
S	L	I	T	■	E	A	S	E	I	N	■	P	A	R	K
E	O	S	■	D	A	R	K	■	C	A	S	E	■	■	■
■	F	L	A	I	L	S	■	D	A	R	T	■	P	Q	R
■	F	A	W	N	S	■	W	E	N	D	Y	■	O	U	I
T	I	T	L	E	■	D	A	F	T	■	L	A	C	E	D
E	C	O	■	T	H	E	F	T	■	P	I	C	K	S	■
X	E	R	■	T	A	F	T	■	G	A	S	K	E	T	■
■	■	■	A	E	R	O	■	T	A	R	T	■	T	I	S
T	O	R	T	■	R	E	L	A	T	E	■	A	V	O	W
I	D	O	I	D	O	■	E	B	O	N	■	L	E	N	O
D	I	A	L	E	D	■	F	O	R	T	■	I	T	E	R
Y	E	N	T	A	S	■	T	O	S	S	■	F	O	R	D

20

D	E	C	C	A	■	R	H	O	S	■	S	H	E	A
I	M	O	U	T	■	E	A	V	E	■	H	O	D	S
F	U	L	L	N	E	L	S	O	N	■	E	V	I	L
■	■	■	D	O	R	I	A	■	■	A	R	E	N	A
A	D	U	E	■	A	C	T	I	O	N	P	L	A	N
K	A	N	S	A	S	■	■	S	A	D	A	■	■	■
I	N	L	A	W	■	D	O	N	H	O	■	T	S	A
S	T	I	C	K	T	O	Y	O	U	R	G	U	N	S
S	E	T	■	W	R	E	S	T	■	R	A	T	E	S
■	■	■	F	A	I	R	■	■	P	A	M	E	L	A
G	O	F	O	R	B	R	O	K	E	■	E	E	L	Y
A	W	A	R	D	■	■	B	A	T	H	S	■	■	■
B	L	U	E	■	F	I	G	U	R	E	H	E	A	D
L	E	N	S	■	E	N	Y	A	■	F	O	R	C	E
E	T	A	T	■	R	A	N	I	■	T	W	E	E	N

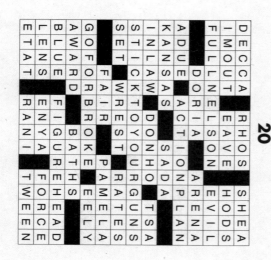

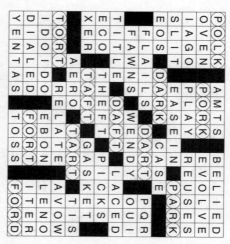

21

A	P	A	C	H	E		F	I	X	E		M	E	H
P	O	S	H	E	R		L	O	R	D		A	L	I
P	O	K	I	N	G	F	U	N	A	T		O	P	T
S	H	A	M	S		R	E	S	T		D	R	A	M
			N	O	S	E	S		E	L	O	I	S	E
R	E	V	E	N	U	E			D	A	W	S	O	N
A	W	A	Y		C	L	V		M	O	N			
J	E	T	S		K	Y	O	T	O		A	S	A	P
			W	E	E		N	E	V		N	O	P	E
A	P	P	E	A	R			M	I	N	D	S	E	T
M	A	D	E	U	P		S	P	E	E	D			
T	R	I	P		U	R	A	L		T	I	B	I	A
R	A	D		U	N	I	T	E	D	F	R	O	N	T
A	D	D		A	C	T	I		O	U	T	A	G	E
K	E	Y		W	H	E	N		E	L	Y	S	E	E

22

C	H	E	E	S	E		W	S	W		S	K	I	L
M	A	R	B	L	E		A	K	A		U	L	N	A
D	I	S	B	A	R		D	U	G		D	E	N	Y
				L	O	R	E	L	E	I		P	I	E
S	A	L	V	O		A	S	K	S	A	F	T	E	R
T	R	I	U	M	P	H				M	O	O		
A	N	T	I		C	R	U	M	B		U	M	P	S
M	I	T	T		P	A	T	T	Y		L	A	L	A
P	E	L	T		S	H	E	E	T		U	N	U	M
		E	O	N				T	E	N	P	I	N	S
C	A	R	N	A	T	I	O	N		O	S	A	K	A
A	S	H		B	U	S	M	A	P	S				
K	A	O	S		L	A	N		E	O	C	E	N	E
E	D	D	Y		I	I	I		C	A	R	R	O	T
S	A	Y	S		P	D	A		S	P	O	N	G	E

23

O	U	T	E	R		F	A	Q		A	B	U	S	E
W	H	A	M	O		A	S	U		F	U	G	U	E
L	U	M	P	S		T	H	E	R	A	C	H	E	L
S	H	A	R	I	F			L	A	R	K			
		G	E	N	I	A	L	L	Y		E	T	C	H
U	F	O	S		V	I	E		S	A	Y	H	E	Y
S	E	T	S		E	R	A			S	E	E	M	E
A	N	C		9	0	S	F	A	D	S		M	E	N
U	N	H	I	P			L	I	E		N	A	N	A
S	E	I	S	M	S		E	W	E		A	C	T	S
A	L	S	O		M	E	T	A	D	A	T	A		
			L	O	U	D			S	M	U	R	F	S
D	R	M	A	R	T	E	N	S		B	R	E	A	K
A	C	U	T	E		N	I	T		L	A	N	C	E
P	A	G	E	S		S	L	Y		E	L	A	T	E

24

I	N	A	T	R	A	P		S	T	R	A	N	D	S
M	E	S	H	U	G	A		T	R	A	V	A	I	L
F	U	S	E	B	O	X		J	U	N	I	P	E	R
I	R	E	N	E			S	O	C	A	L			
N	A	T		S	E	T	T	H	E	T	A	B	L	E
E	L	S	A		L	O	A	N				Y	E	N
			S	E	O	U	L		S	U	I	T	E	D
	O	T	T	O	P	R	E	M	I	N	G	E	R	
S	H	R	I	N	E		M	A	M	I	E			
W	H	O				I	A	M	B		R	U	N	G
M	I	N	U	T	E	S	T	E	A	K		P	A	R
			S	H	A	L	E			A	O	R	T	A
A	S	S	U	A	G	E		F	U	R	C	O	A	T
H	A	I	R	N	E	T		A	R	M	H	O	L	E
H	O	P	P	E	R	S		B	L	A	S	T	E	R

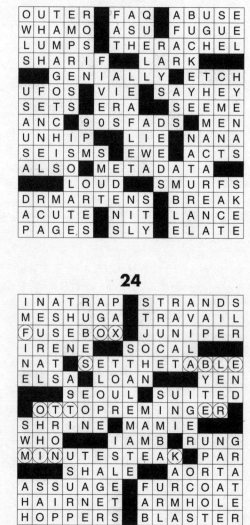

25

S	C	A	T	■	C	A	T	T	Y	■	T	B	A	R
U	H	U	H	■	A	L	O	H	A	■	H	O	P	I
F	E	T	A	■	P	L	A	Y	W	R	I	G	H	T
I	R	O	N	W	O	O	D	■	■	A	N	G	I	E
■	■	■	K	A	N	T	■	S	E	N	■	E	D	S
S	I	S	S	Y	■	■	B	U	T	T	E	D	■	■
E	D	U	■	S	H	A	R	E	H	O	L	D	E	R
R	E	B	A	■	E	L	U	D	E	■	M	O	R	E
B	A	T	T	L	E	F	I	E	L	D	■	W	I	N
■	■	L	E	A	D	I	N	■	■	O	W	N	E	D
A	L	E	■	S	S	E	■	B	O	Z	O	■	■	■
L	A	T	K	E	■	■	F	I	R	E	B	I	R	D
G	R	I	N	D	S	T	O	N	E	■	B	L	U	E
A	V	E	O	■	L	A	R	G	O	■	L	I	M	B
E	A	S	T	■	Y	I	K	E	S	■	Y	A	P	S

26

A	M	O	S	■	L	U	N	G	■	J	A	W	E	D
L	O	R	E	■	E	T	A	L	■	E	N	A	M	I
M	A	C	A	D	A	M	I	A	■	S	I	T	I	N
S	T	A	T	E	S	O	F	M	A	T	T	E	R	■
■	■	■	■	B	E	S	■	■	W	E	A	R	■	■
P	A	S	H	A	■	T	U	B	E	R	■	T	A	O
A	L	T	A	R	S	■	T	A	I	■	M	A	N	N
I	C	E	S	K	A	T	I	N	G	R	I	N	K	S
N	O	A	H	■	I	O	C	■	H	E	C	K	L	E
S	A	M	■	C	L	E	A	R	■	B	E	S	E	T
■	■	B	A	R	E	■	■	A	P	O	■	■	■	■
■	S	O	L	I	D	L	I	Q	U	I	D	G	A	S
D	I	A	L	S	■	E	B	U	L	L	I	E	N	T
O	N	T	O	P	■	D	E	E	S	■	V	E	N	D
Z	E	S	T	Y	■	A	X	L	E	■	E	K	E	S

27

L	S	D	■	S	O	F	A	■	U	N	T	I	D	Y
O	U	R	■	P	O	O	L	■	N	O	O	G	I	E
S	M	A	S	H	H	I	T	■	W	R	O	N	G	S
E	M	I	L	E	■	L	A	F	I	T	T	E	■	■
S	E	N	O	R	A	■	R	U	S	H	H	O	U	R
I	R	E	■	E	L	F	■	R	E	S	■	U	S	O
T	Y	R	A	■	B	U	N	T	■	E	S	S	A	Y
■	■	■	T	R	A	S	H	H	E	A	P	■	■	■
A	D	I	E	U	■	S	L	E	D	■	A	P	B	S
R	U	N	■	T	S	P	■	R	E	T	■	R	A	T
F	I	S	H	H	O	O	K	■	N	E	W	E	R	A
■	■	P	U	L	L	T	A	B	■	C	A	N	I	T
R	E	A	M	E	D	■	H	U	S	H	H	U	S	H
U	N	C	A	S	T	■	L	E	A	N	■	P	T	A
E	V	E	N	S	O	■	O	N	T	O	■	S	A	M

28

B	O	M	B	■	A	T	A	L	L	■	A	T	M	S
O	D	I	E	■	D	E	T	O	O	■	C	O	O	K
B	O	C	A	■	D	E	F	O	G	■	H	O	J	O
O	N	A	D	I	E	T	■	S	I	S	E	N	O	R
■	■	■	■	T	R	I	B	E	C	A	■	■	■	■
K	O	A	L	A	■	M	E	N	■	P	I	Q	U	E
A	M	I	E	■	S	E	N	S	E	■	D	U	L	L
T	A	R	G	E	T	■	■	■	D	A	S	A	N	I
O	R	S	■	T	O	V	■	W	A	X	■	Y	A	Z
■	■	■	H	O	M	E	G	A	M	E	S	■	■	■
S	P	C	A	■	P	S	A	T	S	■	A	M	F	M
L	E	A	S	T	■	P	I	K	■	F	L	O	R	A
A	L	P	H	A	B	E	T	I	Z	A	T	I	O	N
S	L	E	E	P	E	R	■	N	O	W	O	R	S	E
H	A	R	D	E	E	S	■	S	O	N	N	E	T	S

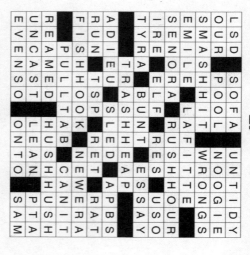

29

C	A	S	H	■	S	L	A	P	S	■	P	O	S	H
L	U	T	E	■	T	O	R	A	H	■	A	N	T	E
A	D	A	M	S	A	P	P	L	E	■	I	B	A	R
S	I	M	I	A	N	■	■	A	M	I	N	O	R	■
S	T	I	N	G	■	H	O	T	P	O	T	A	T	O
I	O	N	■	A	P	A	C	E	■	W	I	R	E	D
C	R	A	B	■	A	R	T	■	■	A	N	D	R	E
■	■	■	A	P	P	E	A	L	I	N	G	■	■	■
S	P	I	R	E	■	■	G	I	N	■	S	A	T	E
A	R	M	E	D	■	R	O	M	A	N	■	M	A	X
T	O	P	B	A	N	A	N	A	■	E	V	E	N	T
■	V	I	O	L	I	N	■	■	E	M	E	R	G	E
F	I	N	N	■	G	L	A	S	S	O	N	I	O	N
E	D	G	E	■	H	O	P	U	P	■	A	C	E	D
Z	E	E	S	■	T	W	E	E	N	■	L	A	D	S

30

S	E	T	S	■	U	H	A	U	L	■	P	S	S	T
I	G	O	T	■	S	A	L	S	A	■	R	I	T	E
L	A	D	I	E	S	T	E	E	S	■	I	D	O	S
O	N	A	P	A	R	■	■	S	T	E	V	E	N	S
■	■	Y	E	T	■	L	O	U	■	L	I	B	Y	A
A	M	O	S	■	P	A	N	P	I	P	E	■	■	■
F	A	N	■	A	O	N	E	■	N	A	S	S	E	R
A	L	L	■	D	O	G	L	E	G	S	■	C	R	O
R	I	Y	A	D	H	■	O	S	L	O	■	O	I	L
■	■	■	L	I	S	S	O	M	E	■	J	U	N	E
S	T	E	R	N	■	U	K	E	■	M	A	N	■	■
H	A	L	O	G	E	N	■	■	C	A	R	D	E	D
I	S	A	K	■	G	O	L	F	C	O	U	R	S	E
E	T	T	E	■	O	C	E	A	N	■	L	E	A	K
D	E	E	R	■	S	O	O	T	Y	■	E	L	I	E

31

G	O	P	■	■	A	D	M	I	T	S	■	H	I	M
O	N	A	■	O	N	A	S	S	I	S	■	A	C	E
T	E	T	■	W	A	Y	N	E	K	N	I	G	H	T
■	■	T	R	A	I	L	■	■	I	S	W	E	A	R
C	L	E	A	R	S	I	G	N	■	■	I	N	T	O
S	U	R	F	■	■	T	A	S	S	E	L	■	■	■
P	I	S	T	O	L	■	H	E	A	T	L	A	M	P
A	G	O	■	R	E	F	■	C	N	N	■	N	O	R
N	I	N	E	B	A	L	L	■	G	A	S	T	R	O
■	■	■	B	E	F	A	I	R	■	■	H	I	E	D
T	O	D	O	■	■	P	L	A	Y	B	I	L	L	S
O	H	I	O	A	N	■	■	N	U	O	V	A	■	■
B	A	C	K	C	O	U	N	T	R	Y	■	B	A	D
E	R	E	■	C	A	R	P	E	T	S	■	O	D	E
Y	E	S	■	T	H	I	R	D	S	■	■	R	O	W

32

P	A	I	D	■	E	Y	E	■	■	M	E	D	A	L
D	R	N	O	■	C	O	X	■	D	A	R	E	M	E
F	E	N	G	S	H	U	I	■	R	U	S	S	E	T
■	■	■	S	H	O	R	T	W	I	N	T	E	R	S
A	U	D	I	O	■	■	■	E	P	A	■	R	I	N
W	H	I	T	E	H	O	P	E	■	L	E	T	G	O
E	F	S	■	■	A	C	E	■	■	O	N	P	O	T
■	■	C	R	Y	S	T	A	L	B	A	L	L	■	■
C	U	R	I	E	■	■	B	I	O	■	■	A	I	D
O	N	E	A	L	■	R	O	C	K	C	A	N	D	Y
M	E	D	■	L	A	A	■	■	■	U	N	T	I	E
P	A	I	R	O	F	J	O	K	E	R	S	■	■	■
O	T	T	A	W	A	■	W	E	N	T	W	I	L	D
S	E	E	G	E	R	■	N	E	V	■	E	D	G	E
E	N	D	E	D	■	■	S	P	Y	■	R	O	A	N

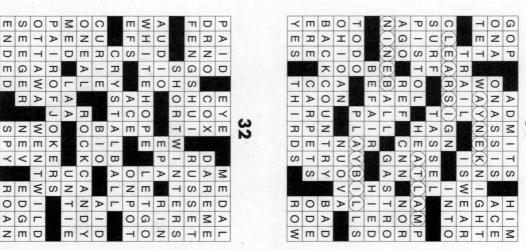

33

C	A	R	G	O	■	E	P	S	■	P	A	N	T	S
A	B	H	O	R	■	N	E	O	■	A	C	U	R	A
S	L	O	P	E	■	C	R	U	■	R	O	D	I	N
K	E	M	O	■	C	H	O	R	E	■	R	I	P	E
■	■	B	O	W	L	I	N	G	L	A	N	E	■	■
■	■	■	F	O	U	L	■	R	A	P	S	■	■	■
T	S	P	■	R	E	A	L	A	L	E	■	P	T	A
A	T	O	L	L	■	D	I	P	■	S	W	I	R	L
M	O	O	E	D	■	A	T	E	■	U	N	T	I	L
P	A	L	A	C	E	S	■	S	K	I	B	A	G	S
■	■	T	H	U	R	■	■	■	A	T	A	B	■	■
B	R	A	■	P	O	C	K	E	T	S	■	R	A	T
L	A	B	S	■	I	R	I	S	H	■	L	E	N	O
U	G	L	Y	■	C	A	N	T	I	■	O	A	T	S
R	U	E	D	■	A	W	G	E	E	■	O	D	E	S

34

A	T	H	O	L	■	S	A	S	■	A	S	L	A	N
S	H	A	M	U	■	T	U	T	■	C	H	A	M	P
F	R	Y	E	R	■	E	R	A	■	C	R	Y	E	R
O	E	R	■	E	F	R	O	N	■	R	E	A	R	■
R	E	I	N	D	E	E	R	■	S	A	W	B	I	T
M	A	D	E	■	L	O	A	M	Y	■	D	E	C	K
E	M	E	R	I	L	■	S	A	N	D	■	T	A	O
■	■	■	D	O	F	F	■	I	D	I	D	■	■	■
S	T	P	■	C	L	U	B	■	R	O	O	T	L	E
S	H	A	M	■	A	L	A	M	O	■	W	H	A	M
W	R	Y	E	S	T	■	H	A	M	O	N	R	Y	E
■	O	H	N	O	■	D	R	Y	E	R	■	E	E	R
S	W	E	A	R	■	O	A	T	■	F	E	A	T	S
P	I	E	C	E	■	N	I	A	■	E	N	D	T	O
A	N	D	E	S	■	A	N	G	■	O	L	S	E	N

35

G	L	I	B	■	C	R	I	M	E	■	F	O	U	R
R	O	M	A	■	A	E	S	O	P	■	A	N	N	A
O	N	A	N	■	S	E	A	B	I	S	C	U	I	T
K	I	C	K	B	A	C	K	■	■	P	A	S	T	E
■	■	■	R	U	B	E	■	C	H	A	D	■	■	■
Z	A	D	O	R	A	■	G	O	O	D	E	G	G	■
E	X	A	L	T	■	B	E	L	L	E	■	O	E	R
S	I	L	L	■	B	R	E	A	D	■	M	A	N	E
T	O	E	■	S	E	U	S	S	■	M	E	T	R	E
■	M	Y	S	P	A	C	E	■	W	E	A	S	E	L
■	■	■	L	A	K	E	■	N	A	S	T	■	■	■
O	A	S	I	S	■	■	C	A	P	S	L	O	C	K
S	T	U	D	M	U	F	F	I	N	■	O	P	E	N
H	O	M	E	■	G	R	O	V	E	■	A	E	R	O
A	M	O	R	■	H	O	S	E	R	■	F	L	A	X

36

S	P	A	R	■	D	R	E	■	■	N	E	S	T	S
O	U	T	E	R	E	A	R	■	M	I	N	T	E	D
P	R	O	V	I	D	E	R	■	A	P	R	O	N	S
P	E	L	O	S	I	■	■	A	E	S	O	P	■	■
Y	E	L	L	■	C	A	R	D	S	■	B	O	S	S
■	■	■	T	I	A	R	A	S	■	H	E	R	T	Z
A	T	T	■	S	T	E	W	■	M	I	D	D	I	E
P	A	W	■	H	E	A	D	S	U	P	■	E	L	L
P	H	O	B	O	S	■	E	A	R	P	■	R	E	L
T	O	B	A	T	■	S	A	I	D	O	K	■	■	■
S	E	A	L	■	T	U	L	L	E	■	E	L	I	S
■	■	G	L	A	R	E	■	■	R	E	N	A	T	A
F	I	G	A	R	O	■	E	C	O	N	O	M	I	C
I	C	E	D	I	N	■	S	A	N	D	B	A	N	K
B	U	R	S	A	■	■	E	V	E	■	I	R	A	S

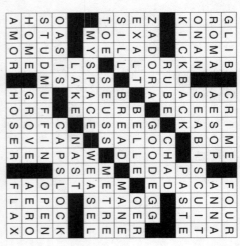

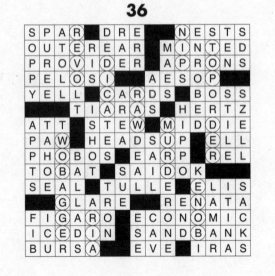

37

A	B	A	N	G		K	I	T	E		I	T	I	N
L	E	R	O	I		A	D	I	N		B	O	N	O
L	A	N	T	Z		B	O	T	T	O	M	R	O	W
S	T	E	A	M	R	O	L	L	E	R		E	R	A
E	L	S		O	E	O		E	R	R		O	B	I
T	E	S	S		M	M	L	I			S	P	I	T
			C	S	I		E	S	T	R	E	E	T	
		M	R	I	N	B	E	T	W	E	E	N		
	F	O	U	N	D	E	R		E	D	Y			
C	L	U	B			H	Y	P	E		A	S	H	E
O	U	R		A	M	O		O	Z	S		T	O	G
L	M	N		P	A	L	M	R	E	A	D	I	N	G
A	M	F	M	R	A	D	I	O		R	I	L	E	D
D	O	U	R		M	E	N	U		A	N	T	S	Y
A	X	L	E		S	R	I	S		H	A	S	T	E

38

S	E	R	F	S			F	L	U		D	O	L	T
A	L	E	R	T	S		A	I	R	C	O	V	E	R
G	A	P	E	A	T		D	E	L	E	G	A	T	E
E	L	O	N	G	A	T	E			A	L	L	O	K
			E	E	G	S		E	A	S	E			
G	R	I	M	M		A	P	P	L	E	G	A	T	E
R	U	N	Y	O	N		O	I	L		S	W	I	M
I	R	T		M	U	S	I	C	A	L		A	R	M
E	A	R	L		D	E	N		H	O	C	K	E	Y
F	L	O	O	D	G	A	T	E		S	H	E	D	S
			W	R	E	N		T	A	T	A			
I	C	A	R	E			T	A	I	L	G	A	T	E
N	A	V	I	G	A	T	E		W	O	R	D	U	P
C	R	O	S	S	F	I	T		A	V	I	A	T	E
H	A	W	K		T	E	E			E	N	S	U	E

39

P	E	P	S	I	■	A	F	R	O	■	A	N	D	S
A	V	I	A	N	■	S	O	P	H	■	L	E	A	H
T	E	S	L	A	■	P	R	I	M	E	T	I	M	E
■	■	■	A	W	A	I	T	■	Y	V	O	N	N	E
R	H	Y	M	E	S	C	H	E	M	E	■	S	S	N
L	O	O	I	E	S	■	■	L	Y	N	X	■	■	■
E	W	W	■	K	A	P	U	T	■	S	Y	N	C	S
S	I	Z	E	■	M	E	T	O	O	■	Z	O	L	A
S	E	A	L	Y	■	D	A	N	K	E	■	T	A	U
■	■	■	F	O	R	A	■	■	E	N	D	S	I	T
A	B	A	■	W	E	L	C	O	M	E	H	O	M	E
B	I	G	W	I	G	■	A	R	O	M	A	■	■	■
B	L	A	M	E	G	A	M	E	■	I	R	O	N	Y
I	B	I	D	■	I	D	E	O	■	E	M	C	E	E
E	O	N	S	■	E	S	O	S	■	S	A	T	A	N

40

A	B	E	D	■	A	B	A	F	T	■	A	B	C	S
L	E	V	I	■	R	I	D	E	R	■	L	O	U	T
B	E	E	S	■	M	O	O	L	A	■	E	Z	R	A
A	B	R	A	H	A	M	S	L	I	N	C	O	L	N
■	■	■	G	E	N	E	■	■	N	U	T	■	■	■
■	H	A	R	R	I	S	O	N	S	F	O	R	D	■
R	A	Z	E	D	■	■	R	E	E	F	■	O	U	T
C	I	T	E	■	P	I	C	O	T	■	B	A	B	E
A	T	E	■	L	E	D	A	■	■	C	O	R	A	L
■	I	C	H	I	R	O	S	S	U	Z	U	K	I	■
■	■	■	Y	E	S	■	■	O	N	A	N	■	■	■
F	R	E	D	D	I	E	S	M	E	R	C	U	R	Y
R	E	A	R	■	A	R	U	B	A	■	E	T	A	L
O	S	S	O	■	N	I	M	E	S	■	R	A	G	E
S	T	Y	X	■	S	C	O	R	E	■	S	H	A	M

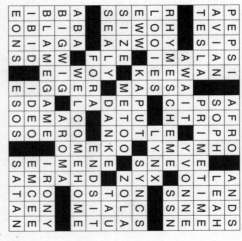

41

S	O	Y	A	■	C	O	S	T	S	■	P	R	E	K
A	S	E	C	■	D	O	N	H	O	■	L	A	C	E
A	L	O	H	A	S	H	I	R	T	■	A	S	H	E
B	O	W	E	N	■	■	P	A	R	T	Y	H	O	P
■	■	■	F	E	E	D	■	S	U	E	D	■	■	■
■	S	H	O	W	M	E	T	H	E	M	O	N	E	Y
H	O	U	R	■	M	F	A	■	■	P	H	O	N	E
A	D	M	■	B	A	Y	M	A	R	E	■	I	D	A
L	O	O	I	E	■	■	E	M	O	■	A	C	E	R
F	I	R	S	T	R	E	S	P	O	N	D	E	R	■
■	■	■	S	T	A	N	■	S	T	U	D	■	■	■
S	E	Q	U	E	N	C	E	■	■	N	I	N	E	S
C	L	U	E	■	G	O	L	D	E	N	C	A	L	F
A	L	I	T	■	I	R	K	E	D	■	T	R	I	P
R	E	P	O	■	N	E	O	N	S	■	S	C	A	D

42

A	B	C	S	■	C	L	O	W	N	■	I	N	S	O
H	A	H	A	■	A	E	G	I	S	■	S	E	E	R
S	L	A	V	■	E	A	R	L	W	E	A	V	E	R
■	C	T	A	■	S	K	E	D	■	D	I	A	S	■
J	O	H	N	J	A	Y	■	■	■	D	A	D	A	S
I	N	A	N	E	R	■	T	O	N	Y	H	A	W	K
M	Y	M	A	N	■	S	A	A	B	■	■	N	S	A
■	■	■	H	A	R	T	C	R	A	N	E	■	■	■
E	N	S	■	■	O	U	I	S	■	O	A	S	E	S
T	O	M	S	W	I	F	T	■	M	O	R	A	L	E
C	R	E	P	E	■	■	■	B	I	R	D	M	A	N
■	I	L	E	A	■	M	O	O	G	■	R	A	P	■
P	E	T	E	R	F	I	N	C	H	■	U	R	S	A
A	G	E	D	■	E	L	E	C	T	■	M	I	E	N
W	A	D	S	■	N	O	S	E	Y	■	S	A	D	O

43

I	D	I	N	G	■	T	I	M	E	■	K	A	L	B
M	A	N	I	A	■	A	N	E	W	■	A	M	I	E
B	R	O	K	E	N	B	O	N	E	■	B	E	B	E
E	E	N	■	L	E	O	I	■	■	M	O	N	E	T
A	M	I	N	■	V	O	L	L	E	Y	B	A	L	L
T	E	T	O	N	■	■	■	A	L	A	■	B	E	E
■	■	■	T	E	A	P	O	T	S	■	O	L	D	S
■	■	D	I	N	N	E	R	T	A	B	L	E	■	■
S	P	O	T	■	T	A	K	E	S	T	O	■	■	■
P	A	N	■	A	I	R	■	■	■	U	R	B	A	N
A	L	A	R	M	C	L	O	C	K	■	D	O	P	E
M	E	T	O	O	■	■	R	H	E	A	■	O	P	S
M	A	I	A	■	W	E	R	E	A	L	L	S	E	T
E	L	O	N	■	A	R	I	A	■	M	E	T	A	L
D	E	N	S	■	R	E	N	T	■	A	I	S	L	E

44

B	E	A	D	■	I	P	O	D	■	D	O	G	G	Y
A	X	L	E	■	S	A	R	A	■	A	T	L	A	S
R	E	D	L	E	T	T	E	R	■	S	T	O	V	E
S	C	O	W	S	■	H	O	T	S	H	O	W	E	R
■	■	■	E	T	R	E	S	■	H	E	M	■	■	■
H	A	S	B	R	O	■	■	S	O	D	A	P	O	P
A	I	R	B	U	B	B	L	E	■	■	N	A	P	A
U	L	T	■	S	E	A	B	E	E	S	■	G	R	R
L	E	A	S	■	■	H	O	R	S	E	M	E	A	T
S	Y	S	T	E	M	S	■	■	T	R	A	S	H	Y
■	■	■	P	D	A	■	S	P	E	E	D	■	■	■
B	O	N	E	W	H	I	T	E	■	N	E	R	V	E
E	V	I	T	A	■	G	O	O	N	A	H	E	A	D
D	E	T	E	R	■	O	R	N	E	■	A	N	N	A
S	N	E	R	D	■	R	E	S	T	■	Y	E	S	M

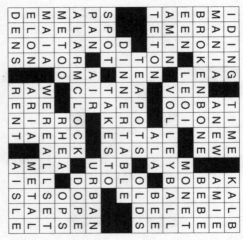

45

H	A	S	H	■	H	O	L	E	■	R	E	H	A	B
E	L	M	O	■	A	M	E	N	■	E	R	O	D	E
R	O	U	T	■	L	I	A	M	■	P	I	V	O	T
B	U	T	T	O	F	T	H	E	J	O	K	E	■	■
■	■	■	E	L	M	■	■	S	O	S	■	R	A	T
■	H	E	A	D	O	F	T	H	E	T	A	B	L	E
S	E	X	■	S	O	A	R	■	■	S	T	O	O	P
P	A	P	A	■	N	A	A	C	P	■	M	A	H	I
E	V	E	R	Y	■	■	S	H	O	W	■	R	A	D
N	E	C	K	O	F	T	H	E	W	O	O	D	S	■
T	N	T	■	D	R	U	■	■	D	E	N	■	■	■
■	■	E	Y	E	O	F	T	H	E	S	T	O	R	M
P	E	D	A	L	■	F	O	U	R	■	O	R	E	O
H	A	L	L	E	■	E	D	G	E	■	U	S	S	R
D	R	Y	E	R	■	T	O	E	D	■	R	O	T	E

46

K	E	G	S	■	R	A	V	E	D	■	A	J	A	R
U	G	L	Y	■	I	T	I	N	A	■	H	O	L	E
D	O	O	R	■	P	H	O	N	E	L	I	N	E	S
U	N	W	I	S	E	■	L	I	D	O	■	A	X	E
■	■	W	A	N	N	A	■	S	A	Y	W	H	A	T
B	O	O	■	O	S	S	O	■	L	A	I	■	■	■
A	D	R	A	W	■	S	H	O	U	L	D	E	R	S
R	I	M	S	■	B	O	G	U	S	■	E	Z	E	K
R	E	S	O	U	R	C	E	S	■	S	N	I	D	E
■	■	■	N	N	E	■	E	T	T	U	■	O	D	D
S	I	Z	E	T	W	O	■	S	O	P	U	P	■	■
U	N	E	■	I	S	P	Y	■	S	E	P	I	A	S
M	A	P	L	E	T	R	E	E	S	■	S	N	A	P
A	L	P	O	■	E	A	T	I	T	■	E	Z	R	A
C	L	O	T	■	R	H	I	N	O	■	T	A	P	S

47

M	A	R	X	■	I	S	O	L	D	E	■	K	O	A
A	V	E	R	■	D	O	M	A	I	N	■	E	L	L
P	I	N	A	C	O	L	A	D	A	S	■	E	D	O
S	A	T	Y	R	■	■	H	E	N	■	O	P	E	N
■	■	■	S	A	L	S	A	D	A	N	C	I	N	G
A	S	L	■	W	O	O	■	■	■	O	T	T	■	■
D	E	A	D	L	A	S	T	■	O	V	E	R	D	O
D	A	Z	E	■	F	O	A	L	S	■	T	E	A	T
S	T	Y	L	E	S	■	R	O	A	D	S	A	L	T
■	■	S	U	E	■	■	■	U	M	A	■	L	E	O
D	O	U	G	L	A	S	A	D	A	M	S	■	■	■
A	N	N	E	■	T	A	S	■	■	N	O	B	L	E
R	E	D	■	T	O	S	S	E	D	S	A	L	A	D
K	I	A	■	I	N	H	E	R	E	■	R	O	V	E
S	L	Y	■	M	E	A	T	A	X	■	S	W	A	N

48

I	M	O	F	F	■	M	T	I	D	A	■	S	M	U
C	R	U	D	E	■	O	A	R	E	D	■	T	A	R
E	S	T	R	E	E	T	B	A	N	D	■	U	G	G
■	■	■	■	T	R	I	O	■	■	■	E	D	G	E
S	K	Y	Y	■	I	F	O	R	M	A	T	I	O	N
P	L	E	A	S	E	S	■	A	O	S	C	O	T	T
H	E	L	L	O	■	■	L	G	B	T	■	■	■	■
■	E	P	L	U	R	I	B	U	S	U	N	U	M	■
■	■	■	■	R	E	L	O	■	■	T	O	P	I	C
M	A	R	A	C	A	S	■	M	A	E	S	T	R	O
I	L	O	V	E	P	A	R	I	S	■	H	O	O	P
S	A	M	E	■	■	■	O	C	H	S	■	■	■	■
E	S	C	■	O	H	E	N	R	Y	T	W	I	S	T
R	K	O	■	W	A	L	D	O	■	Y	I	K	E	S
S	A	M	■	N	Y	L	O	N	■	E	I	E	I	O

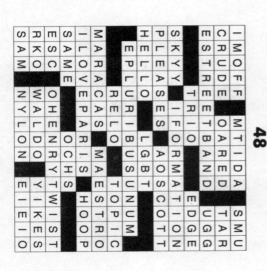

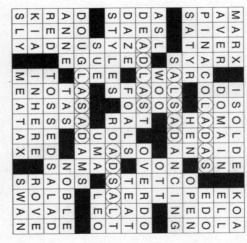

49

P	B	J	■	T	A	M	P	A	■	A	S	F	A	R
L	I	E	■	H	A	S	O	N	■	U	T	I	L	E
E	N	D	R	E	S	U	L	T	■	T	A	R	S	I
A	S	I	A	N	■	■	L	I	G	H	T	S	O	N
■	■	■	M	E	R	C	■	■	L	O	S	T	■	■
A	T	H	■	R	O	O	S	T	E	R	■	B	E	T
T	W	E	L	V	E	N	O	O	N	■	K	E	R	R
B	Y	A	G	E	■	M	A	R	■	A	G	G	I	E
A	L	D	A	■	R	E	V	E	R	T	B	A	C	K
R	A	H	■	M	I	N	E	R	V	A	■	N	A	S
■	■	O	H	I	O	■	■	O	S	L	O	■	■	■
B	A	N	I	S	T	E	R	■	■	A	L	T	O	S
L	U	C	R	E	■	R	E	D	U	N	D	A	N	T
O	T	H	E	R	■	I	N	E	R	T	■	S	T	Y
G	O	O	D	S	■	K	O	A	L	A	■	S	O	X

50

R	O	D	S	■	C	O	M	F	Y	■	E	S	S	O
U	T	A	H	■	I	S	E	R	E	■	T	T	O	P
H	O	M	E	■	S	W	E	E	T	■	H	O	M	E
R	E	O	R	G	■	A	C	E	■	L	A	P	E	L
■	■	N	E	E	D	L	E	P	O	I	N	T	■	■
U	T	A	■	N	U	T	■	R	T	E	■	H	A	D
P	I	N	A	T	A	■	■	■	O	L	D	E	L	I
C	E	D	I	L	L	A	■	P	H	O	E	B	E	S
■	■	P	S	Y	■	S	T	E	■	W	F	L	■	■
I	D	Y	L	■	T	H	R	E	E	■	I	E	D	S
N	I	T	E	■	S	T	O	R	Y	■	B	E	R	T
D	O	H	■	■	H	O	U	S	E	■	■	D	E	R
I	D	I	A	M	I	N	■	A	L	U	M	I	N	A
R	E	A	P	E	R	S	■	T	E	N	A	N	C	Y
A	S	S	E	N	T	■	■	■	T	H	I	G	H	S

51

A	D	W	A	R			A	C	I	D	W	A	S	H
B	I	A	S	E	D		B	A	R	R	E	T	T	E
E	R	N	A	N	I		I	M	M	O	B	I	L	E
			M	T	A		G	R	A	Z		V	E	L
A	P	P	I	A	N	W	A	Y			K	A	O	S
F	O	E			A	H	I		S	U	N	N	I	
T	O	D	O	S		E	L	N	I	N	O			
A	R	I	Z	O	N	A	W	I	L	D	C	A	T	S
			O	N	A	T	I	P		O	K	N	O	W
	D	I	N	G	Y		L	A	T			T	O	E
S	A	M	E			A	L	T	A	R	W	I	N	E
A	S	A		K	O	F	I		H	A	I			
M	A	G	N	O	L	I	A		O	S	C	A	R	S
O	N	E	A	L	A	R	M		E	T	C	H	E	S
A	I	R	W	A	V	E	S			A	A	N	D	W

52

L	A	I	D	U	P		G	I	R	T		O	D	E
O	L	D	I	S	H		I	D	E	A		R	O	S
C	L	I	P	C	Y	C	L	O	P	S		I	N	K
A	M	O	S		L	O	L	L		K	A	N	J	I
L	A	T		F	A	U	N	A	S		L	O	O	M
A	L	I	B	I		P	E	T	P	S	Y	C	H	O
D	E	C	A	L	S		T	R	E	A	S	O	N	
			T	E	E	M		Y	A	Y	S			
	R	A	T	T	R	A	P		R	H	U	M	B	A
B	I	L	L	S	I	N	A	I		E	M	I	R	S
O	B	I	E		F	O	N	D	L	Y		D	I	S
U	M	B	R	A		H	O	L	A		A	S	E	A
N	E	A		S	E	M	P	E	R	S	C	I	F	I
C	A	B		A	N	A	L		D	E	N	Z	E	L
E	T	A		P	O	N	Y		S	T	E	E	D	S

53

■	G	A	L	P	A	L	■	I	M	C	O	O	L	■
P	A	L	E	A	L	E	■	D	O	O	R	M	E	N
A	L	B	E	R	T	A	■	A	R	R	A	N	G	E
D	E	A	R	T	H	■	■	■	E	N	L	I	S	T
■	■	■	■	Y	E	S	D	E	A	R	■	■	■	■
I	N	F	■	F	A	T	I	G	U	E	■	L	A	Y
M	I	A	T	A	■	I	G	O	■	L	A	I	L	A
A	N	N	E	V	■	P	D	T	■	I	N	K	U	P
X	A	C	T	O	■	P	E	R	■	S	T	E	M	S
■	■	Y	E	R	■	L	E	I	■	H	E	M	■	■
H	E	P	■	■	Z	E	P	P	O	■	■	I	T	S
O	R	A	N	G	E	■	■	■	N	A	R	N	I	A
O	R	N	U	R	S	E	■	C	I	C	A	D	A	S
H	O	T	D	A	T	E	■	F	O	R	G	E	R	S
A	R	S	E	N	A	L	■	O	N	E	A	D	A	Y

54

R	E	P	O	R	T	S	■	R	W	A	N	D	A	N
A	T	H	E	A	R	T	■	A	R	G	O	N	N	E
W	H	O	O	P	I	E	■	G	A	R	B	A	G	E
B	I	N	■	S	P	F	S	■	T	O	O	T	E	D
A	C	E	D	■	E	A	R	T	H	■	D	E	L	I
R	A	M	I	S	■	N	A	T	■	D	Y	S	O	N
S	L	E	E	P	Y	■	S	O	H	O	■	T	U	G
■	■	■	M	A	D	E	■	P	A	L	E	■	■	■
O	C	S	■	T	S	A	R	■	G	O	L	E	M	S
R	A	I	L	S	■	C	O	P	■	R	E	M	A	P
I	R	M	A	■	S	H	O	U	T	■	M	E	T	E
G	A	M	B	L	E	■	F	R	E	E	■	R	I	C
A	V	E	R	A	G	E	■	I	N	S	T	A	N	T
M	A	R	A	C	A	S	■	S	T	A	N	L	E	E
I	N	S	T	Y	L	E	■	T	H	U	N	D	E	R

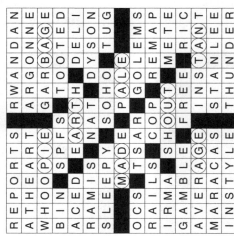

55

I	T	E	M		R	A	Z	E			K	A	Y	O
M	O	V	E		I	C	E	R		S	E	N	O	R
P	R	O	T	E	S	T	E	R		P	A	D	U	A
U	R	N		Y	E	S		O	P	E	N	E	R	
T	I	N	K	E	R		P	R	O	C	U	R	E	R
E	D	E	N			F	I	S	T			S	O	O
			O	P	A	R	T		A	L	M	O	N	D
		P	R	O	V	O	C	A	T	I	O	N		
D	E	A	R	I	E		H	R	O	S	S			
I	A	N			R	H	E	A			E	C	R	U
P	R	O	P	O	S	E	R		L	U	S	H	E	S
	D	R	I	V	E	L		P	E	Z		E	W	E
B	R	A	V	E		P	R	O	F	I	L	E	R	S
R	U	M	O	R		M	I	N	T		E	S	A	U
A	M	A	T			E	D	G	Y		D	E	P	P

56

T	R	U	E	D	A	T		P	R	E		D	E	M
W	I	N	S	O	M	E		O	E	R		U	T	A
I	A	S	S	U	M	E		P	O	O	L	B	O	Y
N	A	H		B	A	N	T	U		S	O	L	I	D
		A	T	T	N		O	P	T		G	I	L	A
R	O	V	E	S		H	U	S	H	M	O	N	E	Y
O	P	E	D		D	O	C	T	O	R	S			
D	E	N		W	I	T	H	O	U	T		C	H	E
			B	O	R	D	E	R	S		B	O	O	T
A	N	D	R	E	G	I	D	E		B	R	A	N	D
L	O	R	I		E	G	O		S	E	A	T		
I	V	I	N	S		G	N	A	W	S		T	K	O
B	E	N	G	A	L	I		R	I	T	E	A	I	D
I	L	K		G	E	T		A	S	I	N	I	N	E
S	S	S		A	N	Y		T	H	E	O	L	D	S

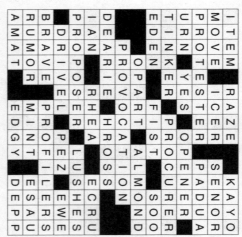

57

S	A	R	I	S		S	K	A		G	U	C	C	I
C	H	I	N	A	S	H	O	P		O	S	R	I	C
R	O	C	K	Y	H	O	A	R		A	B	A	T	E
A	M	I		S	A	W		S	O	W		Z	I	T
P	E	N	N	A	M	E	S		N	O	S	Y		
			C	L	E	R	I	C	A	L	H	E	I	R
T	A	B	O	O			D	U	I		H	Y	D	E
I	C	U		T	H	R	E	E	R	S		E	L	I
E	M	M	A		O	A	T			O	G	D	E	N
R	E	A	R	V	I	E	W	M	E	R	E			
		S	K	I	S		O	U	T	C	L	A	S	S
P	O	M		E	T	A		S	H	E		T	C	U
A	D	O	L	F		S	H	E	E	R	T	E	A	R
T	O	K	Y	O		I	S	U	R	E	W	I	L	L
S	N	E	E	R		A	T	M		R	A	N	D	Y

58

L	A	P	P		A	B	B	E	S	S		R	C	A
A	M	E	S		T	E	L	L	T	O		A	H	I
T	A	R	T		T	R	A	Y	D	I	P	P	E	R
E	R	S		W	A	R	N			T	A	P	E	S
P	A	P	E	R	R	A	C	K	B	I	T	E	R	
A	N	I	M	A				L	O	S	E	R	S	
S	T	R	U	T		B	E	E	R					
S	H	E	S	H	E	A	V	I	N	G	L	O	A	M
					A	T	O	N		A	I	N	T	I
	O	R	B	A	C	H				M	E	L	T	S
	L	E	I	G	H	S	H	O	V	E	S	Y	O	U
A	D	D	E	R			A	V	E	R		O	R	S
T	H	E	B	E	A	T	L	E	S		A	N	N	E
M	A	Y		E	S	C	O	R	T		I	C	E	R
S	T	E		S	H	U	N	T	S		D	E	Y	S

59

S	T	E	E	P	S	■	P	A	A	R	■	P	A	P
P	E	A	R	L	E	■	A	N	N	E	■	O	U	I
E	X	T	R	A	V	I	R	G	I	N	■	P	T	A
E	T	S	■	Y	E	N	T	L	■	A	M	M	O	■
D	E	A	F	■	R	I	V	E	R	M	O	U	T	H
O	R	T	O	N	■	■	■	■	V	E	R	S	U	S
■	■	■	R	A	D	I	A	T	E	■	A	I	N	T
■	D	I	A	P	E	R	S	E	R	V	I	C	E	■
H	I	N	T	■	T	A	K	E	S	I	N	■	■	■
I	O	D	I	Z	E	■	■	■	■	P	E	A	C	H
D	R	Y	M	A	R	T	I	N	I	■	S	T	L	O
■	A	C	E	D	■	R	E	A	D	E	■	R	A	W
A	M	A	■	O	L	I	V	E	R	T	W	I	S	T
J	A	R	■	R	A	K	E	■	I	T	I	S	S	O
A	S	S	■	A	V	E	R	■	S	A	N	K	A	S

60

S	P	L	I	C	E	■	A	M	S	■	■	A	T	M
N	O	U	G	A	T	■	C	U	P	S	■	L	O	A
A	W	N	U	T	S	■	T	R	I	M	O	T	O	R
C	E	D	E	■	■	F	I	R	E	O	P	A	L	S
K	R	I	S	H	N	A	■	A	L	O	E	■	■	■
■	■	■	S	M	E	L	L	Y	■	T	R	A	C	T
D	O	H	■	S	I	D	E	■	S	H	A	L	L	I
I	P	A	D	■	L	O	T	T	O	■	S	O	A	K
V	E	N	I	A	L	■	B	A	R	S	■	T	M	I
E	N	G	E	L	■	S	E	T	T	L	E	■	■	■
■	■	■	T	T	O	P	■	E	A	R	L	E	S	S
S	T	R	E	T	C	H	E	R	■	■	N	A	P	A
A	A	A	R	A	T	E	D	■	A	N	I	M	A	L
N	C	R	■	B	E	R	G	■	S	E	N	E	C	A
D	O	E	■	■	T	E	E	■	L	O	O	S	E	D

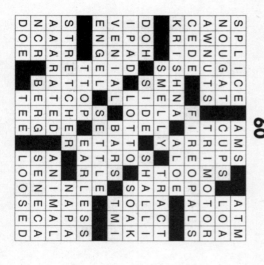

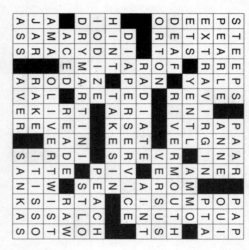

61

S	M	I	T	E	■	F	E	D	■	I	T	E	M	S
M	A	N	I	A	■	T	R	E	■	A	W	A	R	D
O	T	T	E	R	■	L	I	E	■	M	I	T	E	S
O	C	H	S	■	S	E	E	P	A	S	T	■	■	■
T	H	E	T	I	M	E	S	■	R	A	T	I	O	■
■	■	M	O	M	A	■	■	I	M	M	E	N	S	E
A	P	O	■	A	S	H	E	S	■	■	R	D	A	S
L	A	M	■	T	H	E	Y	A	R	E	■	I	G	O
I	D	E	S	■	■	R	E	O	I	L	■	G	E	S
T	U	N	A	S	U	B	■	■	C	I	A	O	■	■
■	A	T	N	O	S	■	A	C	H	A	N	G	I	N
■	■	■	C	I	A	G	A	T	E	■	T	I	L	T
E	M	I	T	S	■	O	N	E	■	T	H	R	E	E
L	A	R	U	E	■	A	D	A	■	M	E	L	D	S
I	T	S	M	E	■	T	E	M	■	I	M	S	E	T

62

S	N	A	P	T	O	■	C	O	O	P	■	A	M	P
T	E	L	L	O	N	■	HE	N	C	E	■	L	O	X
R	O	L	E	O	S	■	R	E	T	R	A	C	T	S
I	C	HE	A	T	E	D	■	S	E	E	T	HE	■	■
P	O	R	T	■	T	R	A	I	T	■	A	M	B	I
S	N	E	E	R	■	I	T	E	■	T	R	I	A	L
■	■	■	D	U	P	L	E	■	H	O	I	S	T	S
R	HE	A	■	B	A	L	L	O	O	N	■	T	HE	A
O	N	C	A	L	L	■	I	N	N	E	S	■	■	■
A	N	I	C	E	■	R	E	P	■	S	H	A	M	S
R	A	D	O	■	P	E	R	O	T	■	I	C	O	N
■	■	HE	L	I	U	M	■	T	U	N	A	HE	R	O
D	E	A	D	S	P	O	T	■	N	O	T	F	A	R
O	K	D	■	T	I	T	HE	■	I	N	S	O	L	E
W	E	S	■	O	L	E	O	■	S	O	U	R	E	D

63

S	P	I	E	L	■	P	U	N	T	S	■	S	K	I
G	E	C	K	O	■	A	L	O	H	A	■	T	O	M
T	A	K	E	C	O	N	T	R	O	L	■	O	R	E
S	K	Y	D	I	V	E	R	■	■	■	A	R	E	A
■	■	■	■	■	U	M	A	T	H	U	R	M	A	N
■	R	E	P	E	L	■	■	R	A	N	T	■	■	■
M	I	D	D	L	E	C	L	A	S	S	■	A	R	F
S	C	I	F	I	■	A	I	D	■	A	G	R	E	E
S	E	T	■	C	E	N	T	E	R	F	I	E	L	D
■	■	■	S	I	L	O	■	■	E	E	N	S	Y	■
A	L	L	A	T	I	N	G	L	E	■	■	■	■	■
R	A	I	D	■	■	■	E	A	S	T	A	S	I	A
U	S	E	■	D	E	A	T	H	E	A	T	E	R	S
B	E	G	■	O	R	B	I	T	■	S	T	E	A	K
A	R	E	■	C	A	C	T	I	■	E	A	R	N	S

64

R	A	F	T	S	■	A	D	S	■	H	E	M	E	N
E	L	I	H	U	■	T	I	L	■	M	Y	O	P	E
H	O	L	E	I	N	O	N	E	■	M	E	D	I	C
A	H	E	M	■	O	A	K	E	N	■	D	E	C	K
B	A	R	A	C	U	S	■	P	E	C	O	S	■	■
■	■	■	F	A	N	T	A	S	T	I	C	T	W	O
A	M	B	I	T	S	■	G	I	S	T	■	F	E	N
S	A	L	A	D	■	D	E	N	■	A	T	E	A	M
T	I	A	■	O	B	A	N	■	A	D	H	E	R	E
O	N	C	L	O	U	D	T	H	R	E	E	■	■	■
■	■	K	A	R	M	A	■	O	I	L	R	I	G	S
K	I	L	O	■	P	I	O	N	S	■	A	P	S	O
A	N	I	T	A	■	S	W	E	E	T	F	O	U	R
R	O	S	S	I	■	T	I	S	■	O	L	D	I	E
O	T	T	E	R	■	S	E	T	■	M	U	S	T	S

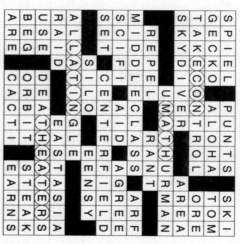

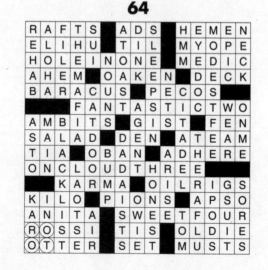

65

V	E	R	B	S	■	■	J	A	M	S	■	M	A	T
I	T	A	L	I	C	■	U	R	G	E	■	O	D	E
N	A	T	U	R	A	L	D	I	S	A	S	T	E	R
■	■	■	E	E	R	I	E	■	■	R	A	I	L	S
W	H	O	L	E	B	E	A	N	C	O	F	F	E	E
I	O	W	A	■	■	■	■	E	A	V	E	■	■	■
C	R	E	W	S	■	S	N	I	P	E	■	C	B	S
C	N	N	■	I	N	T	E	G	E	R	■	L	I	P
A	S	S	■	P	O	O	C	H	■	S	N	A	R	L
■	■	■	W	H	O	M	■	■	■	■	A	N	T	I
R	A	T	I	O	N	A	L	T	H	O	U	G	H	T
O	R	R	I	N	■	■	E	R	U	P	T	■	■	■
I	M	A	G	I	N	A	R	Y	F	R	I	E	N	D
D	O	M	■	N	O	G	O	■	F	A	L	L	O	N
S	R	S	■	G	R	E	Y	■	■	H	I	L	D	A

66

E	B	B	S	■	P	R	O	N	G	■	O	I	L	S
R	E	A	P	■	S	A	U	C	E	■	K	N	O	W
M	A	R	I	E	A	N	T	O	I	N	E	T	T	E
A	M	S	T	E	L	■	■	■	C	O	Y	O	T	E
■	■	■	T	O	M	A	R	N	O	L	D	■	■	■
■	T	R	A	C	■	N	E	O	■	L	O	L	A	■
A	M	O	K	■	A	D	M	I	T	■	K	I	N	K
L	A	Y	E	T	T	E	■	S	I	L	E	N	T	E
E	N	O	■	A	M	A	■	E	M	O	■	D	E	N
■	■	R	O	B	I	N	■	S	E	R	T	A	■	■
L	E	B	R	O	N	■	■	■	S	E	R	E	N	A
O	M	I	G	O	S	H	■	M	I	N	I	V	A	N
C	O	S	A	■	I	O	W	A	N	■	P	A	N	G
A	T	O	N	■	D	R	A	N	K	■	U	N	O	S
L	E	N	S	■	E	A	S	E	S	■	P	S	S	T

67

N	E	I	G	H	■	S	C	A	B	■	E	N	D	S
A	R	N	I	E	■	A	L	F	A	■	V	E	E	P
K	O	A	L	A	■	Y	A	R	D	■	A	W	A	Y
E	D	W	A	R	D	S	N	O	W	E	D	I	N	■
D	E	E	■	D	U	H	■	■	O	X	E	N	■	■
■	■	■	J	O	D	I	E	F	R	O	S	T	E	R
M	O	T	I	F	S	■	T	O	D	D	■	O	R	O
R	A	H	M	■	■	C	H	E	■	■	T	W	I	X
S	H	E	■	A	P	S	E	■	B	O	U	N	C	Y
C	U	R	T	C	H	I	L	L	I	N	G	■	■	■
■	■	E	V	E	R	■	■	U	N	A	■	E	P	A
■	B	A	R	R	Y	C	O	L	D	W	A	T	E	R
P	O	L	O	■	G	A	L	L	■	H	I	H	A	T
E	L	M	O	■	I	S	L	E	■	I	D	O	L	S
P	O	E	M	■	A	T	A	D	■	M	E	S	S	Y

68

A	D	E	L	P	H	■	■	■	T	E	M	O	N	E
L	I	T	E	R	A	T	■	C	E	M	A	K	E	R
A	N	D	S	O	D	O	■	O	N	I	Z	I	N	G
S	O	S	■	M	A	U	■	C	A	L	■	E	E	O
■	■	■	P	O	N	T	■	O	N	I	A	■	■	■
J	A	M	E	S	I	■	■	■	T	A	L	I	C	S
A	T	I	T	■	P	L	A	N	S	■	E	N	C	E
D	A	N	■	■	■	O	H	O	■	■	■	B	I	G
E	R	S	T	■	K	N	A	V	E	■	M	E	N	U
N	I	K	O	L	A	■	■	■	D	B	A	D	G	E
■	■	■	G	O	T	T	■	L	I	E	D	■	■	■
W	C	S	■	T	R	O	■	O	T	A	■	F	E	E
H	O	T	C	H	I	L	■	N	I	T	S	E	L	F
O	P	E	R	A	N	D	■	G	N	O	R	E	I	T
S	A	M	U	R	A	■	■	■	G	N	I	T	E	S

69

L	I	M	E	■	U	R	B	A	N	■	D	U	E	S
E	M	A	C	■	L	O	R	N	A	■	I	N	S	T
T	E	C	H	■	T	A	I	N	T	■	P	I	S	A
T	A	H	O	E	■	S	T	A	G	G	■	T	E	N
E	N	O	■	L	S	T	S	■	E	N	B	A	N	C
R	I	N	G	I	N	■	■	B	O	U	R	R	E	E
■	T	E	A	H	O	U	S	E	■	■	A	D	S	■
■	■	■	S	U	B	M	E	R	G	E	S	■	■	■
■	A	B	S	■	■	P	A	N	E	L	I	S	T	■
S	L	E	E	V	E	S	■	■	S	A	L	A	A	M
C	I	T	R	O	N	■	K	I	T	T	■	S	P	A
R	E	A	■	A	R	T	O	O	■	E	T	H	E	R
I	N	M	E	■	A	S	A	N	A	■	K	I	R	I
P	E	A	S	■	P	A	L	I	N	■	O	M	E	N
T	E	X	T	■	T	R	A	C	T	■	S	I	D	E

70

S	T	I	F	L	E	■	■	M	R	R	O	P	E	R
P	O	G	O	E	D	■	W	A	Y	A	B	O	V	E
L	O	U	N	G	E	■	A	U	N	T	I	E	E	M
A	M	A	Z	O	N	V	I	N	E	■	E	T	N	A
Y	E	N	■	■	■	I	T	A	■	■	■	I	S	P
■	Y	A	H	O	O	P	O	L	I	T	I	C	O	■
■	■	S	O	P	H	■	N	O	B	U	T	S	■	■
■	■	■	V	A	Y	A	■	A	I	R	S	■	■	■
■	■	H	E	R	O	I	N	■	Z	O	O	L	■	■
■	V	U	L	T	U	R	E	G	A	W	K	E	R	■
D	O	S	■	■	■	T	G	I	■	■	■	C	H	E
I	L	K	S	■	C	R	A	S	H	S	I	T	E	S
S	A	I	L	B	O	A	T	■	E	A	S	E	U	P
C	R	E	A	M	P	I	E	■	E	X	A	R	M	Y
S	E	R	B	I	A	N	■	■	D	E	N	N	Y	S

71

A	H	E	M	■	A	B	E	T	■	G	A	P	E	D
M	A	D	E	■	L	E	A	R	■	A	L	I	V	E
A	B	I	T	■	T	A	R	A	■	L	U	C	A	S
Z	I	T	I	C	O	U	N	C	I	L	M	A	N	■
E	T	H	E	R	■	■	■	E	C	O	■	■	■	■
■	■	■	R	O	L	L	S	■	E	N	D	U	R	E
M	O	C	■	C	O	A	C	H	■	■	A	B	E	L
O	R	Z	O	I	T	W	O	U	L	D	S	E	E	M
S	E	A	L	■	■	S	U	G	A	R	■	R	K	O
T	O	R	E	R	O	■	R	E	P	O	S	■	■	■
■	■	■	■	A	W	L	■	■	■	O	H	A	R	E
■	P	E	N	N	E	A	N	T	E	P	O	K	E	R
M	E	R	I	T	■	D	E	A	L	■	R	I	G	A
A	L	I	K	E	■	E	M	M	A	■	E	T	A	S
S	T	E	E	D	■	N	O	E	L	■	S	A	N	E

72

A	M	M	O	■	■	S	T	E	■	■	S	T	A	B
L	A	U	D	■	E	T	H	N	O	■	E	W	E	R
M	U	S	E	U	M	O	(2)	H	I	S	T	O	R	Y
A	L	I	■	C	U	R	E	A	L	L	■	T	O	N
■	■	C	A	L	■	E	R	R	■	A	G	O	■	■
A	Q	A	B	A	■	S	I	M	■	B	E	N	I	N
N	U	L	L	■	L	I	M	O	S	■	N	E	R	O
V	I	N	E	■	E	G	A	N	S	■	E	C	O	N
I	T	O	■	F	A	N	G	I	R	L	■	A	B	E
L	I	T	R	E	■	S	E	C	■	A	R	R	O	W
S	T	E	E	L	■	■	■	■	■	T	E	S	T	S
■	■	■	S	L	A	G	■	A	C	E	D	■	■	■
N	I	C	O	I	S	E	■	W	A	F	T	I	N	G
I	M	E	A	N	I	T	■	E	R	E	A	D	E	R
L	O	O	K	I	N	(1)	■	D	(3)	E	G	A	T	E

(1) G♯/A♭ (2) F♮/E♯ (3) E♭/D♯

73

S	L	E	D			O	W	E			S	P	U	N
A	E	S	O	P		R	A	Y		B	O	I	S	E
N	A	T	U	R	E	P	R	E	S	E	R	V	E	S
T	H	E	R	I	C	H		T	I	R	E	O	U	T
A	Y	E		S	H	A	P	E	L	Y		T	P	S
			M	O	O	N	J	E	L	L	Y			
A	L	V	I	N		E	S	T		L	O	U	P	E
B	O	O	K	E	N	D		H	A	I	R	P	I	N
B	O	L	E	R	O				P	U	E	B	L	O
E	P	T		S	L	O	W	J	A	M		R	A	T
S	H	E	L		A	T	E	I	T		C	A	S	E
S	O	F	E	W		T	I	M		B	R	I	T	S
	L	A	D	Y	M	A	R	M	A	L	A	D	E	
	E	C	O	L	A	W		I	R	A	T	E	R	
	S	E	N	E	C	A		E	M	B	E	D	S	

74

A	T	A	D		C	A	M	U	S		B	A	R	I
T	H	E	E		O	Z	O	N	E		O	D	E	D
L	E	O	N		L	U	C	I	A		B	U	N	S
	F	L	I	VV	E	R		T	I	O		L	E	A
C	L	I	M	B	S		T	E	C	H	S	A	VV	Y
Y	E	A		A	L	A	I		E	M	O	T	E	S
D	A	N	S		A	L	E	C		A	L	E	R	O
			H	I	VV	A	C	C	I	N	E			
A	S	L	A	N		S	L	E	D		D	E	C	K
P	E	O	R	I	A		I	D	O	S		P	O	I
R	E	VV	I	N	G	U	P		L	A	S	H	A	T
I	T	T		K	A	N		C	I	VV	I	E	S	
O	H	I	O		S	T	A	R	Z		E	D	T	V
R	E	D	D		S	I	R	E	E		G	R	E	W
I	D	E	E		I	L	I	E	D		E	A	R	S

75

E	L	M	I	R	A		J	O	K	E		P	H	I
F	A	U	C	E	T		A	X	E	L		A	O	N
F	R	I	E	D	O	N	I	O	N	S		U	N	O
S	A	R	D	I	N	E			T	E	F	L	O	N
				N	A	V	A	L			O	R	R	
	P	I	C	K	L	E	D	P	E	P	P	E	R	S
P	A	L	S			R	O	S	S	I		V	O	L
U	G	L	I	E	R				A	N	G	E	L	A
N	E	B		V	O	I	D	S			O	R	L	Y
S	T	E	W	E	D	T	O	M	A	T	O	E	S	
	U	T	A			S	H	A	M	U				
M	R	H	Y	D	E			C	O	N	S	I	S	T
O	N	E		D	R	U	N	K	E	N	C	O	O	K
P	E	R		A	T	R	A		B	E	A	T	I	T
E	R	E		Y	E	L	P		A	L	T	A	R	S

76

P	E	S	T	O		A	R	I	A	S		N	O	D
O	N	E	U	P		B	A	N	D	E		E	D	U
P	R	E	V	E		U	N	A	D	V	I	S	E	D
S	A	T	A	N	I	S	T	S		E	S	T		
U	G	H		T	O	E		C	A	N	T	E	E	N
P	E	E	R	A	T		C	R	U		O	G	R	E
			N	B	A	D	R	A	F	T		G	I	T
A	R	I	A	L		R	E	P		O	A	S	E	S
C	O	N		E	V	A	P	E	R	O	N			
E	M	U	S		A	M	T		O	K	S	A	N	A
V	E	N	T	U	R	A		T	A	N		P	O	G
		D	A	M		T	U	R	N	O	F	E	V	E
W	H	A	T	A	P	I	T	Y		T	O	X	I	N
H	O	T		M	A	Z	E	S		E	R	E	C	T
O	W	E		I	N	E	P	T		S	A	S	E	S

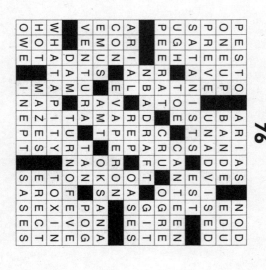

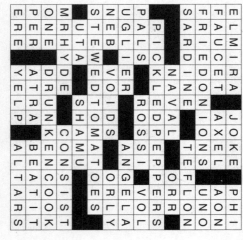

77

W	A	S	T	E	■	■	M	R	T	■	M	O	S	S
O	C	E	A	N	S	■	I	O	U	■	A	B	L	E
N	E	X	T	D	A	Y	A	I	R	■	O	L	I	N
■	■	■	T	R	U	S	T	■	N	A	R	I	T	A
■	A	B	O	U	T	L	A	S	T	N	I	G	H	T
T	H	E	O	N	E	■	■	C	A	N	■	E	Y	E
D	A	T	A	■	■	A	E	R	I	A	L	■	■	■
S	T	A	R	T	I	N	G	A	L	L	O	V	E	R
■	■	■	T	O	M	T	O	M	■	■	V	I	V	A
S	H	O	■	O	P	E	■	■	P	I	E	C	E	S
L	O	N	G	L	O	S	T	F	A	T	H	E	R	■
U	N	L	E	S	S	■	H	O	W	S	O	■	■	■
I	C	O	N	■	T	R	I	P	L	E	T	I	M	E
C	H	A	T	■	O	U	R	■	S	L	E	D	G	E
E	O	N	S	■	R	E	D	■	■	F	L	A	S	K

78

H	A	L	■	E	S	T	D	■	C	C	U	P	■
A	P	P	L	E	P	I	E	■	S	A	T	I	N
L	O	G	I	C	A	L	F	A	L	L	A	C	Y
O	P	A	L	■	■	L	I	V	E	C	H	A	T
■	■	■	A	D	O	■	N	E	W	■	■	■	■
E	B	E	C	A	U	S	E	(C)	I	R	C	U	L
S	E	X	■	Z	I	P	■	■	S	O	U	S	A
N	A	T	■	E	J	E	C	T	■	T	B	A	R
E	C	R	U	■	A	D	L	I	B	■	A	G	R
S	O	A	K	S	■	■	O	A	R	■	N	E	E
O	N	S	E	K	A	M	G	N	I	N	O	S	A
■	■	■	■	I	G	O	■	T	E	E	■	■	■
C	R	A	S	S	E	S	T	■	■	A	S	T	I
B	E	G	T	H	E	Q	U	E	S	T	I	O	N
C	E	E	L	O	■	U	N	F	R	O	Z	E	N
■	D	R	O	P	■	E	A	T	S	■	E	D	S

79

P	A	S	S	E	■	A	C	E	D	■	A	S	S	N
F	A	K	E	R	■	G	U	A	R	A	N	T	E	E
C	H	E	M	I	C	A	L	T	E	S	T	I	N	G
■	■	E	P	C	O	T	■	■	■	K	I	N	D	A
T	O	B	E	■	M	E	A	L	T	I	C	K	E	T
S	T	A	R	R	■	S	L	A	I	N	■	O	R	E
P	I	L	F	E	R	■	G	I	G	■	■	■	■	■
■	C	L	I	M	A	T	E	C	H	A	N	G	E	■
■	■	■	■	■	I	E	R	■	T	H	O	R	A	X
A	T	O	■	S	T	A	I	R	■	A	R	I	S	E
D	I	R	E	C	T	M	A	I	L	■	S	L	E	D
D	R	A	M	A	■	■	■	V	O	W	E	L	■	■
S	A	T	E	L	L	I	T	E	C	A	M	P	U	S
O	N	O	R	A	B	O	U	T	■	W	E	A	N	S
N	A	R	Y	■	J	U	G	S	■	A	N	N	I	E

80

O	P	T	E	D	■	I	M	D	B	■	I	D	I	G
V	E	R	V	E	■	D	E	E	R	■	L	E	N	O
O	N	E	A	N	D	O	N	L	Y	■	O	S	S	O
I	N	S	■	N	U	L	L	A	N	D	V	O	I	D
D	A	B	■	I	S	S	O	■	■	J	E	T	T	A
A	M	I	D	S	T	■	■	S	L	I	P	O	U	T
L	E	E	R	■	■	C	E	S	S	N	A	■	■	■
■	S	N	A	T	C	H	A	N	D	G	R	A	B	■
■	■	■	W	A	F	E	R	S	■	■	I	M	A	N
H	O	T	S	P	O	T	■	■	U	P	S	I	D	E
A	L	I	T	O	■	■	T	A	P	E	■	C	D	C
V	I	M	A	N	D	V	I	G	O	R	■	A	R	K
E	V	E	R	■	A	I	D	A	N	D	A	B	E	T
N	I	L	E	■	M	O	E	T	■	A	D	L	A	I
S	A	Y	S	■	E	L	S	E	■	Y	A	Y	M	E

81

B	A	T	S	■	O	H	Y	E	S	■	G	I	S	T
E	U	R	O	■	P	A	U	L	A	■	A	L	P	O
S	T	E	P	H	E	N	K	I	N	G	B	O	O	K
T	O	E	R	I	N	G	■	T	K	O	■	V	I	E
■	■	■	A	T	L	■	S	E	I	N	F	E	L	D
I	R	O	N	S	I	D	E	■	N	E	A	P	■	■
D	O	Y	O	U	N	E	E	D	■	■	B	A	N	S
I	D	S	■	P	E	N	T	A	D	S	■	R	O	I
G	E	T	S	■	■	S	O	M	E	T	H	I	N	G
■	■	E	A	T	S	■	I	N	S	E	A	S	O	N
P	A	R	T	Y	H	A	T	■	S	R	I	■	■	■
A	R	C	■	P	U	P	■	M	E	E	R	K	A	T
P	E	R	S	O	N	A	L	P	R	O	N	O	U	N
E	S	A	U	■	T	R	E	A	T	■	E	C	R	U
R	O	B	E	■	S	T	O	A	S	■	T	H	A	T

82

S	A	R	A	H	PAL	I	N	■	O	H	S	N	A	P
O	V	E	R	E	A	S	Y	■	PAL	O	M	I	N	O
R	E	G	A	T	T	A	S	■	S	L	I	C	E	S
E	R	S	■	■	I	B	E	T	■	I	L	E	N	E
■	■	■	A	L	A	E	■	I	N	S	E	R	T	S
S	A	Y	H	E	L	L	O	T	O	M	Y	■	■	■
E	I	E	I	O	■	■	N	U	N	■	S	O	P	■
PAL	L	S	■	S	P	I	E	S	O	N	■	N	E	PAL
■	S	T	P	■	A	N	A	■	■	E	M	C	E	E
■	■	■	L	I	T	T	L	E	F	R	I	E	N	D
L	A	D	A	N	S	E	■	R	A	F	T	■	■	■
O	B	E	Y	S	■	L	A	I	C	■	■	L	S	U
R	A	PAL	B	U	M	■	B	E	E	R	T	E	N	T
E	L	M	O	R	E	■	A	P	PAL	A	C	H	I	A
S	L	A	Y	E	D	■	S	A	M	S	M	I	T	H

83

B	T	W	■	E	T	H	N	O	■	L	A	S	S	O
A	H	A	■	N	A	T	C	H	■	A	P	N	E	A
T	E	L	E	V	I	S	I	O	N	C	R	U	E	T
H	O	S	N	I	■	■	S	H	O	E	■	C	D	S
S	C	H	E	R	Z	O	■	■	R	I	S	K	■	■
■	■	■	M	O	U	N	T	A	I	N	D	U	E	T
U	G	L	Y	■	N	E	O	S	■	T	I	P	S	Y
N	A	E	■	G	I	O	R	G	I	O	■	O	P	P
L	E	A	V	E	■	F	R	A	N	■	E	N	N	E
V	A	N	I	T	Y	F	E	R	R	E	T	■	■	■
■	■	I	N	F	O	■	■	D	E	N	S	E	L	Y
A	N	N	■	U	G	G	S	■	■	A	E	R	I	E
M	A	G	A	Z	I	N	E	R	A	C	Q	U	E	T
P	L	O	T	Z	■	A	G	E	N	T	■	C	G	I
M	A	N	L	Y	■	W	A	N	D	S	■	T	E	S

84

L	A	C	E	■	D	O	S	E	S	■	C	H	E	W
I	M	U	P	■	O	P	E	R	A	■	O	A	T	H
N	A	S	H	■	L	A	T	I	N	■	N	I	C	O
E	R	T	E	■	C	H	I	C	K	E	N	(R)	■	■
A	N	O	M	I	E	■	■	■	A	E	O	L	(U)	S
L	A	M	E	(S)	■	B	B	C	■	G	R	O	A	(N)
■	■	■	R	I	(T)	E	A	I	D	■	■	S	E	L
■	■	W	A	T	E	(R)	S	L	I	D	E	S	■	■
C	I	A	■	■	D	R	(E)	I	D	E	L	■	■	■
A	P	N	E	A	■	A	D	(A)	■	B	O	O	S	T
D	O	N	N	Y	(B)	■	■	■	(M)	I	N	N	O	W
■	■	A	N	N	A	(R)	B	O	R	■	M	E	R	E
V	I	B	E	■	R	O	(O)	M	Y	■	U	S	E	R
I	D	E	A	■	B	A	Y	(O)	U	■	S	I	L	K
E	S	T	D	■	S	N	O	O	(K)	■	K	E	Y	S

85

T	W	O	S	■	W	A	C	O	■	G	H	O	S	T	S
A	E	R	O	■	A	F	R	O	■	O	I	L	C	U	P
G	R	A	N	D	S	L	A	M	■	O	D	D	O	N	E
G	E	T	■	C	H	O	M	P	E	D	■	E	R	I	C
I	W	O	J	I	M	A	■	H	A	T	T	R	I	C	K
N	O	R	A	■	E	T	A	■	T	O	I	■	A	S	S
G	L	I	N	T	■	■	R	O	U	G	E	S	■	■	■
■	F	O	U	R	T	E	E	N	P	O	I	N	T	S	■
■	■	■	S	E	E	N	A	T	■	■	N	O	R	A	D
A	R	C	■	E	A	R	■	O	O	F	■	W	I	L	E
F	O	U	L	S	H	O	T	■	N	O	N	S	E	L	F
R	A	T	A	■	O	N	E	P	A	R	T	■	D	O	E
A	R	E	Y	O	U	■	T	O	U	C	H	D	O	W	N
M	I	S	E	R	S	■	R	O	T	E	■	R	U	E	S
E	N	T	R	E	E	■	A	R	O	D	■	E	T	R	E

86

L	I	E	N	■	I	S	H	■	M	O	P	P	E	D
A	N	N	O	T	A	T	E	■	U	P	R	O	O	T
M	A	S	S	A	G	E	R	■	D	R	O	W	N	S
B	L	U	E	G	R	A	S	S	D	A	T	E	■	■
S	L	E	D	■	E	L	H	I	■	H	E	R	B	S
■	■	■	U	T	E	■	E	L	K	■	G	E	E	K
W	O	O	D	Y	■	P	L	E	A	S	E	D	A	Y
A	R	I	■	P	A	L	■	N	Y	E	■	O	R	E
F	A	L	S	E	D	A	R	T	■	W	I	N	D	Y
E	T	T	E	■	D	Y	E	■	G	N	C	■	■	■
R	E	Y	E	S	■	E	T	T	U	■	E	B	B	S
■	■	C	H	I	L	D	R	E	N	S	D	O	R	Y
T	B	O	O	N	E	■	I	N	S	T	O	R	E	S
Y	E	O	M	E	N	■	E	T	H	E	R	N	E	T
R	E	N	E	W	S	■	S	O	Y	■	M	E	D	S

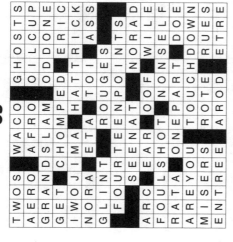

87

C	H	A	S	M	■	O	A	T	■	C	A	V	E	D
H	A	I	K	U	■	M	L	I	■	A	L	I	V	E
E	L	L	I	S	B	E	L	L	■	M	I	N	I	M
N	O	S	■	L	A	G	O	■	V	E	N	E	T	O
■	■	■	■	I	S	A	K	D	I	N	E	S	E	N
B	E	D	I	M	S	■	■	W	E	E	■	■	■	■
A	R	I	D	■	E	A	S	E	■	A	C	H	E	S
R	O	B	E	R	T	G	A	L	B	R	A	I	T	H
E	S	S	A	Y	■	A	S	T	A	■	R	E	N	O
■	■	■	■	E	S	P	■	■	R	I	P	S	A	W
G	E	O	R	G	E	E	L	I	O	T	■	■	■	■
R	E	B	O	R	N	■	A	N	N	A	■	Y	E	S
A	N	I	M	A	■	A	N	D	Y	S	T	A	C	K
S	I	T	E	S	■	I	C	E	■	C	I	R	R	I
P	E	S	O	S	■	R	E	X	■	A	N	N	U	M

88

T	N	A	R	G	■	■	R	O	P	E	■	P	E	S
C	I	R	U	A	■	S	E	N	A	T	■	A	D	E
A	B	B	A	J	■	T	H	E	S	A	U	R	U	S
■	■	■	S	A	B	U	T	■	A	V	A	T	A	R
C	I	M	O	N	O	G	R	E	■	I	T	A	L	O
S	T	E	G	O	R	■	O	V	A	L	■	S	C	H
I	O	L	E	■	■	■	N	A	N	A	S	■	■	■
D	N	E	T	S	E	W	■	E	A	S	T	M	A	N
■	■	■	S	T	F	I	S	■	■	■	A	I	R	Y
B	B	E	■	O	T	T	O	■	S	A	R	D	I	S
E	U	Q	I	P	■	T	U	R	N	S	T	I	L	E
S	T	U	O	P	S	■	T	O	L	L	S	■	■	■
E	L	A	S	E	T	I	H	W	■	O	O	M	P	H
T	E	T	■	R	E	V	E	S	■	P	U	P	A	E
S	R	E	■	S	W	E	Y	■	■	E	T	H	Y	L

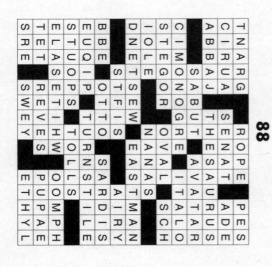

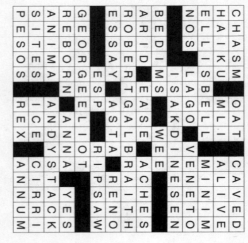

89

R	O	S	A	■	A	M	E	S	■	S	C	R	E	W
E	N	T	R	■	M	I	N	T	■	T	I	A	R	A
D	E	A	R	S	A	N	T	A	■	L	A	R	R	Y
T	O	B	E	O	R	N	O	T	T	O	B	E	■	■
O	N	L	A	T	E	■	M	U	M	■	A	B	E	D
P	E	E	R	■	T	O	B	E	I	S	T	O	D	O
■	■	■	■	A	T	M	S	■	■	S	T	O	I	C
C	A	S	I	N	O	S	■	R	E	T	A	K	E	S
A	L	I	S	T	■	■	B	O	Y	S	■	■	■	■
T	O	D	O	I	S	T	O	B	E	■	S	W	A	N
S	T	E	T	■	I	O	N	■	H	O	P	E	T	O
■	■	D	O	O	B	Y	D	O	O	B	Y	D	O	O
C	H	O	P	S	■	C	A	L	L	S	I	G	N	S
O	B	O	E	S	■	A	G	E	E	■	N	I	C	E
T	O	R	S	O	■	R	E	O	S	■	G	E	E	S

90

■	A	D	M	A	N	■	S	O	D	A	■	D	E	G
I	D	E	A	L	S	■	I	R	I	S	■	A	G	E
T	V	C	R	E	W	■	M	A	R	A	T	H	O	N
S	E	R	E	R	■	F	O	N	T	■	O	L	I	O
W	R	E	S	T	L	I	N	G	■	P	R	I	S	M
A	S	P	■	S	O	N	■	E	D	A	M	A	M	E
R	E	I	D	■	A	D	E	■	O	N	E	■	■	■
■	■	T	R	A	N	S	P	A	R	E	N	T	■	■
■	■	■	U	N	E	■	A	C	E	■	T	E	T	S
F	A	R	M	E	R	S	■	U	M	A	■	N	O	E
A	L	I	S	T	■	E	S	T	I	M	A	T	E	D
C	I	N	E	■	C	A	R	E	■	A	L	A	N	A
A	B	S	T	R	A	C	T	■	S	N	O	C	A	T
D	I	E	■	S	T	O	A	■	A	D	E	L	I	E
E	S	S	■	T	O	W	S	■	E	A	S	E	L	■

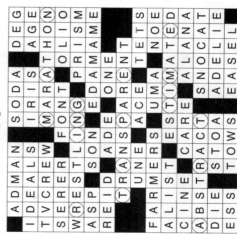

91

A	V	A	■	F	A	M	I	N	E	■	S	A	M	E
M	O	C	■	O	C	E	L	O	T	■	T	R	A	Y
A	N	T	A	R	C	T	I	C	C	I	R	C	L	E
Z	A	I	R	E	■	H	A	H	■	R	E	S	T	S
E	G	O	I	S	M	■	D	E	F	O	E	■	■	■
D	E	N	■	E	E	L	■	■	O	N	T	A	P	E
■	■	■	S	E	N	A	T	O	R	■	R	H	E	A
T	H	A	T	S	A	M	O	O	T	P	O	I	N	T
H	A	I	R	■	C	A	R	R	I	E	D	■	■	■
E	N	D	I	V	E	■	■	T	E	N	■	F	A	T
■	■	■	K	E	S	H	A	■	S	I	M	O	N	E
I	R	K	E	D	■	O	R	E	■	T	O	R	T	S
F	A	N	T	A	S	Y	B	A	S	E	B	A	L	L
S	N	O	W	■	P	A	Y	S	I	N	■	Y	E	A
O	T	T	O	■	A	S	S	E	R	T	■	S	R	S

92

A	J	A	R	■	B	L	O	B	■	A	C	R	I	D
C	O	V	E	■	Y	O	Y	O	■	B	U	E	N	O
T	H	E	P	R	I	M	E	S	U	S	P	E	C	T
L	A	N	■	U	T	E	R	U	S	■	■	B	O	T
I	N	G	O	T	S	■	■	N	O	T	H	O	M	E
K	N	E	W	H	E	W	A	S	C	O	O	K	E	D
E	A	R	N	■	L	I	D	■	■	R	O	S	S	I
■	■	■	■	A	F	T	E	R	H	E	■	■	■	■
S	L	E	E	T	■	■	A	A	A	■	G	U	S	H
W	A	S	G	R	I	L	L	E	D	B	Y	T	H	E
A	N	T	O	I	N	E	■	■	A	L	M	I	R	A
P	E	E	■	■	G	A	Z	E	B	O	■	L	I	V
P	O	L	I	C	E	D	E	T	E	C	T	I	V	E
E	N	L	A	I	■	T	A	T	E	■	S	T	E	T
D	E	E	M	S	■	O	L	A	F	■	P	Y	R	O

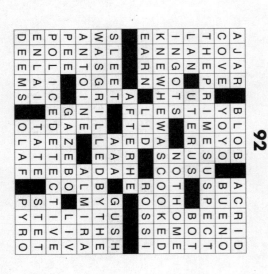

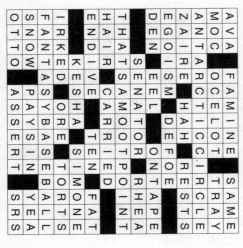

93

A	M	O	■	J	A	F	F	A	■	D	R	A	K	E
S	E	N	■	I	N	A	L	L	■	W	O	M	A	N
C	A	S	H	M	O	N	E	Y	■	A	W	A	R	E
A	D	L	A	I	■	D	U	S	K	Y	■	T	A	M
P	E	A	R	■	C	A	R	S	O	N	C	I	T	Y
■	■	U	T	U	R	N	■	A	D	E	E	■	■	■
A	L	G	■	R	A	G	U	■	■	■	O	O	P	S
J	O	H	N	N	Y	O	N	T	H	E	S	P	O	T
A	T	T	A	■	■	■	A	W	O	L	■	E	D	U
■	■	■	R	O	M	A	■	I	R	K	E	D	■	■
B	E	N	C	H	P	R	E	S	S	■	A	P	S	E
A	D	A	■	C	H	A	R	T	■	F	R	I	E	D
K	I	D	D	O	■	R	O	T	T	E	N	E	G	G
E	N	E	R	O	■	A	D	O	R	E	■	C	E	E
D	A	R	Y	L	■	T	E	P	I	D	■	E	R	R

94

S	L	A	V	S	■	E	T	A	S	■	L	O	A	M
T	U	L	I	P	■	S	A	L	E	■	U	N	P	C
A	M	A	T	I	■	Q	U	I	C	K	T	I	P	S
R	E	M	A	K	E	S	■	B	O	N	Z	O	■	■
S	T	O	L	E	N	■	F	I	N	E	■	N	B	A
■	■	■	S	L	O	M	O	■	D	E	B	R	I	S
A	N	G	I	E	■	A	X	I	S	■	L	I	L	T
R	O	U	G	E	■	R	H	O	■	S	I	N	G	E
O	V	E	N	■	S	T	O	W	■	A	N	G	E	R
M	E	S	S	U	P	■	L	A	I	R	D	■	■	■
A	L	T	■	G	A	P	E	■	M	A	S	A	L	A
■	■	S	I	G	M	A	■	O	P	T	I	M	A	L
T	A	P	A	S	B	A	R	S	■	O	D	I	S	T
A	T	O	M	■	O	V	A	L	■	G	E	S	S	O
J	E	T	S	■	T	O	G	O	■	A	S	H	E	S

95

B	L	E	W	I	T	■	C	M	I	X	■	M	A	D
J	A	N	I	C	E	■	E	A	S	E	■	A	X	E
O	Y	S	T	E	R	■	D	R	E	D	■	I	L	E
R	B	I	■	I	N	T	I	M	E	■	S	T	R	■
K	A	G	A	N	■	I	L	O	■	F	A	R	O	E
■	R	N	C	■	A	L	L	T	H	E	B	E	S	T
■	E	S	T	R	A	D	A	■	E	L	U	D	E	S
■	■	■	■	E	N	E	■	S	L	O	■	■	■	■
A	S	G	A	R	D	■	S	P	I	N	A	C	H	■
C	I	R	C	U	M	F	L	E	X	■	D	U	O	■
U	S	A	I	N	■	R	E	N	■	S	O	R	T	A
■	E	N	D	■	S	A	I	D	A	H	■	A	S	U
A	N	O	■	R	A	N	G	■	G	A	R	C	O	N
L	O	L	■	I	N	C	H	■	U	M	L	A	U	T
I	R	A	■	M	E	E	T	■	A	E	S	O	P	S

96

JACK	A	S	S	■	A	M	A	J	■	JACK	P	O	T	S
F	R	A	T	■	T	A	R	A	■	C	O	M	B	O
R	A	V	E	M	U	S	I	C	■	H	O	G	A	N
O	B	I	W	A	N	■	■	K	E	E	L	■	■	■
S	L	O	■	L	E	O	N	I	N	E	■	D	I	E
T	E	R	S	E	■	R	U	N	S	S	H	O	R	T
■	■	■	A	S	S	E	T	■	L	E	A	D	O	N
S	P	O	T	■	P	L	E	B	E	■	R	O	N	A
A	L	K	A	L	I	■	L	I	R	A	S	■	■	■
S	E	A	T	U	R	T	L	E	■	W	H	E	L	P
S	A	Y	■	M	A	H	A	L	I	A	■	R	A	H
■	■	■	A	B	L	E	■	■	B	R	A	I	N	O
O	V	A	T	E	■	B	E	L	I	E	V	E	I	N
F	A	V	O	R	■	O	Y	E	Z	■	E	P	E	E
F	L	A	P	JACK	■	X	E	N	A	■	C	A	R	JACK

97

B	U	C	K	O	■	A	N	T	I	■	E	H	U	D
S	T	E	E	R	■	T	E	A	R	■	N	A	M	E
H	O	L	D	E	N	T	A	N	K	■	D	I	P	S
A	P	E	S	■	B	I	T	■	■	F	O	R	T	E
R	I	B	■	B	A	C	O	N	P	O	W	D	E	R
P	A	S	S	E	■	■	■	U	A	E	■	Y	E	T
■	■	■	C	R	A	T	E	R	S	■	M	E	N	S
■	■	D	A	N	S	O	N	S	H	O	E	S	■	■
N	A	I	R	■	I	N	S	E	A	M	S	■	■	■
E	L	A	■	G	A	G	■	■	■	S	A	L	S	A
W	A	L	K	E	N	S	T	I	C	K	■	L	O	L
A	M	T	O	O	■	■	O	N	E	■	A	B	L	E
G	O	O	D	■	L	A	N	D	O	N	G	E	A	R
E	D	N	A	■	A	S	T	I	■	T	R	A	C	T
R	E	E	K	■	W	H	O	A	■	H	A	N	E	S

98

T	A	L	C	U	M	■	D	E	F	■	K	N	O	B
I	M	P	O	S	E	■	R	D	A	■	R	A	V	E
A	I	S	L	E	S	■	A	N	I	■	O	P	E	D
■	■	■	O	R	C	■	P	A	R	T	N	E	R	S
C	A	R	R	I	A	G	E	■	G	O	O	■	■	■
L	I	E	I	D	L	E	■	B	A	R	R	E	L	S
A	K	I	N	S	■	L	L	A	M	A	■	M	A	P
W	I	N	G	■	F	A	I	R	E	■	N	I	T	A
A	D	E	■	M	A	T	T	E	■	C	O	L	I	C
T	O	R	T	O	N	I	■	L	E	O	N	I	N	E
■	■	■	B	O	Z	■	H	Y	M	N	B	O	O	K
M	A	J	O	R	I	T	Y	■	A	S	A	■	■	■
E	C	O	N	■	N	A	P	■	J	O	S	T	L	E
L	A	K	E	■	E	X	E	■	O	L	I	V	I	A
D	I	E	D	■	S	I	S	■	R	E	C	A	N	T

99

O	B	I	■	F	R	I	L	L	S	■	L	P	G	A
F	U	N	■	L	A	T	O	Y	A	■	E	L	E	C
F	I	F	T	Y	F	I	R	S	T	S	T	A	T	E
S	L	U	R	■	T	S	A	■	■	A	M	I	S	■
I	T	S	Y	■	S	I	X	T	H	S	E	N	S	E
D	I	E	O	F	■	■	■	H	A	H	■	E	E	L
E	N	S	U	E	S	■	M	O	M	■	A	R	T	S
■	■	■	T	H	I	R	D	R	A	I	L	■	■	■
R	B	I	S	■	N	O	S	■	S	O	L	D	A	S
E	R	N	■	W	E	T	■	■	■	S	C	A	N	T
F	I	F	T	H	W	H	E	E	L	■	A	S	T	O
■	T	I	R	E	■	■	T	B	A	■	S	H	O	P
A	N	D	A	N	O	T	H	E	R	T	H	I	N	G
R	E	E	D	■	C	H	A	R	G	E	■	N	I	A
K	Y	L	E	■	D	E	N	T	E	D	■	G	N	P

100

D	O	C	K	S	■	T	Y	R	O	■	■	J	A	N
O	B	O	E	S	■	R	O	A	R	■	C	O	R	E
M	O	P	E	A	R	O	U	N	D	■	R	U	G	S
■	L	A	P	■	C	I	R	C	A	■	A	L	O	T
■	■	C	A	S	A	■	■	H	I	P	N	E	S	S
C	O	A	T	I	■	A	D	O	N	A	I	■	■	■
H	U	B	■	N	O	I	R	S	■	L	U	B	E	S
A	T	A	■	E	R	G	O	■	G	I	M	L	E	T
L	I	N	A	C	S	■	P	L	U	M	■	O	R	E
K	E	A	N	U	■	T	I	E	T	O	■	O	I	E
■	■	■	A	R	G	O	T	S	■	N	A	D	E	R
G	O	R	G	E	O	N	■	■	M	Y	M	Y	■	■
L	I	A	R	■	T	E	A	S	E	■	U	M	P	■
A	L	D	A	■	S	A	N	T	A	C	L	A	U	S
R	E	A	M	■	E	R	T	E	■	B	E	R	L	E
E	R	R	■	■	T	M	E	N	■	S	T	Y	L	E

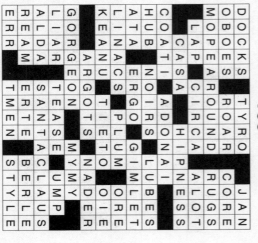

101

J	E	D	I	M	A	S	T	E	R		S	P	A	M
A	L	O	H	A	S	T	A	T	E		N	O	N	E
M	I	R	A	C	L	E	M	A	X		A	L	A	N
E	X	I	T		A	P	P	S			P	A	C	S
S	I	T	E		N	S	A		I	N	A	R	O	W
	R	O	I	L				A	C	E	T	O	N	E
			T	O	Y	B	O	X	E	S		I	D	A
A	S	H		G	O	A	L	I	E	S		D	A	R
U	T	A		J	U	R	A	S	S	I	C			
D	E	N	M	A	R	K				E	A	R	L	
I	M	G	A	M	E		S	M	U		S	E	E	S
E	W	O	K			O	T	O	S		E	V	A	N
N	A	V	E		C	H	O	R	U	S	L	I	N	E
C	R	E	D		D	O	M	E	A	F	A	V	O	R
E	E	R	O		S	H	A	L	L	O	W	E	N	D

102

S	C	R	A	P	S		S	T	R	A	W	M	A	N
M	O	O	L	A	H		T	H	E	P	I	A	N	O
I	M	W	A	Y	A	H	E	A	D	O	F	Y	O	U
T	O	S	S	A	C	O	I	N		P	I	O	N	S
				S	K	U	N	K						
D	E	C	R	Y		R	E	G		R	O	M	A	S
I	G	L	O	O	S		R	O	B	O	C	A	L	L
E	G	O	S	U	R	F		D	E	T	E	N	T	E
G	O	N	E	G	I	R	L		T	I	L	T	E	D
O	N	E	N	O		E	E	L		S	O	A	R	S
						E	M	I	R	S				
S	H	O	W	S		M	O	V	I	E	F	O	N	E
L	I	M	O	U	S	I	N	E	D	R	I	V	E	R
O	V	E	R	L	O	U	D		E	I	L	E	E	N
G	E	N	D	A	R	M	E		S	E	E	N	T	O

103

I	N	S	■	R	I	B	S	■	■	D	I	C	E	Y
D	O	T	H	E	M	A	T	H	■	A	D	O	R	E
I	F	E	E	L	F	R	E	E	■	F	I	L	E	S
D	A	I	R	Y	■	G	E	M	■	T	O	D	A	Y
S	I	N	E	■	G	A	R	I	■	■	T	O	D	O
O	R	S	■	A	R	I	■	N	Y	U	■	P	E	U
■	■	■	T	R	A	N	S	G	E	N	D	E	R	■
■	■	A	I	N	T	I	A	W	O	M	A	N	■	■
■	D	O	M	A	I	N	N	A	M	E	S	■	■	■
L	O	L	■	Z	A	G	■	Y	E	T	■	G	I	G
A	G	R	A	■	■	C	O	E	N	■	M	O	N	O
S	P	A	S	M	■	H	R	S	■	B	A	N	J	O
H	A	D	T	O	■	I	N	Q	U	I	R	E	O	F
E	R	I	E	S	■	P	O	U	N	D	C	A	K	E
S	K	O	R	T	■	■	T	E	E	S	■	R	E	D

104

T	V	D	R	A	M	A	■	S	C	R	A	W	L	S
H	I	R	E	D	O	N	■	T	H	E	S	O	U	P
A	T	A	C	O	S	T	■	R	A	T	H	O	L	E
T	A	G	O	R	E	■	R	O	N	D	E	L	L	E
S	M	O	R	E	■	M	U	N	G	■	S	L	E	D
H	I	N	D	■	C	O	N	G	E	R	■	Y	D	S
O	N	E	S	■	A	D	S	P	E	A	K	■	■	■
W	A	T	E	R	M	E	L	O	N	S	E	E	D	S
■	■	■	T	A	B	L	O	I	D	■	E	X	I	T
A	M	O	■	M	O	R	O	N	S	■	P	A	G	E
M	O	R	E	■	D	O	S	T	■	D	A	M	U	P
P	R	A	C	T	I	C	E	■	M	R	P	I	N	K
U	N	C	L	O	A	K	■	Y	O	U	A	N	D	I
L	A	L	A	N	N	E	■	I	N	B	R	E	E	D
E	Y	E	T	E	S	T	■	P	O	S	T	E	R	S

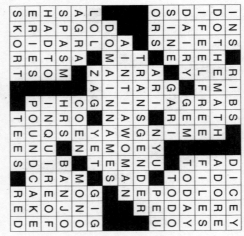

105

D	R	E	A	M	G	I	R	L	S	■	P	O	S	H
D	O	G	G	I	E	D	O	O	R	■	A	S	T	O
A	N	O	I	N	T	I	N	G	S	■	S	C	A	M
Y	A	N	N	I	■	D	D	S	■	S	T	A	R	E
■	■	■	C	O	S	M	O	■	S	H	O	R	T	O
■	P	H	O	N	E	Y	■	P	S	I	■	W	S	W
L	I	E	U	■	A	B	S	O	R	P	T	I	O	N
A	L	A	R	M	■	E	E	C	■	S	O	L	V	E
C	O	T	T	O	N	S	W	A	B	■	O	D	E	R
E	T	E	■	V	E	T	■	H	U	S	K	E	R	■
R	E	N	N	E	T	■	C	O	S	T	A	■	■	■
A	R	G	O	S	■	P	A	N	■	U	S	E	M	E
T	R	I	M	■	L	E	T	T	E	R	T	R	A	Y
E	O	N	S	■	B	R	E	A	K	D	A	N	C	E
D	R	E	G	■	J	E	R	S	E	Y	B	O	Y	S

106

T	H	E	S	I	S	S	T	A	T	E	M	E	N	T
R	O	S	I	E	T	H	E	R	I	V	E	T	E	R
U	P	P	E	R	P	A	L	A	T	I	N	A	T	E
S	P	A	N	I	S	H	O	M	E	L	E	T	T	E
T	I	N	A	■	■	■	S	I	R	■	S	I	L	T
S	N	O	■	C	H	E	■	S	S	A	■	S	E	A
■	G	L	A	R	E	A	T	■	■	N	O	M	S	G
■	■	■	N	E	X	T	O	F	K	I	N	■	■	■
E	A	P	O	E	■	■	M	A	I	T	A	I	S	■
N	S	A	■	K	G	B	■	B	A	A	■	B	E	A
S	O	R	B	■	R	A	D	■	■	■	Y	E	L	L
I	N	T	I	M	A	T	E	A	P	P	A	R	E	L
L	A	I	D	I	T	O	N	T	H	E	L	I	N	E
E	N	T	E	R	I	N	T	O	D	E	T	A	I	L
S	T	A	T	E	A	S	S	I	S	T	A	N	C	E

107

P	A	W	N	■	S	T	E	A	L	T	H	I	E	R
E	P	E	E	■	W	A	L	L	A	W	A	L	L	A
R	E	N	O	■	I	N	M	E	M	O	R	I	A	M
U	N	C	L	O	G	S	■	■	■	■	R	A	T	S
■	N	E	A	P	■	■	Z	I	P	C	O	D	E	■
S	I	S	T	E	R	S	I	N	L	A	W	■	■	■
O	N	L	I	N	E	P	O	K	E	R	■	M	E	W
D	E	A	N	■	N	I	N	J	A	■	R	O	N	A
A	S	S	■	L	A	D	I	E	S	F	I	R	S	T
■	■	■	H	O	M	E	S	T	E	A	D	A	C	T
■	P	R	E	T	E	R	M	■	■	V	E	T	O	■
A	R	A	L	■	■	■	■	S	E	A	S	O	N	S
W	I	N	E	S	E	L	L	E	R	■	O	R	C	A
O	Z	O	N	E	L	A	Y	E	R	■	F	I	E	F
L	E	N	S	C	O	V	E	R	S	■	F	A	D	E

108

P	H	O	T	O	B	O	M	B	■	S	T	A	I	D
R	O	B	R	E	I	N	E	R	■	L	I	T	R	E
O	O	L	O	N	G	T	E	A	■	A	L	T	O	S
M	T	A	P	O	■	A	T	L	■	P	L	A	N	K
P	E	T	E	■	C	R	U	E	L	■	■	G	I	S
T	R	E	S	■	L	I	P	S	E	R	V	I	C	E
■	■	■	■	G	O	O	■	S	N	E	E	R	A	T
I	S	S	U	E	S	■	■	■	S	P	E	L	L	S
T	H	I	N	N	E	D	■	E	C	O	■	■	■	■
C	I	N	D	E	R	E	L	L	A	■	S	L	O	T
A	V	G	■	■	S	C	O	O	P	■	T	U	B	A
N	E	S	T	S	■	L	A	P	■	F	A	T	T	Y
T	R	O	U	P	■	A	D	I	N	I	T	I	U	M
B	E	N	D	Y	■	R	E	N	E	R	U	S	S	O
E	D	G	E	S	■	E	R	G	O	M	E	T	E	R

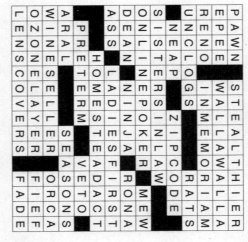

109

A	S	T	R	I	D	■	■	■	G	E	T	S	A	T
S	W	E	E	P	E	A	■	C	L	A	R	I	C	E
C	A	S	T	O	F	T	H	O	U	S	A	N	D	S
O	T	S	■	D	E	R	A	L	T	E	■	K	E	L
T	H	E	N	■	N	O	I	S	E	■	I	S	L	A
S	E	R	A	■	S	I	T	O	N	■	S	I	C	S
■	D	A	N	T	E	S	I	N	F	E	R	N	O	■
■	■	■	E	V	A	■	■	■	R	E	A	■	■	■
■	P	O	T	A	T	O	P	E	E	L	E	R	S	■
S	E	N	T	■	T	R	A	D	E	■	L	A	T	E
K	N	E	E	■	O	N	T	A	P	■	I	T	A	L
I	T	O	■	F	R	A	C	T	A	L	■	E	N	D
B	A	C	K	I	N	T	H	E	S	A	D	D	L	E
I	N	A	T	R	E	E	■	S	T	R	I	P	E	R
B	E	T	S	E	Y	■	■	■	A	D	A	G	E	S

110

A	H	B	L	I	S	S	■	■	■	■	■	N	E	T
E	A	R	A	C	H	E	S	■	■	■	F	O	R	E
G	U	I	D	E	R	A	I	L	■	G	A	S	E	S
I	L	S	■	R	E	A	G	A	N	O	M	I	C	S
S	I	T	Z	■	K	I	N	D	A	S	O	R	T	A
■	N	O	O	K	■	R	E	I	S	S	U	E	S	■
■	■	L	E	N	T	■	E	N	C	A	S	E	■	■
■	■	■	S	E	A	R	■	G	A	M	A	■	■	■
■	■	P	A	L	L	E	T	■	R	E	M	O	■	■
■	B	E	L	L	E	V	U	E	■	R	O	B	B	■
S	A	R	D	I	N	E	C	A	N	■	S	T	E	M
M	R	F	A	N	T	A	S	T	I	C	■	R	A	Y
E	K	I	N	G	■	L	O	S	E	A	T	U	R	N
L	E	D	A	■	■	■	N	I	C	E	I	D	E	A
T	R	Y	■	■	■	■	■	T	E	N	N	E	R	S

111

I	M	U	P	■	B	L	I	G	E	■	C	A	S	T
N	A	N	O	■	O	U	T	E	R	■	A	C	H	Y
S	U	N	T	A	N	N	I	N	G	■	K	C	A	L
O	N	E	P	L	E	A	S	E	■	P	E	E	V	E
L	A	R	I	A	T	■	D	R	P	E	P	P	E	R
E	L	V	E	S	■	B	E	A	R	C	A	T	S	■
N	O	E	S	■	M	A	C	L	E	A	N	■	■	■
T	A	D	■	D	E	N	I	Z	E	N	■	P	T	A
■	■	■	C	E	L	A	D	O	N	■	B	A	R	R
■	L	E	A	V	E	N	E	D	■	R	O	R	E	M
W	E	L	L	R	E	A	D	■	S	E	R	V	E	R
U	N	I	T	Y	■	B	L	O	N	D	E	A	L	E
R	A	T	E	■	T	O	Y	P	O	O	D	L	E	S
S	P	E	C	■	B	A	S	E	R	■	O	U	S	T
T	E	S	H	■	S	T	O	N	E	■	M	E	S	S

112

M	A	M	A	B	E	A	R	■	D	O	U	B	L	E
A	L	A	C	A	R	T	E	■	A	U	K	L	E	T
W	O	R	N	D	O	W	N	■	W	R	E	A	T	H
S	P	E	E	D	D	A	T	I	N	G	■	C	H	A
■	■	■	■	E	E	R	■	B	R	A	C	K	E	N
O	B	A	M	A	S	■	P	I	A	N	O	S	■	■
B	A	B	E	L	■	V	I	S	I	G	O	T	H	S
I	N	S	T	■	W	I	P	E	D	■	P	O	O	L
S	A	T	I	R	I	Z	E	S	■	T	E	N	O	R
■	■	A	M	I	D	S	T	■	S	H	R	E	D	S
S	P	I	E	G	E	L	■	O	N	E	■	■	■	■
I	O	N	■	V	E	A	L	M	A	R	S	A	L	A
C	R	E	P	E	Y	■	O	N	P	A	T	R	O	L
E	T	R	A	D	E	■	S	I	P	P	Y	C	U	P
M	O	S	S	A	D	■	S	A	Y	Y	E	S	T	O

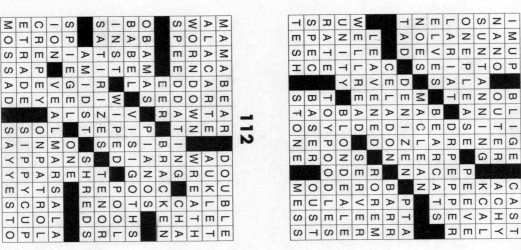

113

G	A	W	P	■	O	D	I	C	■	U	N	G	E	R
A	C	H	E	■	H	O	R	A	■	N	A	O	M	I
G	R	A	N	D	S	T	A	N	D	S	E	A	T	S
A	E	T	N	A	■	S	E	N	A	T	■	T	S	K
■	■	M	E	R	C	■	■	E	N	O	L	A	■	■
A	M	O	D	E	S	T	P	R	O	P	O	S	A	L
M	A	R	■	D	I	A	R	Y	■	S	O	N	D	E
P	R	E	V	■	S	K	I	R	T	■	N	A	D	A
A	S	C	I	I	■	E	M	O	R	Y	■	I	L	K
S	H	A	I	L	E	N	E	W	O	O	D	L	E	Y
■	■	N	I	L	L	A	■	■	U	K	E	S	■	■
A	N	I	■	B	E	B	O	P	■	E	X	P	A	T
J	E	S	S	I	C	A	C	H	A	S	T	A	I	N
A	B	A	F	T	■	C	H	I	N	■	E	C	R	U
R	O	Y	C	E	■	K	O	L	N	■	R	E	S	T

114

A	C	I	D	W	A	S	H	■	R	A	B	B	I	T
D	O	T	O	A	T	E	E	■	A	T	T	A	C	H
D	R	U	G	W	A	R	S	■	B	O	W	S	E	R
I	N	N	■	A	L	I	■	R	I	M	■	I	M	O
N	E	E	R	■	L	E	B	O	N	■	G	L	I	B
G	A	S	O	L	■	S	R	S	■	S	A	I	L	S
■	■	■	S	E	L	F	I	E	S	T	I	C	K	■
■	■	M	A	D	E	I	N	C	H	I	N	A	■	■
■	L	O	N	G	I	N	G	E	Y	E	S	■	■	■
B	O	O	N	E	■	A	I	R	■	S	O	M	M	E
A	C	N	E	■	A	L	T	E	R	■	N	A	C	L
T	A	R	■	D	R	E	■	M	O	I	■	R	A	M
I	R	O	B	O	T	■	H	O	W	S	L	I	F	E
K	N	O	L	L	S	■	O	N	E	L	I	N	E	R
S	O	F	T	L	Y	■	P	Y	R	E	N	E	E	S

115

L	O	C	A	V	O	R	E	■	■	H	I	P	P	O
L	O	A	D	E	D	U	P	■	A	E	N	E	I	D
A	L	S	O	R	A	N	S	■	N	E	A	T	L	Y
M	O	I	■	B	Y	E	■	G	O	D	D	E	S	S
A	N	N	E	■	■	■	L	O	U	■	A	R	E	S
■	G	O	L	D	I	L	O	C	K	S	Z	O	N	E
■	■	■	M	I	D	A	I	R	■	K	E	S	E	Y
A	S	T	■	D	A	B	■	A	L	I	■	E	R	S
C	O	R	D	S	■	O	O	Z	I	N	G	■	■	■
C	R	Y	Y	O	U	R	E	Y	E	S	O	U	T	■
I	C	A	N	■	H	E	D	■	■	■	O	R	E	S
D	E	C	A	T	U	R	■	M	B	A	■	B	E	N
E	R	A	S	E	R	■	H	E	A	T	W	A	V	E
N	E	S	T	E	A	■	O	N	E	O	W	N	E	R
T	R	E	Y	S	■	■	B	U	Z	Z	F	E	E	D

116

W	E	M	E	T	■	F	A	Z	E	■	S	L	A	B
I	V	O	R	Y	T	O	W	E	R	■	T	I	V	O
N	O	S	Y	P	A	R	K	E	R	■	A	M	E	X
S	L	A	K	E	D	■	■	■	O	W	N	E	R	S
A	V	I	A	S	■	M	O	I	R	E	■	A	T	E
T	E	C	H	■	B	A	N	G	■	C	A	D	E	T
■	■	■	B	I	O	D	E	G	R	A	D	E	D	■
■	■	C	A	M	D	E	N	Y	A	R	D	S	■	■
■	J	U	D	G	E	W	A	P	N	E	R	■	■	■
K	A	B	U	L	■	A	M	O	K	■	E	O	N	S
I	N	S	■	A	D	R	E	P	■	F	S	T	O	P
D	E	C	A	D	E	■	■	■	M	U	S	T	D	O
O	D	O	N	■	B	U	T	T	E	R	B	E	E	R
R	O	U	T	■	I	S	M	E	L	L	A	R	A	T
Y	E	T	I	■	T	A	C	T	■	S	R	S	L	Y

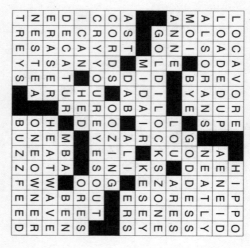

117

F	I	A	T	■	■	A	C	A	I	■	C	O	L	A
E	N	N	I	S	■	H	O	L	D	■	O	V	A	L
M	O	N	T	E	V	E	R	D	I	■	K	E	E	L
B	R	A	■	N	O	M	D	E	G	U	E	R	R	E
O	B	L	A	D	I	■	S	R	I	S	■	A	T	A
T	I	E	R	O	D	S	■	S	T	O	U	T	E	R
■	T	E	N	F	O	U	R	■	■	■	T	E	S	S
■	■	■	O	F	F	E	N	B	A	C	H	■	■	■
E	M	I	L	■	■	■	S	Y	L	L	A	B	I	■
D	A	W	D	L	E	S	■	E	C	O	N	O	M	Y
I	D	A	■	C	L	U	E	■	O	N	T	I	M	E
B	E	N	E	D	I	C	T	X	V	I	■	L	E	A
L	I	T	E	■	S	C	H	O	E	N	B	E	R	G
E	R	I	K	■	H	O	A	X	■	G	O	R	S	E
S	A	N	S	■	A	R	N	O	■	■	Y	S	E	R

118

H	A	S	I	T	M	A	D	E	■	P	E	R	S	E
E	P	I	D	E	R	M	I	S	■	A	L	E	T	A
F	I	X	I	E	B	I	K	E	■	L	A	M	A	R
N	E	T	■	M	I	N	T	■	■	■	T	A	R	P
E	C	H	O	■	G	U	A	C	■	B	E	R	T	H
R	E	S	I	N	■	S	T	A	T	U	S	Q	U	O
■	■	■	L	O	B	■	S	L	O	T	■	U	P	N
B	R	O	S	N	A	N	■	M	A	L	T	E	S	E
R	E	F	■	A	J	A	X	■	D	E	E	■	■	■
I	N	F	O	M	A	N	I	A	■	R	E	C	U	R
S	T	Y	L	E	■	A	P	T	S	■	N	O	S	E
T	R	O	D	■	■	■	H	O	E	S	■	B	E	E
L	O	U	S	Y	■	B	O	N	E	H	E	A	D	S
E	L	G	A	R	■	M	I	A	M	I	V	I	C	E
S	L	O	W	S	■	I	D	L	E	H	A	N	D	S

119

C	A	P	E	F	E	A	R	■	N	E	W	T	O	Y
A	L	O	E	L	A	C	E	■	O	X	H	I	D	E
V	A	M	O	O	S	E	D	■	T	A	I	L	O	R
E	M	P	■	R	E	S	■	G	O	M	P	E	R	S
B	O	O	M	E	D	■	J	U	R	I	S	■	■	■
A	D	U	L	T	■	G	E	M	I	N	I	S	■	■
T	O	S	S	■	B	E	T	W	E	E	N	U	S	■
S	M	A	■	P	E	N	S	E	T	S	■	R	I	G
■	E	S	C	A	P	E	K	E	Y	■	F	E	T	A
■	■	S	U	B	A	R	I	D	■	L	O	Y	A	L
■	■	■	T	A	T	A	S	■	R	O	B	O	T	O
N	O	S	T	R	I	L	■	B	O	A	■	U	H	S
I	M	L	I	K	E	■	S	A	N	D	R	A	O	H
S	E	A	M	E	N	■	O	H	D	E	A	R	M	E
I	N	V	E	R	T	■	U	S	E	R	F	E	E	S

120

T	H	I	S	J	U	S	T	I	N	■	C	A	L	F
H	A	V	E	I	T	M	A	D	E	■	O	L	E	O
A	T	A	L	L	T	I	M	E	S	■	S	P	A	R
Y	E	N	■	L	E	T	I	N	■	■	T	A	S	K
E	R	I	S	■	R	E	A	T	A	■	A	C	H	E
R	S	V	P	S	■	S	M	I	T	H	■	I	L	E
■	■	■	E	E	K	■	I	T	S	A	S	N	A	P
D	R	E	A	M	U	P	■	Y	E	L	L	O	W	S
R	O	C	K	I	D	O	L	■	A	V	E	■	■	■
I	M	O	■	S	O	W	E	D	■	A	W	A	I	T
N	A	N	S	■	S	H	O	E	D	■	S	I	N	E
K	N	O	T	■	■	A	P	R	I	L	■	R	T	E
S	I	M	I	■	S	T	A	M	P	A	L	B	U	M
T	A	I	L	■	P	A	R	I	S	I	E	N	N	E
O	N	C	E	■	A	N	D	S	O	T	O	B	E	D

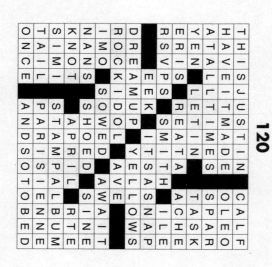

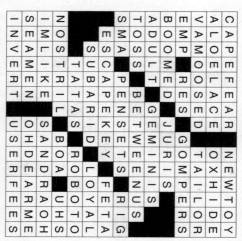

121

B	E	D	■	A	B	D	U	L	J	A	B	B	A	R
R	P	I	■	C	A	R	T	O	O	N	L	I	K	E
O	H	S	■	C	H	E	E	R	L	E	A	D	E	R
W	E	P	T	■	R	I	S	E	S	■	B	E	L	A
■	M	A	R	T	A	■	■	N	O	G	■	N	A	N
P	E	R	I	W	I	G	S	■	N	A	B	■	■	■
D	R	A	C	O	N	I	A	N	■	S	E	P	T	A
F	A	T	E	S	■	F	H	A	■	K	A	R	O	L
S	L	E	P	T	■	T	I	T	L	E	R	O	L	E
■	■	■	S	E	T	■	B	L	O	T	C	H	E	S
Z	A	C	■	P	A	D	■	■	U	S	A	I	R	■
E	D	O	M	■	I	R	A	N	I	■	T	B	A	R
R	A	D	I	O	L	O	G	I	S	T	■	I	B	O
O	N	E	T	W	O	P	U	N	C	H	■	T	L	C
G	A	R	T	E	R	S	N	A	K	E	■	S	E	A

122

T	A	U	T	■	N	O	S	I	R	E	E	B	O	B
A	R	N	E	■	C	R	I	M	E	S	C	E	N	E
L	A	S	H	■	I	L	L	B	E	T	H	E	R	E
C	L	O	R	I	S	■	E	R	L	E	■	R	A	T
U	S	U	A	L	■	O	N	U	S	■	C	M	D	R
M	E	N	N	O	N	I	T	E	■	L	O	U	I	E
S	A	D	■	V	A	S	T	■	T	I	N	G	O	D
■	■	■	P	E	T	E	R	F	A	L	K	■	■	■
T	A	M	A	L	E	■	E	A	R	L	■	J	E	B
A	N	I	T	A	■	B	A	R	E	I	T	A	L	L
B	O	D	S	■	C	O	T	E	■	A	I	S	L	E
I	T	T	■	G	L	A	M	■	A	N	E	M	I	A
T	H	E	H	E	I	R	E	S	S	■	R	I	S	K
H	E	R	E	A	N	D	N	O	W	■	E	N	O	L
A	R	M	W	R	E	S	T	L	E	■	D	E	N	Y

123

R	A	S	H	A	D	■	L	A	C	E	R	A	T	E
E	Z	P	A	S	S	T	O	L	L	L	A	N	E	S
H	E	A	V	Y	C	A	S	U	A	L	T	I	E	S
A	R	M	E	E	■	B	S	I	D	E	S	■	■	■
B	A	S	■	■	A	B	O	■	■	■	■	P	G	A
■	■	■	T	A	K	E	F	O	R	A	F	O	O	L
■	■	F	E	M	I	N	I	N	E	W	I	L	E	S
■	B	A	R	I	T	O	N	E	S	A	X	E	S	■
M	O	U	N	T	A	I	N	B	I	K	E	R	■	■
T	H	R	E	E	S	T	O	O	G	E	S	■	■	■
A	R	E	■	■	■	■	C	T	N	■	■	T	A	G
■	■	■	O	M	E	L	E	T	■	O	S	A	G	E
A	M	E	R	I	C	A	N	L	A	R	C	H	E	S
M	A	D	E	C	O	N	C	E	S	S	I	O	N	S
P	A	U	L	K	L	E	E	■	L	O	S	E	T	O

124

B	R	O	A	D	E	N	S	■	■	G	R	O	S	S
B	O	X	S	O	C	I	A	L	■	M	E	L	E	E
Q	U	E	S	T	L	O	V	E	■	C	O	D	E	X
P	R	Y	■	H	A	B	I	T	■	■	I	N	K	S
I	K	E	A	■	T	E	N	D	■	S	L	O	S	H
T	E	S	T	S	■	■	G	O	U	T	■	R	O	O
■	■	■	T	H	A	T	S	W	H	A	T	S	U	P
■	F	A	I	R	L	Y	■	N	O	T	Y	E	T	■
P	E	N	C	I	L	P	U	S	H	E	R	■	■	■
A	R	T	■	N	Y	E	S	■	■	D	O	D	O	S
R	A	I	S	E	■	C	O	S	T	■	L	E	S	H
A	L	D	A	■	■	A	S	H	E	R	■	N	P	R
S	C	O	L	D	■	S	H	A	R	E	W	A	R	E
K	A	T	E	Y	■	T	O	P	S	E	E	D	E	D
I	T	E	M	S	■	■	W	E	E	K	D	A	Y	S

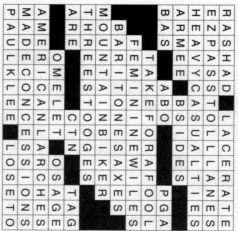

125

M	I	N	I	C	A	R			S	T	R	A	F	E
O	N	T	H	E	M	A	P		I	B	A	N	E	Z
I	D	E	A	L	I	Z	E		T	A	N	G	L	E
R	U	S	T		R	E	N	O	I	R		E	L	K
E	S	T	E	E			C	N	N		E	L	O	I
				L	A	V	I	E		C	R	E	P	E
		T	R	A	V	E	L	C	H	A	N	N	E	L
	L	E	S	T	E	R	P	E	A	R	S	O	N	
S	I	L	V	E	R	B	U	L	L	E	T	S		
P	E	E	P	S		O	S	L	E	R				
Y	A	P	S		A	S	H			S	O	S	A	D
W	H	O		G	R	E	E	N	S		H	O	L	Y
A	E	R	I	A	L		R	O	E	V	W	A	D	E
R	A	T	T	L	E		S	T	E	W	O	V	E	R
E	D	S	E	L	S			A	N	S	W	E	R	S

126

S	T	J	U	D	E			N	U	D	I	S	T	S
C	H	E	N	I	N		L	O	V	E	S	E	A	T
H	E	A	V	E	D		O	N	E	L	L	A	M	A
M	O	N	E	T	S		S	C	A	L	A	W	A	G
A	D	A	S	H		M	I	I		S	N	A	R	E
L	O	U	T		S	A	N	T	A		D	Y	A	D
T	R	E	E	H	U	G	G	I	N	G				
Z	E	L	D	A	F	I	T	Z	G	E	R	A	L	D
				M	I	C	H	E	L	L	E	W	I	E
A	M	F	M		S	C	E	N	E		S	E	N	T
M	A	R	O	N		H	P	S		J	U	D	G	E
P	R	O	P	O	S	A	L		H	A	R	D	E	N
S	I	N	E	S	T	R	O		E	N	G	I	R	T
U	N	D	R	E	A	M	T		W	I	E	N	I	E
P	A	S	S	E	R	S			S	E	D	G	E	S

127

P	E	N	P	A	L	■	■	S	L	O	W	J	A	M
A	V	I	A	T	E	■	S	T	O	N	E	A	G	E
C	E	L	L	O	S	■	P	A	P	E	R	C	U	T
K	N	E	E	L	■	H	A	T	S	■	E	K	E	S
■	■	■	A	L	S	A	C	E	■	P	O	L	■	■
H	A	L	L	■	T	I	E	S	■	I	N	E	P	T
O	B	I	E	■	A	R	R	A	N	T	■	M	O	A
H	A	N	S	O	L	O	■	V	I	T	A	M	I	N
U	S	E	■	R	E	F	L	E	X	■	B	O	N	G
M	E	R	G	E	■	T	O	N	E	■	U	N	T	O
■	■	N	A	S	■	H	O	U	S	E	D	■	■	■
O	D	O	R	■	R	E	N	E	■	S	H	E	E	T
H	A	T	E	R	A	D	E	■	S	T	A	B	L	E
O	D	E	T	O	J	O	Y	■	P	E	B	B	L	E
H	A	S	H	T	A	G	■	■	A	R	I	S	E	N

128

D	R	A	W	S	■	■	■	M	E	A	N	S	I	T
R	O	S	I	N	■	■	M	O	M	J	E	A	N	S
I	D	Y	L	L	■	M	A	R	M	A	D	U	K	E
F	E	E	L	■	T	E	X	M	E	X	■	C	S	T
T	O	T	A	L	I	D	I	O	T	■	S	E	T	S
■	■	■	C	O	L	U	M	N	■	E	A	P	O	E
■	■	L	A	M	E	S	A	■	S	A	T	A	N	S
■	C	E	T	E	R	A	■	R	A	T	I	N	E	■
M	A	T	H	I	S	■	C	O	V	E	N	S	■	■
A	S	H	E	N	■	D	O	T	E	R	S	■	■	■
S	T	E	R	■	M	E	M	O	R	Y	H	O	L	E
S	A	R	■	C	O	V	E	R	S	■	E	X	I	T
I	N	C	A	H	O	O	T	S	■	D	E	L	L	A
F	E	R	R	A	R	I	S	■	■	A	T	I	L	T
S	T	Y	M	I	E	D	■	■	■	E	S	P	Y	S

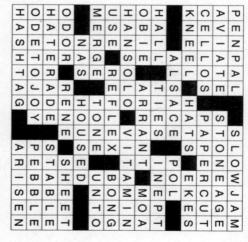

129

O	R	A	L	B		S	O	F	T		M	O	A	T
D	O	P	E	R		C	L	O	I	S	O	N	N	E
D	U	E	T	O	B	U	D	G	E	T	C	U	T	S
S	E	D	U	C	E	D		G	R	A	S	S	E	S
			P	A	L			Y	A	Y				
U	S	S		D	O	G	S		C	A	S	A	B	A
T	H	E	N	E	W	Y	O	R	K	T	I	M	E	S
I	O	N	A			R	A	E			T	A	R	P
C	R	O	S	S	W	O	R	D	P	U	Z	Z	L	E
A	E	R	A	T	E		S	O	U	P		E	E	N
				A	B	C			R	R	S			
A	N	O	S	M	I	A		R	I	O	T	A	C	T
W	I	L	L	E	N	D	T	O	M	O	R	R	O	W
O	C	E	A	N	A	R	I	A		T	A	E	B	O
L	E	S	T		R	E	A	M		S	W	A	B	S

130

G	A	P	T	O	O	T	H	E	D		U	P	C	S
E	T	H	A	N	F	R	O	M	E		M	O	A	T
W	H	O	L	E	F	O	O	D	S		P	O	R	E
G	E	N	E		S	O	R	E	A	T		H	O	P
A	N	I	S	E		P	A	N	D	A		P	L	O
W	A	C		D	A	S	H		E	N	J	O	I	N
			B	U	S	H	S	R		L	E	O	N	I
H	I	B	A	C	H	I		E	P	I	T	H	E	T
O	H	A	R	A		P	E	D	A	N	T			
G	E	T	S	T	O		M	L	L	E		S	O	P
W	A	H		E	M	C	E	E		S	P	A	C	Y
A	R	M		D	E	A	R	T	H		E	V	E	L
R	Y	A	N		G	U	I	T	A	R	S	O	L	O
T	O	T	O		A	L	T	E	R	A	T	I	O	N
S	U	S	S		S	K	I	R	E	S	O	R	T	S

131

B	A	D	D	A	Y	■	■	■	L	A	P	C	A	T
O	T	O	O	L	E	■	■	T	E	A	R	O	S	E
N	A	U	S	E	A	■	F	U	N	H	O	U	S	E
A	N	G	E	R	■	S	A	R	A	■	B	R	U	T
M	E	H	■	T	A	P	I	N	■	K	E	T	C	H
I	N	N	S	■	W	A	T	S	O	N	■	S	H	E
■	D	U	N	C	A	N	H	I	N	E	S	■	■	■
■	■	T	A	L	K	I	N	G	H	E	A	D	■	■
■	■	■	G	O	E	S	O	N	A	D	I	E	T	■
A	I	R	■	A	S	H	M	A	N	■	D	A	R	K
S	P	E	A	K	■	M	O	L	D	S	■	D	I	E
K	H	A	N	■	P	A	R	S	■	H	O	B	B	Y
F	O	R	T	E	R	I	E	■	F	I	R	E	U	P
O	N	E	I	R	O	N	■	■	A	R	C	A	N	A
R	E	D	C	A	P	■	■	■	X	R	A	T	E	D

132

M	O	F	F	A	T	■	■	C	H	A	N	N	E	L	S
E	C	L	A	I	R	S	■	C	O	P	Y	E	D	I	T
R	A	Y	K	R	O	C	■	C	U	T	A	B	O	V	E
G	L	E	E	C	L	U	B	■	N	T	H	■	P	E	A
E	A	R	■	A	L	F	R	E	D	O	■	G	E	R	M
■	■	■	T	R	I	F	O	L	D	■	N	O	R	M	■
O	S	B	O	R	N	■	M	O	O	■	O	N	I	O	N
T	H	E	B	I	G	B	A	N	G	T	H	E	O	R	Y
C	E	L	I	E	■	A	N	G	■	H	A	R	D	E	E
■	L	I	A	R	■	S	C	A	R	E	R	S	■	■	■
B	L	T	S	■	P	I	E	T	I	S	M	■	S	M	L
A	G	T	■	D	I	N	■	E	V	I	D	E	N	C	E
T	A	L	L	O	N	E	S	■	E	R	O	T	I	C	A
O	M	E	L	E	T	T	E	■	S	E	N	A	T	O	R
R	E	D	C	R	O	S	S	■	■	N	E	L	S	O	N

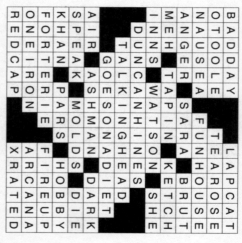

133

F	A	L	S	I	E	S	■	B	A	R	T	A	B	S
I	S	A	I	D	N	O	■	E	X	U	R	B	A	N
G	U	Y	C	O	D	E	■	L	O	S	E	S	T	O
T	S	E	■	L	O	V	E	I	N	S	■	O	R	R
R	U	T	H	■	R	E	Y	E	S	■	B	L	O	T
E	A	T	A	T	■	R	E	B	■	T	A	U	P	E
E	L	E	V	E	N	■	D	E	S	I	S	T	E	D
■	■	■	E	N	I	D	■	R	I	M	S	■	■	■
C	H	A	N	D	L	E	R	■	R	E	S	E	A	L
H	A	L	O	S	■	R	A	H	■	D	A	R	L	A
E	M	I	T	■	T	R	I	O	S	■	X	R	A	Y
W	B	A	■	C	H	I	L	L	A	X	■	A	M	O
T	O	S	P	A	R	E	■	D	U	B	S	T	E	P
O	N	E	O	V	E	R	■	E	C	O	C	I	D	E
Y	E	S	I	S	E	E	■	M	E	X	I	C	A	N

134

B	A	M	B	O	O	S	H	O	O	T	■	M	S	G
I	M	E	A	N	R	E	A	L	L	Y	■	C	E	O
B	A	R	R	E	L	C	H	A	I	R	■	C	A	N
■	■	R	I	M	E	■	A	N	N	O	T	A	T	E
F	B	I	C	A	S	E	S	■	■	■	A	F	A	R
R	A	E	■	N	S	A	■	A	D	E	X	E	C	S
A	S	S	E	S	■	R	A	N	O	U	T	■	■	■
G	E	T	T	H	E	W	R	O	N	G	I	D	E	A
■	■	■	H	O	L	I	S	T	■	E	P	O	X	Y
P	E	R	I	W	I	G	■	C	N	N	■	L	I	E
A	L	E	C	■	■	■	C	H	E	E	Z	I	T	S
G	L	A	S	S	J	A	R	■	A	L	I	T	■	■
A	I	D	■	H	O	M	O	E	R	E	C	T	U	S
N	O	M	■	I	N	T	A	K	E	V	A	L	V	E
S	T	E	■	M	Y	S	T	E	R	Y	M	E	A	T

135

S	M	A	R	T	Y	P	A	N	T	S	■	G	P	A
M	A	D	E	Y	O	U	L	O	O	K	■	R	A	M
O	R	D	E	R	O	N	L	I	N	E	■	E	S	P
T	I	T	L	E	■	■	E	D	G	I	N	E	S	S
E	N	O	S	■	R	A	R	E	■	N	E	N	E	■
■	■	■	■	C	O	N	G	A	■	■	P	E	D	I
B	I	R	T	H	D	A	Y	■	D	R	A	G	O	N
O	V	A	R	I	E	S	■	N	A	I	L	G	U	N
Z	Y	D	E	C	O	■	S	O	L	O	I	S	T	S
O	L	I	N	■	■	W	I	L	E	S	■	■	■	■
■	E	A	C	H	■	A	N	O	S	■	P	U	M	A
C	A	T	H	O	L	I	C	■	■	F	I	N	E	R
A	G	O	■	L	I	V	E	A	L	I	T	T	L	E
F	U	R	■	E	M	E	R	G	E	N	C	I	E	S
E	E	S	■	S	P	R	E	A	D	S	H	E	E	T

136

R	A	G	E	Q	U	I	T	■	G	Y	M	R	A	T
O	H	I	D	U	N	N	O	■	S	O	R	E	L	Y
S	E	N	D	A	W	A	Y	■	T	U	M	B	L	R
S	A	G	■	D	E	C	O	R	■	H	E	S	S	E
I	D	E	S	■	D	A	T	A	S	E	T	■	■	■
■	■	R	O	T	■	N	A	F	T	A	■	R	U	M
O	H	A	R	A	S	■	S	T	A	R	G	A	Z	E
R	O	L	E	X	E	S	■	S	T	D	E	N	I	S
E	Y	E	L	E	V	E	L	■	S	M	E	R	S	H
M	A	S	■	V	E	G	A	S	■	E	S	A	■	■
■	■	■	R	A	R	E	B	I	T	■	E	M	M	A
T	O	G	A	S	■	L	A	T	H	E	■	P	A	S
A	R	A	B	I	A	■	M	A	R	S	B	A	R	S
L	A	Z	B	O	Y	■	B	R	O	M	A	N	C	E
E	L	A	I	N	E	■	A	S	B	E	S	T	O	S

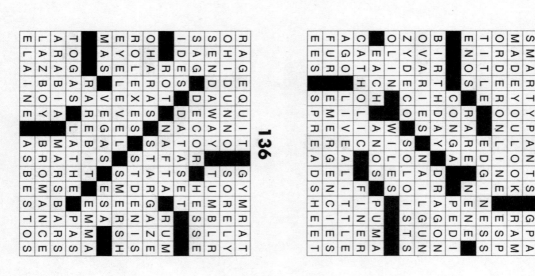

137

F	I	V	E	A	M	■	J	E	T	B	L	A	C	K
A	C	A	D	I	A	■	I	N	R	E	A	S	O	N
B	Y	L	I	N	E	■	G	O	O	D	T	I	M	E
■	S	U	E	T	■	■	S	U	P	■	I	D	E	A
S	T	E	■	I	D	T	A	G	■	S	N	E	R	D
H	A	M	S	T	E	R	W	H	E	E	L	■	■	■
O	R	E	L	■	L	E	S	■	T	R	O	V	E	■
P	E	N	A	L	T	Y	■	H	E	A	V	I	N	G
■	S	U	M	M	A	■	F	O	R	■	E	R	G	O
■	■	■	P	A	S	S	I	O	N	F	R	U	I	T
T	A	B	O	O	■	U	N	D	E	R	■	S	N	O
A	L	O	E	■	S	N	L	■	■	E	A	S	E	■
S	O	R	T	D	A	T	A	■	T	E	R	C	E	T
T	H	E	R	A	V	E	N	■	S	T	M	A	R	K
E	A	S	Y	R	E	A	D	■	E	V	E	N	S	O

138

F	A	C	E	P	L	A	N	T	■	A	N	K	H	S
S	T	A	T	I	O	N	E	R	■	R	E	N	E	W
H	E	G	O	T	G	A	M	E	■	O	X	E	Y	E
A	M	E	N	H	O	T	E	P	■	S	T	E	L	E
R	P	I	■	■	N	O	S	A	L	E	■	H	O	P
P	O	N	C	E	■	M	E	N	U	■	J	O	V	E
■	■	■	A	N	T	I	S	■	G	A	O	L	E	R
S	H	O	P	V	A	C	■	M	A	S	H	E	R	S
L	A	U	R	Y	N	■	K	A	R	E	N	■	■	■
A	S	T	I	■	G	A	N	G	■	A	Q	A	B	A
P	T	S	■	G	O	B	A	N	G	■	■	S	A	N
J	O	C	K	O	■	A	V	E	R	A	G	I	N	G
A	R	O	A	R	■	S	E	T	A	B	L	A	Z	E
C	U	R	V	E	■	E	R	O	S	I	O	N	A	L
K	N	E	A	D	■	D	Y	S	P	E	P	S	I	A

139

■	■	C	A	R	D	C	A	T	A	L	O	G	■	■
■	G	A	M	E	O	F	T	H	R	O	N	E	S	■
G	O	T	I	N	T	O	H	O	T	W	A	T	E	R
L	A	S	S	O	E	S	■	U	S	S	T	A	T	E
O	T	C	■	■	■	■	■	■	■	■	■	T	S	P
S	E	A	L	A	B	S	■	I	T	S	L	A	T	E
S	E	N	E	G	A	L	■	S	A	T	I	N	O	N
■	■	■	A	R	N	O	■	B	R	A	T	■	■	■
C	J	C	R	E	G	G	■	N	O	G	U	C	H	I
H	A	R	N	E	S	S	■	S	T	E	P	H	E	N
A	G	A	■	■	■	■	■	■	■	■	■	I	R	E
S	U	N	D	O	W	N	■	P	L	A	N	F	O	R
M	A	K	E	T	H	E	B	E	S	T	O	F	I	T
■	R	E	C	R	I	M	I	N	A	T	I	O	N	■
■	■	D	O	A	G	O	O	D	T	U	R	N	■	■

140

P	O	N	I	A	R	D	S	■	M	A	C	P	R	O
I	M	O	N	F	I	R	E	■	U	P	R	O	A	R
S	I	G	H	T	G	A	G	■	S	T	A	R	V	E
A	T	O	E	■	S	M	E	L	T	■	F	O	A	L
■	■	A	R	M	■	A	R	A	B	■	T	U	G	S
T	H	R	E	A	D	S	■	L	E	T	S	S	E	E
O	H	E	N	R	Y	■	T	A	N	S	■	■	■	■
W	H	A	T	S	N	E	W	W	I	T	H	Y	O	U
■	■	■	■	H	A	L	O	■	C	R	E	E	P	S
M	A	R	R	Y	M	E	■	R	E	A	D	S	T	O
A	Q	U	A	■	I	N	T	O	■	P	O	W	■	■
D	U	M	B	■	C	A	R	D	S	■	N	E	M	O
R	I	B	B	E	D	■	A	M	E	R	I	C	A	N
I	N	L	I	E	U	■	C	A	S	H	S	A	L	E
D	O	E	S	S	O	■	I	N	S	O	M	N	I	A

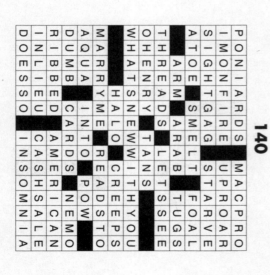

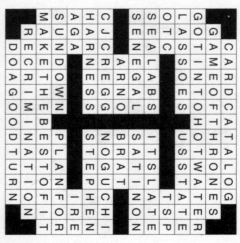

141

P	A	J	A	M	A	B	O	T	T	O	M	S	■	■
I	M	A	G	I	N	E	D	R	A	G	O	N	S	■
V	A	N	E	S	S	A	W	I	L	L	I	A	M	S
E	Z	I	N	E	■	■	A	B	L	E	■	R	A	T
N	E	E	D	■	S	P	L	A	Y	S	■	E	R	E
■	■	■	A	P	P	A	L	L	■	■	H	D	T	V
S	A	G	■	A	R	I	A	■	F	I	E	R	C	E
E	T	E	R	N	A	L	■	S	I	C	H	U	A	N
A	T	T	E	S	T	■	C	O	R	E	■	M	R	S
G	A	B	S	■	■	T	R	U	S	T	S	■	■	■
R	C	A	■	T	S	H	I	R	T	■	P	R	I	G
A	K	C	■	A	T	O	M	■	■	C	R	U	D	E
M	A	K	E	M	I	N	E	A	D	O	U	B	L	E
■	D	A	T	I	N	G	A	G	E	N	C	I	E	S
■	■	T	A	L	K	S	N	O	N	S	E	N	S	E

142

S	N	O	C	O	N	E	S	■	■	■	S	O	U	R
L	O	C	A	V	O	R	E	■	■	T	H	I	N	E
A	V	E	M	A	R	I	A	■	T	O	I	L	E	D
G	E	L	A	T	I	N	■	R	W	A	N	D	A	N
■	L	O	R	I	■	■	J	O	E	T	O	R	R	E
■	■	T	O	O	L	C	A	S	E	■	L	I	N	C
■	■	■	S	N	O	O	Z	E	D	■	A	L	E	K
I	B	M	■	S	A	W	Z	A	L	L	■	L	D	S
P	E	R	M	■	N	B	A	T	E	A	M	■	■	■
R	E	P	O	■	W	A	G	E	S	W	A	R	■	■
O	V	E	R	D	O	N	E	■	■	F	L	O	G	■
M	E	A	S	U	R	E	■	F	A	U	L	T	E	D
I	N	N	E	E	D	■	C	E	L	L	M	A	T	E
S	O	U	L	S	■	■	O	L	D	L	A	T	I	N
E	M	T	S	■	■	■	P	L	A	Y	P	E	N	S

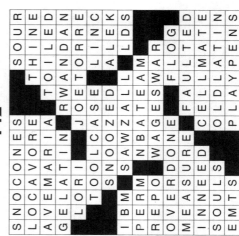

143

R	O	G	E	R	T	H	A	T	■	B	O	T	C	H
A	R	O	M	A	R	A	M	A	■	A	C	H	O	O
R	E	F	U	S	E	N	I	K	■	R	H	E	T	T
E	G	O	■	H	A	G	■	E	M	E	R	G	E	S
G	A	R	B	E	D	■	B	O	A	■	E	I	R	E
A	N	T	I	S	■	F	O	N	D	A	■	R	I	A
S	O	H	N	■	I	T	O	■	O	U	T	L	E	T
■	■	E	G	G	M	C	M	U	F	F	I	N	■	■
A	N	J	O	U	S	■	B	F	F	■	T	E	N	K
S	O	U	■	M	A	G	O	O	■	M	I	X	I	N
P	U	G	S	■	F	A	X	■	C	O	S	T	C	O
E	R	U	P	T	E	D	■	M	E	N	■	D	E	C
C	I	L	I	A	■	G	U	E	S	T	B	O	O	K
T	S	A	R	S	■	E	A	R	T	H	T	O	N	E
S	H	R	E	K	■	T	R	E	A	S	U	R	E	D

144

M	I	S	A	P	P	R	O	P	R	I	A	T	E	S
T	H	E	G	R	E	E	N	L	A	N	T	E	R	N
G	A	V	E	I	T	A	N	O	T	H	E	R	G	O
E	T	E	R	N	A	L	O	P	T	I	M	I	S	T
S	E	N	■	C	L	E	■	■	A	S	P	■	■	■
■	■	T	M	I	■	R	A	N	I	■	O	T	I	S
I	M	H	I	P	■	■	R	O	L	F	■	U	M	A
M	E	D	A	L	■	J	E	D	■	O	D	S	O	N
D	N	A	■	E	D	E	N	■	■	R	O	C	K	S
B	U	Y	S	■	E	T	A	T	■	C	I	A	■	■
■	■	■	L	A	S	■	■	I	L	E	■	L	A	I
H	A	D	A	H	E	A	R	T	O	F	G	O	L	D
U	N	I	V	E	R	S	A	L	R	E	M	O	T	E
G	I	V	E	M	E	O	N	E	R	E	A	S	O	N
S	T	A	R	S	T	U	D	D	E	D	C	A	S	T

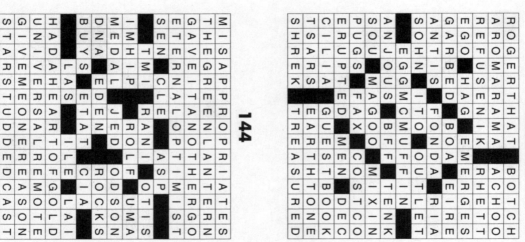

145

S	C	R	A	M	B	L	E	S		H	A	W	E	D
W	H	A	T	A	J	E	R	K		O	V	A	T	E
M	A	N	I	C	O	T	T	I		T	A	X	O	N
			L	A	R	S	E	N		M	I	E	N	S
B	A	R	T	O	K			F	U	E	L	S		
A	M	E				G	I	L	L	S		P	E	T
R	I	A	L		L	E	N	I	N	S	T	O	M	B
O	G	L	E		E	R	I	C	A		D	E	B	I
N	O	T	A	G	B	A	C	K	S		S	T	A	R
S	S	R		R	O	L	E	S				I	N	D
		O	N	E	N	D			S	H	O	C	K	S
B	L	O	A	T		F	A	T	T	E	N			
L	A	P	A	Z		O	P	I	O	N	E	E	R	S
A	L	E	C	K		R	I	C	O	C	A	S	E	K
H	A	R	P	Y		D	E	S	D	E	M	O	N	A

146

Z	I	P	P	E	R				G	L	A	C	E	S
S	N	A	R	L	U	P			R	E	S	U	L	T
A	S	S	E	S	S	E	D		I	N	S	T	I	R
Z	O	T		A	T	T	E	L	E	T		G	T	I
S	N	O	B		S	E	L	I	G		B	L	I	P
A	G	R	I	P		S	U	L		C	E	A	S	E
			G	A	L	A	X	Y	Q	U	E	S	T	
		N	A	T	O	M	E	M	B	E	R	S		
	H	I	P	H	O	P	M	U	S	I	C			
C	A	N	E	S		R	O	N		N	A	T	T	Y
O	N	E	S		H	A	D	S	T		N	E	H	I
A	S	I		R	O	S	E	T	E	A		S	E	P
T	O	R	N	U	P		L	E	T	S	S	L	I	P
E	L	O	I	S	E			R	E	T	R	A	C	E
D	O	N	N	E	D				S	O	I	S	E	E

147

S	C	A	G	G	S			S	C	A	L	P	S
C	A	P	U	L	E	T		A	L	C	O	T	T
A	V	E	N	U	E	B		M	A	R	A	C	A
M	E	R	C	E	D	E	S		P	E	T	R	I
P	A	C	O		Y	A	N	G		S	H	U	N
S	T	U	N	T		M	A	R	T		S	I	L
			T	I	C		C	A	B	O	O	S	E
S	H	E	R	L	O	C	K	H	O	L	M	E	S
C	O	L	O	N	E	L	S	A	N	D	E	R	S
O	N	E	L	O	V	E		M	E	H			
F	O	G		W	A	R	S		S	I	N	E	W
F	R	A	T		L	I	E	S		C	O	L	E
L	A	N	E	S		C	R	A	C	K	P	O	T
A	R	T	L	A	B		F	L	O	O	R	I	T
W	I	L	L	D	O		S	U	C	R	O	S	E
S	A	Y	Y	E	S			D	A	Y	B	E	D

148

A	D	O	L	E	S	C	E	N	T	S		M	A	D
C	E	S	A	R	R	O	M	E	R	O		I	R	E
T	E	C	H	N	O	M	U	S	I	C		S	T	P
I	R	A	T	E		E	S	T		I	S	S	E	L
V	E	R	I	S	M	O		E	C	O	C	I	D	E
				T	O	P	C	A	T		A	D	I	T
B	A	R	B	I	C	E	L		S	T	R	A	T	I
O	L	E	A	N		N	I	T		W	A	H	O	O
H	I	N	D	E	R		O	H	I	O	B	O	R	N
E	M	E	R		E	L	S	E	I	F				
M	O	G	A	M	B	O		B	I	O	D	A	T	A
I	N	E	P	T		S	M	U		R	A	M	O	N
A	I	D		W	A	T	E	R	L	O	V	I	N	G
N	E	O		T	R	O	M	B	O	N	I	S	T	S
S	S	N		F	I	N	E	S	S	E	S	H	O	T

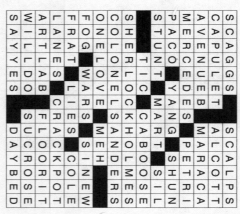

149

N	E	O	P	E	T	S		C	A	U	C	U	S	E	D
E	M	P	E	R	O	R	P	A	L	P	A	T	I	N	E
B	A	T	T	L	E	O	F	T	H	E	S	E	X	E	S
U	N	I	T	E			I	N	I	N	K		I	M	S
L	A	C	Y		L	I	Z	A	R	D		B	R	I	E
A	T	A	T		I	N	E	P	T		W	O	O	E	R
E	E	L	Y		E	R	R	S		M	A	I	N	S	T
			R	A	G	E			G	I	R	L			
E	S	T	A	T	E		B	E	A	R		E	W	E	S
B	O	R	N	E		T	A	B	L	E		R	A	S	P
O	M	I	T		B	Y	R	O	A	D		M	I	S	O
N	E	R		T	U	R	B	O			O	A	T	E	N
I	H	E	A	R	Y	O	U	K	N	O	C	K	I	N	G
C	O	M	P	O	U	N	D	S	E	N	T	E	N	C	E
S	W	E	E	T	P	E	A		G	E	O	R	G	E	S

150

	S	A	L	A	M	I	S		W	A	L	D	O	
R	A	T	S	B	A	N	E		A	M	I	E	N	S
A	L	O	U	E	T	T	E		K	I	S	M	E	T
G	U	N		S	E	L	F	I	E	S	T	I	C	K
E	T	O	N				I	N	N	S		J	A	I
D	E	F	O	R	E	S	T	S			S	O	R	T
			P	A	R	I		T	O	P	T	H	A	T
A	C	C	U	R	S	T		I	N	T	E	N	T	S
T	O	O	L	A	T	E		L	E	A	F			
H	U	M	P			M	A	L	L	S	A	N	T	A
E	S	P		S	O	A	R				N	E	E	R
I	C	A	N	E	X	P	L	A	I	N		G	A	T
S	O	D	O	P	E		I	N	T	I	M	A	T	E
M	U	R	R	A	Y		S	K	E	L	E	T	A	L
	S	E	A	L	E		S	A	M	E	S	E	X	